A History of British Pewter

A History of British Pewter

JOHN HATCHER
Lecturer in History
University of Kent at Canterbury

and **T. C. BARKER**
Professor of Economic and Social History
University of Kent at Canterbury

**Longman
1724-1974**

LONGMAN GROUP LIMITED
LONDON
AND LONGMAN INC., NEW YORK
ASSOCIATED COMPANIES, BRANCHES AND
REPRESENTATIVES THROUGHOUT THE WORLD

© THE MASTER WARDENS AND COMMONALTY OF THE
MYSTERY OF PEWTERERS OF THE CITY OF LONDON

ALL RIGHTS RESERVED. NO PART OF THIS PUBLICATION MAY BE REPRODUCED, STORED IN A RETRIEVAL SYSTEM, OR TRANSMITTED IN ANY FORM OR BY ANY MEANS, ELECTRONIC, MECHANICAL, PHOTOCOPYING, RECORDING, OR OTHERWISE, WITHOUT THE PRIOR PERMISSION OF THE COPYRIGHT OWNER

FIRST PUBLISHED 1974

ISBN 0582 50122·9
LIBRARY OF CONGRESS CATALOG CARD NUMBER
73–93118

SET IN GARAMOND TYPE FACE
AND PRINTED IN GREAT BRITAIN
BY THE UNIVERSITY PRESS, ABERDEEN

COMMISSIONED BY
THE WORSHIPFUL COMPANY OF PEWTERERS
TO COMMEMORATE THE FIVE-HUNDREDTH
ANNIVERSARY OF THEIR ROYAL CHARTER
OF INCORPORATION 1474–1974

Contents

Introduction		1

PART ONE: PEWTER BEFORE 1700

1	From early times to the Norman Conquest	5
2	The Middle Ages	24
3	The sixteenth and seventeenth centuries	81
4	Pewterers' gilds and the regulation of the industry	142
5	Manufacturing and marketing	209

The techniques of manufacture p. 209; the supply of raw materials p. 228; industrial structure p. 241; internal trade p. 251; overseas trade p. 263.

Appendix A Data extracted from London Company records: 1451–1700   270

Appendix B The retail price of pewterware, before 1700   275

PART TWO: PEWTER IN MODERN BRITAIN

6	The decline of pewter	279
7	The Company and the craft	302

Bibliography	323
Index	341

LIST OF FIGURES

1.1	Central and border decoration on pewter dishes found at Appleshaw	15
2.1 2.2 }	Royal feasts of the fourteenth century	48
2.3	A royal feast of the early sixteenth century	49
5.1	The distribution of substandard Walsall pewter in 1640, by maker.	259
5.2	The distribution of substandard pewter made by Thomas Cotton of Marlborough, 1676 and 1677.	260
5.3	The distribution of substandard pewter made by Samuel Bourne of Worcester, 1676 and 1677.	261

LIST OF TABLES

1	The composition of Romano-British pewter finds	17
2	Pewter in churches in the patronage of St Paul's Cathedral, 1249–1458	29
3	Holdings of pewter mentioned in some fifteenth-century wills and inventories	55–6
4	Average annual exports of pewter, 1471–1547	76
5	Probate inventories analysed by period	92–3
6	Probate inventories analysed by wealth	94–5
7	Towns visited and pewterers recorded by London Company searchers, 1635–41 and 1669–83	120–2
8	Estimate of holdings of pewter in late seventeenth-century England	129
9	London pewterers and staff in 1457 and 1459	242
10	The London Company's country search of 1640	255–8
11	Exports of pewter to West Africa, 1673–1704	268
12	London Company shop and apprentice data, 1451–1700	272

13	Average annual admissions to the freedom of the London Company, 1611–1700	273
14	Yeomanry data in annual averages, 1551–1635	274
15	The retail price of pewterware, 1411–1700	276
16	Estimates of employment in the pottery trades of England and Wales, 1680–1770	284
17	Domestic earthenware and china in samples of inventories between the 1680s and the 1730s	285
18	Estimates of annual tin production and annual exports of tin in tin blocks and in pewter in the early, mid, and later eighteenth century	291
19	Number of enrolments to the freedom of the Pewterers' Company by apprenticeship and by patrimony, 1700–99	294
20	Location of those who described themselves as pewterers in the London area in the census of 1841	297
21	Location of men and women outside the London area who described themselves as pewterers in the census of 1841	299

LIST OF PLATES

1 A pewter flask from Abydos, Egypt

2, 3 Romano–British ewers from the Fens

4 Hoard of Romano–British pewter from Manton, Wiltshire

5 A font bowl bearing late Anglo-Saxon decoration

6 Ecclesiastical cruet (thirteenth-fourteenth century), from Weoley Castle

7, 8 Plates from a hoard found in Southwark

9 Set of three 'Spanish trencher' plates

10 Wine measures (baluster form)

11 Elizabethan ecclesiastical flagon
12 Porringer, with two ears of crude 'trefoil' pattern, cast in one piece with the bowl
13 An array of English flagons
14 Charger and two dishes
15 A group of Stuart flat-topped tankards and a flagon
16 The earliest touch-plate of the Worshipful Company of Pewterers
17 A broad-rimmed dish
18 A 'wriggled-work' plate
19 Lidless tavern mugs
20 A selection of seventeenth century pieces
21 A turner using a pole lathe, 1395
22 Lathe driven by wheel and cord, 1568
23 Selection of pewtering tools
24 Steel assaying tool
25 A pewterer casting from an old mould
26 A French pewter workshop, c. 1750
27 A selection of fine Georgian pewter
28 A long range of bulbous, lidless tavern measurers of Imperial measure
29 A range of eighteenth- and nineteenth-century tankards
30 Fine tableware made by Thomas Chamberlain, London, c. 1760
31 A selection of contemporary pewter
32 A selection of representative pieces of Britannia metal

Acknowledgements

We should like to take this opportunity of expressing our gratitude to all those who with help and encouragement assisted in the production of this book. Our primary debt is to the Worshipful Company of Pewterers, for commissioning this book and for giving us every assistance in the writing of it. We also benefited from frequent meetings with the Company's Land and General Purposes Committee. Charles Grant, the Clerk, and Cyril Jossé Johnson, the Chairman of the Committee, kindly read and commented on sections of the book in draft, and supplied much information on the Pewterers' Company and the pewter industry in recent times. Christopher Peal, Secretary of the Pewter Society, kindly read a complete draft and enabled the authors to derive inestimable benefit from his expert knowledge of pewter from Roman times to the present day. Thanks are also due to Major G. S. Johnson and Derrick Mundill for discussions and correspondence on a range of matters; in addition Mr Mundill allowed the authors to plunder the fine library of the Pewter Society in his custody. The premature death of Ronald Michaelis in March 1973 not only deprived the authors of an incomparable guide, but also the pewter collecting fraternity of its foremost authority. Finally, we acknowledge the assistance of Dr David Richardson, Mrs Lorna Weatherill and Mr D. W. Crossley on matters connected with the Pewterers' Company since 1700, the English pottery industry, and Britannia metal respectively. The imperfections which remain are entirely our own responsibility. Part One, *Pewter before 1700*, was written by Dr Hatcher and Part Two, *Pewter in Modern Britain*, by Professor Barker.

We are grateful to the following for permission to reproduce photographs: Ashmolean Museum, Oxford, for plate 1; Museum of Archaeology and Ethnology, Cambridge, for plates 2 and 3; City Museum and Art Gallery, Birmingham, for plate 6; Devizes Museum for plate 4; Dover Publications Ltd. for plate 26 (from Diderot's *Pictorial Encyclopedia of Trades and Industry*, 1959); C. C. Minchin Esq. for plate 13 (from *British Pewter*, R. Michaelis, Ward Lock, 1969); R. Mundey Esq. for plates 10 and 32 (from *British Pewter*, R. Michaelis, Ward Lock, 1969); C. A. Peal Esq. for plates 5, 8, and 29 (from *British Pewter and Britannia Metal*, John Gifford, 1971); Sotheby and Co. for plate 30; The Worshipful Company of Pewterers for plates 11, 12, 14–20, 23, 24, 27, 28, and 31.

Introduction

Pewter the alloy does not lend itself to easy definition. In practice it is unacceptable to exclude any amalgam of metals of which tin forms the bulk, which is relatively soft and easily worked, and possesses a dark silvery colour. Consequently alloys consisting at one extreme of more than 99 per cent tin and at the other of almost 50 per cent lead can legitimately be designated pewter. But many pewter alloys, because they did not command widespread usage, are of more interest to the metallurgist than the historian, and from the late thirteenth century two standard alloys came to be adopted in western Europe. The superior of the two, consisting of pure tin tempered by the addition of relatively small quantities of hardening agents, such as copper, bismuth or antimony, was called 'fine' pewter, and the other, consisting of three or four parts of tin to one of lead, was called 'lay' pewter.

Definition of the alloy, however, is not sufficient to delimit the scope of this book. Pewter alloys have been used in such diverse processes as the manufacture of organ pipes, solder, engine bearings, type metal and coins, and in electroplating. But such applications do not concern us here, for our attention is devoted to the main use of tin-rich alloys, namely pewterware, and to the vast range of tableware and household utensils that were made by pewterers, including plates, dishes, salt-cellars, basins, porringers, spoons, ewers, flagons, cups, tankards, candlesticks, chamberpots, teapots, coffeepots, pepperpots, and inkpots.

One further distinction remains: the method of manufacture. Pewterware was traditionally cast in moulds and then turned and hammered, and we have therefore felt justified in making only passing mention of Britannia metal. Britannia metal, which first assumed commercial importance in Sheffield in the later eighteenth century, was unquestionably a pewter alloy and was also used for the production of household utensils; but it was fabricated in an entirely different way, namely by spinning and stamping from sheets of metal.

Pewter has attracted much attention from collectors of old metalwork, and pewter collecting is now a leading branch of the antiques trade. Many fine books have been written on British pewter in the last seventy-five years or so by connoisseurs such as Massé, Bell, Ingleby Wood, Cotterell, Michaelis and Peal, and they have been of great assistance to the present writers. But the emphasis of these books has lain, quite naturally, more upon the recording of information useful to collectors, such as the nature of surviving pieces, changes in style, and the identification of makers and their marks, than upon the industrial and commercial aspects of pewtering.

The aim of this book is not only to provide a fuller historical background for the connoisseur and collector, but also to bring pewter to the attention of the historian and to place it in the context of the economic and social history of Britain. For more than four hundred years, from the early fourteenth century until the mid-eighteenth century, articles cast from pewter were among the most common of all manufactured goods; in Tudor and Stuart England pewter was to be found in substantial quantities in every household in the realm, apart from the humblest dwellings of the poor. It was also encountered in almost every other institution, lay or ecclesiastical. The weight of pewter in the land at the height of its popularity may well have approached 40,000 tons. In this study emphasis has been placed not only upon the industry and its gilds, but also upon the consumption and distribution of pewter, and upon its role in the household, where usage was influenced by changes in diet as well as in the ritual and etiquette which surrounded the meals of our forefathers.

Part One

❁ *Pewter before 1700*

I ── *From early times to the Norman Conquest*

Tin was a scarce, expensive and highly prized metal in antiquity, and articles made of pure tin or even of tin-rich alloys were extremely rare. By far the greatest amount of available tin went into the manufacture of bronze. The discovery that the addition of relatively small quantities of tin to copper, a fairly common metal in those times, resulted in a far harder and stronger metal than either of its constituents, was one of the most important innovations to be made in early metallurgy, and it facilitated a major advance in the history of mankind by allowing the production of more efficient and durable tools, weapons and utensils. The widespread use of bronze in northern Europe dates from the middle of the second millennium BC, and in south-east Europe and south-west Asia from as early as 3000 BC.[1] At first, however, many bronzes contained little tin, the copper being hardened, probably accidentally, by the presence of arsenic or antimony.[2] The manufacture of true bronzes, eventually to contain the standard proportions of 10 per cent tin to 90 per cent copper, appears to have occurred first in the eastern Mediterranean. Finds in Mesopotamia dating from the early and middle third millennium confirm that the Ur smiths of that period had mastered the metallurgy of copper, tin and bronze, and by 2000 BC true bronzes were being manufactured in large quantities in Sumer, Troy, Crete, Cyprus and the Aegean.[3]

Although European and Malayan deposits were to comprise virtually the sole source of the known world's tin supplies from classical times until the nineteenth century, the earliest tin deposits

---

[1] R. J. Forbes, *Studies in Ancient Technology* (Leiden, 1964), vol. ix, ch. 2 *passim*.
[2] J. R. Maréchal, *Prehistoric Metallurgy* (Lammersdorf, 1963), pp. 24–39; R. F. Tylecote, *Metallurgy in Archaeology* (1962), pp. 40–3.
[3] Forbes, ix, 144–5, 151.

to be exploited, and in fact exhausted, were the many small fields of Asia Minor, Caucasia and Persia; even Egypt appears once to have possessed her own supplies.[1] Whereas tin deposits in these regions were discovered and worked in the third millennium, it is unlikely that any European tin was in use before the close of the second millennium. Nevertheless, supplies available to the civilizations of the Mediterranean and Asia Minor in the third and second millennia do not appear to have been adequate, and tin continued to be treated as a semiprecious metal at least until the increased exploitation of Cornish deposits from about 500 BC.[2] Even as late as Neo-Babylonian times (*c.* 600 BC) the price of tin was eight times that of copper.[3] Some authorities have explained the survival of so few tin or tin-rich artefacts from pre-Christian times by the disintegration of the metal through tin disease,[4] but a far more likely explanation is that the scarcity of tin severely limited the uses to which it was put, and thereby ensured that pewter was not manufactured in significant quantities.

The earliest known example of pewterware was found in a grave at Abydos in Egypt, and can be confidently ascribed to the XVIIIth Dynasty (1580–1350 BC). It is a flask-shaped utensil with a hinged lid and two handles, and when analysed was found to contain 93 per cent tin, 6 per cent lead, and 1 per cent copper with traces of zinc and iron; it now resides in the Ashmolean Museum, Oxford.[5] A bezel of a finger ring of pure tin and a ring of a gold-tin alloy of the same date were also found at Abydos,[6] and are probably more representative of the type of object then made from tin. The great majority of surviving tin pieces from ancient times are jewellery; the earliest of which is probably the pure tin bangle found at Thermi (Lesbos), believed to date from about 2600 BC.[7] A necklace consisting of beads of tin and pieces of

---

[1] *Ibid.*, ix, 130–7, fig. 22; A. Lucas, 'Notes on the early history of tin and bronze', *Journal of Egyptian Archaeology*, xiv (1928), 99–105.
[2] F. M. Heichelheim, *An Ancient Economic History, from the Palaeolithic Age to the Migrations of the Germanic, Slavic and Arabic Nations*, 3 vols (Leiden, 1958–70), i, 237; J. H. Gladstone, 'On metallic copper, tin and antimony from Ancient Egypt', *Proceedings of the Society of Biblical Archaeology* (1892), 226.
[3] Forbes, ix, 153.
[4] For example, J. A. Smythe, 'Notes on ancient and Roman tin and its alloys with lead', *Transactions of the Newcomen Society*, xviii (1937–8), 255.
[5] E. R. Ayrton, C. T. Currelly, and A. E. P. Weigall, *Abydos*, iii (1904), 50; E. S. Hedges, *Tin in Social and Economic History* (1964), p. 70.
[6] A. Lucas, *Ancient Egyptian Materials and Industries* (3rd edn, 1948), p. 286.
[7] W. Lamb, *Excavations at Thermi in Lesbos* (Cambridge, 1936), pp. 165, 171–3, 215.

amber, and odd tin beads dating from the middle of the second millennium have also been found in Holland and Wiltshire respectively.[1] Homer, writing in the ninth or tenth century BC, testifies that tin was also highly prized for decorative work in Mycenean Greece, and that it was used in place of silver for embellishing the shields of Agamemnon and Achilles and the war chariot of Diomedes.[2]

With the increased exploitation of European tin deposits objects of tin gradually became more common in western Europe, and many of them have survived. A wide range of jewellery and other small objects made partly or wholly of tin have been recovered from the excavation of Swiss lake-dwellings, from Scandinavia have come wooden bowls decorated with tin, from Ireland tin armlets and a twisted neck ring, and from Glastonbury a cast tin pendant and a most unusual tin sceptre.[3] Late Bronze Age and Iron Age spindle whorls and buttons made of tin and tin-lead alloys are quite common,[4] and in about 50 BC tin-rich bronze coins were introduced into Britain.[5] But over all these centuries household utensils made of tin or tin-rich alloys—pewterware—are conspicuous only by their absence.

It was in Rome that the use of pewter utensils first assumed some significance in western Europe. Although finds from outside Britain are rare, and comprise only a handful of pieces of probable fourth century provenance, of which a vase discovered on the site of the ruins of Néris, a small pot discovered at Bétricourt, and a vase dredged up at Zaltbommel are perhaps among the most significant,[6] it is possible to gain further insight into the use of pewter from the works of classical writers. As early as the second century BC Plautus described a banquet served in *vasis stagneis*, though some doubt must persist as to whether he meant that the vessels were made of tin or of a lead-silver alloy.[7] Less open to dispute is the reference in the story told by Suetonius against the emperor Vitellius (AD 15–69) who, while proconsul in Africa, is

[1] Hedges, *Tin in Social History*, p. 103.
[2] *Iliad*, xi, 25, 34; xviii, 474, 565, 574, 613; xx, 271; xxi, 592; xxiii, 503, 592.
[3] Hedges, *Tin in Social History*, pp. 102–3; Forbes, ix, 125; A. Fox, *South West England* (1964), pp. 81, 101.
[4] Tylecote, pp. 68–9.   [5] *Ibid.*, pp. 159–60.
[6] G. Bapst, *Études sur l'étain dans l'antiquité et au moyen âge* (Paris, 1884), pp. 41–2; A. J. G. Verster, *Old European Pewter* (1958), p. 71.
[7] See K. C. Bailey, *The Elder Pliny's Chapters on Chemical Subjects*, 2 vols (1929–32), ii, 191–2 for a discussion of the meaning of *stagnum* and *stannum*.

said to have stolen 'some of the offerings and ornaments from the temples and changed others, substituting tin and brass for gold and silver'.[1] The works of the celebrated naturalist Pliny the Elder (AD 23–79) contain a number of references to pewter vessels (*vasa stannea*) and pewter caskets (*pyxides stagnea*),[2] in which medicinal compounds were to be prepared, thus showing clearly that such utensils were not unknown.[3] We also know that pewter tableware was in use at this time in the eastern Mediterranean. Egyptian documents of the second and third centuries AD mention flasks, vessels and plates of pewter,[4] and from the Roman period in Nubia two finger rings of tin, two tinned bronze bowls and a pewter bowl have so far been discovered.[5]

But there can be little doubt that pewter achieved popularity only in late Roman Britain, where to date almost three hundred pewter finds have been made. The advent of British pewter manufacture was the result of the confluence of a series of favourable factors, amongst which the renewed exploitation of Cornish tin deposits is perhaps the most important. The large-scale production and export of Cornish tin in the late Bronze and Early Iron Ages is attested both by archaeological evidence and the descriptions of many Roman commentators.[6] The latter culminate in the remarkably detailed picture drawn in about 8 BC by Diodorus, who tells how the inhabitants of west Cornwall, well civilised because of their intercourse with foreign merchants, extracted tin ore, and smelted and worked it into pieces the shape of knucklebones (*astragali*) to be shipped to Gaul, and thence conveyed overland to Narbonne and Marseilles.[7]

Yet in Imperial times, after the conquest of Britain, there is scarcely a trace of British tin. Roman commentators dealing with the sources of the Empire's tin speak only of north-west Spain, and furthermore archaeological evidence points conclusively to a virtually complete cessation of mining in south-west England

---

[1] Suetonius, Vitellius, v. The translation is that of J. C. Rolfe, Suetonius Tranquillus, G., *Works*, 2 vols (1959–60), ii, 255.
[2] The lack of distinction in Latin between tin and pewter means that we cannot be sure that the utensils were not made of pure tin, but it is most unlikely that they were. Furthermore we consider it justified to term even utensils of pure tin 'pewterware'.
[3] For example, *Historia Naturalis*, xxix, 35; xxx, 38, 57.
[4] T. Frank, ed., *An Economic Survey of Ancient Rome*, 6 vols (1933–40), ii, 47.
[5] Lucas, *Ancient Egyptian Materials and Industries*, p. 286.
[6] J. Hatcher, *English Tin Production and Trade before 1550* (Oxford, 1973), pp. 9–13.
[7] Diodorus Siculus, v, 22, 2; 35, 5; 38, 4.

from the occupation in AD 43 until the middle of the third century.¹ It is clear that although the Romans quickly overran the region as far west as Exeter they then stopped, and made no great efforts to advance further. In contrast to Mendip lead, which was mined within six years of the Conquest, the rich tin deposits of the south-west were not thought worth exploiting. The Romanisation of Britain at first affected Cornwall hardly at all: she received no towns, no roads, no villas, and no troops. The tin veins of northern Spain, with their ample and easily worked surface deposits readily accessible to Rome, rendered the exploitation of the resources of south-west England, for the time being at least, an unnecessary exercise.² About the middle of the third century, however, conditions changed and the systematic occupation of Cornwall by the Romans began as her tin once again became important. Inscriptions and milestones suggest the construction of roads in mining regions, and the increased number of late third and fourth century coins found in mid and west Cornwall suggest a measure of prosperity. The reason for this activity was undoubtedly the collapse of the Spanish mines and the increased demand for tin caused by the minting of massive quantities of debased tin-rich coins called *antoniniani*. The period from the mid-third to the mid-fourth century, while most of the Roman Empire was in the throes of severe economic and political crises, therefore appears to have been the most prosperous for British tin mining.³

As a consequence tin once again became plentiful in Britain, a necessary precondition of pewter manufacture. But other factors also played an important part in stimulating the pewter industry, for, as we have seen, pewter manufacture does not appear to have taken place on a significant scale in the centuries preceding the Conquest when tin was similarly plentiful. In Roman Britain, however, tastes and fashions were moulded anew, and the demand from affluent members of society for high quality and even luxurious personal and household fittings, already discernible in Belgic times, grew rapidly under the influence of Romanisation. In the first two centuries of Roman Britain the demand for

[1] O. Davies, *Roman Mines in Europe* (Oxford, 1935), pp. 146–7.
[2] *Victoria County History, Cornwall*, pt 5, 'Romano-British Cornwall' (1924), pp. 18–21.
[3] *Ibid.*, pp. 21–4; J. Liversidge, *Britain in the Roman Empire* (1968), pp. 204–7; M. P. Charlesworth, *The Lost Province or the Worth of Britain* (Cardiff, 1949), pp. 50–4.

distinctive tableware, to be used as best by families of middling wealth, was satisfied by vast imports of brilliant red-glazed Samian pottery, made first in Italy and later in southern and central Gaul, in a wide range of designs and ornamentation to suit both taste and pocket. For more wealthy and discriminating customers there was a wide range of bronze wares and, from late in the first century AD, an increasing volume of fine Rhenish glass wares, while for the very rich there was imported silver tableware.[1]

As the second century progressed British craftsmen began to compete with many of these imports, usually by producing cheaper copies. It was in the latter part of this century, for example, that the Castor potteries, one of the most important of Romano-British industries, were established. The incentive to produce substitutes for foreign wares was greatly increased as the third century progressed and piracy and continental wars at first disrupted and finally destroyed many sources of supply. Just as the chief centre of the Samian pottery industry, Lezoux in central Gaul, ceased production in about AD 260, so a further major centre was established in Britain in the New Forest.[2]

Paradoxically Britain enjoyed a considerable measure of prosperity from the later third century until the end of Roman occupation, an era when the empire at large was torn by strife and dogged by economic depression. It was Haverfield who first viewed the fourth century as the 'golden age' of Roman Britain, and although the enthusiasm with which this assertion was made might now be questioned there is no doubt that the countryside, in particular the large-scale farmers, did prosper, and that as a consequence much rebuilding and requipping of villas took place. It was in these favourable circumstances, when the disruption of foreign trade led to a substantial shortfall in the supply of imported consumables in the face of increasing demand, that the British pewter industry arose.

With the exception of a number of pieces found in the Walbrook in London, all Romano-British pewter can be assigned on the basis of considerable positive evidence and a lack of negative evidence to the period *c.* AD 250 to *c.* 420. Well over half of extant Romano-British pewter consists of plates and dishes; in

[1] Liversidge, *Britain in the Roman Empire*, pp. 156–61; I. A. Richmond, *Roman Britain* (rev. edn, 1963), pp. 137–41; R. Merrifield, *Roman London* (1969), pp. 163–6.
[2] Liversidge, *Britain in the Roman Empire*, pp. 158, 205.

addition there are considerable numbers of ewers, jugs, cups and bowls, and a few spoons and tazza.[1] The largest hoards so far discovered, and probably the most significant also, are those of Appleshaw (Hampshire), Icklingham (Suffolk), and Appleford (Berkshire–Oxford border). The Appleshaw hoard was found, apparently deliberately hidden, on the site of a Roman house near Andover, and it probably comprises the complete household stock of pewter, consisting of thirty-two pieces in all, and including ten large circular dishes with diameters of between 22 and 15 inches, a large square dish, two smaller dishes, two small plates, eight bowls with diameters of between 8 and 4 inches, two saucers, four cups, two jugs and a vase.[2] The major Icklingham hoard, found on the site of a Roman villa, is of similar proportions, comprising forty pieces in all including twelve large dishes and a number of bowls, saucers, cups and jugs.[3] The Appleford find is smaller, but amongst its twenty-two pieces there are no less than fourteen large dishes with diameters of between 12 and 18 inches.[4]

The distribution of Romano-British pewter finds is most uneven. The great majority of major discoveries, with the exception of those in London, have been concentrated within a belt of land approximately 60 miles wide crossing central southern England, with a northern boundary extending from the Bristol Channel to the Lincolnshire coast of the Wash, and a southern boundary from Portland Bill to Lowestoft. Furthermore even within the confines of this belt the spread of finds is irregular, with a notable absence of pewter over much of the central regions comprised by Gloucestershire, south Warwickshire, Oxfordshire, Buckinghamshire, Hertfordshire, and Bedfordshire. The paucity of pewter from the south-eastern counties of Middlesex, Essex, Kent, Sussex, Surrey and east Hampshire, and from the south-western counties of Cornwall, Devon and Dorset may also be of significance.

[1] W. J. Wedlake, *Excavations at Camerton* (Camerton, 1958), pp. 88–93, gives a list of the chief pewter finds in Britain. For a more recent estimate of the numbers of plates and dishes see C. A. Peal, 'Romano-British pewter plates and dishes', *Proceedings of the Cambridgeshire Antiquarian Society*, lx (1967), 19.
[2] C. H. Read, 'List of pewter dishes and vessels found at Appleshaw and now in the British Museum', *Archaeologia*, lvi, pt 1 (1898), 7–12.
[3] *British Museum Guide to the Antiquities of Roman Britain* (1st edn, 1951), p. 42. A further hoard was found close by in 1956 (J. Liversidge, 'A new hoard of Romano-British pewter from Icklingham', *Proc. Cambridge Antiquarian Society*, lii (1959), 6–10).
[4] *The Times*, 11 December 1969.

But it must be readily admitted that the distribution of finds can provide only a rough guide to the actual distribution of pewter in Roman times, for there is a fortuitous element in both survivals and discoveries and, unlike pottery which was worthless when broken, scarcely any pewter was wilfully discarded. The richness of archaeological evidence of all sorts emanating from East Anglia, for example, owes much to the Norse raids which encouraged the burying of hoards, as well as to the deep ploughing and construction of airfields of more recent times. Moreover, as finds continue to occur the area of Britain which has yielded no pewter continues to shrink. A number of significant finds have been made in northern England and east Wales, for example, including a hoard of plates at Manchester, a flagon at Stokesley in the North Riding, cups at Carrawburgh and High Rochester, and a jug and a plate at Caerwent.

Nevertheless, one is forced to give weight to the present distribution of finds, and on this basis it would appear that pewter achieved its greatest popularity in four regions: the first comprised by north Somerset, Wiltshire, Berkshire, and west Hampshire, the second by the Norfolk, north Suffolk, north Cambridgeshire Fenland and Breckland region, the third by Northamptonshire, and the fourth by London. Thus it does not appear that pewter formed a normal part of the furnishings of villas throughout Romanised Britain, but it is possible that future finds may indicate a wider consumption pattern than present evidence would allow.

Evidence of manufacturing sites is limited, but in recent years a number of possible workshops have been unearthed. The most positive identification of a large-scale manufacturing site is at Camerton, situated close to Bath alongside the Fosse Way which ran from the north Devon coast to Lincoln.[1] Here two stone moulds for casting pewter have been found. The first, designed for casting oval dishes, is fashioned from local Bath stone, and measures $15\frac{1}{2}$ inches in length, 9 inches in width at widest, and is $2\frac{1}{2}$ inches deep; it was found on the floor of a third century building close to a sunken furnace. The second, a smaller and smoother mould fashioned from local white lias, was probably used for casting circular skillets or flat-bottomed saucepans, the handles of which were cast separately, using the top of the mould.

[1] Wedlake, pp. 87–93.

A further piece of Bath stone found a few feet from the second mould may well have been the inner mould for a large dish or pan. In addition the site has yielded a number of pieces of pewter and the remains of a coal tip which undoubtedly supplied fuel for the furnace. Camerton's pewter and iron industries were obviously successful, for we can discern the erection in the late third century of a number of simple rectangular buildings on the site, presumably to house artisans; the occupation layers thereafter are characterised by a black appearance, no doubt due to the use of coal and the smelting operations. Camerton was an ideal site for pewter manufacture, lying adjacent to lead deposits in the Mendip hills and in the centre of the small Somerset coal field, both of which were worked in Roman times, and even the stone for the moulds was on hand. Tin was the only material not available locally, and this had only to be transported from Cornwall.

A number of other significant discoveries have also been made in the Bath region. A series of stone discs, similar in workmanship to those of Camerton, were found at Lansdown within a small settlement that appears to have been occupied for most of the Roman period. Some of these have no lips and do not seem suitable for casting, but they could well have been used for beating plates and dishes into shape.[1] Further moulds, possibly used for pewter casting, have been discovered on nearby Oatland Down, at Nettleton in Wiltshire, and at Silchester in Berkshire. In all fragments of almost twenty moulds are housed in Bath Museum.[2]

Evidence of manufacture outside the Bath region continues to mount. A particularly fine pair of matching moulds, used for casting dishes of a fairly common type, has been found in St Just in Penwith in Cornwall,[3] and recent work has shown that there is a strong possibility that pewter was manufactured in a number of sites in East Anglia. A Romano-British settlement at Brampton, near Norwich, has yielded a piece of limestone with curved grooves which could be a segment of a dish mould of some 30 inches diameter, and a pewter ingot and pewter waste have been found at Hockwold. Perhaps even more convincingly, excavation of a Romano-British site at Hacheston, Suffolk, has

[1] Richmond, p. 137.
[2] Peal, 'Romano-British pewter plates and dishes', p. 20.
[3] P. D. C. Brown, 'A Roman pewter mould from St. Just in Penwith, Cornwall', *Cornish Archaeology*, ix (1970).

yielded, in addition to three plates and two cups of pewter, two pieces of scrap pewter found on a workshop floor which appear to be genuine industrial waste and not the result of pillage or fire.[1] Furthermore a mould found at a villa at Langton, Yorkshire, suggests that pewter was also manufactured in the north.[2]

In the absence of substantial evidence to the contrary it must remain unlikely that manufacture was restricted to a handful of sites.[3] The production of much pewterware was a relatively simple process, tin and lead were available in highly refined ingots, and for even greater convenience ingots of ready-mixed pewter were available.[4] Further information on the degree to which manufacturing was centralised or dispersed might, at some stage, be forthcoming from an analysis of the various styles of extant pieces. This has been attempted for plates and dishes by C. Peal, who has used rim types and decoration to place them into four major and twenty minor categories.[5] Unfortunately, as might be expected given the small size of the available sample, the results are inconclusive. Certain tendencies of interest have emerged, however, and in particular the wide range of rim types found in single hoards. In the Appleshaw group of ten plates, for example, there are four distinct rim types, while out of seven classifiable plates from the first Icklingham hoard, five have different rims. At present local types seem seldom to have emerged, but it must be remembered that we are dealing with pewterware made over a long period of time, and in Roman Britain changes in the tastes and fashions of both producers and consumers occurred with surprising frequency.

The manufacture of simple articles of pewter would not have presented serious problems to British craftsmen. The low melting and fusing points of tin and lead meant that the alloy could be easily prepared by heating earthenware crucibles on hearths surrounded by coal or charcoal. The crucibles that were used

[1] Reported in Peal, 'Romano-British pewter plates and dishes', p. 23.
[2] Brown, p. 108.
[3] Bronze working was widely diffused, and probably existed in most large towns (R. G. Collingwood and J. N. L. Myres, *Roman Britain and the English Settlements*, 2nd edn, Oxford, 1937, p. 234).
[4] A number of pewter bun ingots, containing between 80 per cent and 72 per cent tin and weighing from $6\frac{1}{2}$ to $16\frac{1}{2}$ pounds, have been found in the Thames at Battersea (R. G. Collingwood and I. A. Richmond, *The Archaeology of Roman Britain* (rev. edn, 1969), p. 205; Tylecote, p. 68).
[5] Peal, 'Romano-British pewter plates and dishes'.

were probably hemispherical in shape, similar to those of the bronzesmith, with the rounded base helping to melt the ore speedily while minimising the effects of heat on the vessel.[1] When molten, the alloy would be poured into stone moulds, which would probably also have been heated in order to facilitate clean casting. The opposite members of mould were bound or clamped together. One of the Camerton moulds has incised cut marks around its outer edge which were probably to ensure that the binding which held the two halves together did not slip, and an iron clamp was also found in association.[2] The upper section of the pair of Cornish moulds mentioned earlier could also have formed the base of another in a nest of moulds. More complex pieces, such as ewers and jugs, were fashioned by a combination of casting, beating and welding.

Most casting resulted in a rough product, and it was common for circular objects to be finished on the lathe, and perhaps also beaten to remove imperfections. The lathe enabled rough edges to be trimmed and, because of the softness of the alloy, craftsmen could readily relieve surfaces with concentric circles and other simple devices. Many surviving dishes and plates still bear circular

Fig. 1.1 Central and border decoration on pewter dishes found at Appleshaw

[1] Liversidge, *Britain in the Roman Empire*, pp. 204–5.
[2] Wedlake, pp. 83–4.

lathe marks, and a few also have pieces of untrimmed waste on their outer edges.[1]

Simple decoration was sometimes effected in casting (a few lias moulds have dents or nicks on their rims) and sometimes added afterwards with a chisel or a file. The ornamentation of the finer pieces was of a quite different order. The intricate chasing, frequently of geometrical design, found on a number of the Appleshaw dishes, for example, was obviously the work of highly skilled craftsmen, as too was the fabrication of the better pieces of holloware, such as the magnificent ewer found in the Fens at Burwell. The ornamentation of the Appleshaw plates appears to have been accomplished by following the lines of a traced pattern with a wedge-shaped chisel, used as a punch; in addition the resulting design was sometimes emphasised by filling it with a black bituminous material.[2] Indeed the standard of craftsmanship exhibited on a number of pewter articles is so high that it led Professor Richmond to suspect that some decorated silverware may have been fashioned by similarly talented British craftsmen and not imported.[3]

The composition of Romano-British pewter alloys fluctuated widely. Analyses have shown variations in lead and tin content from more than 99 per cent tin (the Appleshaw 'fish' dish) to more than 50 per cent lead (the Brislington cup and a dish from the Fens).[4] As an exception there is the unique flagon from Bosence which contains 85 per cent tin, 3 per cent lead, 2 per cent iron, and 10 per cent copper.[5] Items within the same hoard frequently reveal wide variations in composition, and even articles made in the same style, and perhaps even by the same craftsman, are often not metallurgically consistent. But the extremes of variations instanced in Table 1 are more apparent than real, and the bulk of vessels that have been analysed have tin-lead ratios that lie within the limits of 2 : 1 to 3 : 1. To some extent variations were accidental and stemmed no doubt from the haphazard manner in which producers composed the alloy, and the practice of remelting obsolete pieces. In addition it should be noted that

[1] Read, p. 8; Liversidge, 'A new hoard of Romano-British pewter', p. 6.
[2] W. Gowland, 'Analyses of metal vessels found at Appleshaw, Hants, and of some other specimens of Roman pewter', *Archaeologia*, lvi, pt 1 (1898), 20. Mention must also be made of the unique dish found recently at Shingham, Norfolk, with its border of mythical beasts (A. S. Mottram, 'Roman pewter dishes from Shingham', *Norfolk Archaeology*, xxxv, pt 1, 1970). [3] Richmond, p. 137.
[4] Table 1 below. [5] Brown, p. 110.

the composition of the pewter can vary by as much as 4 per cent in large vessels, owing to the fact that segregation in the constituent metals commences as soon as the alloy begins to solidify.[1]

Table 1

Composition of Romano-British pewter finds

Object	Locality	Tin (%)	Lead (%)
'Fish' dish [a]	Appleshaw (Hants)	99·18	0·14
Circular dish [a]	Appleshaw	90·55	8·31
Small dish [a]	Appleshaw	72·36	26·09
Circular dish [a]	Appleshaw	64·75	34·66
Tableware [b]	Icklingham (Suffolk)	79	21
Octagonal dish [b]	Icklingham	45·75	53·34
Tableware [b]	Mildenhall (Suffolk)	74·3	25·8
Tableware [b]	Mildenhall	57	43
Dish [b]	Burwell (Cambs)	57	43
Tableware [b]	Sutton (Cambs)	62·2	37·8
Tableware [b]	Sutton	67·8	32·2
Tableware [b]	Abington Piggots (Herts)	62·3	37·7
Tableware [b]	Abington Piggots	70	30
Plate [a]	Southwark	72·9	26·7
Cup [c]	Brislington (Som)	54·8	45·38
Cup [d]	High Rochester (Northumberland)	97·7	2·73

Sources
[a] Gowland, 'Analyses of metal vessels', p. 17.
[b] Liversidge, 'A new hoard of Romano-British pewter', p. 9.
[c] Smythe, 'Notes on ancient and Roman tin', p. 262.
[d] I. A. Richmond and J. A. Smythe, 'A Roman cup of tin', *Proc. Univ. Durham Philosophical Soc.* x (1938) 48–55.

It is not yet possible to determine whether variations in the constituents of Roman pewterware had anything to do with the progress of the industry. It has been suggested that the earliest pieces to be manufactured were those consisting of almost pure tin, and that by trial and error a harder and more flexible alloy was achieved by the addition of a greater proportion of lead.[2] In fact much Romano-British pewter is composed of the most tenacious alloy of tin and lead. But doubtless another reason for the high lead content of pewter lay in the relative cheapness of lead; in Pliny's day tin fetched 80 denarii a pound in

[1] Gowland, p. 18; Liversidge, 'A new hoard of Romano-British pewter', pp. 9–10.
[2] Peal, 'Romano-British pewter plates and dishes', pp. 19–20.

Rome while lead fetched only 7 denarii.[1] There can be no doubt that pewter containing more than about 25 per cent lead constitutes a health hazard; in the Middle Ages the highest permissible lead content was 20 per cent. The Romans, while not unaware of the dangers of plumbism, chose to disregard them: they drank water piped through lead pipes and stored in lead tanks, ate food cooked in lead-lined pots, and smeared themselves with lead-based unguents. No wonder then that many skeletons show an abnormally high lead content and that historians continue to speculate on the possibility of plumbism being an important contributory factor in the infertility of so many Roman families.[2]

The Romano-British pewter industry, as stated earlier, appears to have flourished for little more than a century and a half, and even at its peak it was dwarfed by competitive industries making tableware out of other substances. It is probable that pewter tableware captured only a relatively small segment of the market in high-quality furnishings for affluent households, in which silver, glass, bronze, fine pottery and even gold were competitors; and as we have seen pewter appears to have achieved popularity only over a relatively limited geographical area. Pewter was, of course, far beyond the reach of the vast mass of the people, who had to make do with pots and dishes roughly fashioned from clay, wood and stone. Although many finds of pewter have been casual with little or no indication as to date, those that can be satisfactorily dated have been assigned to the period between the mid-third century and the first quarter of the fifth century.[3] Firm evidence from the contexts of at least a dozen major finds points to the fourth century as the most productive for the industry, while the lack of contrary evidence confirms the absence of pewter manufacture in Britain before about AD 250 and after the withdrawal of the Roman armies.[4] Unfortunately style at present offers relatively little assistance in dating, although it is reassuring to note that pewter jugs and ewers conform closely to those fashioned from other metals which

---

[1] *Historia Naturalis*, xxxiv, 161.
[2] See, for example, J. P. V. D. Balsdon, *Life and Leisure in Ancient Rome* (1969), p. 83.
[3] Wedlake, pp. 87–93, gives the approximate dates of many finds.
[4] For example: Appleshaw not earlier than AD 284 and not later than AD 351; Manton, Wilts, early fifth century; Brislington, nr Bristol, AD 265–361; Meare, Somerset, *c.* AD 388; Shapwith, Somerset, late fourth century–early fifth century; St Albans, Hertfordshire, fourth century.

have been ascribed conclusively to the late third and the fourth centuries.¹

The only finds at present difficult to fit into this late Roman timespan are those from the Walbrook in London. Among the numerous metal finds in the streambed of the Walbrook, objects made of pewter are by no means uncommon, and include plates, spoons and boxes, as well as a cup and a ewer. The problem arises from the fact that the metal finds that can be closely dated, namely coins and brooches, all belong to the first century of Roman occupation; the coin series in fact ends abruptly in AD 155. Furthermore the plates themselves are quite unlike any other known pewter plates. Despite the unwillingness of some authorities to accept the implications of the evidence, it must remain extremely unlikely that all the Walbrook pewter was manufactured in the latter half of the third century or even later, and far more likely that it belongs to the main series of second century Walbrook finds. This does not mean that the accepted duration of the British pewter industry must be amended; on the contrary pewter was being produced elsewhere in the Empire long before the third century and there must remain a distinct possibility that some, if not all, of the Walbrook pewter was imported.²

The disintegration of trade and industry which followed close on the heels of the departing Roman armies doubtless speedily brought about the cessation of pewter production, along with the production of most goods which depended upon more than local markets. There is no evidence whatsoever about English pewter in the fifth, sixth or seventh centuries, and the implication must be that this is because none, or virtually none, was produced. The regression which took place in commercial and industrial life in these centuries can, however, be clearly traced in pottery, a far cheaper and more basic product than pewter. The pottery of the Roman period with its hard, skilful, kilnfired and wheel-made wares produced on a large scale by potteries geared to distant markets, contrasted sharply with the handmade, soft, ill-fired wares of the pagan period.³ Furthermore, whereas large

¹ For the changing forms of metal jugs see *London in Roman Times*, ed. R. E. M. Wheeler (1946), pp. 113–16.
² For discussion of the Walbrook pewter see Merrifield, pp. 162–3; I am grateful to Mr Merrifield for further information on the provenance of the Walbrook pewter.
³ G. C. Dunning, *et al.*, 'Anglo-Saxon pottery: a symposium', *Medieval Archaeology*, iii (1959), 7–9.

quantities of pots can be identified as having been produced in each of the many great centres of the industry throughout Roman Britain and the western Empire, for the pagan Saxon period it is rare to find two or more pots so similar as to be likely to have come from the same workshop; and even when discovered they are usually not merely in the same cemetry but in contiguous graves, thereby suggesting that they are the products of one family, or at most a small domestic industry.[1] It is small wonder therefore that conditions which combined to prevent the commercial production of even the poorest clay pots did not favour the survival of the pewter trade.

Indeed it appears probable that tin production, of which south-west England possessed a monopoly, was itself at a virtual standstill for much of the fifth and sixth centuries, with only some intermittent, small-scale exploitation of deposits taking place. The first tentative indications of a revival of English tin production occur in the seventh century in the form of references to a cargo of tin shipped from England to Alexandria, recorded in the biography of an Alexandrian patriarch, the sale of tin by Saxon merchants at fairs near Paris, and the sending by Alcuin, Abbot of St Martin of Tours, of tin for a bell to the Abbey of Lindisfarne in Yorkshire.[2] But it is not until the ninth and tenth centuries that substantial and conclusive archaeological evidence of tin-working is available,[3] and it is also from this time that tin can clearly be seen as a regular item of European commerce, being transported along the major trade routes to eastern and southern Europe.[4]

It is not surprising, therefore, to find that in the Dark Ages tin was once again a scarce and expensive metal and that, as a consequence, objects made of pure tin or pewter were extremely rare throughout Europe. Tinning (i.e. coating with tin), however, appears to have been frequently practised. Isidore of Seville, writing in the seventh century, draws attention to the tinning of copper, bronze and iron, and also to the manufacture of tin mirrors.[5] The tinning of the inside of copper vessels to obviate the unpleasant metallic flavour and green colour (verdigris) imparted to food and drink by copper, a practice which, according

[1] *Ibid.*, 12–13. [2] Hatcher, pp. 14–16.
[3] F. Haverfield, 'Cornish Tin', *Mélanges Boissier* (Paris, 1903), pp. 253–5; H. O'N. Hencken, *The Archaeology of Cornwall and Scilly* (1932), ch. 7.
[4] Hatcher, pp. 16–17. [5] Bapst, pp. 113–14.

to Pliny the Elder, dated back at least to the first century AD,[1] was widespread throughout the Middle and Far East and probably also followed in western Europe.[2] Tinned bronze buckles are often found in late Merovingian graves, while tinned brooches and bangles occur in lesser numbers. Of particular note in Britain is the Sutton Hoo burial treasure (AD *c.* 650), which contains an iron helmet covered with ornamental bronze plates, each of which is tinned and divided into panels by fluted ribs of tin.[3]

The addition of even a small quantity of tin to most metals produces a brittle alloy, and although tin by itself does not produce much sound when struck, by hardening other metals it can make them sonorous. Bells were usually made of copper mixed with tin, conventionally in the proportions of 23–26 parts tin to 100 parts copper, and have often been seen, probably with justification, as the major use for tin in the Dark Ages and early Middle Ages.[4]

The first indisputable references to the rebirth of our product occur in the early ninth century, and relate exclusively to ecclesiastical usage. From the excellent documentation of Carolingian France, which unfortunately has no counterpart in Britain, we learn that pewter vessels, although extremely rare, were in use in these times. The *Capitulare Aquisgranense* of 812, for example, mentions a cruet or small flagon of pewter, and in the following year a list of the relics of St Richarius records a similar utensil (*canna ex stanno*).[5] The constitutions of the monks of Cluny, dating from the foundation in 918, refer to a large basin made of tin which was used for washing chalices, and to three pewter amphorae, one used for holding wine, one for washing hands, and one for washing chalices. Because of its scarcity tin enjoyed an extremely high reputation, a measure of which was provided

---

[1] *Historia Naturalis*, xxxiv, 48 ('When copper vessels are coated with *stagnum* the contents have a more agreeable taste and the formation of destructive verdigris is prevented').
[2] J. Hawkins, 'On the intercourse which subsisted between Cornwall and the other commercial states of antiquity, and on the state of the tin-trade during the Middle Ages', *Trans. of the Royal Geological Society of Cornwall*, iii (1824), 126; R. Hunt, *British Mining* (2nd edn, 1887), p. 46.
[3] Hedges, pp. 107–8.
[4] G. R. Lewis, *The Stannaries*, Harvard Economic Studies, iii (Cambridge, Mass., 1903), p. 57; V. Biringuccio, *Pirotechnia*, ed. C. S. Smith and M. T. Gnudi (New York, 1942), pp. 60–1, 210–11, 260–77.
[5] Bapst, p. 98. It is just possible that an occasional pewter chalice was in use in France in the seventh century, but the evidence is scanty (*ibid.*, pp. 87–8).

by the ecclesiastical Council of Rheims of 803 or 813 which ordained that only chalices made of gold, silver or tin were to be used in church services.[1] The mention of a pewter chalice among the goods left by the bishop of Vigue in Spain in 909 provides indisputable evidence of the dissemination of pewter.[2] It is probable that the attempts of ecclesiastical authorities to prohibit the use of chalices of such humble materials as wood, stone, earthenware, and bronze provided a strong, albeit highly selective, boost to the use of pewter. Nevertheless, the poverty of many churches in these early centuries would not have permitted even the use of pewter, and total demand was almost certainly of tiny proportions.

Even by the late Saxon period the metal industries and trades in England operated on a very small scale. Surprisingly few iron ore deposits appear to have been worked in the eleventh century, and tin production was almost certainly very low despite the fact that Devon and Cornwall still possessed the only productive tin fields in the known world.[3] Only lead seems to have been mined in quantities comparable with those extracted in later centuries. Furthermore, although highly skilled Saxon craftsmen achieved an international reputation for their fashioning of gold and silver, smiths and general metalworkers, who do not appear to have been a numerous body, occupied a humble station in English society.[4] Very few households possessed cups, plates, jugs or dishes made of metal, and although many must have possessed a metal pot or two for use in cooking and serving, these were far more likely to have been made from iron, copper or bronze than from tin-rich alloys. It is interesting to note that although the role of metals was limited, the *Gerefa*, an early eleventh-century account of the duties of manorial reeves, included among the skilled workmen to be found on agricultural estates a *leodgotan*, and among the equipment required on manors a range of cauldrons, pans and pots, of which many were obviously metal and a few at least are referred to as leaden.[5] *Leodgotan*

[1] *Ibid.*, pp. 112; 82–83; 90.
[2] *Archdeaconry of Norwich: Inventory of Church Goods, 1368*, ed. A. Watkin, Norfolk Record Society, xix, pt 2 (1948). lxxxi.
[3] Tin is not mentioned in Domesday. The tin deposits of Bohemia and Saxony were not exploited until the mid-twelfth century at the very earliest.
[4] H. R. Loyn, *Anglo-Saxon England and the Norman Conquest* (1962), pp. 100–6.
[5] The *Gerefa* is printed, together with an English translation, in W. Cunningham, *Growth of English Industry and Commerce*, i (5th edn, 1910), 571–6.

literally translated means leadworker or plumber, but it seems likely that such estate craftsmen served as general metalworkers. The restricted supply of tin inevitably limited its usage. Bells, bronze, the coating of bronze, copper and iron, and the manufacture of jewellery and ecclesiastical pewter appear to have been the uses to which tin was put, and possibly in this order of importance. Thus from Saxon England there is abundant evidence of bells, of a wide range of tinned articles including spurs, and some splendid pewter jewellery,[1] but there is no trace of pewter utensils. By inference from continental sources it would appear legitimate to argue that some ecclesiastical pewter must have existed in England by the tenth century, but there can be little doubt that the quantity was exiguous.

The scarcity of tin thus ensured that pewterware was extremely rare before the Norman Conquest, and indeed only once can it be considered to have achieved even a modest popularity. This was in the late third century and the fourth century; and even then, as we have seen, it remained the acquisition of the wealthy within a restricted geographical area. In the half millennium and more preceding and succeeding this brief period of importance, pewter, though known, was too expensive and too rare to put to any but occasional ceremonial and decorative uses.

[1] A fine hoard of eleventh-century pewter brooches and rings is housed in the Guildhall Museum, London.

2 The Middle Ages

In this chapter an attempt is made to trace, illustrate and analyse the increasing popularity of pewter in the course of the Middle Ages, an occurrence which was dependent on a wide range of diverse factors, including the availability and price of tin, and changes in etiquette, fashion, and the scale and distribution of wealth. The sources of information concerning the production and consumption of pewter in such early times are, as one would expect, deficient in many respects, but the survival on the one hand of a substantial body of gild records and export statistics, and on the other of a range of wills, inventories, household expenditure accounts, and books on household management and domestic manners, enables this task to be tackled with conviction. In addition the physical evidence of both surviving pieces of pewter and of contemporary drawings and paintings of domestic scenes, contributes a further invaluable dimension.

The Church was without doubt the leading consumer of pewter, both in Britain and in Europe, from the Dark Ages until at least the dawn of the fourteenth century. As mentioned in the previous chapter, pewter enjoyed a special position amongst the base metals and alloys owing to the scarcity of tin, and while at no point achieving the status of silver its rarity in the world at large made it ideally suited for ecclesiastical use, and enabled it to play a role in setting churches and their furnishings apart from everyday life. For the historian this is a fortunate state of affairs, because in an era when documentary evidence of all aspects of social and economic life is slight, ecclesiastical records are among the most numerous and informative.

The high regard in which pewter was held in the early Middle Ages is demonstrated clearly by the many references in these years to pewter chalices achieving acceptance as alternatives to those of precious metals and in preference to those of wood, stone, earthenware, horn, copper, bronze and lead[1]—the chalice being one of the most sacred possessions of the parish church. The earliest reference by far to this practice is the pronouncement agreed at the Council of Rheims at the beginning of the ninth century,[2] which precedes the more famous analogous dictum of the Synod of Rouen by more than two and a half centuries. The latter has, however, survived in a more direct and detailed form and from it we learn that whereas wooden chalices were categorically forbidden those made from pewter were permitted when economic circumstances dictated that vessels of precious metals could not be provided.[3] An identical resolution was adopted for England at the Council of Winchester held two years later in 1076.[4]

It will be noticed that the support for pewter chalices sprang from negative motives: gold and silver were the only truly acceptable substances, but the poverty of many churches and congregations was an unpleasant reality, and pewter at least ensured that the use of what were considered to be even baser materials could largely be avoided. Nevertheless it was inevitable that when circumstances changed, or ecclesiastical authorities became more stringent, the suitability of pewter for such exalted functions should once again be held in doubt. It is in this light, and in the light of the slow growth in the use of pewter for domestic utensils, that the bewildering succession of resolutions, some prohibiting and some sanctioning the use of pewter, can be understood. Thus we find that in 1175 at the Council of Westminster it was the turn of pewter to be relegated from certain sacred offices, and bishops were commanded to consecrate only vessels of gold and silver.[5] The statutes of Fulk Basset, bishop of London (1245-59), are particularly forceful in their condemnation of vessels of copper and tin which were not to be consecrated because they induced nausea (*provocat ad nauseam*).[6] But the mere condemnation of pewter chalices could not secure their removal

---

[1] Bapst, *Études sur l'étain*, pp. 77–83.
[2] Above, p. 22.   [3] Bapst, p. 80.
[4] D. Wilkins, *Concilia Magnae Britanniae et Hiberniae*, 4 vols (1737), i, 385.
[5] M. Bell, *Old Pewter* (1913), p. 53.
[6] F. M. Powicke and C. R. Cheney, ed., *Councils and Synods and other documents relating to the English Church*, ii (Oxford, 1964), p. 651. For other references to chalices of tin see pp. 379, 599.

from all parish churches, and it may well have been that substantial numbers of churches were prevented by poverty from providing silver chalices, at least before the mid-thirteenth century.[1] French ecclesiastical authorities adopted a more realistic attitude and continued to allow poorer churches to use pewter chalices in the celebration of Mass.[2]

Records of visitations of churches, which often provide detailed inventories of utensils and furnishings, suggest that by the later thirteenth century most churches had succeeded in acquiring chalices of silver or silver-gilt. The earliest of these records, which derives from a series of visitations of churches in the patronage of St Paul's Cathedral in the mid-thirteenth century, shows that with scarcely an exception each had at least one silver chalice, while some had two.[3] Admittedly these churches were situated in one of the wealthiest regions of the country, but even in Devon and Cornwall parish churches by the late thirteenth century invariably possessed silver chalices.[4] In 1368 of the 358 churches in the Archdeaconry of Norwich 344 had silver chalices, 75 of which were gilded, 9 had gilt chalices of an unspecified material, and 2 had chalices of pure gold.[5]

Fortunately for the prosperity of the pewter industry, while the increasing wealth of churches in the thirteenth century meant that chalices used at High Mass were only rarely made of pewter, it also made possible the provision of a wider range of furnishings and utensils, thus enabling each utensil to perform a special function. The constitutions of 1229 of William de Blois, bishop of Winchester, for example, provide for two chalices in each church, one of silver for Mass and one 'unconsecrated and fashioned from tin' to be placed with its accompanying paten in the coffin of the priest at his burial[6]; this practice continued into the fifteenth century. A considerable number of sepulchral chalices and patens

---

[1] The melting down of church plate to contribute towards the ransom of Richard I in 1194 may well have necessitated the restoration of much pewter.
[2] Bapst, p. 92.
[3] 'Visitations of churches belonging to the Dean and Chapter of St Paul's Cathedral in the years 1249–52', ed. W. S. Simpson, *Camden Miscellany*, Volume Nine (Camden Society, new ser. liii, 1895); 'Visitations of certain churches in the patronage of St Paul's Cathedral Church between the years 1138 and 1250', ed. W. S. Simpson, *Archaeologia*, lv, pt 2 (1897).
[4] Exeter Cathedral Archives, Dean and Chapter MSS 3672, 3672a (visitations of churches in the Diocese of Exeter undertaken in 1281 and 1301).
[5] *Archdeaconry of Norwich: Inventory of Church Goods*, pp. lxxix–lxxx.
[6] *The Church Plate of the County of Wiltshire*, ed. J. E. Nightingale and E. H. Goddard (Salisbury, 1891) p. 5.

survive, and it is clear that many were merely representations specially manufactured for this purpose; among the best specimens are those from Westminster Abbey, Abbotsbury Abbey and Exeter Cathedral.[1] In addition there is strong evidence that unconsecrated pewter chalices were kept in increasing numbers of churches for giving communion to the sick, and in the thirteenth century a whole succession of ecclesiastical pronouncements urged that they should be provided for this purpose.[2] Moreover, it was customary for the laity to drink unconsecrated wine after receiving communion, and we may confidently assume that pewter chalices were frequently used in this manner.[3]

Confirmation of both the decline of consecrated pewter chalices and the growing adoption of unconsecrated, is provided by church inventories of the thirteenth and fourteenth centuries: whereas in 1249 none of the fourteen churches belonging to St Paul's possessed a pewter chalice, by 1297 eight did[4]; and in the Norfolk inventories of 1368 no less than 250 of the 358 churches possessed a pewter chalice in addition to one or more of silver.[5]

We have perhaps dwelt too long upon chalices, for they comprised only a small fraction, albeit one of the most sacred, of the metal utensils and ornaments of medieval churches. The importance of other ecclesiastical pewter is exemplified in the earliest detailed church inventory, that of St Augustine's, Watling Street, London, dating from somewhere between 1160 and 1181, which records the holdings of the church as a silver-gilt chalice with silver paten, two pewter cruets, a pewter water pitcher, two copper candlesticks and two wooden, and two small bowls of unspecified material.[6] From the mid-thirteenth century inventories of the goods of the Hertfordshire, Essex and Middlesex churches belonging to St Paul's we learn that every church had at least one

[1] See, for example, *Proceedings of the Society of Antiquaries of London*, 2nd ser., viii (1879–81), 159–63; *ibid.*, 2nd ser., xxii (1907–9), 392–3; H. J. L. J. Massé, *Pewter Plate: a historical and descriptive handbook* (1910), pp. 86–8; R. F. Michaelis, *Antique Pewter of the British Isles* (1955), p. 68.
[2] *Archdeaconry of Norwich: Inventory*, p. lxxxi; Powicke and Cheyney, pp. 296, 1005. In 1301 an inventory of the furnishings of Dawlish parish church noted 'a pewter chalice for the infirm' (Exeter Cathedral Archives, Dean and Chapter MS 3672 f. 29).
[3] *Archdeaconry of Norwich: Inventory*, p. lxxxi.
[4] 'Visitations of churches, 1249–52'. *Visitations of Churches belonging to St Paul's Cathedral in 1297 and 1458*, ed. W. S. Simpson (Camden Society., new ser. lv, 1895).
[5] *Archdeaconry of Norwich: Inventory*, p. lxxx.
[6] 'Visitation of churches 1138 and 1250'.

item of pewter and that most had four or five. Furneaux Pelham, Hertfordshire, had the most substantial holdings of pewter, namely four candlesticks, four cruets (old), a chrismatory and a pyx.[1]

It can be seen from Table 2 that the amount of pewter kept by these churches had substantially increased by 1297, and at this time averaged more than six items per church. Cruets, small covered vessels used to store the wine and water for Mass, were the most numerous pewter items in medieval churches and seem rarely to have been made of any other metal. It is no mere coincidence that the early twelfth-century technologist Theophilus used the cruet to illustrate the technique of pewter making.[2] The finer medieval cruets may well have resembled the two surviving examples, probably dating from the thirteenth or fourteenth century, found in the moats of Ludlow and Weoley castles. Both cruets display a high standard of workmanship and bear a close resemblance to each other, both being hexagonal with relief-cast panels and reserves depicting religious scenes.[3] Next in order of magnitude were candlesticks, used either for processions or for standing on the altar or altar steps, and then basins, in which the priest ceremonially washed his hands before Mass; ewers or pitchers for use with the basins were also frequently made of pewter. Common additional pewter items were locked caskets in which the Eucharist was reserved (pyxes), locked containers for holy oils (chrismatories), censers, incense boats and their spoons, holy water vats and sprinklers, small wine barrels, font bowls, and small bells.[4] Mention must also be made of the unique bowl decorated by the chip carving method, almost certainly used as a font bowl, which was discovered recently and ascribed to a period between the twelfth and fourteenth centuries.[5]

Some approximation to the scale of the demand for ecclesiastical pewter in the late thirteenth and fourteenth centuries can be gauged from the supposition that each of some 9,000 or so parish churches possessed five or six items of pewter, and that much

[1] *Ibid*; 'Visitatian of Churches 1249-52'.
[2] *On Divers Arts: The Treatise of Theophilus*, ed. J. G. Hawthorne and C. S. Smith (Chicago, 1963), pp. 179–83.
[3] R. F. Michaelis, *British Pewter* (1969), pp. 12–13.
[4] For a discussion of the form and function of medieval ecclesiastical utensils see *Archdeaconry of Norwich: Inventory*, pp. lxxix–xcix.
[5] C. A. Peal, *British Pewter and Britannia Metal for Pleasure and Investment* (1971), pp. 82–4.

more besides lay in other institutions such as cathedrals, monasteries, abbeys, nunneries, chantries, the chapels of religious gilds, and numerous other private chapels. Account must also be taken of vessels which were lost or broken; items recorded on one visitation were frequently found to be missing on the next. It must be stressed, however, that such quantities were probably tiny in comparison with the amounts of domestic pewterware in the realm by the end of the fourteenth century.

Table 2

Pewter in churches in the patronage of St Paul's Cathedral

Date	Number of Churches	Cruets	Candlesticks	Basins	Ewers	Chrismatories	Pyxes	Incense Boats	Spoons	Chalices	Total
1249	14	24	18	5	8	7	3	0	0	3	68
1297	14	36	21	14	7	6	0	4	3	8	99
1458	7	25	13	2	0	4	1 a	1	1	0	47

a Described as a cup. For the use of cups for storing the Eucharist, see Watkin, *Archdeaconry of Norwich: Inventory*, p. lxxxii.

Furthermore, there are strong indications that the fourteenth century may well have experienced the peak of the consumption of ecclesiastical pewter, and that the fifteenth and sixteenth centuries witnessed a sharp decline in this usage. Surviving inventories of the fifteenth century reveal some decrease in the amount of pewter held by parish churches, and the mass of mid-sixteenth century inventories compiled to assess the value of church goods prior to confiscation, from which the historian can sample holdings in most parts of the country, demonstrates a substantial increase in the numbers of utensils made from silver, latten, bronze, brass, and copper, with a corresponding decline in those of pewter. In the thirty-six Huntingdonshire churches surveyed in 1552, for example, all chalices were silver or silver-gilt, and censers, pyxes, and candlesticks were almost exclusively latten, although a few were silver or copper.[1] In contemporaneous inventories from Bedfordshire and Oxfordshire there is scarcely

[1] *The Edwardian Inventories for Huntingdonshire*, ed. S. C. Lomas and T. Craib (Alcuin Club Collections, vii, 1906).

a mention of pewter,[1] and while pewter appears more frequently in those of Surrey churches its usage was confined to one or two small items of little value.[2] Inventories of northern churches reveal a similar picture, with an abundance of bronze, latten and brass but the use of pewter largely confined to cruets.[3] No doubt the same motives and resources which inspired the re-building of so many parish churches in such magnificent style in the late Middle Ages also accomplished a corresponding increase in the quality of their furnishings. Thus we can pardon the exaggeration of an Italian visitor to England at the turn of the fifteenth century, who remarked 'above all are their riches displayed in church treasures; for there is not a parish church in the kingdom so mean as not to possess crucifixes, candlesticks, censers, patens, and cups of silver'.[4]

Although pewter was extensively used by the Church many centuries before it became popular in the household, we have perhaps been guilty of dwelling too long on ecclesiastical pewter, and must now turn our attention to domestic pewter. Ideally we would wish to discover precise details of when pewter once again began to find a place in the household, of how and why it grew in popularity, of the social groups that consumed it, of the quantities that were produced, of the uses to which it was put, and so on. Unfortunately such precision is unattainable. Yet the careful and imaginative study of a wide range of sources of varying degrees of utility does enable answers to be attempted, and at once it becomes evident that the popularity of domestic pewter followed a course which was diametrically opposed to that of ecclesiastical pewter.

A number of medieval wills are extant, but as a source reflecting the consumption of pewter they have many defects. Firstly, relatively few wills are earlier than the fifteenth century; secondly, a large proportion of those of all periods concerns the estates

[1] *The Edwardian Inventories for Bedfordshire*, ed. F. E. Eeles and J. E. Brown (Alcuin Club Collections, vi, 1905); *Chantry Certificates and Inventories of Church Goods*, ed. R. Graham (Oxfordshire Record Series, i, 1919).
[2] *Inventories of the Goods and Ornaments in the Churches of Surrey, in the reign of King Edward the Sixth*, ed. J. R. D. Tyssen (1869). For additional Surrey inventories see those edited by R. A. Roberts, *Surrey Archaeological Collections*, xxi–xxiv.
[3] *The Inventories of Church Goods for the Counties of York, Durham, and Northumberland*, ed. W. Page (Surtees Society, xcvii, 1897).
[4] *Italian Relation of England: a relation or rather a true account of the Island of England*, ed. C. A. Sneyd (Camden Society, xxxvii, 1847), p. 29.

of persons of great wealth—royalty, nobility and upper clergy; and thirdly, they invariably provide only partial lists of the deceaseds' possessions, and while, understandably enough, devoting considerable space to the most valuable items, such as plate and fine textiles, they either ignore or make only passing reference to general household utensils, gathering them together under such headings as 'kitchenware', 'furniture' or merely 'the residue of my goods'. Inventories, many of which were drawn up in order to guard against fraud and excessive claims upon the estate, are a more useful source, but compared to the veritable flood which confronts the historian of the sixteenth and seventeenth centuries medieval inventories are scarce, and what is more they frequently suffer from the deficiencies of medieval wills already enumerated. Notwithstanding, inventories and wills are among the most revealing, albeit also potentially the most treacherous, sources for the consumption of pewter. Another invaluable insight can be gained from the accounts of expenditure by noble and great ecclesiastical households which, from the late thirteenth century onwards, enable one to extract some particulars of purchases of furniture and tableware. Finally there are a number of contemporary handbooks on etiquette and household management which contain, among a wealth of fascinating detail on everyday life and domestic manners, evidence of both a direct and an indirect nature on the uses of pewter.

From these and other sources it is apparent that the turn of the thirteenth century was the critical period in the re-emergence of pewter in the household. No pewter tableware has been revealed in England before the opening decades of the fourteenth century, and although prudence dictates that we must not assume that domestic pewter was entirely unknown before this date it must surely have been extremely rare.

The earliest glimpses of household expenditure are provided by the accounts kept on behalf of royalty, which stretch back well into the thirteenth century, and exist in considerable numbers from the reign of Edward I onwards.[1] Unfortunately, very few of the detailed particulars of the purchases of the separate household departments have survived, and those of the scullery—a subdepartment of the kitchen responsible among other things

[1] The Public Record Office (PRO) collection is catalogued under Exchequer Accounts Various (E. 101); see also those held by the British Museum (Nero, C, VIII, etc.).

for the provision and maintenance of non-precious tableware—are especially rare. Nevertheless a number of scullery accounts do exist for the late thirteenth and early fourteenth centuries, and they contain no mention of pewter. Instead it appears that important members of the household and their guests frequently ate and drank from vessels of gold or silver, of which prodigious quantities were kept,[1] while vessels of clay and wood served for other guests and other purposes. Purchases of vast quantities of vessels of clay and wood are revealed in late thirteenth and early fourteenth century accounts, at prices so low as to have rendered them attractive in comparison with all possible substitutes, even having regard to their short life. In 1264 almost 3,000 pitchers were purchased on behalf of Henry III at an average price of less than 30s per thousand,[2] in the following year 1,000 dishes were purchased for the Countess of Leicester at a cost of 6s8d,[3] and in 1290 100 dishes, 100 platters and 125 salt-cellars were purchased for Edward I at a cost of 7d, 14d, and 4d respectively.[4] Although the materials from which these vessels were made are not given, their cost quite clearly identifies them as wood or clay; dishes, platters, and salt-cellars were usually made of wood, and pitchers of clay.[5] In the later scullery accounts we find reference to 2,000 dishes, 2,000 platters, and 2,000 salt-cellars of wood purchased in 1307 at Nottingham at a total cost of £6.2s8d, and also to various vessels purchased in Dover from Andrew, Roger and Robert *le tornour*.[6]

A similar picture emerges from the expenses of the household of a great ecclesiastic, Richard de Swinfield, bishop of Hereford, which are enumerated in minute detail for 1289–90. Once again we find that huge quantities of clay and wooden vessels were bought to supplement substantial holdings of gold and silver plate, but there is not a trace of pewter.[7] In like manner inventories

---

[1] See, for example, the inventories of cups, dishes, basins, salt-cellars and other utensils of gold and silver held by Henry III and Edward I (PRO E. 101. 394/14, 15; 356/23, 25; 365/1).
[2] *Calendar of Liberate Rolls* (CLR), *1260–67*, pp. 145, 191, 210, 252.
[3] *Manners and Household Expenses of England in the Thirteenth and Fourteenth Centuries, Illustrated by Original Records*, ed. T. H. Turner (1841), p. 13; for other purchases see pp. 3, 43.
[4] S. Lyons, 'Extracts from the *Rotulus Familiae*, 18 Edward I', *Archaeologia*, xv (1806).
[5] H. E. J. Le Patourel, 'Documentary evidence and the medieval pottery industry', *Medieval Archaeology*, xii (1968), pp. 101–2.   [6] PRO E. 101. 369/17, 370/20/17.
[7] *The Household Roll of Richard de Swinfield, Bishop of Hereford for 1289–90*, ed. J. Webb, 2 vols (Camden Society, old ser. lix and lxii, 1853–55).

made by the executors of the Bishops of London and Exeter, who died in 1303 and 1310 respectively, describe in detail holdings of copper, bronze and iron, but do not mention pewter; utensils of wood and clay were almost certainly omitted because of their scant value. Silver tableware, however, was held in abundance by the bishops: London's estate contained forty-six dishes, thirty-six salt-cellars and a range of cups, spoons, saucers, and pitchers of this metal, and that of Exeter fifty-six dishes, eight saucers, eight basins and various cups, salt-cellars and spice boxes; in addition both possessed a small quantity of gold plate.[1] Thus, once again it seems proper to deduce that the tableware of these households consisted of two extremes, gold and silver on the one hand and wood and clay on the other, with no serviceable yet attractive middle range—the position subsequently to be held for many centuries by pewter.

So far as one can judge the absence of pewter from great households was paralleled by the households of those of middling wealth. In London, a centre of fashion as early as the fourteenth century, even the most minutely itemised of surviving wills and inventories fail to allude to pewter. For example, the schedule annexed to the will of Juliana Fussell, dated 1 November 1305, lists three bronze basins with ewers, five silver cups, eighteen silver spoons, five bronze pots, a bronze dish and 'all the bronze and wooden utensils pertaining to the hall, chamber and kitchen of Doningtone', but no pewter[2]; a few months later Edith Paumer bequeathed a whole range of bronze pots, pans, and cauldrons, but once again pewter fails to make an appearance.[3] A comparable absence of pewter is repeated many times in the early decades of the fourteenth century in wills and inventories from various parts of the country.[4]

[1] *Accounts of the Executors of Richard Bishop of London 1303, and of the Executors of Thomas Bishop of Exeter 1310*, ed. W. H. Hale and H. T. Ellacombe (Camden Society, new ser., x, 1874).
[2] *Calendar of Wills proved and enrolled in the Court of Hustings, London, 1258–1688*, ed. R. R. Sharpe, 2 vols (1889–90), i, 173–4 (hereafter cited as *Hustings Wills*). Although referred to as brass by contemporaries and historians alike the ubiquitous *ollae eneae, patellae eneae* etc., were in fact invariably made of bronze alloys consisting of copper mixed with from 10 to 25 per cent tin and occasionally lead (Hatcher, p. 35).
[3] Sharpe, *Hustings Wills*, i, 175–6.
[4] See, for example, *Wills and Inventories illustrative of the History, Manners, Language, Statistics, etc., of the Northern Counties of England from the Eleventh Century Onwards*, i, ed. J. Raine (Surtees Society, 1835); *Wills and Inventories from the Registers of the Commissary of Bury St Edmunds and the Archdeacon of Sudbury*, ed. S. Tymms (Camden Society, Old ser., xlix, 1850).

The rare survival of lists of chattels valued for the payment of lay subsidies on the personal property of inhabitants of Colchester and neighbouring villages in 1296 and 1301 provides a most welcome addition to our range of sources and enables us to study the metal goods held by a large number of persons of comparatively modest wealth, namely the merchants, traders, craftsmen, and artisans of a flourishing provincial town.[1] The 1301 lists are the more detailed of the two and contain schedules of the goods of 384 persons. Although these schedules clearly do not give complete lists of chattels, metal items tended to be recorded since they were amongst the most valuable possessions of the taxpayers. From these lists we find that a large proportion of the wealthier taxpayers possessed the conventional bronze ewer and basin for the washing of hands before and after meals, and perhaps also a cup of silver or of decorated maple wood (mazer) and a couple of silver spoons, in addition to the essential range of bronze cooking pots and pans. The metal goods of poorer households, by contrast, were invariably confined to bronze cooking utensils and iron grates and tripods. Thus once again our impression of the extreme rarity of household pewter at this time is reinforced, since not one of almost 400 such lists contains a mention of pewter. Metal cooking utensils were clearly essential, but the needs of the table were adequately and cheaply served by vessels of clay and wood, with greater wealth and status displayed by the possession of the odd item of silver and a bronze ewer and basin.

The earliest mention of domestic pewter to have come to light in English sources is of the export from London in 1307 of a small quantity of 'pitchers, dishes, and salt-cellars of pewter' worth 13s by an English merchant named Nicholas le Graunt.[2] This reference is curious since it occurs in a period when detailed export accounts are extremely rare, and also because at this time pewter manufacture on the Continent appears to have existed on a far larger scale and in a more highly developed form than in England.

Evidence from France, Germany and the Low Countries at the turn of the thirteenth century suggests a greater usage of

[1] *Rotuli Parliamentorum*, 6 vols (1767–77), i, 228–38, 243–65. Colchester had approximately 4,500 inhabitants in 1377 (J. C. Russell, *British Medieval Population* (Albuquerque, 1948), p. 142).
[2] PRO E.122.68/22 ('*picher*', *disc' et salsar' de stagno*').

pewter than in England, although there also pewter tableware was rare.¹ An early household inventory of the Templars in Caen, dated 1307, reveals that the many pots, plates and vessels used at table were made of wood, copper, bronze, and clay, but not of pewter; significantly, however, it also reveals a sizeable quantity of pewter in the cellar, where it was used for storage vessels and for measures.² Indeed further evidence from many parts of north-west Europe confirms that pewter was rapidly superseding copper, bronze and earthenware for the storage of liquids—a sensible advance since copper and bronze vessels were liable to impart an unpleasant taste and odour to their contents caused by the formation of verdigris, and those of earthenware were fragile. Nevertheless, although the use of pewter for tableware was rare before the early fourteenth century it was not unknown, for we learn that in 1286 a canon of Troyes Cathedral possessed more than seventy-five dishes, platters, pots, flagons, and measures, all made of pewter; no doubt firsthand experience of the qualities of ecclesiastical utensils made of pewter had encouraged him to introduce it into his household.³

The progress of pewter in north-west Europe can also be gauged from the production side, from the records of gilds and associations of pewterers. Fortunately these are sufficiently numerous and informative to confirm the belief that England lagged far behind her neighbours. With the possible exception of an association of pewterers which is thought to have existed in Bordeaux as early as 1093,⁴ the first European tin-workers' gild was probably that of Paris which, according to the *Livre des métiers* of Étienne Boileau, was in existence in the mid-thirteenth century and included in its membership potters, hammermen, toy-makers, nail-makers, saddlers and lorimers; the nail-makers no doubt produced pewter nails which were used to decorate leather, and the saddlers and lorimers used buckles and ornamentation fashioned from tin.⁵ Evidence from Parisian tax records suggests that a growth of pewterers took place at the expense

---

¹ The abundance of ecclesiastical pewter on the Continent in the twelfth and thirteenth centuries is fully documented by Bapst, pp. 77–109.
² *Ibid.*, pp. 147–8.
³ Bapst, pp. 168–9. For pewter in Dordrecht in 1284 see Verster, p. 12.
⁴ Hedges, *Tin in . . . History*, p. 86.
⁵ Bapst, pp. 210–13; G. Fagniez, *Études sur l'industrie et la classe industrielle à Paris, au treizième et au quatorzième siècle* (Paris, 1877), pp. 7–19.

of workers in wood and clay in the late thirteenth century.[1] By 1304 there were nineteen master pewterers at work in the city.[2] In fact by the time we learn of a craft of pewterers in London in 1348, gilds and associations of pewterers had been in existence in many European cities for decades. For example, there is proof of gilds in Nüremberg, Lübeck and Frankfurt before 1300, Bruges by 1303, Augsburg by 1324, Ath by 1328, and Poitiers by 1333.[3]

The importance of French pewterers is confirmed by the role played by France in the consumption and distribution of English tin; indeed it seems likely that the greater part of the tin which left England in the thirteenth and early fourteenth centuries was destined for French ports. Substantial quantities of tin went direct to Normandy and Brittany for local consumption and for redistribution to the major urban centres of the region and the fairs for Champagne, but the route *par excellence* was that which linked the ports of south-west England and London to the ports of south-west France. La Rochelle, Bordeaux, Bayonne and Oléron were the major ports of the region and they regularly received large quantities of English tin; the merchants of Bayonne and La Rochelle played such an important part in this trade that for a time the English government informed their mayors and leading citizens of any changes in policy which might affect the production and sale of tin.[4] On the other hand the development of pewter industries in German cities no doubt owed much to the exploitation of the tin resources of Bohemia and Saxony, which commenced in the mid-thirteenth century, or even earlier.[5]

Considering that England for centuries had been virtually the sole producer of tin in Europe, her failure to provide a sizeable pewter industry before the mid-fourteenth century is striking. But on further reflection this particular lack of enterprise can be seen as just another symptom of the general inability of the English economy of the thirteenth and early fourteenth centuries to seize the opportunities which presented themselves. The experience of pewter closely paralleled the failure, before the mid-fourteenth century, to develop a cloth industry capable of generating a substantial export trade, despite the advantage of having the

[1] Bapst, p. 214.   [2] Hedges, *Tin in . . . History*, p. 86.
[3] Tardy, *Les Étains français* (Paris, 1959); Bapst, pp. 217–24, Hedges, *Tin in . . . History*, p. 88.
[4] Hatcher, pp. 21–4.   [5] *Ibid.*, pp. 25–6.

best wool in Europe produced at home. Comparable shortcomings can also be found in the fields of shipping and finance, where English merchants played second fiddle to aliens.

Notwithstanding, the manufacture of pewter was pursued in England in the twelfth and thirteenth centuries and, as we have seen, it was geared to the provision of ecclesiastical utensils and ornaments. It is probable, however, that this pewter was the work of general metalworkers rather than specialist pewterers; the demand for pewter before the fourteenth century was neither so continuous nor so great as to encourage men to specialize solely in its production. It is significant that the manufacturing process described by Theophilus in the early twelfth century was the 'lost wax' method, which was suited only to the production of very small numbers of articles.[1] If we may judge from the two surviving cruets of thirteenth or fourteenth century date discussed earlier, a number of pieces were of exceptionally fine quality and highly decorative, and therefore likely to have been produced by skilled craftsmen who may also have worked in precious metals. Simpler pieces of pewter may well have been cast and hammered by men who also worked in bronze and copper, latten and iron, and perhaps also as bell-founders.

The potters, founders, latteners, and braziers of thirteenth and early fourteenth century London were such a body of men. In addition to their normal employment of casting bronze pots and pans and making spurs, buckles, stirrups, bowls, and candlesticks, we also find them making brass lecterns, copper angels, weather vanes, gilt bronze effigies, bells and even lavatories. It was William Torel, goldsmith, who, using the casting techniques of the bell-founder, created the bronze effigies of Henry III and Queen Eleanor for Westminster Abbey.[2] The manufacture of pewter before the fourteenth century was undoubtedly in the hands of men such as these; indeed the small-scale production and repair of pewter by general metalworkers and itinerant tinkers continued into the nineteenth century, particularly in country areas.

Yet from the early fourteenth century craftsmen specializing in the manufacture of pewter begin to emerge from the records of

[1] *On Divers Arts*, pp. 179–83.
[2] G. Unwin, ed. *Studies of Finance and Trade under Edward III* (1918), pp. 31–4; E. M. Veal 'Craftsmen and the economy of London in the fourteenth century', *Studies in London History*, ed. A. E. J. Hollaender and W. Kellaway (1969), pp. 145–8.

English cities with, as one would expect, those of London very much to the fore. The first positive identification of a pewterer occurs in 1311 when, coincidentally, no less than three can be found in different documents: William de Suttone, who was admitted to the freedom of the City,[1] Lambert le Peuterer of Middlesex, who gave lands in Westminster to the abbot and convent of Vale Royal, Cheshire,[2] and John le Peuterer, who appeared as a juror in a case heard before the mayor.[3] Furthermore, although not a single person with the occupational surname of pewterer occurs in the London subsidy roll of 1292, no less than four appear in that of 1319: Geoffrey, John, Thomas and William 'le Peautrer'.[4] Occupational surnames of the early fourteenth century are no longer a sure guide to the occupation of the bearer, but the prefix 'le' appears to leave only negligible doubt that these men were pewterers. The London subsidy rolls are a good source for early pewterers and in those of 1332 we discover William and Thomas le Peautrer,[5] while Roger and Margery le Peautrer appear in other London records dated 1331 and 1333 respectively.[6] Nevertheless many pewterers at this date had names which give no clue to their occupation, we have already noticed William de Suttone, and the men chosen to 'oversee and keep' the ordinances of the Craft of Pewterers in 1348 and 1349 were named Stephen le Straunge, John Syward, Nicholas de Ludgate and Ernald Schipwaysshe[7]; only Nicholas de Ludgate appears sometimes to have been known as Nicholas 'le Peudrer'.[8]

The registration in 1348 of ordinances for the control of pewtering within London can thus be seen as a natural development from the growth of the industry. These ordinances, which provide the first proof of the existence of an organisation of

[1] *Calendar of Letter Books preserved among the archives of the city of London at Guildhall*, ed. R. R. Sharpe, 12 vols (1894–1912), *Letter Book D*, pp. 35–179.
[2] *Descriptive Catalogue of Ancient Deeds*, i, A.1538; P. H. Reaney, *A Dictionary of British Surnames* (1958), p. 249.
[3] *Calendar of Letter Books, Book D*, p. 190.
[4] Three resided in Cheap Ward and the other in Langebourne (E. Ekwall, ed., *Two Early London Subsidy Rolls* (Lund, 1951), pp. 243, 292, 298, 300; Reaney, p. 249).
[5] Both resided in Cheap Ward (M. Curtis, 'The London lay subsidy of 1332', in *Studies in Finance and Trade*, ed. Unwin, pp. 70, 71).
[6] *Calendar of Letter Books, Book E*, p. 259; G. Fransson, *Middle English Surnames of Occupation, 1100–1350* (Lund, 1935), p. 139.
[7] *Memorials of London and London Life in the XIIIth, XIVth, and XVth Centuries*, ed. H. T. Riley (1868), p. 244.
[8] *Hustings Wills*, i, 502–3.

pewterers within Britain, show clearly by their detail and complexity that pewter manufacture had strong traditions and a sophisticated body of technical and trade rules. In addition to regulations concerning, among other things, standards of workmanship and the admission of members, the ordinances also list some of the wide range of articles which were already being made of pewter, including 'pottes, salers, dysshes, platers, and othir thinges' and 'disshes, Saucers, platers, Chargeours, pottes square, Cruets square, Crismatories, and othir thinges that they make square or Cistils' and candlesticks.[1]

Unfortunately it is not possible to estimate the size of the London pewter industry before the start of the Company records in the mid-fifteenth century, since the registers of admission to the freedom of the City, unlike those of York, have not survived. But by a fortunate chance the names and occupations of persons made free during the years 1309–12 were entered in one of the extant London Letter Books.[2] During this troubled period in London's politics 253 persons were admitted to the freedom by apprenticeship and 656 by redemption; in addition a number of enrolments of apprentices were also recorded. Of the 909 new freemen, from over 120 occupations, there was only a single pewterer: William de Suttone who was admitted on 25 July 1311 on payment of 10s[3]; no apprentice pewterers were admitted. Thus, despite the scope and complexity of the ordinances of 1348 one is forced to conclude that pewtering as a specialist occupation emerged as late as the opening decades of the fourteenth century. On the other hand, however, there can be no doubt that a rapid expansion of the industry took place in the brief period encompassed by the second and fifth decades, an expansion of such proportions that in 1360 Nicholas le Peudrer, perhaps acting on behalf of a syndicate of London pewterers, was able to write to the Black Prince, the lord of the stannaries, offering to 'come to the next coinage after Easter to buy a great part of the tin and pay promptly for the coinage thereof'.[4]

[1] This is the early English version preserved amongst the Company's records; strangely it omits candlesticks, which appear on the original Norman-French and Latin version (C. Welch, *History of the Worshipful Company of Pewterers of the City of London*) (2 vols, 1902) i, 2–6; *Memorials of London*, p. 242).
[2] *Calendar of Letter Books, Book D*, pp. 35–179. See also the analysis by A. H. Thomas in *Calendar of Plea and Memoranda Rolls 1364–81* (1929), pp. xxxii–vi, l–lvi.
[3] *Calendar of Letter Books, Book D*, p. 72.
[4] *The Registers of Edward the Black Prince, 1346–65*, 4 vols (1930–3), ii, p. 170.

Although London was clearly by far the most important centre of the English pewter industry, pewterers were at work in other parts of the country. The York Freemen's Rolls, which provide a continuous record of enrolments to the freedom of the city from 1272 onwards, record their first pewterer, William de Ordesale, in 1348, and the second, Thomas de Weston, a year later.[1] We also learn of a John Peautrer at work in Norfolk in 1350.[2] A sizeable body of pewterers was at work in Cornwall in the 1340s although in this case they were probably the agents of the nefarious forces which were at work to defraud the Duchy of Cornwall of the tax paid on tin produced within the county. In 1343 it was asserted that 'whereas the coinage of tin in the said county and profit thereof pertains to the Duke so that no tin ought to be carried from the county or vessels worked therefrom until the tin has been coined many pewterers daily work vessels out of uncoined tin', and that these pewterers were aided and abetted by the leading tin merchants of the county, with the result that the Duke had 'lost his profit to a very large sum'.[3] It was also repeatedly claimed in this decade that substantial quantities of pewter vessels were being smuggled out of Cornwall.[4] Finally, in 1346, the Duchy sought to restrict these illegal activities by declaring that 'no pewterer is to work in the Duchy except two, to wit, one in the castle of Launceveton and the other in the castle of Restormel, (and) that the tin to be worked by them is to be seen and examined by the prince's receiver before being worked'.[5] It appears that these illegal practices were gradually brought under control, although the lack of immediate success is attested by the need for further action in 1348 and 1350 against those who continued to export pewter made from uncoined tin.[6] Unfortunately by their very nature these pewter shipments have left no record on contemporary customs accounts, and there are no means by which they can be quantified.

Behind the growth in the pewter industry outlined above lay a massive increase in the production of tin. The small-scale and intermittent exploitation of tin deposits which took place between the departure of the Romans and the Norman Conquest has been

[1] *Register of the Freemen of the City of York, 1272–1558*, ed. F. Collins (Surtees Society, xcvi, 1896), pp. 41, 42.   [2] Fransson, *Middle English Surnames*, p. 139.
[3] *Calendar of Patent Rolls (CPR) 1343–45*, p. 75.
[4] *CPR 1340–43*, p. 582; ibid., *1343–45*, p. 71; ibid., *1345–48*, p. 390.
[5] *Registers of the Black Prince*, i, pp. 26–7.   [6] *CPR 1348–50*, pp. 74, 519.

noted above, and when the series of records of the taxes levied on tin production commence in 1156 annual output was little more than 65 tons.[1] But the late twelfth century was a watershed in the history of the stannaries, a period when output and employment was poised on the brink of a truly phenomenal expansion, and by 1214 output was almost ten times higher than in 1156. Unfortunately records cease in 1214 and are not available again until the early fourteenth century, when it is clear that a subsequent major depression in output had been experienced, for by 1301 production had been almost halved to 279 tons. Doubtless the expansion of English production, combined with the intensive exploitation of the tinfields of central Europe a few decades later, had saturated the market and induced a drastic curtailment of supply. By the fourteenth century, however, the market for English tin was once again expanding rapidly, partly due no doubt to the growing popularity of pewter. Consequently Cornish production which, after substantial increases in the first decades of the century, had attained almost 450 tons in 1324, suddenly embarked on a further burst of exceptional expansion and by 1332 reached the unprecedented level of 734 tons, and although contracting slightly thereafter it continued to average over 550 tons per annum in the succeeding decade.[2] Of further stimulus to the pewter industry was the fact that this striking advance in tin production was achieved without significant increases in price: after rises in the later thirteenth century tin prices were relatively stable in the first half of the fourteenth at $1d$ to $1\frac{1}{2}d$ per pound in Cornwall and $1\frac{1}{2}d$ to $2d$ per pound in London and Oxford.[3] Unfortunately, there is no direct evidence of the price of pewter at this time, but from current tin prices and wage rates it was unlikely to have been more than $2\frac{1}{2}d$ per pound in London.

Although it is inevitable that the use of pewter in the household preceded our earliest record of it, there can be no doubt whatsoever that before the early fourteenth century such use was

[1] Hatcher, Appendix A.
[2] Unfortunately the Devon stannaries were farmed for most of the fourteenth century; Cornish production, however, appears to have been eight to ten times greater than that of the neighbouring county.
[3] Based on prices of tin purchased for building work in Cornwall, Oxford and London (Hatcher, p. 90).

extremely rare. It is possible to amass a considerable body of evidence illustrating consumption, complementary to that of the production side already discussed, which bears witness to the increasing popularity of domestic pewter in the fourteenth century in preference to articles made of cheaper materials such as wood, clay, stone and leather. Surprisingly, two of the earliest records of domestic pewter come from Durham: from the first we learn that in 1312 Finchale Priory purchased a dozen pewter plates for 3s,[1] and from the second that *ij picheri de stagno* were among the goods left on the death of John Fitz Marmaduke, Lord of Horden, at Silksworth in 1318.[2] But even more telling are those records which clearly show pewter succeeding cheaper materials: such as the purchase of pewter pitchers in 1340 by the bursar of Durham Cathedral Priory for the feast of St Cuthbert, in preference to the clay pitchers which he had purchased for the same feast four years before,[3] or the fact that whereas the cellarers of Battle Abbey thought clay or wooden dishes were suitable for the visit of Edward I in 1275–76, by 1359–60 pewter dishes, plates, and cruets were being purchased for the monks' own use.[4] The wills of the merchant classes are also revealing, for in contrast to the opening decades of the fourteenth century, when they displayed no trace of pewter, from the fifth decade small quantities begin to appear with mounting frequency. Among the wills of London merchants who died in the 1340s we find a number of references to pewter. In 1345, for example, both Thomas Corp, pepperer, and Richard Constantyn, draper, bequeathed pewter, the will of the former speaks of 'divers vessels of mazer, vessels of silver and of bronze, *peutre*, and iron', and that of the latter refers to 'all his vessels and utensils of silver, bronze, iron, wood, stone, and tin, and all his household furniture'.[5]

In 1369 on the death of William Cosyn, a London potter, his wife inherited 'all his utensils of gold, silver, wood, lead and tin'.[6] Leaden vessels are also mentioned in a number of other

[1] J. E. T. Rogers, *A History of Agriculture and Prices in England*, 7 vols (Oxford, 1866–1902), ii, 569.
[2] *Wills and Inventories of the Northern Counties*, i, 19.
[3] *Extracts from the Account Rolls of the Abbey of Durham*, ed. J. T. Fowler, 3 vols (Surtees Society, xcix, c, ciii, 1898–1901), i, 533.
[4] *The Accounts of the Cellarers of Battle Abbey, 1275–1513*, ed. E. Searle and B. Ross (1967), pp. 42, 60; see also p. 80 for '12 pewter vessels garnys' purchased for 13s in 1384–5.
[5] *Hustings Wills*, i, 477, 482.
[6] Ibid., ii, 129.

wills. For example, that of Nicholas Miller of Medomsley, Durham (d. 1334), refers to *'omnia vasa lignea et plumbea et utensilia domui meae'*,¹ whilst that of Thomas atte Vigne (d. 1349), a London woolmonger, refers to 'his entire chamber, with all vessels and utensils of silver, iron, lead and wood'.² The exact nature of these leaden vessels is obscure, but it is probable that they were made of a lead–tin alloy, cheaper to produce than good quality pewter but far softer, unpleasant to use, and even injurious to health— precisely the sort of inferior wares that the ordinances of the London pewterers were designed to eliminate.³

Both the number of surviving wills and the frequency with which they mention pewter increase sharply from the later fourteenth century; furthermore it becomes more usual for the type and quantity of pewter to be specified. In London wills of the 1370s and 1380s, for example, we learn of 'dishes of peautrer and four large chargeours', 'two candelabras of tin', 'half a dozen peutrevessel',⁴ and a 'lavour of peuter with the basin of led'.⁵ But the use of pewter was by no means confined to London or to the merchant classes. Indeed the outstanding features of the consumption of pewter in the fourteenth century were the speed and thoroughness with which it was disseminated throughout the country and the social hierarchy, with the obvious exception of the poorer classes. To take two examples from opposite ends of the country, pewter was used in the households of John Blake of Bodmin (d. 1352),⁶ and Adam de Stanton of Suffolk (d. 1370).⁷ The spread of pewter to the households of some richer peasants is examined below (pp. 57-9).

Naturally the nobility quickly found a use for pewter tableware and kitchenware: it conveniently bridged the gap between costly vessels of gold and silver and those of wood and clay to be found in the homes of common peasants, and it was eminently suited to the needs of itinerant households for whom the transport of

---

[1] *Wills and Inventories of the Northern Counties*, i, 25.
[2] *Hustings Wills*, i, 552-3.
[3] The Pewterers' ordinances of 1348 specifically forbade members of the craft to make 'privily in secret vessels of lead, or of false alloy' (*Memorials*, p. 243). It was a great temptation to use more than the permitted amount of lead because it was on average four to five times cheaper than tin (Rogers, *A History of Agriculture and Prices*, ii, 530-4).
[4] *Hustings Wills*, ii, 202, 271, 277.
[5] *The Fifty Earliest English Wills in the Court of Probate, London*, ed. F. J. Furnivall (Early English Text Society, 1882), p. 2.
[6] Duchy of Cornwall Office, 5 (pewter worth 3s4d).
[7] *Bury Wills and Inventories*, p. 1 (old pewter worth 4s2d).

gold and silver was a risky undertaking. We learn that as early as 1354 the household of Edward the Black Prince used pewter, when the receiver of Cornwall was ordered to send 'vessels of tin' from Restormel to Sonning, near Reading.[1] The Prince may well have started a fashion amongst his retinue for in July 1357 his clerk, Sir Richard de Wolveston, purchased 500 lb of tin in Cornwall 'to make vessels thereof for his own use', and a month later a further 500 lb 'as the original 500 lb weight bought by him did not suffice to make the vessels he intended'.[2]

Evidence from continental Europe presents a similar picture to that from England, although one suspects that even as late as the close of the fourteenth century the consumption of pewter per head in many parts of France, Germany and the Low Countries remained greater than in England. Bapst in his pioneering work on French pewter found that by the outbreak of the Hundred Years War in 1337 a veritable revolution in tableware and kitchenware was in progress, with utensils of copper, wood and clay giving way to pewter.[3] Instead of the occasional references to pewter storage vessels and pewter held by church dignitaries noted earlier, we now find substantial quantities appearing in the houses of the nobility, gentry and bourgeoisie all over France. An inventory made in 1344 of the possessions of Jeanne de Presles, for example, lists the following wealth of pewter kitchenware:

> Deux chauderons blans ... trois grans plas d'estain, VIII moiens plas, quarante-cinq escuelles, tous d'estain. Item trois grans plas d'estain, douze solz. Item huit plas d'estain, seize solz. Item quarante-six escuelles d'estain, que bonnes que mauvaises, quarante solz. Item deux quartes d'estain, six pintes quarrées d'estain et deux chopines d'estain, et un pot d'estain à aumosnes, tous vint solz.[4]

In 1380 we find the king himself, Charles VI, purchasing six dozen dishes and twelve dozen porringers from Michelet le Breton, a Paris pewterer,[5] and in 1393 in the kitchens of the celebrated *bon viveur*, Baron Pichon, we find ten dozen dishes, six dozen small and two and a half dozen large platters, eight quart pots, two dozen pints, and two 'poz à aumosnes'.[6]

[1] *Registers of the Black Prince*, ii, 68.
[2] *Ibid.*, ii, 116, 124.
[3] Bapst, pp. 150–1.
[4] *Ibid.*, p. 171.
[5] Bell, pp. 59–60.
[6] Bapst, p. 172.

As one would expect the homes of the French ecclesiastical nobility were well stocked with pewter in the later fourteenth century. The Bishop of Troyes in 1370–71, for example, had fourteen dozen pewter dishes in his palace at Troyes, and a further four dozen at Aix-en-Othe, while in 1380 a mere Canon of Sainte-Chapelle boasted eighteen plates and forty-five dishes of pewter. From an inventory of the estate of the Archbishop of Rheims, compiled in 1389, we find a hint of the complex and highly decorated styles that later were to become so popular on the Continent, for in addition to huge quantities of unspecified pewter listed by weight it records: 'Plats, escuelles, une grande escuelle à aumosne, quarte, avec et sans couvercles, carrées, rondes, à façon d'argent, chopines et pintes en étain pesant 155 livres'.[1]

Nor was pewter limited to the homes of the nobility, for the bourgeoisie in France, as in England, were quick to use pewter; Guillaume de Bosc senior in distant Normandy, for example, possessed at least seventeen large and nine small platters, three and a half dozen dishes, six saucers, seven salt-cellars and a large assortment of pots and drinking vessels made of pewter. And also, as in England, there is evidence of pewter reaching the homes of artisans and peasants.[2]

Naturally the number of pewterers grew in concert with the demand for their wares, established centres of manufacture expanded, and many towns gained a pewterers' gild for the first time, as did Rouen, Hamburg, Dijon and Limoges, whose gilds are first mentioned in 1369, 1375, 1382 and 1394 respectively.[3] Furthermore, both the popularity of pewter on the Continent and the rapid expansion of the English industry is attested by the customs accounts of the later fourteenth century, which in 1390–91 recorded exports by alien merchants of almost 20 tons from London alone.[4]

At first sight it may well appear paradoxical to argue that the production of a commodity increased in the course of a century which experienced a decline in total population of the order of

[1] *Ibid.*, pp. 148, 166–8. It is also interesting to note in this context that in 1323 Jean de Jeandun stated that there were a number of chasers of gold, silver, pewter and copper on the Grand Pont in Paris (*ibid.*, p. 215).
[2] *Ibid.*, p. 154. For the stock of pewter held by an enterprising farming curé in Burgundy in 1377 see G. Duby, *Rural Economy and Country Life in the Medieval West* (1968 edn), p. 341.
[3] Hedges, *Tin in . . . History*, p. 87; Bell, p. 59.
[4] PRO E.122. 71/8. For further discussions of the export trade see below p. 64.

upwards of 30 per cent, largely as a result of epidemic plague.¹ Indeed historical controversies have tended to centre on whether *per capita* production rose or fell rather than on the course of absolute production, which is invariably assumed to have declined.² Nevertheless, whereas it is clear that the output of most basic commodities tended to fall in the course of the later fourteenth and the fifteenth centuries, thereby contributing to the downward tendencies exhibited by most sectors of internal and international trade, it is possible that the changed consumption patterns consequent upon the massive redistribution of wealth and opportunity which followed upon the heels of population decline resulted in increases in the output of a smaller range of commodities. Woollen textiles are a case in point, where the rise in general living standards may well have inspired an augmentation in the *per capita* consumption of cloth of an order of magnitude sufficient to offset the decrease in population.³ In the case of pewter there can be no doubt that just such an augmentation did take place, and that far more pewter was produced after the Black Death than before.

The size of the market for pewter depended on a range of factors in addition to its price, among which tastes and preferences and the distribution of wealth were the most important, while on the supply side the availability of tin was obviously a crucial variable. In order to demonstrate and explain the increased consumption of pewter in the later Middle Ages it is perhaps simplest to look first at the general improvements which took place in the quality and quantity of household furniture and equipment, and second at the redistribution of wealth which enabled greater numbers of households to afford pewter.

One of the most striking features of early medieval households, even the richest, was the small number of rooms and the sparseness and rudeness of their furnishings. The wooden furniture

¹ For general discussions of late medieval demographic history see: K. Helleiner, 'The population of Europe from the Black Death to the eve of the vital revolution', in *Cambridge Economic History of Europe*, iv, (Cambridge, 1967); M. M. Postan, 'Some economic evidence of declining population in the later Middle Ages', *Economic History Review*, 2nd ser., ii (1950).
² For a general discussion of late medieval economic developments see: M. M. Postan, 'The trade of medieval Europe: the North, the age of contraction', in *Cambridge Economic History of Europe*, ii (Cambridge, 1952). A. R. Bridbury, *Economic Growth: England in the later Middle Ages* (1962), presents a controversial interpretation of the period which stresses the benefits of population decline.
³ For a tentative statement of this view see E. M. Carus-Wilson, *Medieval Merchant Venturers* (1954), p. 261 n.

of the hall of a noble house, the most important room, would commonly consist of the chief table raised up on a dais across the upper end with subordinate tables arranged at right angles to it, and seating composed of benches with an occasional chair; there might also be a dresser to display the most handsome items of tableware. The tables themselves were merely boards placed on trestles, although it gradually became more common for the chief table to be a dormant or stationary table. In the wealthiest households the walls of the hall would be hung round with tapestries or curtains, but the floor was rarely carpeted, rushes being the normal covering. Chambers were on the whole more comfortably furnished than the hall, with walls hung with tapestries or curtains, floors sometimes carpeted, chairs, often a cabinet or two against the wall, and a number of chests for clothes and valuables, and, of course, a bed.[1] In fact the bed soon became the object of conspicuous expenditure, and it was a matter of pride to furnish it with the finest possible coverings, such as cloth of gold, velvet, and arras.[2]

The table and the kitchen are, however, our true concern, and here also we find the simplicity and lack of variety displayed elsewhere in the household. From contemporary illustrations and descriptions of meals it is clear that tables were usually laid with only salt-cellars, knives, jugs, and drinking vessels, none of which were assigned to individual guests; neither plates nor forks were used. The food was usually served in larges dishes from which two or more guests would select portions with their fingers, assisted occasionally by a shared knife or spoon, setting them down on thick slices of bread called trenchers. It was also customary for more than one guest to share the same cup.[3] In the kitchen the range of utensils was necessarily far greater and included, according to the late-twelfth-century *Liber de Utensilibus* of Alexander Neckam and the mid-thirteenth-century *Dictionarius* of John

[1] T. Wright, *A History of Domestic Manners and Sentiments in England during the Middle Ages* (1862), pp. 120–40, 153–4, 244–6, 256–66; M. W. Labarge, *A Baronial Household of the Thirteenth Century* (1965), pp. 18–37.
[2] A. P. Eames, 'Documentary evidence concerning the character and use of domestic furnishings in England in the fourteenth and fifteenth centuries', *Furniture History*, vii (1971), 42–7.
[3] Wright, *History of Domestic Manners*, pp. 158–61, 276–7; Labarge, p. 124; see also the instructions for laying a table etc. in John Russell's 'Boke of Nurture' and 'The Boke of Curtasye', *Early English Meals and Manners*, ed. F. J. Furnivall (Early English Text Society, 32, 1868). Even as late as the turn of the fifteenth century a visitor wrote that Englishmen did not consider it an inconvenience 'for three or four persons to drink out of the same cup' (*Italian Relation of England*, p. 21).

Garlande, cauldrons, frying-pans, saucepans, and pots of bronze; tripods, gridirons, and spits of iron; various aids to cooking such as peppermills, handmills, and mincers; and an assortment of barrels, jugs, dishes, platters, and saucers, for the storing and serving of food and drink.[1]

Fig. 2.1 A royal feast of the fourteenth century

Fig. 2.2 A royal feast of the fourteenth century

[1] T. Wright, *A Volume of Vocabularies* (1882).

The Middle Ages 49

Fig. 2.3 A royal feast of the early sixteenth century

From the later fourteenth century, however, it is evident that the standard of housing and furnishings enjoyed by most classes was undergoing a substantial improvement.[1] Houses of the nobility and gentry often contained far more rooms than hitherto, and of particular note was the increasing popularity of comfortably appointed parlours for audiences and entertaining.[2] Textiles and plate still comprised the most valuable elements in

---

[1] Wright, *History of Domestic Manners*, p. 359; M. W. Barley, *The English Farmhouse and Cottage* (1961), pp. 19–20; Eames, pp. 53–4.
[2] Wright, *History of Domestic Manners*, pp. 370–3.

household goods, but wooden furniture was being kept in greater quantities and in more elaborate and varied forms, while dressers for the ostentatious display of plate became almost obligatory.¹ On the table many more utensils were used: individual plates, drinking vessels, and even salt-cellars became more common, as did the use of platters under the slice of trencher bread.² And whereas silver, or perhaps even gold, continued to be provided for the most important members of the household and their guests, the desire to impress often dictated that pewter be substituted for pottery and wood on the lower tables.

At the turn of the fourteenth century it would appear that each noble household possessed substantial quantities of pewter, and that purchases of this commodity increased in the course of the fifteenth century.³ In royal household accounts modest purchases of pewter occur frequently, and by 1526 £40 a year was thought to be an acceptable sum for pewter for Henry VIII's household at Eltham, which compares with £20 for ashen cups and £5 for leather pots,⁴ and the parsimonious Elizabeth spent £14.13s8d on the purchase and repair of pewter during her residence at Hatfield in 1551–52.⁵ That some of this expenditure went on replacing stolen vessels is indicated by the instructions given to the porters of the Duke of Clarence's household in 1469, who were 'to see that no vitaills, silver plate, pewter vessels ne none other stuffe of the household be enbeselled out'.⁶

The tastes of the English crown were shared by the king of Scotland, who in 1430 had eight dozen pewter vessels shipped northwards from London,⁷ and by Clement VI of France, who in 1422 purchased 64 dishes and 158 porringers from a pewterer of Tours.⁸ In fact pewter, especially if it was of English manufacture,

¹ *Ibid.*, pp. 379–81; for contemporary instructions on how to display plate see *Early English Meals and Manners*, ed. Furnivall, p. 15.
² Compare the illustrations of a thirteenth-century feast with that of a fifteenth-century feast, pp. 48–9. See also *Early English Meals and Manners*, pp. 202–4, 350–6; Wright, *History of Domestic Manners*, pp. 369–70.
³ See, for example, the regular purchases for the household of the Duke of Norfolk from 1462 to 1471 (*Manners and Household Expenses*, ed. Turner, pp. 273, 279, 416).
⁴ *A Collection of Ordinances and Regulations for the Government of the Royal Household* (Society of Antiquaries, 1790), pp. 195–6.
⁵ 'Household expenses of Princess Elizabeth during her residence at Hatfield, 1.10.1551–30.9.1552', *Camden Miscellany Volume Two* (Camden Society, lv, 1853), 23–4.
⁶ *Ordinances and Regulations for the Royal Household*, p. 92.
⁷ *Foedera, Conventiones, Litterae, etc.*, ed. T. Rymer, 4 vols in 7 parts (Record Commission, 1811–59), x, 470.
⁸ Bell, p. 64.

was not eschewed by the papacy: in 1382 'certain vessels of pewter namely six great chargers, 24 dishes, 24 large saucers and an inkwell of tin' were purchased in England on behalf of the pope, probably Urban VI, and we also learn of the export from Southampton in 1387 of 'a barrel filled with vessels of pewter with the pope's arms thereupon ... purveyed within the realm for the pope's use'.[1] But even this was not the first pewter to find its way into the household of a pope, for in 1379 there were at least thirty-nine dishes and six plates of pewter in the rival Clement VII's residence at Avignon.[2]

It is clear that in households which possessed an abundance of silver and even gold, pewter still had some part to play. For example, in 1400 Thomas de Dalby, Archdeacon of Richmond, a great and wealthy ecclesiastic whose jurisdiction covered a large part of north Yorkshire, north Lancashire and south Cumberland, in addition to silver tableware valued at more than £200, and ready money in excess of £800, possessed fifty-five dishes and twenty-one salt-cellars of pewter.[3] Even the fabulously wealthy Sir John Fastolf, hero of Agincourt and property and business entrepreneur extraordinary, who left on his death in 1459, in addition to some gold plate, almost 20,000 ounces of silver including at least 100 dishes, 50 bowls and basins, 85 platters and chargers, 80 saucers, 50 spoons, 20 salt-cellars, 40 flagons, 30 pots, 50 cups, and 30 candlesticks, as well as numerous unclassifiable pieces of exotic design, at least had two 'chamber basins', four chargers, six platters, and six saucers of pewter in his home, even though they were doubtless only for the use of servants.[4]

The use of pewter by noble households on travels and expeditions is strikingly illustrated in the accounts of expenditure by the Earl of Derby on sojourns in Prussia and the Holy Land in 1390–91 and 1392–93. While in Prussia in 1391 a large quantity of pots and dishes was purchased from 'Hans Peutrer of Conyngsburg' at a cost of £65 Prussian, and on return to England a further ten dozen dishes and fifty-six salt-cellars of pewter were purchased

[1] *CCR 1382–85*, p. 56; *ibid., 1385–89*, p. 232.
[2] Bapst, p. 166.
[3] *English Historical Documents*, vol. iv, ed. A. R. Myers (1969), 699–703.
[4] T. Amyot, 'Transcript of two rolls containing an inventory of effects formerly belonging to Sir John Fastolfe, 1459', *Archaeologia*, xxi (1827), 232–80. See also 'The will and inventory of Robert Morton, Gentleman, 1486–8', *Journal of the British Archaeological Association*, xxxiii (1877), 308–30.

for the household. On the second expedition, to the Holy Land, further pewter was purchased in Venice.[1] It is interesting to note that vast quantities of wooden cups and dishes were also used by Derby's household in these years. Also of interest is the fact that not all the pewter used by noble households was bought outright: some was hired. In 1512, for example, in addition to purchasing two garnishes of 'counterfeit vessels' and six dozen 'Rugh Pewter Vessell', the treasurer of Henry Percy, fifth Earl of Northumberland, also hired 40 dozen 'Rugh Pewder Vessell' on four monthly contracts.[2]

The hire of pewter specifically for large dinners and feasts was a more common occurrence, and many pewterers kept large stocks for this purpose. In London in 1476–77 Robert Turnour hired out at least 148 dozen garnishes of pewter and Thomas Langtofte 120 garnishes.[3] The quantities of pewter used at feasts increased along with the vogue for even larger and more ostentatious occasions. For the Lord Mayor's feast in 1505, for example, over 9,000 pieces of pewter were hired, comprising 'in platters gret and small xij^{xx} x dozen [250 dozen = 3,000], item dyshis gret and small xij^{xx} x dozen, item in saucers gret and small xij^{xx} x dozen, item in chargers gret and small x dozen'; the drinking vessels were made of clay, ash and stone.[4] This was undoubtedly a particularly flamboyant occasion, but in 1467 when Sir John Howard and Thomas Brewse gave a feast at Ipswich for the voters of Suffolk, in celebration of their being adopted knights of the shire, the hire and loss of pewter comprised some $2\frac{1}{2}$ per cent of the total cost.[5]

Improvements in housing and domestic furnishings in the later Middle Ages were by no means confined to the upper classes; on the contrary, perhaps the most significant developments took place in the middle strata, with the redistribution of wealth and opportunity consequent on massive population decline leading to a growth in the numbers of persons of substance who were

[1] *Expeditions to Prussia and the Holy Land made by Henry Earl of Derby in the years 1390–1 and 1392–3*, ed. L. Toulmin-Smith (Camden Society, new ser., lii, 1894), 101, 154, 211, 233.
[2] *The Regulations and Establishment of the Household of Henry Algernon Percy the fifth Earl of Northumberland at his castles of Wresill and Lekinfield in Yorkshire, begun A.D. 1512*, ed. T. Percy (1827), pp. 17, 19.
[3] Welch, I, 49–52.
[4] *Early English Meals and Manners*, pp. 363–4.
[5] The pewter cost 19s4d out of a total expenditure of £40.17s8d (*Manners and Household Expenses*, p. 400).

neither nobility nor gentry, a development which had profound effects on the consumption of pewter. The later fourteenth and the fifteenth centuries have been seen as 'an age of ambition' and pronounced social mobility, when the upper bourgeoisie of merchants and landowners was assimilating itself with the gentry through marriage and the adoption of 'gentle' life styles, the lesser bourgeoisie of shopkeepers and skilled artisans was proliferating and prospering, and yeomen were emerging from the ranks of the peasantry with sufficient capital to build and furnish fine houses or take over the manses vacated by their lords.[1] Furthermore, lower down the scale a virtual doubling of real wages, consequent on labour shortage and falling food prices, accomplished a substantial improvement in the standards of life of the masses.

With the cherished hierachy of status and wealth under such determined assault it is scarcely to be wondered at that the upper classes sought to defend their position. The spirit of the age, which combined acute awareness of the blurring of status divisions with a strong disapproval, is expertly grasped by Henry Knighton, who wrote in 1388 of 'the elation of the inferior people in dress and accoutrements in these days, so that one person cannot be discerned from another in splendour of dress or belongings, neither poor from rich, nor servant from master, nor priest from layman, but everybody tried to imitate the other, till the magnates had to decide on a remedy'.[2] One of the remedies decided on was the sumptuary statutes which repeatedly attempted, with a notable lack of success, to halt 'the outrageous and excessive apparel of divers people against their estate and degree' and to regulate personal possessions according to occupation and income.[3] The appearance of a series of books on etiquette devoted to such topics as courtly behaviour, the subtle differences and gradations of rank, and the symbolism and allegory of the intricate rituals of service at meals, should also be seen against this background of increased social mobility.[4]

But all this reaction was of little avail, the nature of society was

[1] See, in particular, F. R. H. Du Boulay, *An Age of Ambition* (1970); S. Thrupp, *The Merchant Class of Medieval London* (Michigan, 1948).
[2] *Knighton's Chronicon*, ii, 299 (quoted by Du Boulay, p. 67).
[3] See, for example, that of 1363 (printed in *English Historical Documents 1327–1485*, ed. A. R. Myers, pp. 1153–5); see also F. E. Baldwin, *Sumptuary Legislation and Personal Regulation in England* (Baltimore, 1926).
[4] A. R. Myers, *The Household of Edward IV* (Manchester, 1959), pp. 2–3.

such that the life styles of the nobility set a pattern which lesser mortals sought to copy to the fullest extent their resources would permit. For the *bourgeois gentilhommes* necessity usually demanded that the pomp and etiquette of seigneurial ostentation was simplified, that its scale was reduced, that cheaper materials were employed; but in essentials there was little attempt to develop alternative modes of behaviour. Consequently we find prosperous yeomen living in large stone houses, with domestic servants, the walls hung with linen and tapestry, sleeping on feather beds, and, in addition to acquiring the odd piece of silver, having pewter to grace the tables from which they ate their ample meals. Pewter was a status symbol and, along with silver, linen, tapestry, and feather beds, it helped to set the rural and urban bourgeoisie quite clearly apart from their lesser neighbours and on the ladder to gentility.[1] It was essential, therefore, that pewter, and other vessels of value, were displayed to the best effect, and to this end the *buffet*, *dressoir*, *vesseller* or *cupboard* was used; in many contemporary illustrations we find the family plate carefully displayed in this fashion in a prominent position in the parlour or hall.[2] Consequently from the end of the fourteenth century we find the middle strata of society—burgesses, yeomen, lesser clergy—frequently owning whole services of pewter, which provide a sharp contrast to the occasional ewer, basin or dish in the homes of their predecessors half a century or so earlier.

The following examples are intended to provide an indication of the scale and range of pewter held by some members of these social groups. With few exceptions they have perforce been selected from wills. Wills are a difficult source to employ, and only those which appear to enumerate a substantial portion of a testator's holdings of pewter have been selected. Unfortunately no estimate of average holdings or of the frequency with which pewter was held can be attempted before the sixteenth century when inventories first become available in substantial numbers.

A further substantial demand for pewter came from institutions. The use of pewter in monasteries and priories, whose extravagant style of living became a public scandal in the late Middle Ages,

[1] Du Boulay, p. 57; see also Bridbury, pp. 103–6, for evidence of the increase in the *per capita* consumption of 'luxuries'.
[2] Wright, *History of Domestic Manners*, pp. 379–81.

Table 3
Holdings of pewter mentioned in some fifteenth-century wills and inventories

London
1391	Richard Toky, grocer (inventory)	2 chargers, 12 platters, 10 dishes, 11 saucers, 9 trenchers, 2 half gallon pots, 3 quart pots, 1 pint, salt-cellars, 1 holy water stoup, 1 candlestick: 86 lb at $2d$ per lb; plus 2 shallow bowls
1426	John Credy, esquire	2½ dozen pewter vessels
1434	Roger Elmesly, waxchandler's servant	1 plate, 2 dishes, 2 saucers
1513	John Hudson, ironmonger	7 platters, 7 dishes, 7 saucers *
1517	Robert Tyde, chaplain	2 dishes, 2 saucers, 2 pots, 2 basins
1519	John Hardyng, rector of Cold Norton	7 platters, 7 dishes, 5 saucers, 1 salt-cellar, 1 basin

Bury St Edmund's
1418	Agnes Stubbard, clothier's widow	½ a garnish (i.e. 6 platters, 6 dishes, 6 saucers) with residue of pewter to be divided amongst 3 other beneficiaries
1437	John Nottingham, grocer	1 garnish, 2 quart pots, 1 'potel pot'
1463	John Baret, clothier	6 trenchers, 12 platters, 8 dishes, 8 saucers of old vessel, a charger of 'myldel syse', 1 pint and 1 quart pot *
1479	John Rokewood, squire	6 dishes, 4 saucers, 3 platters *
1493	William Honyboorn, dyer	1 garnish 'countorfete', 2 basins
1522	Agas Herte, widow	11 platters, 11 dishes, 11 saucers, 6 porringers, a 3-pint pot, 1 quart pot, 2 pint pots (1 'of the olde ffasshon'), 3 basins, 1 salt-cellar, 1 charger, a basin and ewer of hammered pewter

Northern Counties
1420	Roger de Kyrkby, vicar of Gainford, Durham (inventory)	2 dozen vessels, one dozen old vessels, 5 platters and 10 dishes
1427	John Ely, Vicar of Ripon, Yorks	½ a garnish and 2 chargers
1444	John Danby of Alverton, Durham	9 pieces of lead and pewter vessel *

Wiltshire
1476	Richard Gilbert, gentleman, Salisbury (inventory)	22 platters, 19 porringers, 10 saucers, 7 round dishes, 2 chargers, 2 broad dishes, 2 broken dishes, 8 lb old pewter, total 85 lb at $2d$ per lb

continued overleaf

Table 3 continued

Somerset

1501	John Cokur, Wells	2 dishes, 12 plates, 12 porringers, 12 saucers
1501	William Knoyell	'a hoole garnish of vessells' with the residue of vessels to daughters
1510	John Jeffreys, citizen and alderman of Bath	1 charger, 12 platters, 12 porringers, 12 saucers
1511	William Roynyon, esquire	'a hole garnysshe of pewter vessell of the best', 6 'eryd' dishes of pewter, 4 pots 'of the best'
1515	Reginald West, subdean of Wells	2 garnish of counterfeit, 1 garnish of vessel *
1519	John Welshote, mercer	3 garnish *
1520	Richard Holmede, tucker	6 platters, 6 porringers, 6 saucers

Nottinghamshire

1512	Thomas Robynete, Rampton (inventory)	14 pieces of pewter

* These wills are known to give an incomplete record.
Sources. Myers, ed., *English Historical Documents*, iv, 1070, 1152; *Earliest English Wills*, pp. 76, 101; *London Consistory Court Wills, 1492–1547*, ed. I. Darlington (London Record Society, iii, 1967), 30, 49, 50; *Bury Wills and Inventories*, pp. 3–4, 9–10, 23, 53, 81–2, 116–17; *Wills and Inventories of the Northern Counties*, i, 56, 90; Bell, *Old Pewter*, p. 65; *Somerset Medieval Wills, 1501–1530*, ed. F. W. Weaver (Somerset Record Society, xix, 1903), 18, 19, 148, 156, 183–4, 200, 207. *Nottinghamshire Household Inventories*, ed. P. A. Kennedy (Thoroton Society Record Series, xxii, 1963), p. 6.

has already been touched on,[1] and the expansion of education created a further market. In the fifteenth century Oxford and Cambridge colleges made frequent large-scale purchases of pewter; in 1466, for example, vessels weighing 274 lb were bought by King's College, Cambridge, and vessels weighing 100 lb were bought by various Oxford colleges.[2] The expenditure accounts of Winchester College reveal that from 1413 purchases of pewter were made more than four times a decade on average, thereby providing us with one of the best price series,[3] and an inventory drawn up in 1498 of the possessions of the Collegiate Church of Auckland, Durham, where many of the nobility and gentry

[1] See above p. 42. For a good example of the scale of monastic purchases from 1336 onwards see *Extracts from the Account Rolls of the Abbey of Durham*, ed. J. T. Fowler, 3 vols (Surtees Society, xc, c, ciii, 1898–1900), 108, 156, 184, 247, 386, 406, 533.
[2] Rogers, iii, 370–5; iv, 478–9.
[3] W. H. Beveridge, *Prices and Wages in England from the Twelfth to the Nineteenth Century* (1939), pp. 85–90. See also below Appendix B, pp. 275.

of the north were educated, lists twenty pewter platters, twelve pewter dishes, eight salt-cellars, a 'garnishe of vessell', and a 'shavyng Basyn'.[1] The London livery companies and the Inns of Court also had services of pewter, even the Goldsmiths' company which in 1470 spent £1.17s6d on a garnish of two dozen pewter vessels to serve the membership.[2]

Hence we can see that a substantial market for pewter had developed in the course of the fourteenth and fifteenth centuries among nobility, gentry, urban elites, and lay and ecclesiastical institutions. These are exactly the groups one would expect to have purchased a relatively expensive product for which there were many adequate and cheaper substitutes, and writers on medieval pewter have invariably assumed that consumers did not exist farther down the social scale.[3] As has been stated previously the bulk of the available documentation reflecting consumption patterns has a strong bias towards the upper groups in the social hierarchy, but a number of lists of the personal possessions of peasants have recently come to light which reveal that such an assumption is not wholly warranted.

Most lists of the household goods of peasants derive from the right of the lord to the whole or part of the goods of his tenants on their death. In some cases the lord appears to have owned the basic household goods and family equipment, and the tenant who took them over when entering a tenement was obliged to leave them when he gave up the tenure. These goods, which were called the *principalia*, clearly did not include all the movables of a holding, nevertheless there existed a positive correlation between the size of the holding and the range and value of the *principalia*. From the *principalia* of Worcestershire peasants in the late fourteenth and early fifteenth centuries, which have been studied in detail by R. K. Field,[4] we find that the lowest group of tenants, the cottagers with only a few acres, usually possessed bronze cooking pots and pans, and iron hearth equipment, but no other metal household utensils. Moving to the half-virgaters, holding approximately 15 acres, we find that in addition to the ubiquitous cooking pots

---

[1] *Wills and Inventories of the Northern Counties*, i, 101.
[2] Massé, *Pewter Plate*, p. 67.
[3] For example: Massé, *Pewter Plate*, p. 67; Bell, *Old Pewter*, pp. 62, 72; H.-U. Haedeke, *Metalwork* (1970), p. 178.
[4] R. K. Field, 'Worcestershire peasant buildings in the later Middle Ages', *Medieval Archaeology*, ix (1965).

and pans the tenants had drinking bowls or cups of unspecified material, and one had a leaden vessel. The tenants who held a virgate or more formed the peasant aristocracy and, as we might expect, their possessions reflected their enhanced wealth and status. The *principalia* of seven such tenants are listed, and they show that in addition to bronze pots and pans of greater capacity than lesser tenants, two possessed leaden vessels, two possessed ewers and basins, one possessed a silver spoon, and one possessed pewter worth 2*s*. The only tenant to possess pewter out of the twenty-nine whose *principalia* are known was also the most substantial landholder recorded, namely John More of Broadway, who died in 1392 the tenant of no less than five virgates (*c*. 150 acres).

Further invaluable information about peasant household furnishings is obtainable from estates where the lord exercised a right to all or part of the goods accumulated by certain categories of tenant. The exercise of this right necessitated the compiling of inventories, which, unlike the lists of *principalia*, purport to contain all possessions. In practice these inventories also have many deficiencies, but on the whole they provide a fuller picture of peasant standards of life than the lists of *principalia*. The lists compiled for the exercise of a terciar (third part) of the goods of the free and villein tenants on certain Shropshire manors of Wenlock Priory in the third quarter of the fourteenth century have been studied by W. F. Mumford,[1] and although often failing to provide a detailed enough description for our purposes they are worthy of attention. From them we learn that a number of tenants owned tableware, such as dishes, pitchers, and pots, and although the materials from which they were fashioned are not given it is clear from valuations that some were metal; for example, a small pitcher owned by John de Palton was valued at 6*s*, as were two small pitchers owned by John de Shipton. One particularly long and detailed inventory does survive, however, that of John Brice of Clee Stanton, who died in 1377 and left among his sizeable holdings of livestock, corn, and household goods '2 chargers, 7 dishes with 5 pewter saucers' and further pewter valued at 4*s*2*d*. Although an examination of the few surviving inventories of the possessions of Cornish servile tenants of the

---

[1] W. F. Mumford, 'Terciars on the estates of Wenlock Priory', *Transactions of the Shropshire Archaeological Society*, lviii (1965).

Duchy of Cornwall has failed to reveal any pewter,[1] it was a common item in the houses of wealthy tin miners.[2]

From this brief but welcome glimpse of peasant consumption patterns in the later fourteenth and early fifteenth centuries it is clear that the only metal household utensils the vast bulk of the peasantry possessed were cooking pots and hearth equipment; and yet it is also clear that pewter was sought by the upper stratum, the aspiring yeomen, for whom it served, along with costly textiles, bronze basins and ewers, linen, and perhaps a silver spoon or two, to demonstrate in a tangible fashion their superior status in the village and their identification with the life styles of the gentry. John Brice and John More were clearly more akin to yeomen than to peasants, but the fact that they possessed pewter in rural Shropshire and Worcestershire before the end of the fourteenth century is perhaps an even more eloquent testimony to the rapid circulation of this product, in both social and geographical terms, than all the evidence of pewter in the households of noblemen, gentlemen and burgesses.

It is time to consider the potential market for pewter in terms of the availability and price of articles made of alternative materials, although the lack of previous attention devoted to these competitive products must necessarily limit the scope of our discussion. Pewter was fashioned into such a wide range of articles that it was in competition, to a greater or lesser degree, with gold, silver, copper, lead, brass, latten, bronze, fine pottery, coarse pottery, glass, wood, leather, and stone. Of these materials silver, pottery and wood were the most versatile, since the others competed with pewter over only a relatively narrow range of articles. It is clear that the most common form of pewterware in the late Middle Ages was Sadware, also known as counterfeit or flatware, namely chargers, platters, dishes, basins, porringers, and salt-cellars. These articles were also commonly produced in silver and wood; clay was used for salt-cellars but only rarely for dishes and basins, at least in other than peasant households, and copper and bronze tableware went out of vogue early in the fourteenth century.

Pewter fashioned into vessels for storing, measuring, serving, and drinking liquids came next in order of size of production,

[1] For example: PRO SC. 2. 160/25, 160/27; SC. 6. 819/15, 817/1.
[2] For example: PRO SC. 2. 157/2, 157/6.

with those appearing in contemporary documents ranging down in size from half gallons (pottles) to half pints. The main competitors for the storage and serving of drink were clay pitchers and leather blackjacks, but in the fifteenth century a boost was given to pewter by the determined effort which was made to eliminate fraud by insisting on the use of pewter pots of stamped capacity in taverns.[1] The predominance of bronze water ewers and washing basins has already been noted. Although some of the smaller pewter measures were no doubt also used for drinking, wood, both in the form of expensively decorated mazer cups and cheap ash, was much more common for these purposes than pewter; glass drinking vessels are rarely encountered in the documents. At the Lord Mayor's feast in 1505, for example, the use of pewter was restricted to eating utensils, and we find that 800 ashen cups, 6 dozen stone pots, and 60 dozen earthenware pots were used for the wine and ale.[2] Even in royal households in the later fifteenth and the sixteenth centuries, although pewter had ousted eating utensils of cheaper materials, vast numbers of ashen cups, and leather and earthenware pots were used.[3] Pewter spoons are rarely mentioned in medieval wills and inventories, probably because they were of scant value, but many have been excavated and we know that they were made in substantial numbers.[4] Spoons made of latten, wood, and silver were substitutes: latten being stronger, wood cheaper, and silver spoons a popular form of conspicuous consumption amongst the aspiring middle classes. Candlesticks and mortars in the later Middle Ages were most frequently made of latten or bronze, although pewter candlesticks were not uncommon.[5]

Gold can be quickly dismissed as, at ten or twelve times the price of silver, it was beyond the reach of all but the very rich.[6] Silver, however, did enjoy a wide usage among the upper and middle classes. We have seen how the wealthy could afford

[1] See below, p. 68.   [2] *Early English Meals and Manners*, pp. 363–4.
[3] For example, the Black Book of Edward IV decreed that the sergeant of the cellar had the 'kepying of all the pootes and cuppis of sylver, pottes of lether, tankardes of yerthe, asshin cuppis', and the household of Henry VII budgeted £66 for the annual provision of 'ashen cupps' (Myers, pp. 183, 229). In 1526 £20 was provided for ashen cups and £5 for leather pots for Henry VIII's household at Eltham (*Collections of Ordinances and Regulations*, p. 195).
[4] Michaelis, *Antique Pewter*, p. 56; Peal, *British Pewter*, pp. 85–7.
[5] We have already noted the increasing use of candlesticks of latten and bronze in churches.
[6] Rogers, iv, 474–5.

whole services of silver, and how those with less wealth frequently possessed a few silver items, usually goblets, salt-cellars or spoons. But silver and pewter were not close substitutes, for in the fifteenth century an ounce of silver plate cost almost as much as a dozen pounds of pewter.[1] It may well have been the result as much of necessity as of choice that silverware on sale in England in the late fifteenth century seemed to an Italian visitor to be 'all either salt cellars, or drinking cups, or basins to hold water for the hands; for they eat off that fine tin, which is little inferior to silver'.[2]

Compared with our knowledge of pottery in the eighteenth and nineteenth centuries, relatively little is known about the medieval pottery industry, but in a number of recent articles attempts have been made to provide an outline of its fortunes.[3] Of the small country potters producing crude wares on a part-time basis for sale in the immediate neighbourhood, we have scarcely any knowledge, but it must be assumed that they continued to supply most of the needs of the poorest households throughout this period. It is clear, however, that the tendency towards a specialised and commercialised sector of the industry, noted in the previous chapter, was accentuated in the later Middle Ages. One of the most significant developments in the thirteenth century, apart from the expansion of the production of plain utilitarian wares, was the marketing of substantial numbers of highly decorated glazed pots, clearly aimed at prosperous consumers. This practice lasted approximately a century, and drew to a close at just the time that pewter was increasing in popularity. It seems likely, therefore, that the pewterers stole this market from the potters. Thereafter the English pottery industry, although continuing to operate on a large scale, concentrated once more on the production of simple wares. Nevertheless some high-class pottery continued to be imported in the fourteenth and fifteenth centuries, although the quantities do not appear to have been large. Brittany, Normandy, and Aquitaine were the normal sources of these imports, but it is interesting to note pots from Malaga and 'Saracen pots' arriving at English ports.[4] There is no information

[1] *Ibid.*, 488.   [2] *Italian Relation of England*, p. 43.
[3] See in particular Le Patourel, 'Medieval pottery industry', and E. M. Jope, 'The regional cultures of medieval Britain', *Culture and Environment: essays in honour of Sir Cyril Fox*, ed. I. LL. Foster and L. Alcock (1963), pp. 328–43.
[4] Le Patourel, p. 121; S. Pollard and D. W. Crossley, *The Wealth of Britain* (1968), pp. 47–9; *CCR 1413–19*, p. 513.

on the prices of high quality pottery, but simple pots were very cheap in comparison with pewter; in the fifteenth century an average pewter pot at 6*d* cost approximately the same as a dozen or more clay pots.[1]

The type of competition offered by wooden trenchers, platters, and dishes to their counterparts in pewter was very similar to that offered by clay pots to pewter pots, and the price differential appears to have been almost identical. Unfortunately the economics of the manufacture of wooden utensils has received even less attention than that of clay utensils, and archaeology can throw scant light. From craft records, however, it appears that 'turning' was more of an urban occupation than clay potting, although there were many rural craftsmen making wooden tableware, particularly in forest regions.[2] With the exception of mazer cups, there was little scope for the manufacture of high quality wooden utensils, although there is a reference to silver bowls made after the fashion of wooden bowls.[3] In the fourteenth century a small export trade in wooden trenchers was pursued from London.[4]

Although glass-making was carried on in England throughout the Middle Ages it remained on a very small scale, largely confined to a few areas on the fringes of forests, such as the western Weald and south-east Staffordshire, where fuel, potash, sand and clay could be found in suitable combination.[5] Although table glass was not uncommon in Saxon times there is little evidence of its use in late medieval England, and until the expansion of the industry in the later sixteenth century it remained rare and expensive. From the handful of examples found by Thorold Rogers in the mid-sixteenth century it appears that glasses usually cost about 1*s* each.[6]

The price of pewter was primarily determined by the price of tin and the price of labour, and both of these rose sharply after the Black Death.[7] The effect of the plague of 1348–49 on tin

---

[1] Rogers, iii, 544–82. For pre-Black Death prices see Le Patourel, p. 124, and above p. 32. It is interesting to note that an unskilled labourer earned about 4*d* a day at this time.
[2] Little has been written about this craft in the Middle Ages, but see W. C. Hazlitt, *The Livery Companies of the City of London* (1892), pp. 648–50; J. Birrell, 'Peasant Craftsmen in the Medieval Forest', *Agricultural History Review*, 17 (1969), 93–5.
[3] *CLR 1245–51*, p. 6.   [4] For example, PRO E.122.71/16.
[5] D. W. Crossley, 'The performance of the glass industry in sixteenth-century England', *Economic History Review*, 2nd. ser., xxv (1972), 426–7; Birrell, p. 102.
[6] Rogers, iii, 547, 573, 581; iv, 612.
[7] For the money wages of building craftsmen and labourers see E. H. Phelps Brown and S. V. Hopkins, 'Seven centuries of building wages', *Economica* (1955).

output was little short of catastrophic. In the 1350s little more than a third of the annual output of tin attained in the 1330s and, 40s was realised, and the price more than doubled. But, after many setbacks, production at the turn of the century was once again at levels comparable with the highest attained before the Black Death, and prices retreated to $1\frac{1}{2}d$ to $2d$ per pound in Cornwall and $2\frac{1}{2}d$ to $3d$ in London and Oxford. This impressive recovery was of limited duration, however, and after 1414 tin output fell almost continuously until it reached its nadir in the early 1460s, thereby registering a contraction of fully 50 per cent in half a century. Despite sharply diminishing production tin prices displayed no tendency to rise; on the contrary, they too displayed a falling trend, albeit of less spectacular dimensions.[1]

For the fifteenth century it is possible to compile for the first time fairly reliable series of pewter prices, using the records of the frequent purchases made by Oxford and Cambridge colleges and Winchester College. As can be seen in Appendix B these series correlate closely with each other to produce a U-shaped cycle, with the decennial averages from 1421 to 1470, or even 1490, below the $4s$ per dozen pounds of 1411–20, and with prices in some intervening decades falling as low as $3s$. It is probable that lead prices traced a similar pattern.[2] Unfortunately it is impossible to compile price data for pottery and wooden utensils over the same period.

It would be fruitless to attempt to graft a statistical backbone on to these impressions of an increasing consumption of pewter, since wills and inventories survive in insufficient numbers before the later fifteenth century, and furthermore frequently provide incomplete lists of possessions. But supporting evidence of the growth of pewter consumption is available in the marked expansion of the production side; indeed evidence of pewter manufacture in the later Middle Ages adds a degree of precision not afforded by wills and inventories. Although G. R. Lewis was guilty of overstatement when he wrote that 'the history of English pewter is largely the history of the London pewterers', the capital was in the fourteenth and fifteenth centuries, as it was to remain, by far the most important centre of the industry.[3]

Unfortunately before the excellent series of Company records

[1] Hatcher, pp. 90–1.   [2] Rogers, iv, 488.   [3] *The Stannaries*, p. 45.

begins in 1451 there is little direct evidence of pewter manufacture to be culled from City records. In fact one of the most significant references in City records, after the enrolment of the ordinances of 1348, is to the annulment and rejection of further ordinances made in 1438, which were found by the mayor and aldermen to be 'ayenst the libertes of the cite and ayenst the comen profit and also with out autorite'.[1] Nevertheless for this critical period in the history of the London industry much can be learnt from customs accounts. We have seen how as early as 1307 pewter was being exported from London, and the survival of a number of detailed records of exports in the closing decades of the fourteenth century shows that this trickle had become a substantial trade comprising approximately 15 to 20 tons per annum, perhaps 20,000 to 30,000 items of pewterware.[2] By the 1430s when a further series of records is available, exports from London had at least doubled and were averaging 35–40 tons per annum, with an additional 7–9 tons of predominantly London pewter exported from Southampton.[3] The 1440s saw yet a further decisive upturn: in 1443 over 45 tons of pewter left London; in the eight months from the end of January to the end of September 1446 aliens alone exported over 43 tons, and finally in 1448–49, the date of the last account before 1466–67, exports rose to the unprecedented level of 90 tons,[4] equivalent to almost 20 per cent of current annual tin production and a total not to be surpassed until the late seventeenth century. Exports from Southampton in the 1440s probably averaged 3–4 tons per annum. When the long series of continuous export data begins in the late 1460s, we find that London's pewter shipments were being maintained at levels comparable with the 1440s, and another peak was achieved in 1468–69, this time comprising almost 80 tons; by this time, however, Southampton no longer played a significant part in the trade.[5]

It is, of course, impossible to determine what proportion of total pewter production these exports constituted; the only calculation that can be made, and even the results of this must be

[1] Welch, i, 9.   [2] Hatcher, pp. 170–3.
[3] A number of pewterers were at work at Southampton and Winchester in the later fifteenth century, but substantial quantities of London pewter were also sent to Southampton for export (*The Brokage Book of Southampton, 1443–44*, ed. O. Coleman, 2 vols. [Southampton, 1960], i, pp. xxxii, 166, 277).
[4] PRO E.101. 73/23, 25.   [5] PRO E.356/21.

considered an approximation, is of the amount of tin consumed in England. In the course of the 1430s and 1440s registered tin production declined from about 450 tons per annum to 350–400 tons, of which about half appears to have been exported as raw tin or pewter. In the late 1460s both production and exports were somewhat higher, the latter temporarily, and averaged just over 450 tons and 265 tons respectively.[1] But as for the final destination of the 180–200 tons that remained in England one can say little with precision: the pewter industry was by this time almost certainly the foremost consumer of tin, but substantial quantities also went into the manufacture of bronze, bells, organs and solder, not to mention the lesser amounts used by girdlers, jewellers, toy-makers and others.[2] And, of course, there is the further complication that a substantial proportion of the pewter output was made from old pewter rather than new tin.[3]

The Particulars of Customs list the day-by-day arrivals and departures of all vessels engaged in overseas trade, together with details of the cargoes they carried, the merchants who owned the cargoes, and the customs duties they were charged with. The weight of pewter exports, the number of barrels or casks they were packed in, and their value are usually given, but sadly it is unusual for the accounts to contain any indication of type or quality. One exception was the intermittent small-scale exports of secondhand pewter, which were termed 'old' or 'worn' and assessed at a lower value.[4] From the early fifteenth century it became customary to value pewter at £13.6s8d per thousand-weight of 1,200 lb; this was a third higher than raw tin, and in line with the charges for workmanship imposed by the London Pewterers.[5] Strangely, the occasional small exports of pewter from west country ports were valued no higher than tin, perhaps an indication of their poor quality.[6]

Markets for English pewter appear to have existed in many countries in north-west Europe and the Mediterranean. Pewter exporters were similarly divers and, in addition to

[1] Hatcher, pp. 157–8, 170–5.   [2] *Ibid.*, pp. 35–42.
[3] It was common practice for old pewter to be traded in when buying new; see below, pp. 239–40.
[4] For example, PRO E. 122.73/25.   [5] Welch, i, 57.
[6] For example, pewter exports from Plymouth, Fowey and other Cornish ports 1461–78 (PRO E. 356/21, 22).

Englishmen, were drawn from Genoa, Florence, Venice, Catalonia, Holland, Zeeland, Spain, Portugal, and Hanse towns in Germany and the Low Countries.[1] The demand for English pewter overseas stemmed from two distinct sources: first, and most simply, it catered for the needs of consumers in countries that produced little or no pewter for themselves; and second, it is clear that even countries with substantial pewter industries imported some of the finest English pewter to satisfy the needs of discerning consumers.

English pewter, and in particular the best London pewter, was probably among the finest in late medieval Europe. An Italian visitor to England at the turn of the fifteenth century wrote that English pewterers made 'vessels as brilliant as if they were of fine silver, and these are held in great estimation',[2] and another Italian describing London at a somewhat later date remarked that 'the working in silver, tin or white lead, is very expert here, and perhaps the finest I have ever seen'.[3] Commendations by Englishmen are, as might be expected, not at all difficult to find, but the testimony of Harrison, written in the later sixteenth century, is particularly enlightening since he explains the popularity of English pewter in terms both of the skill of the pewterer and the quality of the tin:

> In some places beyond the sea a garnish of good flat English pewter of an ordinary making ... is esteemed almost so precious as the like number of vessels that are made of fine silver, and in manner no less desired amongst the great estates, whose workmen are nothing so skilful in that trade as ours, neither their metal so good nor plenty so great as we have here in England.[4]

The part played by the excellent quality of English tin in securing a substantial pewter export trade should therefore not be underestimated, for English tin was without doubt the purest as well as the most abundant in the known world. Both to support this statement and to avoid any suggestion of chauvinism we can draw from the testimonials of foreigners, indeed we can draw

[1] Customs accounts *passim*; see below p. 263 ff.
[2] *Italian Relation of England*, p. 11.
[3] *Two Italian Accounts of Tudor England*, ed. C. V. Malfatti (Barcelona, 1953), p. 32.
[4] William Harrison, *The Description of England*, ed. G. Edelen (New York, 1968), p. 367.

exclusively from the testimonials of Italians; the Italians being the leading traders in tin, were in an excellent position to judge its quality. Most Italian relations or reports of England in the late fifteenth and sixteenth centuries devote some space to praising England for the wealth and high quality of the minerals found within her shores. The anonymous Italian of the late fifteenth century wrote: 'This island produces a quantity of iron and silver, and an infinity of lead and tin, the latter which is of the purest quality'.[1] And Giacomo Soranzo's report made to the Venetian senate in 1554, although it erroneously places both tin and lead mines in Cornwall, is quite clear about the matchless quality of their product: 'In Cornwall they have lead and tin mines, from which they extract metal in great quantity, and of such good quality that the like is not to be found elsewhere.'[2] The expert testimony of the celebrated mid-sixteenth century technologist, Vanoccio Biringuccio, provides further confirmation, for he wrote of tin in his *Pirotechnia*:

> According to what I have heard from experienced men, the best and the most abundant that is found in the provinces of Europe is that which is mined in England.... I see that the tin that comes from England, when worked as well as in cakes that show it to be pure, is much more beautiful and better in all works than is that made in Venice.[3]

On the other hand one can also find direct evidence of the relative inferiority of the German product. English commentators frequently extol the incomparable quality of their native tin and point to the deficiencies of that from German mines[4]; and if their evidence is open to doubt the legislation passed in Germany requiring that only English tin be used in certain manufacturing processes provides conclusive proof.[5]

The customs accounts thus reveal that by the mid-fifteenth century a substantial export trade in pewter was being prosecuted. In some respects the growth of this trade from humble origins in the early fourteenth century can be compared with the spectacular increase in English cloth exports over the same period, indeed

[1] *Italian Relation of England*, p. 11.
[2] *Calendar of State Papers Venetian, 1534–54*, p. 543.
[3] Biringuccio, pp. 60, 211.
[4] For example, G. Malynes, *Consuetudo vel Lex Mercatoria* (1629), p. 268.
[5] Bapst, pp. 236–7; H-U. Haedeke, *Zinn: ein Handbuch fur Sammler und Liebhaber* (Brunswick, 1963), pp. 41–8; Hedges, *Tin in ... History*, pp. 16, 87–8.

pewter was second only to cloth in England's restricted list of manufactured exports, although it was, of course, of far less importance to the national economy than this staple product.

Further indications of the expansion of the London pewter industry (to which the mayor's order in 1423 that all ale sold retail should be served in pewter pots 'sealed and open' doubtless gave an additional stimulus[1]) occurred in 1444 when the London pewterers were granted both the right to purchase, at the current market price, a quarter of all tin brought into London for sale, and the right to 'serche and assaie alle tynne hereafter to be multe withinne the said Citee and the Fraunchise thereof' and confiscate any 'befounde deceyvable and untrewe'.[2]

With the start of the long series of Audit Accounts of the London Craft of Pewterers in 1451–52 we can at last look closely at the structure of the industry. Naturally the accounts do not tell us all we would wish to know, but those for 1456–57 and 1458–59 contain invaluable lists of members, together with the journeymen and apprentices they employed.[3] In the former account we find that the craft consisted of a minimum of 41 liverymen, 15 'that be no brotheren and paien quarterage' (i.e. freemen), 35 'covenant men' or journeymen, 97 apprentices, and 5 others who were probably freemen, thus giving a total of 193 craftsmen. We also learn that there were no less than forty-three pewter workshops employing two or more persons and that Thomas Dounton's workshop contained seven journeymen and eleven apprentices, the largest staff to be mentioned in the medieval records of any London craft.[4]

Looked at from another perspective the beginning of formal accounting and the compilation of lists of masters, journeymen and apprentices can be seen as indications of a desire on the part of the craft to increase the efficiency of its organisation and tighten its control over the production of pewter. It is probable that the rapid growth in output and workers in pewter within London and its suburbs in the first half of the fifteenth century had not occurred exclusively within the ranks of the established fraternity; it is certainly strange to learn that Dounton, who had been a mercer

---

[1] W. Herbert, *The Twelve Great Livery Companies*, 2 vols (1834–6), i, 58.
[2] Welch, i, 13–14.
[3] For the 1456–57 list see Welch, i, 20–5; for that of 1458–59 see Guildhall Library MS 7086/1, fol. 18 ff.
[4] Thrupp, *The Merchant Class*, p. 9.

Plate 1 A pewter flask from Abydos, Egypt, c. 1580–1350 B.C.

Plates 2 and 3 Romano-British ewers from the Fens.

Plate 4 Hoard of Romano–British pewter from Manton, Wiltshire.

Plate 5 A font bowl bearing late Anglo-Saxon decoration, c. 1100–1300.

Plate 6 Ecclesiastical sexagonal cruet (thirteenth to fourteenth century), from Weoley castle. Height approximately 5 in.

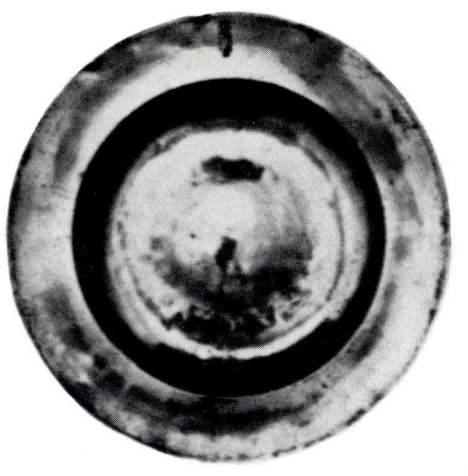

Plates 7 and 8 Plates, diameters 13⅜ in. and 10½ in. Part of a hoard of more than twenty found in Southwark in 1889. The crowned feather punched on the rims is believed to represent the mark of Prince Arthur, eldest son of Henry VII. Probably late fifteenth century.

Plate 9 Set of three 'Spanish trencher' plates. Diameters 6⅛ in., 9¾ in., 12⅜ in. respectively. Probably mid-sixteenth century.

Plate 10 Wine measures (baluster form). Height overall 5⅞ in., 7 in., 7¾ in., 9 in., 10¼ in., 12 in. respectively. This group comprises the earliest known examples of English pewter wine measures, probably mid- to late-sixteenth century.

Plate 11 Elizabethan ecclesiastical flagon. Height to lip 9⅝ in. Late sixteenth century.

Plate 12 Porringer, with two ears of crude 'trefoil' pattern, cast in one piece with the bowl. Diameter of bowl 6⅜ in. Mid- to late-sixteenth century.

since 1422, was admitted to the Pewterers' Craft only in 1457.¹ Thus it was soon appreciated that a royal charter of incorporation, which would confirm old powers and confer new, was essential if these ambitions were to be fulfilled, and the spectacular growth which had taken place in the size of the industry, and the liberality with which charters had been granted by Henry VI, greatly strengthened the Pewterers' case.² Finally in January 1474, after the expenditure of considerable sums of money on legal expenses and straightforward bribery over a period of more than twenty years, the craft was transformed into an incorporated company. The next acquisition, in keeping with this enhanced status, was a hall, and less than two years after incorporation possession was obtained of a site and buildings in Lime Street.³

Although the opposite has frequently been maintained there are good reasons for believing that incorporation was more a ratification of the growth that had already taken place in the London pewter industry than a springboard for further expansion in the immediately ensuing decades. Admittedly no time was lost by the Company in seeking to enforce its charter, and a large number of successful searches and recruiting drives were performed in many parts of the realm, but within a few years these were abandoned and the Company once again turned its attention almost exclusively to London.⁴

The audit accounts conveniently contain annual lists of persons assessed to pay quarterage, a due levied on householders within the Company (that is the liverymen and freemen who had their own shops). The numbers of those who were assessed to pay quarterage and of those who actually paid are given in the accounts, and both declined in the course of the second half of the fifteenth century.⁵ The extent of the decline in the numbers

¹ The audit account for 1456–57 contains under the heading 'receipts of entry of brethren' the sum of 6s8d from Thomas Dounton, Mercer, for his entry into the Craft; in the list of members compiled in this year he is described as a mercer. In 1422 Dounton had been made free in the Mercers' Company by apprenticeship (Thrupp, *The Merchant Class*, p. 9 n).
² For charters granted by Henry VI and Edward IV see G. Unwin, *The Gilds and Companies of London* (4th edn, 1963), pp. 160–3.
³ Welch, i, 18, 34–76; Unwin, *Gilds and Companies*, pp. 164–6.
⁴ Evidence of searches is contained only in the accounts of 1474, 1475, 1476 and 1477; searches were then apparently discontinued and not undertaken again until 1504 when in this and the following two years they were revived on a much reduced scale. In the account of 1486–87 a small group of 'foreign' pewterers is listed including one each of Lewes, Ware, Canterbury, and Suffolk.
⁵ See Appendix A below for an analysis of relevant data extracted from Company records.

paying was from an average of almost sixty in the 1450s to little more than forty in the 1470s and 1480s, and although the numbers liable to pay did not decline to the same extent this increase in indebtedness was in itself a further sign of the difficulties the Company was experiencing. The numbers of freemen admitted each year are also a useful guide to the size and prosperity of the industry, and these too suggest that there was little expansion in this period. The number of freedoms granted by servitude in the last decade of the century, twenty-four, was only one higher than that recorded in the 1450s. Nor was much compensation to be found from the recruitment of country pewterers, for few of them appear to have paid quarterage or maintained close links with the Company.

While it must be admitted that the numbers of masters and the rate of admissions provide only a rough guide to the size of the Company, still less to that of the London pewter industry, when the data of the later fifteenth century are compared with those from the first half of the sixteenth there can be little doubt that the former period was one of stagnation, if not of retrenchment, for the London Company.

The reasons for the absence of further sustained growth in the London pewter industry in the second half of the fifteenth century appear to have lain primarily in the expansion of production outside the capital, both within Britain and overseas. The most obvious and the simplest method of estimating the productive capacity of the industry is through the formation of gilds, and naturally gilds developed in the largest cities, notably in the regional capitals of the north and the west. The first organised craft of pewterers to develop in Britain outside London was that of York, and in 1416 a comprehensive set of *Ordinaciones pewderariorum*, based explicitly on those of London, was accepted by the mayor and aldermen of the city.[1] The next pewterers' gild to enrol its ordinances was that of Bristol, which in 1457 similarly adopted the 'rewle and asay of London'.[2] It is fitting that York and Bristol should have possessed the most highly organised and probably the largest of the provincial pewterers' gilds, for it was with some justification that our late fifteenth-century Italian

[1] *The York Memorandum Book*, ed. M. Sellars, 2 vols (Surtees Society, cxx, cxxv, 1912–15), ii, 211–13.
[2] *The Little Red Book of Bristol*, ed. F. M. Bickley, 2 vols (1900), ii, 184–5.

visitor remarked that 'there are scarcely any towns of importance in the kingdom excepting these two: Bristol, a seaport to the West, and Boraco, otherwise York, which is on the borders of Scotland; besides London to the South'.[1] But although England lagged far behind Italy in the degree to which she was urbanised, the Italian was guilty of exaggeration,[2] for Norwich and Coventry were also sizeable towns with populations in excess of 6,000, and in the course of the fifteenth century they too acquired organisations of pewterers. We learn of the Norwich pewterers from a list of crafts whose members processed through the city on Corpus Christi Day 1449,[3] and our first mention of a pewterers' association in Coventry dates from 1494 when an ordinance was passed regulating the production and trade of our commodity.[4] An association of pewterers at Chester, the leading borough of the north-west, is first revealed in 1490 in a gild of miscellaneous craftsmen which also included smiths, founders, cutlers, cardmakers, girdlers, headmakers, wire-drawers and spurriers.[5]

Medieval York ranked as England's second city, and was the leading industrial and commercial centre of the north; in 1377 its population was probably in excess of 11,000. Although fewer specialist occupations were pursued in York than in London and many other leading European cities, she boasted almost sixty organised crafts in the early fifteenth century. Unfortunately the total numbers in each occupation cannot be determined as no census was ever held, but the remarkably continuous registers of admissions to the freedom of the city provide an invaluable insight into industrial and commercial recruitment, since registration as a freeman was compulsory for anyone who wished to work as a master in York.[6]

From these registers it is possible to extract the numbers of pewterers made free, thereby providing a guide to the fortunes of this industry in the city. It must be stressed, however, that

[1] *Italian Relation of England*, p. 41.
[2] For conservative estimates of the populations of leading English towns, based upon the Poll Taxes of 1377, see Russell, pp. 142–3.
[3] *English Historical Documents*, iv, pp. 1095–6.
[4] *The Coventry Leet Book*, ed. M. D. Harris, 4 vols (Early English Text Society, 134, 135, 138, 146, 1907–13), ii, 554.
[5] R. J. A. Shelley, 'Wigan and Liverpool Pewterers', *Transactions of the Lancashire and Cheshire Historic Society*, xcvii, (1946), p. 2.
[6] J. N. Bartlett, 'Some Aspects of the Economy of York in the Later Middle Ages, 1300–1550' (London Ph.D., 1958); E. Miller, 'Medieval York', in *Victoria County History: Yorkshire: The City of York*.

admissions are no more than a guide to the numbers practising the craft, since the numbers who ceased to practise are not known, and some historians have erred by assuming too close a correlation between admissions and total membership, a critical misjudgment in a period of high mortality such as the fifteenth century, when recurrent plague, and later sweating sickness, ravaged England's cities.[1] Nevertheless, with the exercise of due caution, and by comparing the admissions of pewterers with those of other craftsmen, much of value can be learned from this source.

As we have seen the first York pewterers were admitted just before the Black Death of 1348–49. This catastrophe, together with later outbreaks of plague, may well have contributed to the lack of progress in the industry over the next fifty years when only five pewterers gained licence to practice in York, with none at all admitted in the 1350s or '60s. Furthermore in the York Poll Tax returns of 1381 we find ten potters, a founder, and a lattener, but not a single pewterer.[2] In the fifteenth century, however, a striking improvement took place in the fortunes of the industry, an improvement which was all the more impressive because it was accomplished while the metal industries as a whole were becoming of less importance within the city. No less than twenty-six pewterers were admitted in the first half century, an achievement which was crowned by the election of the first pewterer mayor, Thomas Snaudon in 1432. Snaudon must have been an exceptionally wealthy and influential pewterer for he was one of only twenty mayors, out of the eighty-eight elected between 1399 and 1509, who was not a merchant or a mercer.

Significantly, and in contrast to the experience of the London pewterers, the York industry appears to have enjoyed an even more rapid expansion over the next fifty years when admissions totalled forty-seven and the pewterers became the second largest metalworking craft. The York industry was probably at its peak at the close of the fifteenth century, for in the first half of the sixteenth there were only thirty-six admissions.[3] A measure of perspective is added to these figures by the admissions to the

---

[1] Such a criticism could be levelled at Dr Bridbury's use of burgess admissions data in *Economic Growth*, pp. 61–9. See also R. B. Dobson, 'Admissions to the freedom of the City of York in the later Middle Ages', *Econ. Hist. Rev.*, 2nd ser., xxvi, (1973).
[2] J. N. Bartlett, *The Lay Poll Tax Returns for the City of York in 1381* (1953), p. 15.
[3] Bartlett, *Economy of York*, pp. 14–43.

freedom of the London Company, which between 1451 and 1500 averaged 2·7 persons annually, while in the first half of the sixteenth century an average of almost five new masters were licensed to open workshops in London each year.

Admissions to the freedom of a city are clearly one of the most revealing of medieval sources for our purpose, but of the remaining cities only Norwich has a series comparable with that of York, being continuous and also consistent in the recording of occupations.[1] Our knowledge of the Bristol pewter industry is tantalisingly slight, despite the fact that it was second only to York amongst the provincial industries, and that as early as the 1350s John Peutrer of Bristol attained a position of great power in the regional administration by being appointed to many offices by the crown.[2] For Coventry also the picture is disappointingly partial: we learn that there were at least three pewterers at work in the city at most times in the first half of the fifteenth century, and that in 1450 pewterers were amalgamated in a composite gild of metalworkers, but little else that throws light on the size and prosperity of the craft is at present available.[3] At Norwich, through the admissions which numbered three from 1351 to 1400, four from 1401 to 1450, and nine from 1451 to 1500, we can see that although the craft was far smaller than that of York it followed a similar chronology of development, with the expansion of the second half of the fifteenth century of particular note.[4] Admissions data from Leicester are very patchy before 1465, with many long gaps and frequent omissions of occupations, but we learn that in the thirty-one years for which records exist between 1465 and 1500 nine pewterers joined the burgess ranks.[5]

For the state of the craft elsewhere in England the 'country' craftsmen enrolled by the London Company after its incorporation in 1474 are an extremely valuable guide. In a short series of energetic searches and recruiting drives, conducted from 1474 to 1476 in Norfolk, Suffolk, Essex, Cambridgeshire, Surrey,

[1] The recently published Exeter series is continuous from 1266, but sadly only a small proportion of burgess occupations are recorded before the later sixteenth century (*Exeter Freemen, 1256–1967*, ed. M. M. Rowe and A. M. Jackson (Devon and Cornwall Record Association, extra ser., i, 1973).
[2] For example, *CPR 1354–58*, p. 605.
[3] *Coventry Leet Book*, passim.
[4] *Calendar of the Freemen of Norwich from 1317–1603*, ed. J. L'Estrange and W. Rye (1888).
[5] *Register of the Freemen of Leicester, 1196–1770*, ed. H. Hartopp (Leicester, 1927).

Yorkshire, Somerset, Devonshire, Hertfordshire, Buckinghamshire, Northamptonshire, Leicestershire, Oxfordshire, Berkshire, Gloucestershire and Dorset, considerable quantities of defective pewter were seized and thirty-seven craftsmen from twenty-seven different towns outside London were enrolled, namely Canterbury, Bury St Edmunds, Colchester, Cambridge, Ware, Boston, Wells, Winchester, Coventry (2), Leicester, Brentford, Burford, Bristol (5), Exeter (2), Southampton (3), Salisbury (2), Chichester, Reading, Nottingham, Lincoln, Oxford, Bridgewater, St Albans, Ipswich, Taunton, and Wookey and Montacute in Somerset.[1] In 1488 certain 'foreign' members were listed, including craftsmen from Ware, Lewes, Canterbury and Suffolk, and in 1504 there were six further enrolments of this kind, one from Rutland, two from Cambridge, one from Oxford, one from King's Lynn, and one other; a Gloucester pewterer is mentioned in 1506. Finally in 1536 craftsmen from Taunton, Abingdon, Boston, Lincoln, and Northampton were enrolled. The term craftsmen rather than pewterers is used because amongst the new members there were brasiers, chapmen, and a bell-founder.[2]

These enrolments should not be taken as anything more than a guide to pewter manufacture in the provinces, for they are only a partial record of the towns which contained pewterers and of the numbers of pewterers in the towns that are mentioned. Most obviously we can see that the jurisdiction of the York company was scarcely challenged: there is mention of false pewter being seized at Rotherham in 1476, but northern recruits are notable only by their absence, and it is likely that, in addition to York, pewterers were working in a number of northern towns including Carlisle, Newcastle, Hull, Beverley, and Scarborough. Norwich is also omitted, presumably because its gild was also jealous of its independence, but the omission of many other important towns such as Hereford, Shrewsbury, Chester, Stamford, Yarmouth, Worcester, Derby, Wigan and Ludlow, some of which are known to have possessed pewterers, was almost certainly due to the failure of London officials to visit or recruit. If the searches had not been brought to a virtual halt in 1477 the list of country pewterers would doubtless have been far longer.[3]

[1] The last two towns are named as 'Wokey' and 'Okey', and 'Muntagewe' in the accounts.   [2] Guildhall MS 7086/1.
[3] For Chester pewterers see above; for Wigan see R. J. A. Shelley, *Brief Notes on Wigan Pewterers* (Wigan, 1936), p. 8.

The ease with which pewterers were enrolled in many parts of the country in a short space of time is a powerful testimony to the widespread distribution of pewter manufacture in the late fifteenth century. The evidence from an extensive range of sources which uniformly points to the later fifteenth century as a period of unprecedented expansion of provincial pewtering must also be stressed; and the first mention of an association of pewterers in an Edinburgh gild of Hammermen in 1496, in which it had not been included in 1483, is yet another example of this universal phenomenon.[1] Hence, whereas even by the late fourteenth century there was scarcely any large-scale manufacture of pewter outside London,[2] by the later fifteenth much demand must have been satisfied locally, and we find even discriminating consumers such as John Howard, Duke of Norfolk, resorting only occasionally to London pewterers.[3]

It was undoubtedly this increase in competition and the threat it posed to their livelihoods, that encouraged the London Pewterers to seek, and finally obtain in January 1474, additional powers to control the trade outside the capital, and later to lobby, with York pewterers, for still wider powers to restrict the sale of pewter and maintain standards and prices.[4]

To the effects on London's pewter industry of the growth of manufacture in the provinces must be added comparably deleterious effects caused by the initiation of manufacture in many regions of Europe previously without pewterers, and the expansion of production in old-established European manufacturing centres, which in turn sought to export pewter. The success of English tin exports, which increased by more than 50 per cent in the last quarter of the fifteenth century and then doubled in the first decade of the sixteenth to reach a peak of more than 600 tons per annum, combined with a doubling of the output of the

---

[1] L. I. Wood, *Scottish Pewter-Ware and Pewterers* (Edinburgh, 1905), p. 23.
[2] A preliminary investigation of the occupation data contained in the 1381 Poll Tax returns has confirmed the impression of the scarcity of craftsmen specialising in pewter manufacture in the country at large at this time.
[3] For example, in 1464 Howard purchased half a garnish of counterfeit vessels and half a garnish of plain vessels in Colchester; in 1467 he purchased two pewter basins from an Eastcheap pewterer (*Manners and Household Expences*, pp. 273, 279, 416).
[4] These powers were granted in a series of statutes passed between 1503 and 1541: 19 Henry VII, c. 6; 4 Henry VIII, c. 7; 25 Henry VIII, c. 9; 33 Henry VIII, c. 47; and comprehensive new ordinances were adopted by the Company in 1522 (Welch, i, 106–15).

tin mines of central Europe, similar increases in the production of lead, and the ease with which the basic skills and capital equipment needed to produce low-grade pewter could be acquired, must have greatly facilitated the dissemination of pewter production throughout Europe.[1]

The net result of these European developments was the precipitation of a slump of truly catastrophic proportions in England's pewter exports in the last quarter of the fifteenth century. In the 1470s exports from London averaged less than eight tons per annum—in fact more pewter was exported between Michaelmas 1468 and 20 August following than in the whole of this decade. The closing decades of the century brought no respite; on the contrary London's exports fell to a paltry three tons per annum. Nor was compensation obtained elsewhere, since exports from Southampton and the west country soon fell to a mere trickle. That the slump in English pewter exports was due to long-term rather than short-term factors is exemplified by its persistence into the sixteenth century, for although the 1520s and '30s experienced the next peak in exports they were still less than half those attained in the 1420s and 1460s.

But the loss of export markets and the growth of competition within Britain did not mark the limit of the London pewterers' predicament, for in the late fifteenth century the home market

Table 4
Average annual exports of pewter 1471–1547

Period	London (tons)	Miscellaneous ports (tons)	Total (tons)
1471–80	7·6	*	*
1481–90	2·8	1·8	4·6
1491–1500	3·4	2·2	5·6
1501–10	11·3	4·6	15·9
1511–20	28·7	1·6	30·3
1521–30	31·0	0·9	31·9
1531–40	25·2	1·3	26·5
1541–47	19·0	1·7	20·7

Sources. PRO E.356/22–27. For details of the miscellaneous ports and the division of trade between denizen and alien merchants see Hatcher, pp. 176–93.

[1] For tin output see Hatcher, pp. 119–21, 194; for the expansion of lead production, particularly in central Europe, see *Cambridge Economic History of Europe*, ii, (Cambridge, 1952), 469 ff.

was threatened by imports of low-grade pewter from France and Germany. Nevertheless, despite vociferous protests from pewterers, it is quite clear from customs accounts that these imports were intermittent and extremely small in scale, and furthermore that they consisted not of major items of tableware but rather of miscellaneous small items such as spoons and lids for stone and clay pots.[1]

As we have already seen the major English pewterers' gilds had been given powers to limit competition within Britain in 1474 and 1504, and the loss of export markets and the threat of imports provoked fresh cries for protection. Once again the interests of the pewterers did not go unheeded and further beneficial royal statutes and gild ordinances were passed in the first half of the sixteenth century which, amongst other things, prohibited all imports of pewter, and the employment of foreign workmen and the emigration of English pewterers because of the danger that they might divulge trade secrets.[2]

If we turn to look at the progress of pewter manufacture in fifteenth-century Europe it becomes immediately clear that the fears of the London pewterers were well founded. From the firm base laid in the early fourteenth century the pewter industries of France, Germany and the Netherlands had entered on a phase of rapid expansion which paralleled that experienced by England, and similarly included both the expansion of established centres of production and the development of new. Germany, blessed with its own supplies of tin and lead and a wide expertise in the fabrication of all types of metal goods, was the leading pewter producer in continental Europe, and with gilds and associations of pewterers spread throughout the land and large-scale industries located in Nuremberg, Lübeck, Frankfurt, Augsburg, Breslau, Dresden, Freiberg, Cologne, Leipzig, Munich, Regensburg (Ratisbon) and elsewhere, total production may well have exceeded that of England.[3] With the commercial dominance of the Hanseatic League in the Baltic and eastern Europe, German pewterers were

---

[1] The importation of a wide range of small manufactured articles, including pewter spoons, was prohibited by statute in 1463 and again in 1483 (3 Edward IV, c. 4; 1 Richard III, c. 12). For pewter lids for clay and stone pots see Welch, i, 149.
[2] See below, pp. 152, 198.
[3] For German metalware in general see L. Guicciardini, *The Description of the Low Countreys and of the provinces thereof (gathered into an epitome etc. by T. Danett)*, (1593), p. 36; for German pewter in particular: see L. Mory, *Schönes Zinn* (Munich, 1961); Haedeke, *Zinn*; Hedges, *Tin in . . . History*, p. 88; Bapst, pp. 236–40.

assured of a ready export market for their wares.[1] Another major production area, for pewter as well as for metalwork of all kinds, was the famous industrial region of the Meuse Valley, in which the cities of Namur, Liège, Huy and Dinant figured prominently.[2]

The Hanseatic pewter export trade is perhaps well enough known, but less well appreciated are those that were pursued by a multitude of smaller centres of production, which when aggregated must have played a significant part in the loss of English export markets. This development can be illustrated from the experience of a number of French cities. France was second only to Italy and the east Mediterranean as a consumer of English tin in the later Middle Ages, and a large proportion of the annual output of Cornwall and Devon was shipped direct to Normandy, Brittany, and Gascony for local consumption, redistribution inland, and re-export; the ancient tin route from Bordeaux on the Atlantic to Marseilles on the Mediterranean retained its importance despite the establishment in the early fourteenth century of a direct sea route between England and the Mediterranean.[3] There can be no doubt that the bulk of the demand for tin in France stemmed from the needs of the pewter industry, which by the later fifteenth century was flourishing in many of her leading cities including Paris, Rouen, Mons, Dijon, Bordeaux, Angers, Montpellier, Chartres, Macon, Poitiers, Amiens, Toulouse and Marseilles.[4] The pewter that was produced was not exclusively for home consumption. In the south the pewterers of Marseilles and Toulouse served the needs of Provence and Languedoc, as one might expect, but some pewter

---

[1] Attention should be drawn to the pot-bellied tankards of fourteenth- and fifteenth-century dates, known as Hanseatic tankards, which have been dredged from the North Sea (Haedeke, *Metalwork*, p. 174; Haedeke, *Zinn*, pp. 76–85; Verster, pp. 18–20).

[2] H. Pirenne, 'Dinant dans la Hanse teutonique,' *Annales de la Fédération archéologique et historique de Belgique*, ii (1903), 523–46; Unwin, *Finance and Trade*, pp. 31–4; D. Brouwers, 'Les marchands batteurs de Dinant à la fin XVe siècle, *Bulletin de la Commission Royale d'Histoire*, lxxvii (1909).

[3] M. Mollat, *Le Commerce maritime normand à la fin du moyen âge* (Paris, 1952), pp. 152–4; H. Touchard, *Commerce maritime breton à la fin du moyen âge* (Paris, 1967), pp. 255–6; Hatcher, pp. 126–9. For contemporary comment on the importance of France in the tin trade see *Tudor Economic Documents*, ed. R. H. Tawney and E. Power, 3 vols (1924), iii, 201, 254.

[4] Bapst, pp. 217–35; Mollat, pp. 279–80; T. Malvezin, *Histoire du commerce de Bordeaux depuis les origines jusqu'à nos jours*, 4 vols (Bordeaux, 1892), i, 304; Ph. Wolff, *Commerces et marchands de Toulouse, vers 1350-vers 1450* (Paris, 1954), pp. 289–90; E. Baratier et F. Reynaud, *Histoire du commerce de Marseille, II: de 1291 à 1480* (Paris, 1951), 662–3.

was also exported in Marseilles galleys, and we find it despatched to Sardinia amongst other destinations.[1] In the north pewterers were also at work, and Morlaix, Villedieu and Rouen were the leading centres of production.[2] In the course of the fifteenth century Breton pewter, particularly *les pintiers*, acquired an international reputation and was regularly exported; and we learn that in 1430, for example, a quantity of Breton pots, dishes, platters, and porringers was sent from Morlaix to Portugal.[3]

In addition to the expansion of production in countries which possessed long-established pewter industries, and the development by them of new export trades, there is also indisputable evidence that production spread in the fifteenth century to many countries which had previously satisfied all their needs by imports. From the limited sources at present available we learn of production in eastern Europe, in Russia,[4] Poland[5] and Lithuania,[6] and of more significance for English exports, of the founding of pewter industries, albeit at a later date, in Italy, particularly Venice,[7] in Spain,[8] and perhaps even in Cairo.[9]

The difficulties of the London industry in the latter part of the fifteenth century should not be allowed to blind us to the immense progress made by the pewter industry throughout Europe during the preceding century and a half. During this time pewter had emerged from being a rare alloy used almost exclusively for sacred utensils, to being a common household item, and pewter manufacturing had emerged from the anonymity of being only one of the functions of the general metalworker into a specialised craft which took its place amongst the leading trades in London and the provinces. The extent of the progress of the London company can be measured by its rise in order of precedence among the London gilds to rank fourteenth in 1488,[10] sixteenth in 1513,[11] and fourteenth in 1532,[12] thereby achieving in little more

[1] Wolff, pp. 289–90; Baratier et Reynaud, ii, 827.
[2] Mollat, pp. 133, 160; Touchard, p. 62.
[3] *Ibid.*, p. 283. [4] Hedges, *Tin in . . . History*, pp. 89–90.
[5] Cracow was an important pewter manufacturing centre in the fifteenth century—M. Matowist, 'L'evolution industrielle en Pologne du XIVe siècle', in *Studi in onore di Armando Sapori*, 2 vols (Milan, 1957), i, 580.
[6] *Expeditions to Prussia . . . by Henry Earl of Derby*, p. 101.
[7] Biringuccio, p. 211; *Enciclopedia Italiana di Scienze, Lettre ed Arti*, 36 vols (Rome, 1949–52), *sub: Peltro*.
[8] Bapst, p. 240. [9] Haedeke, *Zinn*, p. 6.
[10] Welch, i, 66–7. [11] Hazlitt, p. 588.
[12] J. Stow, *Survey of London*, ed. C. L. Kingsford, 2 vols (1908), ii, 190.

than a century a status just outside the magic circle of the twelve great livery companies, a position usually reserved for merchant gilds and an achievement all the more impressive when considered in the context of the rapid development in this period of most sectors of London's economy. The order of precedence assumed by the gilds was not a mere reflection of numerical strength, since a number of companies with substantially more freemen than the Pewterers were of lower or only slightly higher status.[1] The wealth of the freemen was therefore of great importance and, if we may judge from men such as Thomas Dounton, William Dere, and John Paris, that enjoyed by pewterers was frequently well above the norm for members of craft gilds. The rapid expansion of provincial manufacture in the second half of the fifteenth century must also be stressed, particularly since it took place in a period of acute urban depression, and in many cities the pewter industry must have provided a rare but welcome growth point. Indeed the pewter industry was one of only a small group of industries whose output grew absolutely after 1350, in the face of prodigious population decline. The growth in demand for pewter, stimulated by changes in tastes and the distribution of wealth has been noted in some detail above, but the position that pewterware had attained at the turn of the fifteenth century, one which admirably combined the qualities of utility and restrained ostentation, cannot be better expressed than by the sentiments of Ann Barrett, widow, of Bury, who in 1504 made the following bequest: 'I wyll that myn executors shall geve to XX^{ti} maydens that be honest to ther maryage, tho that have neede, to yche of them xij pecys of pewtyr, that ys to sey, iiij platers, iiij dysshys, and iiij sawssers, and ych of them a pewter basyn, an ewer therto, or else a quart pot of pewter or of a pottell'.[2]

---

[1] For example, using accounts of quarterage we find that in 1458 the Coopers had 98 householders and the Pewterers 57, in 1495 the Leathersellers had 127 and the Pewterers 56, and in 1497 the Founders had 94 and the Pewterers 60 (Thrupp, *Merchant Class*, p. 46; Guildhall MS 7086/1).
[2] *Bury Wills and Inventories*, p. 97.

3 —— The sixteenth and seventeenth centuries

There can be no doubt that a substantial increase in both the scale and the diversity of industrial production took place in England during the course of the sixteenth and seventeenth centuries; and little doubt that by 1700 industrial output accounted for a greater proportion of the national income, and the industrial workforce for a greater proportion of the national workforce, than ever before.[1] This increase was accomplished in many ways, including the introduction of a range of 'new' industries from the Continent, among which the manufacture of brass, copperas, alum, cannon, gunpowder, sugar, and paper were the most significant; the enormous expansion of industries which had previously operated on a small scale, such as those devoted to the production of iron, soap, and glass; and the growth of long-established staple industries such as textiles, mining, building, salt-production, and leather-working. It has been claimed that these developments constituted an early industrial revolution 'no less important than that of the eighteenth century',[2] but more considered reflection leads one to limit the impact of the 'new' industries on the national economy and also to emphasise the lack of major technical advances in the staple industries.[3] Nevertheless, although the bulk of English industry continued to be organised along conventional lines and reliant upon traditional techniques, the indisputable expansion of production was one of the major economic phenomena of the era.

[1] For a recent introductory discussion see L. A. Clarkson, *The Pre-Industrial Economy in England 1500–1750* (1971), pp. 105–16.
[2] This view was expressed by J. U. Nef (*War and Human Progress*, 1950, p. 13). See also the same author's 'The progress of technology and the growth of large-scale industry in Great Britain, 1540–1640', *Economic History Review*, v (1934).
[3] For example, D. C. Coleman, 'Industrial growth and industrial revolutions' *Economica*, new ser., xxiii (1956).

The most important influence behind this expansion, at least before the later seventeenth century, was demographic, and according to the most generally accepted estimates the population of England and Wales rose from approximately 2·5–3 million in 1500 to approximately 5·5 million in 1700.[1] In addition to generating an increasing demand for foodstuffs and basic necessities, population growth stimulated the production of a wide range of manufactured luxuries and semi-luxuries, not only by helping to increase the size of the landowning, farming, industrial, and commercial communities, but also by providing the bulk of their members with rising incomes. It is within this context that we must consider the fortunes of the pewter industry.

Inflation, nourished principally on population growth with occasional high protein supplements in the shape of increased money supply, was at the heart of much social and economic change in the epoch between the closing years of Henry VIII's reign and the outbreak of the Civil War. During the course of what was little more than a century the average price of agricultural products rose almost 500 per cent, and that of industrial products by more than 250 per cent; in general the rate of increase in money wages tended to keep pace with, or fall a little behind, that of industrial products.[2] Conditions such as these were advantageous to farmers with security of tenure and with farms sufficient to provide a marketable surplus, and those with large farms held in freehold or on long leases reaped considerable profits. The combination of sharply rising agricultural prices, gently rising wages, and stable or gently rising rents, was sufficient to guarantee sizeable increases in incomes for all but the least efficient commercial farmers, and such a combination appears to have been general before the closing years of the sixteenth century.

The obvious result of the increasing wealth of the farming community was a sharp rise in its expenditure on housing and on household equipment and furnishings. Many contemporary com-

[1] See, for example, G. S. L. Tucker, 'English pre-industrial population trends', *Economic History Review*, 2nd ser., xvi (1963); D. V. Glass, 'Gregory King's estimate of the population of England and Wales, 1695', *Population Studies*, iii (1948–49). It must remain a distinct possibility, however, that the population of England and Wales in 1500 was significantly below 2·5 million.
[2] For an introductory discussion see R. B. Outhwaite, *Inflation in Tudor and Stuart England* (1969). For more detail see: E. H. Phelps Brown and S. V. Hopkins, 'Wage-rates and prices: evidence for population pressure in the sixteenth century', *Economica*, xxvi (1959); D. Felix, 'Profit, inflation and industrial growth: the historic record', *Quarterly Journal of Economics*, lxx (1956).

mentators have drawn attention to these developments, but none more perceptively or eloquently than William Harrison, whose account written in 1576–77 has especial value for our study since it draws particular attention to the increased consumption of pewter:

> The furniture of our houses also exceedeth and is grown in manner even to passing delicacy; and herein I do not speak of the nobility and gentry only but likewise of the lowest sort in most places of our South Country that have anything at all to take to. Certes in noblemen's houses it is not rare to see abundance of arras, rich hangings of tapestry, silver vessel, and so much other plate as may furnish sundry cupboards, to the sum oftentimes of £1,000 or £2,000 at the least, whereby the value of this and the rest of their stuff doth grow to be almost inestimable. Likewise in the houses of knights, gentlemen, merchantmen, and some other wealthy citizens, it is not geason [uncommon] to behold generally their great provision of tapestry, Turkey work, pewter, brass, fine linen, and thereto costly cupboards of plate, worth £500 or £600 or £1,000, to be deemed by estimation. But as herein all these sorts do far exceed their elders and predecessors, and in neatness and curiosity the merchant all other, so in time past the costly furniture stayed there, whereas now it is descended yet lower, even unto the inferior artificers and many farmers, who, by virtue of their old and not of their new leases, have for the most part learned also to garnish their cupboards with plate, their joint beds with tapestry and silk hangings, and their tables with carpets and fine napery, whereby the wealth of our country (God be praised therefor and give us grace to employ it well) doth infinitely appear. Neither do I speak this in reproach of any man, God is my judge, but to show that I do rejoice rather to see how God hath blessed us with His good gifts; and whilst I behold how that, in a time wherein all things are grown to most excessive prices and what commodity soever is to be had is daily plucked from the commonalty by such as look into every trade, we do yet find the means to obtain and achieve such furniture as heretofore hath been unpossible.[1]

[1] *Description of England*, p. 200.

Harrison then passes on to 'three things to be marvelously altered in England' within the 'sound remembrance' of 'old men yet dwelling in the village where I remain' (Radwinter in northwest Essex). The first is the 'multitude of chimneys lately erected, whereas in their young days there were not above two or three, if so many, in most uplandish towns of the realm'; the second 'is the great (although not general) amendment of lodging' whereby 'straw pallets on rough mats covered only with a sheet, under coverlets made of dogswain or hapharlots' and a log for a pillow, have been replaced by down or feather beds, pillows and under- as well as over-sheets. He goes on:

> The third thing they tell of is the exchange of vessel, as of treen [wooden] platters into pewter, and wooden spoons into silver or tin. For so common were all sorts of treen stuff in old time that a man should hardly find four pieces of pewter (of which one was peradventure a salt) in a good farmer's house, and yet for all this frugality (if it may so be justly called) they were scarce able to live and pay their rents at their days without selling of a cow or an horse or more, although they paid but £4 at the uttermost by the year. Such also was their poverty that if some one odd farmer or husbandman had been at the alehouse, a thing greatly used in those days, amongst six or seven of his neighbors, and there in a bravery to show what store he had did cast down his purse, and therein a noble or 6*s* in silver, unto them (for few such men then cared for gold, because it was not so ready payment, and they were oft enforced to give a penny for the exchange of an angel), it was very likely that all the rest could not lay down so much against it; whereas in my time, although peradventure £4 of old rent be improved to £40, £50, or £100, yet will the farmer, as another palm or date tree, think his gains very small toward the end of his term if he have not six or seven years' rent lying by him, therewith to purchase a new lease, beside a fair garnish of pewter on his cupboard, with so much more in odd vessel going about the house, three or four feather beds, so many coverlets and carpets of tapestry, a silver salt, a bowl for wine (if not an whole nest), and a dozen spoons to furnish up the suit [set].[1]

[1] *Ibid.*, pp. 201–2.

This personal testimony is well supported by a comprehensive range of less direct evidence. Analysis of Leicestershire inventories, for example, suggests that the median value of the personal estates of farmers in the husbandman category rose from £14.7s1d in 1500–31 to £46.16s8d in 1588, £67.2s4d in 1603, and £74.8s6d in 1638–42.[1] A similar progress has been charted amongst Lincolnshire husbandmen, with the median value of estates between the fifth and the ninth decades of the sixteenth century rising from £10.16s10d to £41.12s0d on the smaller Fenland farms, from £24.16s8d to £70.9s0d on marshlands, from £10.9s4d to £30.10s8d in clay vales, and from £15.4s8d to £49.7s2d on uplands.[2] In both Leicestershire and Lincolnshire the rate of accumulation of wealth was far in excess of the rate of increase in industrial prices, and it is more than likely that farmers in the south-eastern counties closer to the great London market prospered to an even greater extent.[3]

Tudor England has often been thought of as the golden age of the English yeoman, so it is scarcely surprising that the happy experience of the husbandmen was shared, perhaps even exceeded, by yeomen. Indeed one recent authority has gone so far as to state that 'there is every reason to believe that yeomen were advancing as a class both absolutely and relatively more than any other landed group of the time'.[4] Whereas in the fifteenth century the yeomanry was gradually emerging in times of uncertain farming prosperity, an estimate based on records of areas covering a third of the country suggests that the average wealth of this class doubled between the time of Elizabeth and the Civil War. Although the most substantial husbandmen merged indistinguishably with the lower ranks of the yeomanry there was a substantial difference in the average or median wealth of the members of the two strata. The farm of a substantial husbandman was probably of the order of 25 to 50 acres, whereas that of an equivalent yeoman appears to have been approximately 50 to

[1] W. G. Hoskins, 'The Leicestershire Farmer in the seventeenth century', in *Provincial England* (1965), pp. 153, 155.
[2] J. Thirsk, *English Peasant Farming: the agrarian history of Lincolnshire from Tudor to recent times* (1957), p. 456.
[3] For the pull of the London market and its effect on agriculture see F. J. Fisher, 'The development of the London food market, 1540–1640', *Economic History Review*, v (1935); A. Everitt, 'The marketing of agricultural produce', in *The Agrarian History of England and Wales*, iv, ed. J. Thirsk (Cambridge, 1967), 507–16.
[4] G. Batho, 'Landlords in England: noblemen, gentlemen and yeomen', in *ibid.*, 305.

120 acres, depending on fertility and location, with the result that the average yeoman may well have been at least twice as wealthy as the average husbandman, and possessed goods worth at least £200 by the mid-seventeenth century.[1]

As Harrison stated, one of the most notable results of the enhanced wealth of farmers was a marked increase in standards of housing and household furnishings. That this was not due simply to a proportionate rise in expenditure on these items is becoming evident from current studies, indeed it now appears indisputable that there was a tendency among all levels of society to invest a growing share of their total wealth in domestic goods. Among Oxfordshire farmers of the middle range, for example, the proportion of total wealth made up of household goods as opposed to farm stock rose from a quarter in the 1550s to a half by the 1580s.[2] Similar tendencies were displayed not only by those towards the top of the wealth range, but also by the more prosperous agricultural labourers, and in the case of the latter group the domestic proportion rose from 40 per cent to 50 per cent of wealth, comparing 1560–1600 with 1610–1640.[3]

The cumulative effect of rising wealth and a greater proportionate expenditure on housing and household goods was nothing less than 'a revolution in domestic comfort and in living standards generally' for the broad middle strata of rural and urban society, a revolution which is documented in minute and fascinating detail in thousands upon thousands of probate inventories.[4] The most tangible manifestation of these developments took place in housing. From about 1570 onwards farmers all over England were rebuilding their houses, and in the towns the houses of craftsmen and merchants were also improved and enlarged, although the pace of successive phases of urban re-development has resulted in the survival of far less evidence than in the countryside. All over England small, dark, uncomfortable medieval dwellings were being completely or partially transformed into

---

[1] J. P. Cooper, 'The social distribution of land and men in England, 1436–1700', *Economic History Review*, 2nd sər. xx (1967), 426–7; Hoskins, '*Provincial England*', p. 155.
[2] *Household and Farm Inventories in Oxfordshire, 1550–1590*, ed. M. A. Havinden (1965), espec. pp. 32–4; Pollard and Crossley, p. 98.
[3] A. Everitt, 'Farm labourers', *Agrarian History of England*, iv, 421; W. G. Hoskins, *The Midland Peasant: the economic and social history of a Leicestershire village* (1957), pp. 296–7.
[4] Hoskins, *Provincial England*, p. 153.

larger, warmer, and lighter homes, with more fireplaces and chimneys, glazed windows, and more rooms and a greater degree of specialisation between rooms.[1]

Turning to the interiors of these houses we find that the transformation was no less complete. The rise in the average value of estates discussed earlier was to a large extent manifested in more and better soft furnishings, including linens, silks, carpets, curtains, tapestries and 'painted cloths', coverlets and cushions; more and better furniture, much of it 'joined' and made of fine woods, including canopied beds, long tables, a variety of stools and chairs, some covered with leather or fine cloth, presses and cupboards for the display of fine tableware, and an occasional desk or musical instrument; and more and better metalware, including silver and some gold, but more commonly a wide range of bronze, brass, iron, and, of course, pewter utensils for the kitchen, hearth and table.[2]

It would be perverse not to pay especial heed to Harrison's intimation that the pewter industry was one of the main beneficiaries of the rising wealth of the rural and urban middle classes, and a closer inspection reveals his conclusion to be well founded. The advance of the middle strata was, in very general terms, based less on the creation of new wealth than on a redistribution in favour of the centre at the expense of the higher and lower reaches, especially of the latter. It was the same twin phenomena of sharply rising food prices and gently rising money wages, that so benefited farmers selling their produce, that also inexorably drove deeper into poverty the great mass of those who relied solely on manual labour for their livelihood or who possessed exiguous landholdings. The nadir of the Phelps Brown–Hopkins statistical index of building craftsmen's real wages, which covers more than six hundred years, was reached at the turn of the sixteenth century.[3] It is also more than likely that the well publicised

---

[1] *Ibid.*, pp. 131–48; M. W. Barley, 'Rural housing in England', *Agrarian History of England*, iv.

[2] A large-scale systematic study of probate inventories has still to be undertaken, but a substantial body of inventories has been published. A detailed examination of the published collections is undertaken below. For general comments by historians see *inter alia:* Pollard and Crossley, pp. 95–8; Hoskins, *Provincial England*, pp. 153–4; C. Hole, *English Home-Life, 1500 to 1800* (1947), ch. 1. For more detailed discussions of the household goods themselves see F. G. Roe, *English Cottage Furniture* (1961); *Farm and Cottage Inventories of Mid-Essex, 1634–1749*, ed. F. W. Steer (Chelmsford, 1950).

[3] E. H. Phelps Brown and S. V. Hopkins, 'Seven centuries of the prices of consumables, compared with builders' wage-rates', *Economica*, new ser., xxiii (1956).

difficulties of the great aristocratic landlords under Elizabeth and the early Stuarts owed something to the failure of rents to keep pace with prices, at least before the 1590s. As a result of this redistribution of wealth there can be no doubt that the consumption of pewter rose sharply. To use economic terminology the marginal propensity to consume pewter was higher amongst the middle strata than it was amongst the very poor or the very rich; in other words, members of the middle strata were more likely to spend a greater proportion of each additional unit of income on purchases of pewter than were those at the top or bottom of the social scale. It has already been demonstrated from medieval evidence that pewter was not purchased in significant quantities by the vast bulk of town and agricultural labourers, domestic servants, cottagers, paupers, and unemployed, and although in the course of the sixteenth and seventeenth centuries pewter permeated much further down the social scale it was only a modest number of the most prosperous of these groups who had resources to devote to this commodity after satisfying the basic requirements of food and clothing. Neither should the huge quantities of pewter held by the very rich blind us to the fact that the average expenditure on pewter of this sector, expressed as a proportion of income or wealth, was far lower than that recorded by the middle classes.

A major part of the study of any item of personal consumption in the sixteenth and seventeenth centuries, with the exclusion of food, must be based upon probate inventories. The production of a 'trewe and perfyte Inventory of all the goodes, catells, wares, mechaundyses, as well moveable as not moveable' by four honest persons was first made obligatory for executors of wills by the statute 21 Henry VIII, c. 5. Although, as we have seen, a significant number of medieval wills and inventories survive, it was not until the latter part of Elizabeth's reign that the practice became well established. Individuals whose personal estates were worth less than £5 were not required to make a will, and are therefore only rarely represented in the inventories that survive. In addition the majority of the landowning aristocracy and richer gentry, as well as of the richer merchants, are also unrepresented because they preferred to have the probate of their wills granted by the superior Archbishop's Prerogative Court of Canterbury, rather than by their local diocesan court. Finally, anyone owning property in more than one diocese was also required to have recourse to Canterbury, regardless of wealth.¹ Thus although we can learn very little of the small number of very rich and the vast number of very poor from probate inventories, they do provide a unique record of the personal estates of the substantial middle portion of the population. Estimates of the proportion of English households represented in probate inventories inevitably vary, indeed the actual proportion itself was bound to differ from time to time and region to region, but for our purposes it would appear safe to conclude that at least half the households of the realm were excluded, the vast bulk because of poverty.²

Probate inventories, which exist in prodigious numbers for most parts of the country,³ offer one of the most promising lines of investigation into standards of wealth and domestic comfort in Tudor and Stuart England still to be adequately exploited. They can be made to yield a rich crop of data on a wide range of interesting and important problems, such as the relationship between demand and economic development, and the nature of agricultural and industrial structure before the Industrial Revolution. But it is essential that inventories should be handled with care and with an awareness of their many limitations. Many deficiencies stem from the fact that the persons who compiled inventories were not experts, on the contrary they were usually simply the friends, neighbours, and relations of the deceased, and were sometimes barely literate. A number of inventories are clearly only a partial list of the goods of the household in which the deceased lived; many rich widows, for example, are credited with a relatively small range of possessions because they were living in the homes of friends or relatives. Many other partial or misleading inventories exist, such as those of priests and servants, but they are more difficult to detect. The value placed

[1] For the origins of the custom of making inventories and the legal procedures followed see: B. G. Bouwens, *Wills and their whereabouts* (2nd ed., 1951); R. Burn, *Ecclesiastical Law* (1763); *Household and Farm Inventories in Oxfordshire*, pp. 3-4. The inventories of the Prerogative Court of Canterbury are still not available to the public.
[2] Estimates of the proportion of the total population covered by inventories vary from 50 per cent in the Petworth region of Sussex in the later seventeenth century (G. H. Kenyon, 'Petworth town and trades', *Sussex Archaeological Collections*, xcvi (1958), 40-1) to as high as two thirds to three quarters in later sixteenth century Oxfordshire (*Household and Farm Inventories in Oxfordshire*, p. 3). The proportion in the sixteenth century appears to have been higher than that in the seventeenth century, see D. C. Coleman, 'Labour in the English economy of the seventeenth century', *Economic History Review*, 2nd ser., viii (1956).
[3] More than 120,000 inventories survive for the dioceses of Lincoln and Kent alone.

on goods is also a potentially treacherous subject. The legal position was quite clear, the appraisers ought to have specified the price at which the goods could be sold, but obviously in practice the decision depended as much on the knowledge and skill of the appraisers as on the condition and quality of the goods. It should also be noted that inventories do not include freehold property. Furthermore they also vary considerably in the thoroughness with which the outstanding credits and liabilities of the deceased were recorded, although such items frequently comprised a significant proportion of the total value placed upon an estate. More important for our purposes was the frequent failure of the appraisers to list goods of scant value, which means that references to utensils of clay and wood are deceptively few. Finally it must be stressed that inventories, particularly with respect to durable goods such as pewter, do not necessarily accurately reflect the current consumption pattern of the deceased; this point is of particular importance when attempting to date the demise of pewter in the face of competition from new forms of tableware.

For the study of the consumption of pewter many of these defects are of less significance than might appear at first sight. The relative infrequency of inventories of poor households, for example, although serious is not a crucial defect; firstly because despite the lack of legal compulsion a moderate number of estates with a total value of less than £5 were appraised, and special attention can be devoted to them, and secondly because, as has been stated before, this sector of the population was responsible for a relatively slight proportion of total pewter purchases. The scarcity of probate inventories of the richer strata is, perhaps, even less of a hindrance, since many alternative indications of the consumption of pewter by these groups are available, including a selection of privately commissioned inventories. In addition the valuations placed on pewter are rarely as idiosyncratic as those placed on many other goods, since the greater part of the value of pewter lay in the metal, irrespective of the condition of the particular piece under scrutiny.[1]

The following tables incorporate the results of an analysis of well over 1,500 inventories, which is probably a large enough sample from which to draw some tentative conclusions. A variety

---

[1] In the seventeenth century, for example, old pewter generally had a part-exchange value of two-thirds to three-quarters of the price of new.

of methods have been adopted to display the data they contain, in addition to fundamental divisions based upon chronology and wealth. The simplest method, and also the most reliable, is a calculation of the number of inventories which record pewter; this method also makes use of the greatest possible number of inventories, since few have to be discarded. The results of this exercise are contained in columns (i), (ii), and (iii) of Tables 5 and 6. But such an unsophisticated approach leaves much valuable information about the precise nature of holdings of pewter unrevealed, and the subsequent columns contain less accurate but more informative data, based necessarily on a smaller number of inventories. The fourth column of both tables gives the average number of pieces of pewter recorded in those inventories which provide this information. Columns (v), (vi), (vii) and (viii) are based on larger groups of inventories which give the value of pewter holdings. Columns (vi) and (vii) are the least reliable of all, depending as they do on the frequently erratic valuations placed on goods and the exhaustiveness with which outstanding debts and credits are listed; in addition the valuation placed on an estate could be unrealistically affected simply by the holding of a lease instead of a freehold. A division based on the value of estates was preferred to one based on occupational and status data, primarily because occupations are only infrequently given and thus the samples would have been needlessly small. The price of pewter fluctuated considerably in the course of the sixteenth and seventeenth centuries, and these fluctuations must be borne in mind when considering the tables.[1]

Among the important inferences that can be drawn from the data contained in these tables are: first, that from the mid-sixteenth century pewter was virtually ubiquitous in the households of the broad strata represented by inventories; second, that there was a consistent tendency for the size and value of pewter holdings, and the value of each piece of pewter held, to increase sympathetically with the total worth of the estate; third, that the proportion of the estate composed of pewter tended to have an inverse relationship with the total worth of the estate; and finally, and with less certainty, that the number of pieces held by persons within the same wealth range tended to fluctuate within relatively narrow limits from c. 1550 to c. 1700, although the price of pewter increased markedly.

[1] SeeA ppendix B below.

Table 5
Probate inventories analysed by period

Date	(i) Number of inventories	(ii) Number of inventories with pewter	(iii) Percentage of inventories with pewter	(iv) Average number of pieces per inventory	(v) Average value of pewter per inventory (Shillings)	(vi) Average value of inventory (£)	(vii) Value of pewter as a percentage of value of inventory	(viii) Number of inventories used for columns (v–vii)
				NOTTINGHAMSHIRE				
1532–50	37	35	95	20	10.2	33.2	1.5	21
1558–68	65	61	94	26	21.7	59.4	1.8	33
				OXFORDSHIRE				
1550–79	63	60	95	20	14	40.9	1.7	41
1580–90	176	164	93	18	10.6	34.7	1.5	105
				DEVONSHIRE				
1555–1600	30	28	93	22	27.1	121.8	1.1	26
1601–50	134	127	95	28	37.8	203.4	0.9	112
1651–99	70	66	94	26	39.3	231.4	0.9	49
				BEDFORDSHIRE				
1617–20	161	150	93	19	16.7	80.2	1.0	79
				STOURBRIDGE (WORCESTERSHIRE)				
1541–58	20	20	100	20	8.7	14.7	3.0	11

The sixteenth and seventeenth centuries 93

				DUDLEY (WORCESTERSHIRE)				
1551–1601	50	50	100	22	13·4	27·0	2·5	46
1605–85	24	23	96	27	31·1	59·1	3·8	15
				MID-ESSEX				
1635–40	21	17	81	18	25·7	83·7	1·5	14
1658–80	90	87	97	15	34·1	151·4	1·1	57
1681–1700	64	59	92	21	41·5	160·5	1·3	24
1701–44	44	44	100	20	31·5	108	1·5	13
				LICHFIELD (STAFFORDSHIRE)				
1642–60	35	33	94	52	71·9	185	1·9	23
1661–80	126	121	97	26	49·3	91·2	2·7	84
				SEDGLEY (STAFFORDSHIRE)				
1649–99	101	94	93	10	19·4	46·3	2·1	24

Sources. Nottinghamshire Household Inventories, ed. P. A. Kennedy (Thoroton Society Record Series, xxii, 1962); *Household and Farm Inventories in Oxfordshire 1550–1590*, ed. M. A. Havinden (1965); *Devon Inventories of the Sixteenth and Seventeenth Centuries*, ed. M. Cash (Devon and Cornwall Record Society, new ser., xi, 1966); 'Jacobean household inventories', ed. F. G. Emmison, *Bedfordshire Historical Record Society*, xx (1938); *Stourbridge Probate Inventories, 1541–1558*, ed. J. S. Roper (Dudley, 1966); *Dudley Probate Inventories, 1544–1603*, and *Dudley Probate Inventories, 1605–1685*, ed. J. S. Roper (Dudley, 1965, 1966); *Farm and Cottage Inventories of Mid-Essex, 1634–1749*, ed. F. W. Steer (Chelmsford, 1950); *Probate Inventories of Lichfield and District, 1568–1680*, ed. D. G. Vaisey (Staffordshire Record Society, 4th ser., v, 1969); *Sedgley Probate Inventories, 1614–1787*, ed. J. S. Roper (Dudley, 1966).

Table 6
Probate inventories analysed by wealth

Total value of inventory (£)	(i) Number of inventories	(ii) Number of inventories with pewter	(iii) Percentage of inventories with pewter	(iv) Average number of pieces per inventory	(v) Average value of pewter per inventory (shillings)	(vi) Average value of inventory (£)	(vii) Value of pewter as a percentage of value of inventory
NOTTINGHAMSHIRE, 1532–1568							
Under 11	23	18	78	15	4·8	6·6	3·6
11–51	53	52	98	17	10·2	28·7	1·8
51–100	14	14	100	44	26·3	77·3	1·7
over 100	11	11	100	57	57·2	152·5	1·9
OXFORDSHIRE, 1550–1590							
Under 6	44	37	84	7·5	4·1	3·4	6·0
6–11	31	26	84	14	8·6	7·5	5·7
11–21	40	38	95	17	8·3	16·7	2·4
21–51	72	71	99	19	17·5	35·9	2·4
51–100	38	38	100	28	22·6	75·5	1·4
over 100	7	7	100	76	46·7	137·6	1·7
DEVONSHIRE, 1615–1655							
Under 11	8	8	100	9	7	7·8	4·5
11–51	39	35	90	19	20	28	3·6
51–100	36	33	91	21	24·6	67·6	1·8
over 100	52	52	100	45	51·6	368·6	0·7

The sixteenth and seventeenth centuries

						(viii) Value of pewter as a percentage of household goods
ESSEX, 1635–1680						
Under 11	14	12	86	6	6.8	4.4
11–51	44	41	96	19.8	30.5	3.2
51–100	20	19	93	30.1	84.1	1.8
over 100	33	32	97	53.8	321.9	0.8
ESSEX, 1681–1744						
Under 11	7	7	100	10	7	7.0
11–51	31	28	90	28.6	33.6	4.3
51–100	21	20	95	38.6	70.2	2.7
over 100	48	47	98	42.9	246	0.7
LICHFIELD (STAFFORDSHIRE), 1642–1680						
Under 11	18	17	94	7.4	7.1	5.2
11–51	68	64	94	23.8	26.2	4.5
51–100	26	25	96	49.1	74.6	3.1
over 100	43	43	100	105.8	280.0	1.9
BEDFORDSHIRE, 1617–1620						
Under 6	15	12	80	3.8	3.3	5.7 ⎫
6–11	17	14	82	6.5	8.3	3.9 ⎭
11–51	69	66	96	11.8	25	2.3
51–100	16	16	100	23.1	66.2	1.7
over 100	33	33	100	32.8	219	0.6

Sources. Nottinghamshire Household Inventories, ed. P. A. Kennedy (Thoroton Society Record Series, xxii, 1962); Household and Farm Inventories in Oxfordshire, 1550–1590, ed. M. A. Havinden (1965); Devon Inventories of the Sixteenth and Seventeenth Centuries, ed. M. Cash (Devon and Cornwall Record Society, new ser., xi, 1966); 'Jacobean household inventories', ed. F. G. Emmison, Bedfordshire Historical Record Society, xx (1938); Stourbridge Probate Inventories, 1541–1558, ed. J. S. Roper (Dudley, 1966); Dudley Probate Inventories, 1544–1603, and Dudley Probate Inventories, 1605–1685, ed. J. S. Roper (Dudley, 1965, 1966); Farm and Cottage Inventories of Mid-Essex, 1634–1749, ed. F. W. Steer (Chelmsford, 1950); Probate Inventories of Lichfield and District, 1568–1680, ed. D. G. Vaisey (Staffordshire Record Society, 4th ser., v, 1969); Sedgley Probate Inventories, 1614–1787, ed. J. S. Roper (Dudley, 1966).

We have seen in the previous chapter that not only did a substantial market for pewter develop among the nobility, gentry, richer bourgeoisie, and wealthy lay and ecclesiastical institutions in the course of the fourteenth and fifteenth centuries, but also that it came to be purchased in modest but nevertheless significant quantities by some richer peasants and emergent yeomen. Notwithstanding, the remarkably extensive social and geographical distribution revealed in Tables 5 and 6, even in the homes of the lowest stratum represented, testifies to a further massive widening of the market for pewter by the later sixteenth century. Indeed, on the basis of these inventories it is clear that pewter was one of the most common items to be found in middle-class and lower-middle-class homes, and that only a very small group of necessities such as linen, beds and cooking pots approached its level of distribution.[1] On the basis of the evidence of the inventories that have been studied, it would appear justifiable to conclude that from the mid-sixteenth century pewter was being used in at least half the households in England. In the areas, and at the periods, covered by the inventories the number of households without pewter scarcely sinks below one in five, and is usually substantially less than one in ten. So widespread was the distribution at an early date that only one of the fourteen surviving inventories from rural mid-Nottinghamshire between 1532 and 1550 does not contain pewter, despite the fact that the average value of the estates represented was less than £15. Households in and around the small market town of Stourbridge in Worcestershire present a similar picture, with each of the twenty surviving inventories from the period 1541 to 1550 recording some pewter, although the average value of the estates here was less than £19. Moving across to Dudley in the same county we find that all eleven inventories covering the period 1544 to 1570 contain pewter, and in Oxfordshire all fourteen inventories dated 1570 or earlier similarly contain pewter.

Data concerning the widespread distribution of pewter in the earliest available inventories are complemented by evidence exemplifying its diffusion among the poorest households represented, and again the results are surprising. Table 6 shows that in rural and small urban communities in Oxfordshire, Notting-

---

[1] Only a handful of items manage to achieve mention in more than 80 per cent of inventories.

hamshire, Bedfordshire, Worcestershire, Essex, Devonshire and Staffordshire between 80 and 100 per cent of estates worth less than £10 presented for probate contained pewter, and that the average number of pieces per household ranged from almost fifteen in mid-sixteenth-century Nottinghamshire to just over six in mid-seventeenth-century Essex. The Oxfordshire collection contains the highest proportion of 'poor' households, with no less than 20 per cent valued at under £6, so it would be profitable to proceed into greater detail. Table 6 shows that more than four-fifths of these 'poor' Oxfordshire households contained pewter, and probing even more deeply we find that of the eighteen estates valued at under £3 two-thirds contain pewter, of the three valued at less than £1 two contain pewter, and finally that the smallest inventory of all, worth a pathetic 14s 8d, contains pewter valued atabout 1s.

Too many bald statistics can deaden the impact, however, so it would be as well to reinforce the points already made by quoting in full the contents of a number of poor households which contained pewter. The two Oxfordshire inventories of estates under £1 containing pewter were as follows:

Elizabeth Sly of Banbury, taken 21 March 1575:
2 formes, A bedsted, and 2 bordes, 1s 8d: 2 coffers and A pyn chest, 1s 6d; A nowld broken coffer, 2d; owld Ierne, 1d; 2 pewter platters, A dysshe, A sawser, A pyntpot, 2 lettell candulsteckes, A ston salte, 1s 6d; A nowld ladder, 1d; A saw, 4d; A payle, A lome, A pere of bellowes, A pere of scales, and A nowld hachett, 6d; A bras pot, 3 owld kettuls, A pere of cobbordes, A spyt, and A choppyng knyfe, 2s 0d; A pere of sheres, 2d; A red kyrtull, 2 owld petycotes and A wascot and A hat and A cap, 1s 3d; A pyllowbere, 3 carchewes, A napurne, and A cornard carchew, 6d; A matteres, A keverled, 2 pyllowes, 2 wynowshetes, 3 shetes and A halffe, and A nunder cloth, A rowlyng pyn and A stamper, A stole and A kusshyn, 4s 0d; A tabull bord, A pere of tressulls and 4^{ll} of woll and A nowld peynted cloth, 1s 0d; A taynkerd and A showying horne, 1d; an old wheelstoole, 1d; Total, 14s 11d.[1]

Deans Anstie of Banbury, taken 19 February 1588:
1 brasse potte, 1s 0d; a frieingpanne, a kettel, a gridiron, a

[1] *Household and Farm Inventories in Oxfordshire*, pp. 65–6.

sckellet and a spite, 1s 8d; 5 peces of pewter and a cansticke, 1s 6d; towe lomes, 8d; a peacke and halfe stricke, 4d; 3 payer of shettes, 3s; a coverlet, 1s 6d; 12 peaces of linnen, 1s 8d; 2 coffers, 7d; 2 pillowes 8d; a cubberd a table and forme, 2s 0d; Total, 14s 8d.[1]

In Nottinghamshire five of the nine inventories of estates valued at less than £6 contain pewter, but in Stourbridge and Dudley the acquisition of pewter was considered even more essential amongst those of limited means, for all of the fifteen inventories of estates under £6 contain pewter. Furthermore the amounts of pewter held were in many cases substantial and comprised a major portion of the total estate, as some of the following examples show:

Thomas Grene, Old Swynford parish, Stourbridge, taken 1544:
a horse, 13s 4d; certeyne hay, 8s 0d; 2 lytle pannes, 5s 0d; 2 potts, 5s 0d; sheets, 16s 0d; yren, 9s 0d; 3 cawtherns, 2s 0d; 18 pieces of pewter, 5s 0d; 4 candelstycks, 1s 4d; 2 canvasses, 3s 0d; a coverlet, 2s 2d; 5 shurts, 4s 0d; 9 trene dysshes and a ladle, 2d. a skomer, 2d; 4 stonds and a lytle fate, 2s 8d; 2 payles, 4d; the cheyne a potks and a peyre of tongs, 8d; a trame and a straynynge bagge, 2d; a peyre of hamps, 10d; peynted clothes, 12d; a rope and a bucket, 6d; 3 kerchieffes, 12d; in hempe, 2s 0d; a pere coberts, 3d; a bolster, 3d; Total, £4. 3s 10d.[2]

William Smallman, Dudley, taken 2 December 1572:
a galan potte with three or foure houles, 3s 0d; a littell pan of a gallan and halfe, 2s 6d; an olde cautheren, 6d; a candle sticke, 2d; an old hand basket, 2d; one pewter dishe and a sawcer, 8d; a frying panne, 8d; an olde peinted cloth, 1s 0d; an olde coverlet twillie and tow shetes, 1s 0d; one bed stide with one foote borde and one hed borde, 4d; one blacke cowe, £1. 0s 0d; one mare, £1. 0s 0d; one wether, 2s 4d; a pyd cowe, £1. 0s 0d; 8 shippe and 6 lambes, £1. 0s 0d; Total, £4. 14s 10d.[3]

[1] *Ibid.*, p. 258.
[2] *Stourbridge Inventories*, p. 8.
[3] *Dudley Inventories 1544–1603*, p. 18.

William Downing, Dudley, taken 4 June 1588:
one cowe and a heafer, £1. 10s 0d; 3 kettells, one skellet,
2 brase potts, 9s 0d; one skemer, 2 candellstick, 17 pecies of
pewter, 7s 4d; 2 coffers, 2s 0d; one flockebed, 2 bolsters,
2 pelawes, 3 twellies, one covering, 10s 0d; in hemton
flaxen and hordon shettes be to the number of 10 shettes,
8s 0d; 2 pelows beares, one towell, 1s 1d; one Jerkine, one
dublet, one perei of hose, 3s 4d; 2 table Clothes and 3
shortes, 2s 8d; one peare of shewes, one Cappe, 1s 0d;
2 lommes, 2 stoppes, 2 barreles, one paill, one gawne,
3 Chese fatts, 2s 4d; dishes, trenchers, spones and ladell,
2 whelles, 2 wooden platters, a piging chorne, 1s 4d; one
table bord, 3 stolles, one forme, and 2 tresteles, 1s 0d; one
gratt fier sholl, one peare of tonges, 1s 8d; one galle, one
peare of pothokes, and cobbardes, 1s 8d; 9 small painted
Clothes, 2 boxes, 2s 11d; teane pottes and milk pans, 2d;
one friing pan, 3d; Total, £4. 4s 2d.[1]

Elizabeth Bailies, alias Thatcher, Dudley, taken 12 July 1588:
her weringe apparell, 4s 0d; three littell brasse potts, one
littell brasse panne, one littell kettell, one skellet, two
Candelsticks of brasse, 6s 8d; eleven peeces of pewter and
two pewter pottes, 2 sawcers, 5s 0d; one olde Featherbeed
Case with some fethers, and one olde Flockebeed with the
furniture therto belonginge, 3s 4d; two payer of Sheetts
whereof the one is hempton and the other nogen, 2s 0d;
one olde Cubbord, one table bourde with the Tresteles and
forme, two payer of beedsteeds, one Cheste, 3s 0d; six
Elnes of new nogen Cloth, 2s 6d; one fier gratte, one fier
shovell, one payer of Tonngs, a payer of pottegayles, a payer
of Cobberds, and one littell Spytte, 2s 6d; three littell
lomes, 2 olde payles, and other Treene stuffe, 1s 4d; Total,
£1. 10s 4d.[2]

By the seventeenth century the proportion of small estates represented in collections of inventories had decreased sharply, but those that exist exhibit the same characteristics as comparable estates of the previous century, despite the fact that they are drawn from even poorer households owing to the sharp fall which had taken place in the value of money. Twelve of the

[1] *Ibid.*, p. 47.   [2] *Ibid.*, p. 48.

fifteen estates of under £6 in value in the Bedfordshire collection of over 150 inventories from the closing years of the second decade of the seventeenth century contain pewter, while in the Lichfield collection pewter was present in all eight such inventories. The following examples are typical of the possessions listed in these tiny inventories:

Edward Glover, Bedford, St. Cuthberts, 1620:
One chest, one coffer, one cubberd, 11s; one table, 3s 4d; one blankett, one pare of sheetes, three bannes, 2s; one matteris and his waring apparrill, 2s; One cettle, one frying panne, 18d; one peuter dish, one salt, one caster, 6d; Two shirtes, one pillobeare, two pillowes, 2s; Total 22s 4d.[1]

John Stevens of Thorncote in Northill, 21 June, 1619:
One cupboard, 6s 8d; one great penne, 3s 8d; one table, tressles and forms and two coffers and one trough, 5s; foure brasse kettles, a little brasse pot with a paire of pothookes, and pothangers, 13s 4d; one tubb, one frying panne, one spitt, with one cushion and other small commodities, and a sheephooke, 3s 4d; two bedsteads, two bolsters, foure pillowes, one old coverlett, and an undercloth, 18s 4d; foure coffers, 8s 4d; his apparell, 14s 6d; three pewter dishes, one salt, two spoones and two candelstickes and a sawcer, 2s 6d; the painted clothes, one forcer, one hatchell, one plancke, with other small things, 6s 7d; in money, 19s 10d; Total £5. 2s 1d.[2]

Thomas Hammond of Cardington, shepherd, 25 January 1620:
one olld cuppbord, a table, a chaire, a forme 10s; two little puter dishes and a saucer, and two little kettells and some dishes, 3s 4d; the potthangers, a spitt, a candlesticke and a bill, 8d; two troughes, one tubb, one barrell and a skepp and the frying pan, 3s; Two borded bedds with the bedding, 5s; three coffers, a forme, a hopp barrell, 6s; 3 paire of harden sheets, and two pillow beers, fower napkins and a table clothe, 7s; a little cow and some haye, £3; Some fire wood, 5s; his wearinge apparell, 10s; Total £5. 10s 0d.[3]

[1] 'Jacobean inventories', p. 59.   [2] *Ibid.*, p. 75.   [3] *Ibid.*, p. 135.

James Ealy or Heeley, Lichfield, taken 1675:
1 press, 7s 0d; 1 cubbard, 2s 0d; 1 table, 3s 0d; 2 pots,
1 brass and 1 iron, 10s 0d; 1 kettle, 1s 0d; 1 forme, 6d;
3 puter dishes, 1 salt and 1 poringer, 4s 0d; 1 andiron,
1s 8d; 1 friing pann, 10d; 1 pare tongues, 6d; 1 spitt, 6d;
1 bed and all that belongs to it, 18s 0d; 1 table, 2s 0d;
1 cofer, 2s 0d; 1 churne, 1s 4d; 1 shelfe, 6d; 1 prese, 4s 0d;
1 table, 2s 6d; 1 cofer, 2s 0d; 3 boxis, 2s 6d; 1 bed,
blankets and linins, 14s 0d; Total, £3. 19s 10d.[1]

William Winstanley, Lichfield, labourer, taken 12 May, 1673:
Seaven pewter dishes little and greate, three pewter porrengers
and one pewter cann, 6s 0d; two potts and one brasse kettle,
one possnett and one little kettle, 10s 0d; one table, fower
joyne stools, one cupboard, two shelves, one chaire and one
other little table, 6s 8d; one grate, potthookes, firer shovell
and tongs, bellowes and one frying pann, 2s 0d; one feather
bedd, two boulsters, one pillowe, two blanketts, one old
coverledd and a beddstedd, 13s 4d; fower paire of old
sheets, fower nappkins and two pillow beares, 10s 0d;
Two boxes, two coffers and an old truncke, 2s 6d; one
feather bedd and a bedstedd, one old cupboard, two pailes
and one wheele, 10s 0d; all other things nott specified in this
inventory, 3s 4d; Total, £3. 3s 10d.[2]

It is probable that more than one of the tiny estates listed above belonged to labourers, but it would be remiss to pass on without attempting to gain further insight into the household goods of labouring families, for labourers were an extremely important sector of the population, both in terms of numbers and of their contribution to national wealth, and they comprised a large proportion of the employed poor. It has been estimated that labourers and their families formed from a quarter to a third of the entire rural population in Tudor and early Stuart England, while in 1695 Gregory King classed almost a quarter of the national population as 'labouring people and out servants'.[3] Despite the great numbers of labourers, however, inventories of labourers' households comprise only about 8 per cent of total

[1] *Lichfield Inventories*, p. 242.   [2] *Ibid.*, p. 265.
[3] Everitt, 'Farm labourers', *Agrarian History*, iv, 396–9; Coleman, 'Labour in English Economy', p. 283.

surviving inventories, and it is extremely unlikely that more than one in four labourers was sufficiently well-off to leave an inventory.[1] Nevertheless, the upper reaches of the labouring class no doubt shaded into the lesser husbandmen; William Heptinsall of Carleton in the East Riding of Yorkshire probably fell into this category, for his estate in 1611 was valued at £18 and contained nineteen pewter dishes, two salts, four saucers, five porringers, and two candlesticks. Robert Wood of Nuneaton, Warwickshire, was almost as prosperous, for when he died in 1617 he left goods valued at almost £11, including a set of pewter dishes, salts, cups and candlesticks in his hall.[2] The presence of two small pewter dishes in the house of a south Staffordshire coalminer in 1682 is also a pertinent commentary on the wide distribution of our product.[3] Owing to the infrequency with which occupations are given, the Bedfordshire collection of the early seventeenth century is perhaps the only published series to provide an adequate sample of labourers' household goods: it contains twenty-two labourers' inventories, of which nineteen (86·3 per cent) contain pewter; furthermore each of these labourers held an average of ten pieces of pewter, worth approximately 6·8s, which in turn comprised approximately 4·5 per cent of the total value of their household goods.

The conclusion to be drawn from our extended glimpse of the possessions of the poorest households of which inventories were made, including a substantial number of estates worth considerably less than £5, must be that from the second half of the sixteenth century, if not earlier, the purchase of pewter had ceased to be the exclusive privilege of the upper and middle classes. Indeed we have found that the great majority of the poorest households represented contained pewter, and what is more not merely a piece or two but often a range of at least six or seven items. Furthermore, it is clear from Table 6 that pewter consistently comprised a substantially greater proportion of the total value of the estates of the poor than of those of the well-to-do.[4] Thus pewter was no longer considered a luxury or even a semi-luxury and, although a wide selection of more easily available

[1] Everitt, 'Farm Labourers', pp. 419–20; Everitt's estimate that 25 per cent of labourers left inventories may well be too high.
[2] *Ibid.*, pp. 446–7.   [3] *Sedgley Inventories.*
[4] It can be seen in Table 5 that the proportion comprised by pewter fell from c. 6–7 per cent in estates of less than £6 to under 2 per cent in estates of over £50.

and far less costly substitutes existed, it appears that the attractions of pewter as a status symbol were so great that social pressures encouraged even the poorer members of the community to view it as a necessity. Just as in previous centuries pewter had performed this function for the rising middle class of merchants and yeomen so in the sixteenth and seventeenth centuries its attractions permeated down the social scale until widows, labourers, smallholders, and the like devoted a sizeable part of their tiny incomes to its acquisition, after the minimum basic requirements of food, clothing and shelter had been satisfied.

Pewter, of course, is not a truly homogeneous product, and considerable variations of quality of materials, standards of workmanship and general condition must have existed amongst the items appraised in inventories. Much of that held by poorer households was undoubtedly of inferior quality and probably also in poor condition, and it is likely that impecunious purchasers often resorted to the secondhand pewter market or the local tinker rather than to the retailer of fine wares. Such speculations are, in fact, amply borne out by the valuations placed on pewter by the appraisers of estates, which reveal a consistent tendency for the average price per piece to rise with the total value of the estate. In later sixteenth-century Oxfordshire, for example, the average value put on pewter in estates of under £21 was around 6d per piece, in estates of £21 to £100 it was 1s per piece, and in estates of over £100 it was 1s10d, while in Nottinghamshire comparable valuations rose from c. 6d to c. 1s. Although some of this increase was doubtless accounted for by differences in the size and type of article kept by richer households, it is unlikely that a significant part was not also played by quality and general condition. Even at the lowest valuations, however, it took the wage of a whole day's labour to buy one simple item of pewter.

Another significant feature of the data presented in the tables, to which special attention must be drawn, is the remarkable consistency of the proportion of wealth constituted by pewter in estates of comparable size in different parts of the country. The decline in the proportion of wealth constituted by pewter as estates increased in value is also a remarkably consistent trend. But the proportion of total wealth constituted by pewter is perhaps less valuable for our purposes than its contribution to the value of household goods alone. Unfortunately such information is extremely difficult to obtain owing to the haphazard methods used to compile inventories, which frequently make it impossible to separate household goods from other constituents of the estate, such as implements, livestock, crops, leases, cash, and debts. Emmison, when editing early seventeenth-century Bedfordshire inventories did, however, attempt to overcome these difficulties, and an additional column has been added to the section relating to Bedfordshire in Table 6 in order to take advantage of his calculations of the value of household goods. It can be seen that the value of pewter, when expressed as a proportion of the value of household goods, was on average more than four times greater than when expressed as a proportion of total wealth; but perhaps of even greater significance is the fact that the difference between the two calculations was not the same for all sizes of estate. In particular these calculations suggest that the procedure, perforce adopted for other regions, of comparing the value of pewter with the total value of the estate, may tend to give an exaggerated impression of the decline in the proportion of wealth invested in pewter as the value of the estate increased, since it is clear, in Bedfordshire at least, that the proportion of total wealth invested in household goods also tended to decline when wealth increased.

One must beware of drawing too many firm conclusions from the sample of inventories that has been analysed, but the natural tendency for the amount and value of pewter held to move in sympathy with wealth is unlikely not to have been universal. We have already noted the striking increase in the wealth of most sectors of the farming community and urban bourgeoisie during much of this period, and it is further illustrated by the data relating to the value of estates contained in the tables above. These trends were beneficial for the consumption of pewter, and they lend support to Harrison's testimony which clearly ascribes the accumulation of larger stocks of pewter by farmers to their greater wealth.

Although the contribution of pewter to the total value of the estate declined with advancing wealth, the number of pieces held rose sharply. If the inventories of all the series used in Table 6 are averaged we find that estates worth less than £11 contained eight pieces, estates worth £11 to £51 sixteen pieces, estates worth

£51 to £100 twenty-seven pieces, and estates worth more than £100 forty-eight pieces. But such averages provide little more than a convenient generalisation for some markedly divergent figures, and even the averages of holdings in individual regions are in some respects misleading. That some large estates contained no pewter is evident from the first three columns of the table, but what is not revealed is the wide range of deviations from the norm. In a small number of estates of between £51 and £100, for example, pewter constituted more than 5 per cent of total value. When George Atwood, a cordwainer of Dudley, died in 1584, although the total value of his estate including livestock, crops, and leases, was only £55.7s0d his house contained '34 greate Platters, 13 smale pottengers, 25 counterfeyte dishes, 3 Saltes, 2 sawcers, 2 cuppes of pewter, 4 pewter potts and a pynte potte, one chamber potte, 2 pewter bottels, 3 candelsticks of pewter' valued at more than 60s.[1] One of the most valuable holdings of pewter relative to the total estate was that of Joan Barrie, a widow of Crediton who died in 1648, which at 32s comprised over 15 per cent of the total value placed on all her goods.[2]

We have perhaps dwelt overlong with the rural middle classes to the neglect of merchants, shopkeepers, and craftsmen; these groups are, however, represented in all the collections of inventories studied above. In the Oxfordshire collection, for example, more than a quarter of those inventories which give occupation, or allow it to be deduced, belonged to craftsmen and tradesmen, while in the mid-Essex and Devonshire collections the proportion dropped to a fifth or even less. Amongst inventories drawn from the market towns of Sedgley, Dudley and Stourbridge, commercial and industrial persons were, of course, even more numerous and comprised almost half the total, while from those in and around the city of Lichfield, which had a population of approximately 2,500 in the mid-seventeenth century, the proportion rose to almost two-thirds.[3] Although many of the craftsmen and tradesmen represented in these inventories were less wealthy than their counterparts in agriculture, they appear to have had a greater proportion of their wealth invested in household goods in general, and in pewter in particular. This feature

[1] *Dudley Inventories, 1544–1603*, pp. 40–1. [2] *Devon Inventories*, p. 101.
[3] *Lichfield Inventories*, p. 2.

is brought out most clearly in the data from town collections, but it is also present amongst inventories of tradesmen in the predominantly rural collections.

Unfortunately scarcely any inventories from large or medium cities have been published. Those from Worcester, a city of medium size whose population rose from 4,000 to 8,000 between the mid-sixteenth century and the mid-seventeenth, have perhaps received most attention. Worcester inventories reveal a substantial consumption of pewter, especially among the richer merchants, whose butteries were often stacked high with pewterware.[1] The urban middle classes conventionally tended to indulge in conspicuous consumption to a greater degree than their rural counterparts, and this favoured the consumption of pewter. For example, among the household goods of Thomas Yeat, smith, which were valued at approximately £37 in 1563, we find '24 platters, 10 potyngears, 19 sawcers, 11 cownterfett dyshes, 1 basson and a yower, 12 flower cyps, 4 salltes and 2 covers of pewter, 6 pewter pottes, 9 candyllstyckes' valued at about 70s; while in the 'littell buttrey' of James Hill, tanner, in 1602 there were 'ten chargers, and ten platteres, and twelve frute disses, and 18 sawcers, six salltes, and sixe candelstickes, and fyve pewter cuppes, on pottell pewter pott, fyve pewter pottes, and a pynte pott, on dossen and a halfe of spones, on dossen of trenchers', which together with a few stone and wooden utensils were valued at £4, against a valuation of less than £30 put on all Hill's household goods.[2]

Passing upwards into the gentry and aristocracy one naturally encounters even more substantial holdings of pewter, but ostentation and conspicuous expenditure were obligatory in Tudor and Stuart England, and just as the substitution of wooden and clay utensils by pewterware was one of the first priorities, when resources permitted, of those towards the bottom of the scale of wealth, so the substitution of pewterware by utensils of silver and silver-gilt was one of the first priorities of those towards the top of that scale. These aspirations were part of the universal desire to live in a grand style, and as hospitality and

---

[1] A. D. Dyer, 'The City of Worcester in the Sixteenth Century' (Birmingham Ph.D. thesis, 1966), pp. 202–5; 'Probate inventories of Worcester tradesmen, 1545–1614', *Miscellany* II, ed. A. D. Dyer (Worcestershire Historical Society, new ser., v, 1967). [2] *Ibid.*, pp. 21–5, 29–30.

eating were at the centre of this life style, tableware assumed a role of crucial importance.[1]

It is possible to distinguish a number of stages, each determined by wealth, by which pewter was removed from the dining halls of the rich. The first stage, which was not usually greatly prejudicial to the use of pewter, was the acquisition of salts, goblets, tankards, ewers, bowls, spice-boxes and spoons of silver, whilst eating-utensils of pewter continued to be used, thereby echoing the comments of the anonymous Italian visitor to England at the turn of the fifteenth century.[2] The second stage, which required a far greater investment, and was thus restricted to the very rich, was the acquisition of large numbers of silver chargers, platters, dishes and saucers. Of course, there were various intermediate stages, the commonest of which was the provision of smaller numbers of silver eating utensils for the senior members of the household. The tendency for the relative amount spent on pewter to decline with rising income has already been noted among the middle classes, but it is among the richest members of society that the tendency for the absolute amount spent on pewter to decline is discernible for the first time. Hence, while the wealthy yeoman and lesser gentleman with sufficient resources for only a limited range of silver tableware had to invest in great quantities of fine pewter, the richer gentry and nobility strove to relegate pewter to the tables of servants.

The cost of supplanting even the most expensive pewterware with silverware was formidable, and although the price of silver did not increase as rapidly as that of pewter in the sixteenth and seventeenth centuries an ounce of silver cost as much as half a dozen pounds of pewter.[3] Thus in the household of Robert, earl of Essex, in 1588 we find twenty-six silver platters valued at almost £210, while thirty-six platters, forty-two dishes, eleven saucers, and seven pie plates of pewter were thought to be worth a mere £3.6s8d.[4] It must, of course, be remembered that expenditure on plate, unlike conspicuous expenditures on buildings,

---

[1] For the cult of ostentatious expenditure followed by the rich see L. Stone, *The Crisis of the Aristocracy 1558–1641* (Oxford, 1965), esp. ch. 10.
[2] Above, p. 61.
[3] From the later sixteenth century to 1700 the price of an ounce of silver plate averaged 5s6d to 6s, whilst that of pewter fluctuated between 8d and 1s6d per pound. For the price of silver plate see Rogers, v, 501–4; for pewter see below Appendix B.
[4] C. L. Kingsford, 'Essex House, formerly Leicester House and Exeter Inn', *Archaeologia*, 2nd ser., xxiii (1923), 44, 46.

clothes, food and wages, was usually a sound investment which could be readily turned into hard cash in times of need.

The household papers of Henry Percy, ninth earl of Northumberland (1564–1632) are most revealing.[1] At the turn of the sixteenth century the running of the Percy household cost in the region of £4,000 to £5,000 per annum. But whereas the sums expended on either linen, mercery, or upholstery frequently exceeded £100, annual expenditure on pewter rarely exceeded £10.[2] The amount of money Percy invested in plate was truly phenomenal: in 1617–18, for example, silver costing no less than £3,368.11s5d was purchased, and between 1617 and 1622 Percy purchased at least twenty dozen silver dishes and twenty-four dozen silver trencher plates, in addition to large quantities of porringers, fruit and sugar dishes, plates of various designs, ewers and basins, candlesticks, salts, and drinking vessels.[3] Small wonder then that on his death in 1632 the ninth earl left, among goods valued at over £8,000 in his houses at Petworth and Syon, plate worth more than £2,500 and pewter worth less than £20.[4] That Percy was, in this respect at least, representative of his class is exemplified by other household accounts and inventories, including those of Robert, earl of Leicester, who on his death in 1588 left plate valued at more than £1,000 and pewter worth less than £10,[5] and Henry Howard, earl of Northampton, who in 1614 left plate worth almost £2,000, jewels and gold worth about £3,000, but only 300 lb of pewter worth a paltry £5.[6] With holdings of plate as vast as these most guests, even at the largest banquets, could expect to dine off silver; indeed there was among Cardinal Wolsey's collection

> a cupboard as long as the chamber was in breadth, with six deskes in height, garnished with guilt plate, and the nether most deske was garnyshed all with gold plate, having with lights one pair of candlesticks with silver and guilt, being

[1] *The Household Papers of Henry Percy, Ninth Earl of Northumberland (1564–1632)*, ed. G. R. Batho (Camden Society, 3rd ser., xciii, 1962).
[2] For example, £9.10s was spent on pewter in 1585–6 (*ibid.*, p. 71), £6.18s6d was spent on pewter in 1598–9 (*ibid.*, p. 37), and £9.10s was spent on pewter in 1604–5 (*ibid.*, p. 54). [3] *Ibid.*, pp. 94, 108–12. [4] *Ibid.*, pp. 112–30.
[5] Kingsford, 'Essex House'. It should be noted that no account has been taken of chamberpots and closestool pans which were frequently made of pewter.
[6] E. P. Shirley, 'An inventory of the effects of Henry Howard K.G., Earl of Northampton, taken in 1614', *Archaeologia*, xlii, pt. 2 (1869), 347–78.

curiously wrought, which cost three hundred marks. This cupboard was barred round about that no man might come nigh it, for there was none of all this plate touched—there was sufficient besides.[1]

As might be expected expenditure by royal households followed a similar pattern, and £40 was considered by the official who in 1526 drew up the ordinances for Henry VIII's household at Eltham, to be an adequate sum to be spent each year on pewter,[2] while the young Princess Elizabeth spent only £14.13s8d on the purchase and repair of pewter out of a total household budget of almost £4,000 during her residence at Hatfield, in 1551–52.[3] The claim made in 1609 on behalf of William Hurdman, the king's pewterer, for 16,000 lb of tin annually on special terms, was undoubtedly designed to provide him with raw material far in excess of that which he normally used on the king's behalf.[4]

Hence, it is likely that some of the finest as well as the most extensive hoards of pewter resided in the homes of the lesser nobility and the gentry. A systematic analysis of the household goods of these groups must await the eventual release of the inventories attached to wills proved before the Prerogative Court of Canterbury, but inventories drawn from other sources are sufficient in number to provide some valuable insights. That the pewter held by the gentry and lesser nobility was notable not only for its quantity but also for its quality and variety is evident from that belonging to Sir John Gage, of West Firle, Sussex, in 1556. Gage's extensive holdings of plate contained only three dishes, two saucers, two plates and a porringer, but his holdings of pewter were immense:

> Item vj dosyn greate platers of the best sorte. Item ij dosyn and vij platers of a lesser sorte. Item ij dosyn olde platers occupied dayly in the kechyn. Item xxiij disshes of the best sorte. Item vj olde disshes occupied daily in the kechyn. Item ij dosyn and vij sawcers of the best sorte. Item ij dosyn saucers of the worst sorte occupied daily. Item xviij potengers

[1] From the account given by Amadel and Cavendish, quoted in Bell, pp. 91–2.
[2] *A Collection of Ordinances and Regulations for the Government of the Royal Household*, p. 196.
[3] 'Household expenses of Princess Elizabeth during her residence at Hatfield, October 1, 1551, to September 30, 1552', *The Camden Miscellany, Volume the Second* (Camden Society, lv, 1853), p. 23–4.
[4] *Calendar of State Papers, Domestic Series* (CSPD) 1603–10, p. 547.

occupied daily. Item ij square disshes to serve butter in. Item viij rounde dishes to serve butter in. Item ij new chargers. Item ij olde chargers. Item iij plates for bottoms for bake meates. Item a collender of pewter. Item iij basons and ewers of pewter. Item iij rounde deepe basons of pewter, for handes. Item iiij shaving basons of pewter. Item vj dosyn trencher plates of pewter. Item ij dosen plates of pewter for frute. Item v flate lowe candlestickes of pewter, with ij noses the pece. Item ij highe candlestickes of pewter. Item iiij chamb'r pottes of pewter. Item iij chamber basons of pewter. Item ij rownde saltes of pewter for the haule. Item iij other saltes of pewter of a worsse sorte, for the laborers.[1]

The careful distinctions made between the best pewter and that reserved for the servants and labourers are most interesting. At Speke Hall, Lancashire, home of Sir William Norris, we find that in 1624 there was a variety of pewter utensils of all shapes and sizes totalling almost 320 pieces:

IN THE STORE HOWSE: Imprimis one dozen of bigg deep dishes. Item one other dozen of a lesser sort. Item one dozen of a third sort, the one halfe lesser than the other. Item an other dozen of a fourth sort, the one halfe lesser than thother. Item on other dozen of a fift sort, the one halfe lesser than thother. Item one other dozen of a sixt sort, the one halfe lesser then thother. Item one dozen and a halfe of sallett dishes. Item six porrengers. Item xij sowcers, thone halfe lesser then thother. Item v other lytle sowcers. Item iiij bigg dishes. Item iij dishes of a lesser sort. Item viij bigg dishes. Item viij of a lesser sort. Item viij or a third sort. Item xxiij plates. Item one dozen plates of a lesser sort. Item one jellye basen. Item 2 great pastye plates. Item 8 lytle pye plates. Item 2 great voydes. Item 4 basens for ewers. Item 4 hand basens. All these do waighe 34 score poundes, and 3 odd poundes, which att 8d. a pound doth come to £22 15s 4d.

MORE IN THE STORE HOWSE.

Item 2 great flagons, 26s 8d; Item 2 cannes London pewter,

---

[1] R. G. Rice, 'The household goods, etc., of Sir John Gage, of West Firle, Co. Sussex, K.G., 1556', *Collections of the Sussex Archaeological Society*, xlv (1902). Gage was Lord Chamberlain of the Queen's household.

16s. Item 2 flagons & 2 cannes Wigan pewter, 24s. Item 2 other lytle cannes, 6s. Item 4 ewers, 8s. Item 4 candlestickes, 6s. Item 6 chamber pottes, 6s. IN THE DEY HOWSE. Item viij pewter dishes, 6s 8d; IN THE BREAD LOFT. Item a pewter salt seller, 1d; Item iij pewter dishes 18d:
PEWTER IN THE KYTCHIN.
Imprimis: ij voydes, vj broad dishes, 5 pye plates, 8 sallett dishes, ix sawcers, iiij porrengers with eares and 4 without eares, one collynder, 3 dishes Wigan pewter of a bigg sort, 3 dishes Wigan pewter of a second sort, ix dishes of a third sort, vij of a 4th sort, 47s 6d.
FOR THE SERVANTES
One broade dish, 5 of a lesser sort, 3 deep dishes. In all 95 pound att 6d a pound.
IN THE BUTTRY
2 basens and ewers, a toning dishe, 4 voyders, 2 hand basens: 54 pound, att 6d a pound 26s. 2 cannes one bigger than the other, 2 lyverye cannes, in all 19 pound, 14s.[1]

Although in 1594 the plate of Sir William Fairfax of Gilling, Yorkshire, included no plates or dishes, his holdings of pewter were smaller than Norris's, and comprised only six dozen dishes, four dozen platters, three dozen saucers, five chargers, and a few lesser items.[2] Fairfax may well have entertained on a more modest scale than the notorious spendthrift Norris, and he certainly appears to have entertained on a far smaller scale than Sir Thomas Ramsey, Lord Mayor of London in 1577, who left on his death in 1590, plate valued at almost £700, including '10 hanse pots', three dozen 'plate trenchers', two dozen 'old plate trenchers', and a 'nest of goblets', and about a ton of pewter.[3] Occasionally too the pewter of the middling gentry competed with that of their social superiors. We learn, for example, that in 1658 Michael Biddulph, an esquire of Lichfield and Elmhurst, Staffordshire, had pewter worth almost £35 in a comparatively modest estate of less than £900; namely at the house in Lichfield

[1] R. J. A. Shelley, 'Some early inventories of pewter in country houses', *Apollo*, (Oct. 1947), 86.
[2] E. Peacock, ed., 'Inventories made for Sir William and Sir Thomas Fairfax, knights, of Walton and of Gilling Castle, Yorks., in the sixteenth and seventeenth centuries', *Archaeologia*, xlviii (1884), 121–56.
[3] F. W. Fairholt, ed., 'On an inventory of the household goods of Sir Thomas Ramsey, Lord Mayor of London, 1577', *Archaeologia*, xl (1866), 311–42.

> 82 round dishes great and small, and 6 long dishes, £16;
> 12 pewter dishes great and small, 7 trencher plates, a pastry
> plate and a pye plate, 3 basons, a bedpan and closetoole
> pan, 2 great flaggons and 2 canns, 1 brasse caffing dish,
> 3 sawcers, 3 porringers, 1 salt, 5 candlestickes, 1 pynt and
> 11 spoones, £3 16s 0d';

and at Elmhurst

> a voyder and a pewter fountaine; 24 pewter dishes, 41
> plates, 18 great sawcers, a pewter cullender, 2 ewres and 4
> candlestickes, £8 17s 0d; 18 pewter dishes, 13 plates and
> sawcers, 2 pie plates and a custard dish of pewter, a
> cullender, 3 porringers, 1 can, a pewter salt, and 1 candle-
> sticke and a pastry plate £3 15s 0d; 1 flaggon, 6 spoones,
> and a stoolepan, 5 chamber pottes and a quart pott, 15s 0d.[1]

In the sixteenth and seventeenth centuries, as in the Middle Ages, institutional demands constituted a substantial part of the total market for pewter. Even the summary demise of the monasteries inflicted merely a glancing blow on the prosperity of the industry, since many compensations were obtainable elsewhere, particularly the rapid growth of educational and legal institutions. Thorold Rogers concluded after an exhaustive search of documents recording the purchases made by a wide range of such institutions that 'hardly a year passes in any considerable establishment in which pewter dishes and vessels do not figure'.[2] Purchases exceeding a hundredweight a year were often made by individual Oxford and Cambridge colleges, and some items, stamped with the appropriate arms, have survived into our own times.[3] This demand showed no signs of abating as the eighteenth century approached, since the rough treatment meted out to tableware rendered pottery an unacceptable substitute; and in the five years from 1692 to 1696 King's College, Cambridge, bought more than two-thirds of a ton of pewter.[4] In like manner pewter

---

[1] *Lichfield Inventories*, pp. 105–12. For further inventories of the households of gentry and lesser nobility see *inter alia*: 'Probate inventory of Sir John Eliot, late prisoner in the Tower (1633)', *Camden Miscellany XVI*, ed. F. J. Fisher (Camden Society, 3rd ser., lii, 1936); O. Ashmore, 'Household inventories of the Lancashire gentry, 1350–1700', *Trans. Historic Society of Lancashire and Cheshire*, cx (1958); E. W. Crossley, 'Two seventeenth-century inventories', *Yorkshire Archaeological Journal*, xxxiv (1939). [2] Rogers, V, 491.
[3] *Ibid.*, iii, 375–84; iv, 459–71; Massé, *Chats on Old Pewter*, pp. 118–19.
[4] Rogers, v, 492.

purchases by Winchester College increased in frequency from the average of four per decade recorded in the fifteenth century to almost eight per decade between 1560 and 1660.[1] The now notorious proliferation of lawyers in the early modern era also contributed indirectly to the demand for pewter, and it is interesting to note that one of the rules of Clifford's Inn specified that each member was to pay 13d per year for pewter and was bound to have two pewter plates and dishes in the kitchen each day for his own use.[2]

City companies also had large stores of pewter which were used for the frequent festive dinners. In 1602, for example, an inventory of the possessions of the Merchant Taylors' Company revealed the following pewter: 'nine great chargers, twelve 5 lb platters, four dozen 4 lb platters, thirty-four 3 lb platters, three dozen 2 lb platters, four dozen sallet dishes, five dozen plate trenchers, three dozen pie-plates, eight dozen and five saucers, and two dozen pottle pots'; eight years later nearly as much again was purchased.[3] In the early eighteenth century the quantities held by the Clothworkers' Company were so substantial that a pewterer was paid an annual salary of 5s 'for Looking after the Pewter and Beating out Bruses'.[4] Some companies, however, preferred to hire their pewter, and the provision of vessels for hire continued to constitute an important source of income for pewterers. Occasionally debts were incurred, and we learn that in 1561 the Pewterers' Company forbade its members to serve the Sadlers with pewter until an outstanding debt owed to William Lowton had been settled.[5] Lord Mayors' feasts continued to require immense quantities of pewter, but a certain measure of scepticism might be permitted when confronting a claim made in 1609 that 'according to ancient usage' these functions employed at least six tons each year.[6]

The religious history of the sixteenth and seventeenth centuries was so tumultuous that it would neither be a simple nor a profitable task to trace the vicissitudes of ecclesiastical pewter in great

[1] Beveridge, pp. 85–90.
[2] Massé, *Chats on Old Pewter*, p. 120.
[3] *Ibid.*, p. 118.
[4] Records of invoices relating to the supply and repair of pewter were kindly supplied by the Clerk of the Worshipful Company of Clothworkers. The pewterer so employed was John Shorey of Catteaton Street, near Guildhall.
[5] Guildhall MS 7090/2, 7 Nov.
[6] This claim was made by Richard Glover, Thomas Smith and Francis Greves (*Historical Manuscripts Commission: Calendar of Salisbury MSS*, xxi, 144).

detail. Nevertheless, a number of salient points can be discerned. The steady decline in the amount and importance of church pewter in the two centuries before the depredations of Edward VI has already been surveyed, yet although it appears most unlikely that the position enjoyed in the later thirteenth and the fourteenth centuries was ever regained, a substantial measure of recovery was effected. The first major step came with Mary's attempts to recreate the old religion, during which there were many indications that churches were replacing confiscated vessels of silver with pewter replicas.[1] A further boost was given in 1603–04, when it was ordained that the sacramental wine should be 'brought to the Communion table in a clean and sweet standing pot or stoup of pewter—if not of purer metal'.[2] Flagons, which were perhaps the most distinctive and dignified of all items of pewter church plate, had been in use at least since 1547 when the laity was readmitted to Holy Communion, but the seventeenth century saw a considerable increase in their number.[3] It was usual for each flagon to have a plate to stand on. Other common articles of ecclesiastical pewter were candlesticks, offertory plates, and lavers or bowls; the latter were used for the celebrants to wash their hands at Communion just before the consecration.[4] The destruction or removal of fonts from many churches in 1643, soon led to their replacement by pewter basins or large pewter ewers.[5] Yet despite the increase in ecclesiastical pewter which undoubtedly took place in the course of the seventeenth century, and despite the fact that early ecclesiastical pewter has survived in far greater quantities than domestic pewter, in terms of total demand its significance was now small. It is probably true that there was less pewter in seventeenth-century churches than there had been in those of the late thirteenth and early fourteenth, and it is undoubtedly true that the vast expansion of demand for domestic pewter had drastically diminished the importance of the ecclesiastical market for English pewterers.

The remaining major source of demand sprang from the use of pewter vessels as measures and drinking vessels, notably in taverns, ale-houses, and hostelries. The provision of these vessels had constituted a sizeable part of pewterers' business from early

---

[1] Michaelis, *Antique Pewter*, pp. 68–9. [2] Massé, *Pewter Plate*, p. 93.
[3] Peal, *British Pewter*, pp. 93–4; Michaelis, *Antique Pewter*, pp. 69–74.
[4] *Ibid.*, pp. 74–6. [5] Massé, *Pewter Collector*, pp. 83–4.

times, and it was not merely the strictness of the control exercised over this branch of the trade that made 'false potels' the subject of the first recorded case brought against a pewterer for substandard wares,[1] or that ensured that the standard weights and sizes of measures were specified at more frequent intervals than those of any other product.[2] Because of the close control they exercised over members, pewterers' gilds were seen by state and civic authorities as allies in the struggle to ensure that all vessels used for the retailing of wine, ale and beer were of full capacity, and pewter was widely viewed as the most acceptable substance for their manufacture. For their part pewterers' gilds sought to make pewter vessels mandatory for all sales of wine and beer, and the London Company frequently petitioned to this effect.[3] Although legal compulsion was only rarely forthcoming, the multiplication of taverns had a decisive effect upon the trade; as early as the later seventeenth century some London pewterers were able to specialise in the manufacture of tavern pots,[4] and by the nineteenth century this branch of the trade was pre-eminent.

Turning from consumption to production our attention must first be devoted to London, which was in all periods the most important centre of the pewter industry. After the effects of the late fifteenth-century depression had been shaken off, the overall record of the London industry until the close of the seventeenth century was one of substantial and at times even prodigious growth. With production, as with consumption, it is possible to amass a considerable body of quantitative evidence to support and exemplify trends discernible in a wide range of qualitative evidence. The sum of the quantitative evidence is to suggest that the London industry achieved a sevenfold expansion between the early sixteenth century and the mid-seventeenth. The incomparable records of the London Pewterers' Company supply the bulk of the data, allowing calculations to be made not only of the total numbers of freemen and pewter workshops, but also of the annual enrolments of new freemen and apprentices, and of the numbers

[1] The prosecution was brought in 1350 (Riley, *Memorials of London*, pp. 259–60).
[2] Welch, *passim*.
[3] We know that petitions were presented in 1633, 1649 and 1696 (Welch, ii, 90, 113, 167).
[4] See, for example, Sir John Fryer's diary (Guildhall MS 12017, f. 21).

of freemen granted licence to set up in business on their own account. The value of the data, which is set out in full in Appendix A (below, p. 270), in common with all similar data extracted from gild records, depends upon the extent to which Company members were practitioners of the craft and practitioners of the craft were Company members. Further discussions of these and related matters are contained in Chapter 4 and Appendix A, and it will suffice here simply to stress that this data can be used with rare confidence since the Pewterers' Company was exceptional in that even by the later seventeenth century over 90 per cent of its freemen were practising pewterers, while in turn the vast bulk of London pewterers were Company freemen. Furthermore systematic crosschecking of the various sorts of information obtainable from Company records reaffirms their value as indices of the size and prosperity of the London industry, and the scale of the growth that they reveal must be sufficient to tempt even the most sceptical of readers to stifle doubts concerning precise accuracy.

The number of independent masters or shopkeepers provides one of the best guides to the size of the industry, and this rose from just over 50 in the first decade of the sixteenth century to almost 350 by the 1640s. The rate at which freemen were setting up in business is also informative, and this rose from an average of under five per annum in the first half of the sixteenth century to over thirteen in the first half of the seventeenth; while a similar calculation of the average enrolment of apprentices reveals an increase of from seventeen to almost forty per annum. The total number of freemen in the Company is more difficult to determine as journeymen were imperfectly recorded on the yeomanry accounts and did not appear at all on the audit accounts, but it appears likely that there were about 200 liverymen, freemen and journeymen in the 1550s, and well over 400 in the later 1630s.

The severity of the late fifteenth century depression should not be underestimated, however, since it induced a period of stagnation and intermittent retrenchment which persisted for more than half a century. As we noted in the previous chapter the depression was caused partly by provincial competition and partly by the drastic curtailment of exports consequent upon the initiation or expansion of production in countries that had previously relied upon imports from England.¹ The long-term decline in exports, from occasional annual peaks of 60 to 80 tons in the 1440s and 1460s to little more than 5 tons at the turn of the century, was clearly a matter of great concern to the London industry, and it is understandable that its representatives should report to Parliament in 1533 that

> a great Number and Quantity of Pewter Vessel, and other Things of Pewter made in divers Sorts and Fashions, amounting to a great Value, which was daily and continually wont to be carried and conveyed out of this Realm by Merchants into strange Regions and Countries, there to be sold and vended, which hath been in great Estimation as Things very necessary and commodious, and the King's Customs thereby much advanced, is now like utterly to cease and decay, and not to be esteemed as heretofore hath been, but also the said Craft of Pewterers, which at this Day setteth and keepeth in Work and Occupation a great Number of People, shall be utterly undone, and a great Multitude of the King's natural Subjects thereby fall into Idleness, to the great Impoverishment of this Realm, if speedy Remedy for the Redress of the Premisses be not provided.'²

The resulting statutory prohibitions on the emigration of pewterers and the employment of aliens proved, however, to be palliatives rather than remedies. Exports, after a brief recovery, declined slowly to reach an annual average of just over 20 tons in the 1540s, when the fine series of Enrolled Customs Accounts came to an end. The extraction of data from surviving Port Books is a tedious and inevitably inexact business, but sampling suggests that the exports of the second and third decades of the sixteenth century were not to be consistently and convincingly exceeded until the closing decades of the seventeenth century.³ In 1563, for example, London's pewter exports appear to have totalled less than 20 tons,⁴ and between 1592 and 1595 to have averaged little more.⁵ The second year of the second decade of the next century produced exports of about 50 tons,⁶ but by 1640

¹ Above p. 70 ff.   ² 25 Henry VIII, c. 9.
³ Some of the export data quoted in the following sentences was provided by Mr P. Atkinson.   ⁴ PRO E.122.90/11.
⁵ PRO SP.12.256/23.   ⁶ PRO E.190/16/2, 16/8.

they seem once more to have been below 20 tons,[1] and even as late as 1673 exports from London of less than 30 tons were recorded.[2] It is possible that the shortage of tin and the activities of the tin farmers occasionally adversely affected exports. In 1646 it was claimed that the farmers, who had at their time a monopoly of pewter exports, forbade the shipping of pewter to countries importing English tin.[3] The sevenfold expansion of the London pewter industry thereby becomes all the more remarkable, since it was a response to the growth of the home market alone.

Naturally the expansion of the industry, both in relative and absolute terms, took place at an uneven pace. Expansion was somewhat slow to get under way in the early sixteenth century, but spurts occurred in the 1520s and 1550s, and at the close of this latter decade the number of master pewterers in the Company stood at 130, and the number of journeymen at almost 100. Small wonder then that the Court of Assistants remarked that because of 'the greate Encrease of the Company . . . the hall is not able to holde them'.[4] Subsequent growth took place on a more modest scale, and between 1570 and 1600 the membership of the Company appears to have remained fairly stable at around 260 persons.

The turn of the sixteenth century brought a series of grave threats to the prosperity of the industry, the most potent being manoeuvrings by groups of speculators to obtain the right from the Crown to purchase the total product of the Devon and Cornish stannaries. Despite vigorous opposition from the Company the pre-emption of tin became a regular occurrence from the start of the seventeenth century.[5] In the event, however, pre-emption did not bring about the ruin of the English pewter industry, and gloomy prognostications, such as that made in 1601 concerning 'the calamyty and the poverty which is more and more lykely to be by meanes of the small trad that the company hath',[6] were soon proved to be unfounded. On the contrary, it is possible that the favourable terms upon which the Company was able to secure supplies of tin, particularly in the early decades of pre-emption, provided a stimulus to further growth, perhaps at the expense of the provincial industries. At all events the first half of the seven-

---

[1] PRO E.190/43/1, 44/2. [2] PRO E.190/59/1.
[3] John Sweeting, *A Declaration of Sundry Grievances concerning Tinne and Pewter* (1645).
[4] Guildhall MS 7090/2, 11 June 1563.
[5] See ch. 5 below. [6] Guildhall MS 7090/3, 16 Mar.

teenth century experienced yet another period of rapid expansion, despite sharply rising tin prices, and the depredations of recurrent plague and Civil War. Each of the indices obtainable from Company records reached a new peak in this period: the number of apprentices enrolled exceeded an average of forty per annum in the 1620s and reached sixty-nine in 1626; the number of freemen setting-up shop for the first time exceeded fifteen per annum in the same decade, although the peak of twenty-three was reached in 1612; and in certain years in the 1640s the number of master pewterers exceeded 400.

It is apparent from county and parish records that the London pewter industry was still located primarily within the City, notably within the wards of Billingsgate and Bishopsgate which were renowned for their metal trades. Cornhill was also of importance, and Newgate had the largest group of pewterers to be found outside City boundaries.[1]

Sadly but inevitably the sources for the history of the provincial pewter industries are much less informative, and only rarely do they permit quantification or the reconstruction of a rough chronology of development. Nevertheless from scattered references in a wide range of sources, notably borough and town records, muster rolls, tax returns, inventories, and London Company search books, a certain amount of material can be amassed, and it is possible to hazard one or two general conclusions. For the seventeenth century, as for the later fifteenth century, the most compendious sources for provincial pewterers are Company search records. Two books giving details of searches conducted between 1635 and 1641 and between 1669 and 1683 take pride of place amongst such records and are a veritable mine of information on a wide range of important subjects.[2] From these books it is possible to glean precise details of the towns that were visited, the shops that were entered, the wares that were analysed, and frequently also the names of the makers. Between 1635 and 1641 two, and sometimes even three, parties of searchers left London each year to conduct widespread examinations of the stock of provincial pewterers. Later in the century it was usual to conduct only one search annually, but it was frequently ambitious in scope and often involved the inspection of more than

[1] J. L. Archer, 'Industrial History of London', Appendix F.
[2] Guildhall MSS 7105, 7105/1; see also MS 7106 for the rough notes of searches conducted between 1689 and 1691.

fifty pewterers' wares. Searches were well organised, and routes were carefully planned to cover most of the important manufacturing centres, as well as those regions where standards of production were known to be low. Because of its value a sample of the information contained in these books has been reproduced in Table 7. Some towns were visited more than once during each period, and the maximum number of pewterers' premises inspected during a single visit have been indicated. Although the data contained in the search books throw more light on the numbers and distribution of provincial pewterers than any other known source, it must be stressed that this light is still only partial. Many towns containing pewterers were not visited, not all pewterers' premises in the towns that were visited were searched, and finally premises which did not contain substandard pewter do not appear to have been systematically noted. Thus the table provides merely the *minimum* numbers of pewterers in the towns that were visited. On the other hand a number of the pewterers noted doubtless also practised other crafts, such as brazier or founder, while some specialised in retailing rather than manufacturing pewter.

Table 7

Towns visited and pewterers recorded by London Company searchers
(The figures refer to the maximum number of pewterers noted on any single visit)

1635–41

Town	No.	Town	No.
Abingdon	2	Cambridge	2
Alresford (Hants)	1	Chard	1
Alton	2	Chippenham	1
Ashbourne (Derbys)	1	Chipping Norton	1
Ashburton	3	Cley (Norfolk)	3
Atherstone (Warwks)	3	Coventry	3
Aylesbury	1	Crewkerne (Som)	1
Barnstaple	4	Cricklade (Wilts)	1
Bath	2	Derby	2
Blandford Forum (Dorset)	2	Devizes	3
Bolsover (Derbys)	1	Dorchester	2
Braintree	1	Duffield (Derbys)	1
Bridgwater	2	Exeter	4
Bristol	12	Faringdon (Berks)	1
Bruton (Som)	2	Gloucester	6
Burton-on-Trent	2	Harringworth (Northants)	1
Calstock (Cornwall)	1	Hereford	1

Table 7 *continued*

1635–41

Honiton	1	Penryn	2
Ipswich	4	Reading	3
Kingsthorpe (Northants)	1	Ross-on-Wye	1
Launceston	1	St. Columb Major	1
Leicester	3	Salisbury	4
Lichfield	1	Shaftesbury	1
Longford (Warwks)	1	Sherborne	2
Looe (Cornwall)	1	Southampton	2
Lostwithiel	1	Stafford	1
Market Harborough	1	Taunton	4
Marlborough	3	Thame	1
Mitcheldean (Glos)	1	Torrington	1
Montacute (Som)	1	Totnes	1
Monkton-Farley (Wilts)	1	Warminster	1
Newbury	1	Warwick	1
Newnham (Glos)	1	Wells	1
Northampton	2	Winchester	3
Oakham	1	Witney	1
Oxford	3	Woodstock	1
Paignton	2	Worcester	4
Plymouth	2	Yetminster	1

Fairs visited

Atherstone (Warwks)	Probey (Wilts)
Banbury (Oxon)	Stourbridge (Cambs)
Bicester (Oxon)	Tan Hill (Wilts)
Chard (Som)	Thame (Oxon)
Exeter (Devon)	Trowbridge (Wilts)
Odiham (Hants)	Woodbury Hill (Wilts)

1669–83

Abingdon	1	Bromsgrove	1
Alresford	1	Bristol	18
Alton	1	Buckingham	1
Andover	1	Burton-on-Trent	1
Atherstone	1	Bury	3
Aylesbury	2	Cambridge	7
Banbury	2	Chester	4
Bantry	1	Chippenham	1
Bath	1	Chipping Norton	1
Bedford	1	Cirencester	2
Birmingham	4	Colchester	3
Biston	1	Coventry	6
Blandford Forum	2	Crewkerne	1
Boston	3	Daventry	1

continued overleaf

Table 7 continued

1669–83

Derby	2	Northampton	3
Devizes	3	Norwich	7
Diss	3	Oswestry	1
Doncaster	2	Oundle	1
Dorchester	1	Oxford	4
Dunstable	1	Peterborough	1
Durham	3	Pontefract	1
Farnham	2	Reading	5
Gainsborough	1	Ringwood	2
Gloucester	4	Romsey	1
Gt. Yarmouth	2	Ross-on-Wye	2
Halesworth (Norfolk)	2	Salisbury	5
Harleston (Norfolk)	1	Sherborne	1
Harrington	2	Shrewsbury	1
Henley (Warwks)	1	St. Albans	1
Hereford	1	St. Ives (Hunts)	2
Hertford	1	Southampton	3
Hungerford	1	Spalding	1
Ipswich	2	Stafford	2
Kendall	2	Stamford	2
Kidderminster	1	Stratford-on-Avon	1
Kineton (Warwks)	1	Tadcaster	2
King's Lynn	3	Tamworth	2
Leicester	3	Taunton	3
Leominster	1	Tewkesbury	2
Lichfield	1	Uxbridge	2
Lincoln	7	Walsall	2
Longford (Warwks)	2	Warminster	1
Ludlow	2	Warwick	3
Market Harborough	1	Watford	1
Marlborough	3	Wellingborough	3
Milborne Port (Som)	1	Wigan	18
Mountsorrel (Leices)	1	Winchester	1
Newbury	4	Windsor	1
Newcastle upon Tyne	8	Wisbech	1
Newmarket	1	Worcester	9
Newport Pagnell	1	Wrexham	1
Northallerton	2	York	16

Fairs visited

Atherstone (Warwks)
Blackburn (Lancs)
Stony Stratford (Bucks)
Stourbridge (Cambs)
Tetbury (Glos)
Winslow (Bucks)

The suggestion contained in Table 7, that provincial pewter manufacture was widespread but predominantly small in scale, is supported by evidence from a number of studies of the occupational structures of towns and regions. From these studies it appears that the metal trades as a whole usually constituted no more than 10 per cent, and frequently less than 5 per cent, of the skilled workforce of medium and larger towns; well below the numbers of workers in either the clothing and textile trades, the leather and allied trades, or the food and drink processing trades.[1] Of those engaged in the metal industries workers in iron were by far the most numerous, with pewterers relatively few in number.

As pewter was a product which consumers needed to purchase only rarely, pewterers tended to practise in market towns which provided a range of specialised goods and services not offered elsewhere in the locality. Thus in Babergh Hundred in southwest Suffolk, which had a population of just over 10,000 in 1522, the solitary recorded pewterer had his premises in the largest town, Sudbury.[2] The relative infrequency with which pewterers resided outside the larger villages is further exemplified by the fact that among 9,000 rural Worcestershire inventories covering the century 1550 to 1650, of which the occupation of the testator is known, only twelve belonged to pewterers,[3] while among more than 17,000 Gloucestershire persons whose occupations were listed in a 1608 muster roll we find only 16 pewterers, compared with 430 smiths, 23 cutlers, and 54 nailers.[4] Furthermore, only a single inventory can be ascribed tentatively to a pewterer from more than 200 late sixteenth-century Oxfordshire inventories which provide occupational data or allow it to be deduced,[5] while not a single pewterer appears amongst the occupations listed in over 100 Devon inventories covering the period 1531 to 1699,[6] or in over 100 mid-Essex inventories covering the period 1635 to 1744.[7]

Even within medium and larger towns, moreover, it was almost certainly rare to find more than ten or a dozen master pewterers.

---

[1] Data from these studies are tabulated in L. A. Clarkson, *The Pre-Industrial Economy in England, 1500–1750* (1971), pp. 88–9.
[2] J. Patten, 'Village and town: an occupational study', *Agricultural History Review*, xx (1972). [3] J. West, *Village Records* (1962), pp. 126–7.
[4] A. J. Tawney and R. H. Tawney, 'An occupational census of the seventeenth century', *Economic History Review*, v (1934–35).
[5] *Household and Farm Inventories in Oxfordshire*, p. 6. [6] Calculated from *Devon Inventories*.
[7] Calculated from *Farm and Cottage Inventories of Mid-Essex*.

As stressed above, the figures in Table 7 are minima, but corroborative evidence is forthcoming from other sources. For example, a 1524 subsidy roll of the city of Northampton, which probably had a total population of 3,000 to 4,000, lists only three pewterers: John Stanley, who was assessed on goods worth 100*s*, William Byshoptree, who was assessed on goods worth 40*s*, and a journeyman William Ashebourne, who was assessed on his wages of 20*s* a year.[1] The Southampton apprenticeship registers, which run from 1609 to 1740 and contain almost 1,100 entries, record only four apprentice pewterers, of which three were apprenticed to Richard Luke.[2] Even at Norwich, probably the largest provincial city in the land in the sixteenth century with a population of over 12,000, only two pewterers were admitted to the freedom from 1500 to 1529, three from 1530 to 1558, six from 1558 to 1580, and three from 1581 to 1603. Furthermore, occupational breakdowns of the city for 1525 and 1569, admittedly less than comprehensive, reveal only three and four master pewterers respectively.[3]

Consequently there were rarely sufficient pewterers to justify a separate gild, and it is usual to find small groups of pewterers amalgamated with other craftsmen amongst the membership of composite gilds. In some instances, as at Chester, Gloucester, Newcastle, Hull, Norwich, Reading, Dorchester, Salisbury, Hereford, and Doncaster, pewterers shared in gilds primarily devoted to the metal trades, while in others the amalgamations of crafts were unexpected. At Shrewsbury, for example, pewterers shared a gild with mercers, apothecaries and physicians, and at Worcester with glovers and pouch-makers, while at Ipswich they were members of a gild called the Tailors' Company, and at St Albans of the Innholders' Company.[4]

It is unlikely that groups of ten or more master pewterers were to be found at any one time in more than a dozen English towns, excluding London. It is impossible to be precise, but it seems probable that pewter industries of this size, or somewhat larger, were located in later seventeenth-century Gloucester, Coventry,

[1] PRO E.179.155/124.
[2] *A Calendar of Southampton Apprenticeship Registers, 1609–1740*, ed. A. J. Willis and A. L. Merson (Southampton, 1968), pp. xxxvii, 29, 35, 41, 42.
[3] J. F. Pound, 'The social and trade structure of Norwich, 1525–75', *Past and Present*, xxxiv (1966).
[4] F. J. Fisher, 'The Influence and Development of the Industrial Gilds in the Larger Provincial Towns under James I and Charles I' (London, 1931), pp. 260–3; S. Kramer, *The English Craft Gilds* (New York, 1927), pp. 77–9.

Cambridge, Worcester, Newcastle, Lincoln and Norwich; the York and Bristol pewter industries were, of course, consistently much greater. There is scarcely any direct information of the Walsall pewter industry, but solely from the wares inspected by London searchers in shops in western England in 1640 it is possible to compile a list of thirteen Walsall pewterers.[1] The Walsall industry appears to have blossomed for a short time, however, and by the second half of the seventeenth century it had been eclipsed by that of Wigan.

In the late Middle Ages York's pewter industry had been second only to that of London, and it seems to have held this status well into the early modern era. As time wore on admissions to the freedom of the city become an even less reliable guide to the strength of an industry, but they do so by erring further on the side of understatement, and the admission of over eighty pewterers in the sixteenth century, compared with seventy-three in the fifteenth, reflects a modest rate of growth.[2] Nevertheless, it is clear that the York industry did not share fully in the rapid expansion of pewter production which took place under the Tudors and the Stuarts. At the close of the seventeenth century, if one may judge from the signatures appended to decisions reached by the York pewterers' gild, there were about thirty master pewterers in the city,[3] and while this was a substantial number there can be no doubt that York had been overtaken by Wigan, which in a relatively short space of time had risen from comparative obscurity to become the leading pewter manufacturing centre of the north.

The search conducted in Wigan in 1676 was a particularly unsatisfactory guide to the number of pewterers in the town, owing to the warnings which had been received of the approach of the Londoners,[4] but searches amongst Wigan borough records are more revealing and a list of no less than 200 seventeenth-century Wigan pewterers has been compiled.[5] More valuable still is the petition drawn up in 1683 which argued the case for the incorporation of Wigan pewterers by royal charter, a privilege hitherto enjoyed solely by the London Company. The petition does not appear to have been submitted, but its contents, even

---

[1] Guildhall MS 7105/1.   [2] *Register of the Freemen of York.*
[3] Univ. of York Library MS E.54.   [4] Guildhall MS 7105.
[5] R. J. A. Shelley, 'Wigan and Liverpool Pewterers', *Transactions of the Lancashire and Cheshire Historic Society*, xcvii (1946), pp. 21–6.

allowing for considerable overstatement, give a unique insight into the extraordinary scale of the town's pewter industry. The petition starts, for example, with the bland statement 'Wigan consisting chiefly of Pewterers', and goes on to ask for 'a Charter to incorporate them into a body, with power to make by-laws, as the London Pewterers have for regulateing their trade and preventing those abuses, and power to search and try mettle, and punish abuses therein, on the North side of the Trent'. In addition, the Wigan pewterers planned to ask for a supply of tin upon special terms and, as the London industry was thought to consume 200 tons of new tin annually, 40 to 50 tons were claimed for Wigan. Remarkable as these claims may seem to be, they are given credence by the list of 'Aldermen, Balife Peers, Burgesses and Freemen that are Pewterers of Wigan', numbering seventy-five in all, which is appended to the petition. Furthermore among the seventy-five pewterers there were four borough aldermen, twelve ex-bailiffs, and fourteen burgesses, and in the course of the 1680s pewterers held the office of mayor no less than four times.[1] Wigan had thus clearly ousted York as the second most important pewter manufacturing centre in Britain, and was operating on a scale which had hitherto been unprecedented outside London. It is therefore not surprising that Wigan pewter was to be found in substantial quantities throughout northern and western England, including the city of York.[2]

Despite regular imports from England and overseas, pewter manufacture was well established in Scotland by the later sixteenth century.[3] As in England the industry was urban-centred and, outside Edinburgh, invariably small in scale. There were no gilds devoted exclusively to pewterers; instead pewterers were amalgamated with other metalworkers in incorporations of hammermen. The earliest mention of Scottish pewterers occurred in 1496, when they were included amongst the membership of the Edinburgh Hammermen, and fifty years later pewterers formed part of the Hammermen of the adjacent borough of Canongate. Edinburgh remained the largest centre of the industry and in the seventeenth century almost eighty pewterers were admitted to the freedom. Pewterers are also mentioned for the

[1] *Ibid.*, pp. 10–13.   [2] Guildhall MS 7105.
[3] For pewter imports into Scotland see below p. 267. The rest of this paragraph is based on Wood, *Scottish Pewter-Ware and Pewterers*.

first time amongst the Hammermen of Perth in 1546, Dundee in 1587, Aberdeen in 1581, St Andrews in 1619, and Glasgow in 1648. Imperfect documentation remains a serious obstacle, but we can discover that in the course of the seventeenth century only twelve pewterers were admitted to the freedom of Perth and only thirteen to the freedom of Dundee, and that between 1599 and 1620 only four pewterers can be identified at Stirling, and between 1581 and 1765 only eleven at Aberdeen. The poverty of the populace and the lack of indigenous supplies of tin clearly served to limit the growth of the industry.

A similar picture emerges from Ireland. We learn of pewterers in Dublin, Cork and Youghal, and later in Galway, Kinsale and Clonmel, but they always appear to have comprised a relatively minor element in gilds devoted to a wide range of metalworkers.[1] Demand for pewter in Ireland appears to have been less buoyant than in England, to have stemmed in the main from English settlers, and to have been satisfied in part by English imports.[2]

Given the data that has been amassed on the demand for pewter and the numbers and distribution of provincial pewterers, it would be a pity not to attempt quantification on a national scale, even though such an exercise is likely to amount to little more than the drawing of tentative conclusions from uncertain premises. To begin with the number of master pewterers in later seventeenth-century England. The Company search records for 1635 to 1641 and 1669 to 1683 provide us with details of well over 300 pewterers in just under 150 towns. As stated earlier, the searchers did not visit all towns with pewterers, and did not inspect the wares of all pewterers in the towns they visited. There are some obvious omissions: no searches were conducted in Kent, Sussex or Surrey, a number of important towns known to have possessed pewter industries, such as Nottingham, Hull and Liverpool, were not visited,[3] and searches conducted in such towns as York, Wigan, Walsall and Bristol clearly involved only a fraction of the resident pewterers. Using other sources we can assume that there were at least 400 master pewterers in London,

[1] Massé, *Chats on Old Pewter*, p. 76; Michaelis, *Antique Pewter*, p. 7.
[2] Below, p. 267.
[3] For Nottingham, which had two pewterers in 1629, see E. Lipson, *The Economic History of England* (1949–56), iii, p. 346–7; for Liverpool see Massé, *Pewter Collector*, p. 106 ff.; Shelley, 'Wigan and Liverpool Pewterers', pp. 16–17; The Hull pewterers have already mentioned as part of a gild of metalworkers.

60 in Wigan, 30 in York, and 30 in Bristol. Using the search records we can assume that perhaps a further 130 master pewterers were at work in a dozen or so additional major centres including Gloucester, Coventry, Cambridge, Worcester, Newcastle, Lincoln, Norwich and Walsall, and perhaps a further 200 pewterers in forty or so lesser centres including Ashburton, Barnstaple, Exeter, Salisbury, Devizes, Marlborough, Taunton, Winchester, Southampton, Newbury, Reading, Oxford, Leicester, Birmingham, Warwick, Wellingborough, Northampton, Chester, Ludlow, Hull, Durham, Boston, Diss, Bury St Edmunds, King's Lynn, Ipswich, Colchester, and probably also a number of northern centres such as Carlisle, Lancaster, Leeds and Wakefield. This gives a total of about 850 master pewterers in the larger towns. We are now faced with the difficult task of estimating the number of master pewterers who worked in the remaining 700 or so market towns scattered throughout the country.[1] Surviving search records cover less than a quarter of the seventeenth century, and it can safely be assumed that many more towns were visited in other years. Villages like Newnham, Monkton-Farley, Harleston, and Harringworth were probably searched simply because they were situated on or adjacent to routes to larger centres, and many other small towns with one or two pewterers were doubtless neglected because they were less conveniently sited. We can learn from other sources that pewterers worked at some time in the seventeenth century in many towns for which we have no search records, including Rotherham, Petersfield, Canterbury, Tiverton, Evesham, Tavistock, Lewes, and Aulton Priors; and we can be certain that many more remain to be discovered.[2] The brief search of Cornwall in June 1637 involved the inspection of only five pewterers in five towns, but a recent study of Cornish pewterers has revealed a minimum of fourteen towns with pewterers in the seventeenth century.[3] It cannot be assumed, however, that once a pewterer was established in a town the trade continued to be represented in later years. All in all it appears unlikely that less than 400 master pewterers resided in the small market towns and country districts, in which case there

[1] It is generally agreed that there were 700–800 market towns in sixteenth- and seventeenth-century England (*Agrarian History of England*, iv, 467).
[2] See the lists of pewterers in H. H. Cotterell, *Old Pewter, its Makers and Marks* (1929), pp. 145–344 and Massé, *Pewter Collector*, pp. 106–79.
[3] H. L. Douch, 'Cornish potters and pewterers', *Journal of the Royal Institution of Cornwall*, new ser., vi (1969).

may well have been approximately 1,250 master pewterers at work in later seventeenth-century England with a total workforce of perhaps 2,500 to 3,500.[1] To put this total in perspective we should note that it has been estimated that there were possibly 150,000 people engaged in the manufacture of leather and leather goods in England in the early eighteenth century.[2] It should also be noted that not all pewterers worked exclusively in pewter—in the smaller towns it is likely that many also acted as braziers and founders; some too doubtless concentrated more upon retailing than upon manufacturing.

Estimating the total stock of pewter in late seventeenth-century England is perhaps an even more hazardous undertaking, yet the area of uncertainty can be reduced by using the extensive information contained in inventories and Gregory King's remarkably reliable analysis of the structure of England's population in 1688.[3] The results of a highly speculative collation of data from these two sources is contained in Table 8.

Table 8

Estimate of holdings of pewter in late seventeenth-century England

Income per annum	Number of families (approx)	Estimated average holding (lb)	Total (tons)
Over £500 [a]	1,600	500–750	c. 500
£200–500 [b]	22,000	350–550	3,500–5,500
£100–200 [c]	23,000	200–350	2,000–3,500
£50–100 [d]	194,000	100–150	8,500–13,000
£20–50 [e]	260,000	30–50	3,500–6,000
under £20 [f]	850,000	—	c. 500
TOTAL			18–29,000

[a] Includes temporal and spiritual lords, baronets and knights.
[b] Includes esquires, gentlemen, eminent international merchants, and great office-holders.
[c] Includes lesser international merchants, lesser office-holders, and lawyers.
[d] Includes freeholders of the better and lesser sort, naval and military officers, clergymen, and persons in liberal arts and sciences.
[e] Includes farmers, shopkeepers and tradesmen, and artisans and craftsmen.
[f] Ranges downwards from labouring people and outservants to vagrants and beggars.

[1] Assuming an average workforce of three in the larger towns, two in the lesser towns, and 1·5 in the small towns. [2] Clarkson, p. 82.
[3] For holdings of pewter derived from inventories see above; for Gregory King's analysis of families by income see P. Laslett, *The World We Have Lost* (1965), pp. 32–3.

If a further 4,000 to 6,000 tons is allowed for pewter held by the Church, colleges, gilds, corporations, hostelries and so on, we arrive at a total of 22,000 to 35,000 tons. Even this figure may well be a substantial understatement and the total stock of pewter in the nation may have been much higher.[1]

Turning from estimates of the total number of pewterers and the total stock of pewter in later seventeenth-century England to the development of the pewter industry in the century and a half after 1500, one is drawn to conclude that there are strong grounds for doubting that the sevenfold expansion of London pewterers was matched in the provinces. There are many reasons why the rate of growth of the London pewter industry should have been exceptionally rapid, one of the most important being the exceptional rate of growth of the capital's population. Most experts seem to be agreed that whereas the population of the country as a whole probably doubled between 1500 and 1700, the population of London increased six or sevenfold between the early decades of the sixteenth century and the middle of the seventeenth, at which date it stood at approximately 400,000—some 7 per cent of the national total.[2] Furthermore, it was not merely the simple growth of numbers which stimulated industrial activity, but the fact that average consumption per head of most goods and services was far higher in the capital than in the provinces. London at this time has aptly been described as a centre of conspicuous consumption: purchasing power was generated not only by wealthy residents, courtiers, merchants, lawyers, manufacturers and such like, but also by seasonal visits from peers, baronets, knights, gentlemen, squires, and even yeomen and provincial businessmen, who spent in London the incomes they had accumulated elsewhere.[3] By the seventeenth century a house in London had become one of the indispensable trappings of high social status, and a distinct season had evolved which ran from autumn

[1] Evidence of the widespread use of pewter in Pembrokeshire and northern England suggests that the *per capita* consumption in the country as a whole may not have been substantially below that revealed in the areas analysed in Tables 5 and 6. (F. Green, 'Pembrokeshire in by-gone days', *West Wales Historical Records*, ix, 1920–3; *Wills and Inventories . . . of the Northern Counties*).
[2] For recent discussions see E. A. Wrigley, 'A simple model of London's importance in changing English society and economy 1650–1750', *Past and Present*, xxxvii (1967), 44–5; *Agrarian History of England*, iv, 514–15.
[3] F. J. Fisher, 'The development of London as a centre of conspicuous consumption in the sixteenth and seventeenth centuries', *Trans. Royal Historical Society*, 4th ser., xxx (1948); Stone, ch. 10.

to late spring. There can be no doubt that sales of pewter benefited immensely from such an environment. If some of the richest residents and visitors spurned pewter tableware, then some of the London labouring class, encouraged by wages far above the national average, may well have been able to spurn treen and rough pottery.

The downward trend of tin production between 1550 and 1650 is another reason why the rate of growth of the London pewter industry was probably exceptional. Tin production between 1500 and 1700 traced a U-shaped cycle: after reaching new peaks of 800 to 900 tons in the early sixteenth century it fell rapidly to a level of 450 to 550 tons, where it remained until the Civil War precipitated a further, and this time truly disastrous, slump.[1] When account is also taken of the catastrophic effects of the Thirty Years War on Bohemian and Saxon tin production, there can be no doubt that Europe experienced a severe shortage of tin.[2] Price increases were therefore inevitable and, exacerbated by the effects of the monopoly exercised over the output of the stannaries, they took place on a grand scale. As can be seen in Appendix B (p. 275), the price of pewter leapt sharply upwards in the first half of the seventeenth century to reach a peak in the 1650s which was more than four times higher than that of the 1450s, compared with little more than a threefold rise in the price of industrial products generally. In money terms this was a rise from 3d per pound in the first half of the fifteenth century, to 8d in the second half of the sixteenth, and 1s2d by 1650. Such a trend must have exercised some restraint upon the expansion of demand for pewter, but once again the London industry suffered less than those of the provinces. Furthermore, members of the London Company benefited from substantial supplies of tin at reduced prices from the monopolists, and the assurance of additional supplies at market rates.[3]

It would be misleading, however, to imply that the fortunes of the pewter industry rested solely on the supply of new tin. On the contrary, one can be certain that by the seventeenth century the greater part of the raw materials used by the industry came from scrap pewter, which the pewterer either bought or accepted

[1] Lewis, pp. 254–6; Hatcher, pp. 159–63.
[2] According to B. Neumann's estimates Bohemian and Saxon tin production collapsed in the early seventeenth century and did not recover until the eighteenth: *Die Metalle* (Halle a.s., 1904), pp. 249–50.   [3] See ch. 5.

in part exchange for new wares. It is the durability of pewter which reconciles the vast stocks to the relatively small numbers of pewterers. But even allowing for a twenty- or thirty-year lifecycle for the average piece of pewter, many hundreds of tons of scrap pewter must have come into the hands of pewterers for reworking each year. We must not forget that the demand for the services of the pewterer also extended to the repair and furbishing of old and damaged pewter.

Nevertheless, although the link between the supply of new tin and the prosperity of the industry became much less direct than might appear at first glance, it was of considerable importance in the long run. It is possible to make some approximate calculations of the amount of tin devoted to the home market simply by subtracting exports from output—indeed a number of such calculations were made by contemporaries at the turn of the sixteenth century. Broadly, it appears that 200 to 250 tons of tin were devoted to home consumption in the first half of the sixteenth century,[1] and that by the turn of the sixteenth century falling production had reduced this to about 150 tons.[2] Although the pewter industry was by far the largest consumer, allowance must also be made for alternative uses of tin, including bronze-, brass-, and bell-founding, window glazing, soldering, dyeing, printing, the manufacture of organ pipes, and the glazing of pottery.[3]

The spectacular expansion of the pewter industry in the course of the sixteenth and seventeenth centuries was accomplished not only in the face of difficulties caused by the shortage and high price of tin, but also in the face of growing competition from pottery, tinplate and glass. Earthenware had been a prevalent form of tableware from time immemorial, but since the rise of pewter its usage had been largely confined to the homes of the poorer sections of society. The primary reason why earthenware remained unattractive to the middle and upper classes was the failure of European technology to develop pleasing, hard-wearing, impermeable wares. In the course of the seventeenth century significant advances were made in various manufacturing processes, notably in the production of slipware and delftware, but porcelain, the only pottery fine enough to pose a serious threat to

[1] Hatcher, pp. 119–20, 200.
[2] PRO SP.12.256/23; *HMC Salisbury MSS*, v, 136; *Journals of the House of Commons*, i, 619–20.   [3] Hatcher, ch. 2.

Plate 13 An array of English flagons *c.* 1610–1730.

Plate 14 A massive broad rimmed charger, engraved with a coat of arms, a later owner's initials, and the date 1676. Diameter 28 in. Made by James Taudin. A pair of broad-rimmed dishes, diameters 16½ in. Made by Ralph Marsh, Jr., London, *c.* 1660–75.

Plate 15 A group of Stuart flat-topped tankards and a flagon, *c.* 1685–95.

Plate 16 The earliest touch-plate of the Worshipful Company of Pewterers, with pewterers' marks dating to c. 1680.

Plate 17 A broad-rimmed dish engraved with conventional 'wriggled work' decorations. Diameter 16¾ in. Possibly made by Charles Sweeting, London *c.* 1660–5.

Plate 18 A 'wriggled-work' plate. Diameter 8½ in. Made by James Hitchman, London, *c.* 1720–30.

pewter, had to be imported from China and Japan and was consequently difficult to obtain and extremely expensive. Indeed it may well have been the consumption of silver rather than pewter that suffered from porcelain imports, since the high cost and fragility of porcelain restricted its appeal to the wealthy and its usage to decorative rather than functional items. One of the earliest mentions of porcelain tableware occurs in the diaries of John Evelyn, in which he entered for 19 February 1652: 'Invited by my Lady Gerrard, I went to Lond., where we had a greate supper, and all the Vessels, which were innumerable, of Porcelan, which was very extraordinarie, she having the most ample and richest collection of that curiositie in England.'[1] Despite the expansion of the trading activities of the English and Dutch East India Companies porcelain tableware was to remain little more than a 'curiositie' until the eighteenth century.

The finest home-produced pottery at this time was delftware which, as the name suggests, was of Dutch origin. It was a heavy form of earthenware with a fine glaze and brilliant colouring, but the ease with which it could be chipped or scratched and the weakness of the heavy coarse body were major disadvantages. The major centres of production were in London and Bristol.[2] Slipware, which was coarser and softer still, was widely manufactured in seventeenth-century England and traded almost exclusively on a local basis.[3] The name derives from the fact that the surface was decorated by the application of different coloured slips, in much the same way as cakes are decorated with icing. The finest pieces were attractive and displayed a high standard of craftmanship, but they required much labour to produce and, as with delftware, the softness of the glaze and the weakness of the body were severe handicaps which rendered slipware unsuitable for eating utensils.

The disadvantages of earthenware were much less pronounced when it was fashioned into ornaments and drinking vessels, and in the seventeenth century increasing numbers of such articles were produced, encouraged by the rising consumption in

[1] *The Diary of John Evelyn*, ed. E. S. de Beer, 6 vols (Oxford, 1955), iii, 60.
[2] F. H. Garner, *English Delftware* (1948).
[3] R. G. Haggar, *English Country Pottery* (1950). See also L. Weatherill, *The Pottery Trade and North Staffordshire, 1660-1760* (Manchester, 1971), p. 78, for a map showing the areas where slipware, delftware, and coarse pottery were made in the seventeenth century.

fashionable society of warm beverages, such as tea, coffee and chocolate.[1] That pewter never achieved as strong a hold over drinking vessels as it did over those for eating is evident from inventories, household accounts, contemporary comments and paintings. Cups, goblets, and drinking bowls of earthenware and wood were as common in the homes of all social groups in the seventeenth century as they had been in the sixteenth,[2] while those members of the richer strata who could not afford silver plates and dishes invariably possessed some silver drinking vessels. That glasses were popular by the later sixteenth century is evident from Harrison's testimony, as is the lack of pewter drinking vessels:

> As for drink, it is usually filled in pots, goblets, jugs, bowls of silver in noblemen's houses, also in fine Venice glasses of all forms, and for want of these elsewhere, in pots of earth of sundry colours and moulds, where of many are garnished with silver, or at the leastwise in pewter; ... It is a world to see in these our days, wherein gold and silver most aboundeth, how that our gentility, as loathing those metals (because of the plenty), do now generally choose rather the Venice glasses, both for our wine and beer, than any of those metals or stone wherein beforetime we have been accustomed to drink.[3]

A further substantial advance in the popularity of glass followed the migration of Dutch craftsmen to England in the later sixteenth century, and the striking twofold achievement of markedly improved quality at steady or even declining prices.[4] By 1645 even the London Pewterers' Company had succumbed, for the account of this year reveals the purchase of '6 Beere glasses for 2s. 3d.'[5] But even at these prices glass was unsuitable for the rough treatment meted out to vessels in taverns and hostelries, where the most serious competition for pewter came from earthenware mugs. It is strange to learn that in 1696 the Pewterers' Company felt it worthwhile to promise financial support to the extent of £55 for a 'Bill to be preferred this present Session of Parliament

---

[1] It is interesting to note that the Pewterers' Company frequently held committee meetings in London coffee houses (B. Lillywhite, *London Coffee Houses* (1963), no. 388, 670, 1742).
[2] Above, pp. 50, 52.   [3] Harrison, *Description of England*, pp. 127–8.
[4] D. W. Crossley, 'The performance of the glass industry in sixteenth-century England', *Economic History Review*, 2nd ser., xxv (1972).
[5] Guildhall MS 7086/3, 1644–5.

for suppressing the use of Silver Tankards in uttering Beer or ale', for such usage could scarcely have been widespread.[1]

Once again we can turn to inventories for more precise details of household consumption patterns, and in particular the demand for fine pottery and glass utensils. Looking at the probate inventories of the broad middle strata of wealth and status, we find scant evidence of either substance in the sixteenth century, and of only a slow progress in the first half of the seventeenth. Coarse earthenware, for use in the dairy or by servants, is not difficult to find, but fine pottery is encountered in only a small proportion of the inventories of wealthy households, and even then usually in tiny amounts and in the form of ewers and basins, with perhaps a dish or a candlestick or two. Thus in 1617 the inventory of a rich Exeter widow, Jane Sture, mentions '3 basons and ewers whereof one of neld a nother of Carricke and the other of outlandishe Clome' worth 30s. among goods valued at almost £140; while that of Edward Gould a Staverton merchant, mentions, 'A bason and Ewer of Cheyney with some small dishes' worth 10s in an estate valued in 1628 at more than £1,700.[2] By the latter part of the century such references became somewhat more frequent, but the overall pattern changed little, and even in Lichfield fine earthenware or pottery was a rarity.[3] In scarcely a single inventory that has been examined is there clear evidence that pottery tableware was being preferred to that of pewter.

Tinplate consists of thin sheets of iron coated with a layer of tin, which can be beaten to form a wide range of utensils. The practice of coating metal items with a thin layer of tin for decoration or to prevent rusting or verdigris stretches far back into the mists of time, and the tinning of iron was widely practised in the Middle Ages. The production of good quality sheet tinplate, however, involves a number of complex processes and, despite numerous attempts by seventeenth-century British, Swedish, and French entrepreneurs, manufacture was limited almost exclusively to Germany before the eighteenth century.[4] Although tinplate was being produced in significant quantities in sixteenth-century

[1] Guildhall MS 7090/8, 9 Jan.
[2] *Devon Inventories*, pp. 25–6, 38–40; 'neld' = annealed, 'Carricke' = a type of imported pottery, 'outlandishe Clome' = imported pottery, 'Cheyney' = China.
[3] *Lichfield Inventories, passim.*
[4] W. Minchinton, *The British Tinplate Industry* (Oxford, 1957), pp. 2–13; F. W. Gibbs, 'The rise of the tinplate industry', *Annals of Science*, vi (1950), 390–403; vii (1951), 25–61, 113–27.

Bohemia, there was considerable resistance on the part of both German and English consumers, and for a time utensils and household vessels made of tinplate, called tinware, were regarded as an imposture on the part of tradesmen. This prejudice was gradually eroded, however, and by the close of the sixteenth century English craftsmen were producing small quantities of kitchenware, candlesticks, and lanterns, from imported tinplates.

There is considerable evidence of the growth of the production of tinware in seventeenth-century London: the 'wyreworkers alias plateworkers' of Elizabethan times had become the 'tinplate workers alias wireworkers' by the reign of Charles II, and a subsidy of 1641 reveals that a considerable body of tinplate workers had gathered in the vicinity of Crooked Lane, just above the old London Bridge. By the fourth decade of the century pewterers first began to voice fears of the effects of tinware on pewter sales, and in 1635 it was agreed by the court of the London Company that measures should be taken for 'suppressing of the excesse and abusive making of Crooked Lane ware, whereby the so doing and counterfeiting of the recall commodity of Tynn is to the greate deceipt or wrong of his Majesties subjects'.[1] In subsequent years the Pewterers' Company devoted much time and money to the aim of achieving the overthrow of tinplate manufacture. In 1637 after a petition by the poor workmen of the Company 'against the frequent making of severall sorts of ware by the Crooked lane men of forraigne plater counterfaiting the wares formerly made by Pewterers of London of Pewter' £50 was devoted to its suppression; in 1639 one of the four articles put forward by the Company 'to be propounded to his Majestie' asked that 'noe Candlesticks, Pye Plates, Pie Coffines, Chamber potts, Pastie platts, potts, or other dishes be made of white Plate which doth hinder the consumption of Tynn'; and seven years later a further petition claimed in more specific terms that 'the dearnesse of that commodity [tin] has forced the poorer sort of people to buy White Metal, a deceitful outlandish commodity'.[2] Such efforts were in vain, however, and despite objections by the Girdlers and the Pewterers a charter of incorporation was granted to the tinplate workers in 1670.[3] It is also interesting to note that

---

[1] Guildhall MS 7090/4, 19 Mar.
[2] *Ibid.*, 23 Feb. 1637; 3 Oct. 1639; Sweeting, *A Declaration of Sundry Grievances*.
[3] Gibbs, *Annals of Science*, vi, 398.

in the closing decades of the century small quantities of tinware fashioned in England were exported; in 1673, for example, we find shipments leaving London for Cuba, New England, Jamaica, and Scotland.[1]

Although tinware makes an appearance in inventories from the later sixteenth century onwards its dissemination was a slow process, and it is only in the second half of the following century that it can be assumed to have obtained a modest level of popularity. The accuracy of the list of tinplate utensils compiled by the Pewterers' Company in 1639 is confirmed by inventories, where the emphasis was firmly on kitchenware rather than tableware; the tinning of iron kitchen utensils to prevent rust, discoloration, and the imparting of unpleasant flavours, was a great convenience. Consequently we find many 'tinning' dripping pans, pudding pans, pasty pans, and even a 'tinn Apple Roster', but very few tinplate saucers, dishes or platters. Notwithstanding, in the house of James Holmead, a Devon yeomen who died in 1678, we find 'Nine Teening dishes and two saucers' valued at 4s3d, and '9 Puter dishes' valued at £1.11s9½d, which shows clearly the cheapness of tinware.[2] Pewter candlesticks had always faced competition from other metals and alloys, and candlesticks made from tinplate, wire, and brass are frequently encountered in seventeenth-century inventories. The greatly improved quality of English brass was a further source of competition for pewterers.

The London Company records of 1651–53 contain a number of fascinating, but frustratingly brief, references to an alloy called 'Silvorum' which a Major Purling, with the assistance of at least one pewterer, was fashioning into 'dishes plate trenchers and sundry other sorts of wares'.[3] Unfortunately for our purposes the Company was able to put Purling swiftly out of business. The emphasis on tableware suggests that Silvorum was not ordinary tinplate. It is tempting to speculate that it was a fine quality tinplate with a silverlike lustre imparted by the addition of copper to the coating of tin, a trade secret previously confined to Germany, but in honesty its composition must remain a mystery.

By the close of the seventeenth century, therefore, few inroads had been made into the market traditionally served by pewter. Moreover there is considerable evidence that not only was the

[1] PRO E.190. 59/1. [2] *Devon Inventories*, p. 144.
[3] Welch, ii, 116, 117.

pewter industry able to withstand the challenge from pottery and tinware, but also that after the 1650s helped by a series of favourable developments, it experienced a further period of expansion, albeit on a modest scale. Perhaps the most favourable development of all was the sharp fall in the price of pewter. It has already been indicated that the growth in the demand for pewter may well have been restrained by the steep rise in price which occurred in the first half of the seventeenth century, between the 1640s and 1660s, however, the rising trend was arrested, by the 1670s it had been decisively reversed, and by the 1690s a fall in the price of pewter of almost 30 per cent had been registered.[1] This fall in price was linked directly to a parallel fall in the price of tin, which in turn owed much to sharply increased output. English tin production in the 1660s leapt to more than 700 tons per annum, and by the later 1670s had reached over 1,200 tons, a record level which was maintained until the close of the century.[2] Furthermore, a major revival was also taking place in the mines of Bohemia and Saxony, and substantially increased supplies of tin were being obtained by the Dutch from Malaya.[3]

Favourable developments exogenous to our industry were also taking place in the later seventeenth century, which stimulated the demand for pewter along with that for a multitude of other products. Real incomes and the aggregate level of home demand appear to have risen in response to the slowing down of the rate of population growth, gently falling grain prices, and rising productivity.[4] While the level of home demand can only be guessed, that for English products overseas is amenable to measurement, and trade statistics suggest that the annual value of England's exports probably increased by rather more than half between 1663 and 1701.[5] This excellent performance was largely due to the expansion of trade with the extra-European world, a process which augured well for the pewter industry. The stagnation which had enveloped pewter exports since the later fifteenth century was primarily due to the initiation or expansion

[1] See Appendix B.   [2] Lewis, pp. 255–6.
[3] Neumann, pp. 249–50; Lewis, p. 53 n.
[4] See, for example, A. H. John, 'Aspects of English economic growth in the first half of the eighteenth century', *Economica* (1961). Despite the title the author maintains that '1670 or 1680 might be a far more appropriate starting point' for the rising trend.
[5] R. Davis, 'English foreign trade, 1660–1700', *Economic History Review*, 2nd ser., iv (1952).

of pewter production in many European countries and, despite contemporary claims to the contrary, the bulk of English pewter was despatched to a small group of countries with little or no industries of their own, such as Spain, Russia and Scandinavia. The development of trade with America, the British West Indies, West Africa and the East Indies opened up much needed new markets to English exporters, and what is more they were markets with an enormous potential for growth. Lacking industries of their own these countries provided thousands of eager and, in the case of the Americas, captive consumers for British manufactures, and it was their purchases that were largely responsible for the doubling of the exports of metalwares of all kinds from London between 1663–69 and 1699–1701.[1] Exports of pewter appear to have achieved an even faster rate of growth, and from what was probably an annual average of less than 50 tons over much of the sixteenth and seventeenth centuries, they quintupled to a record average of more than 250 tons between 1697 and 1700, the first four years of the Customs Ledgers.[2]

It would be misleading, however, to imply that the buoyancy of the English pewter industry in the closing decades of the seventeenth century was wholly due to favourable price and export trends outside the control of pewterers. On the contrary, far from being merely the passive beneficiary of the bounty of improved trading conditions, it is clear that the industry reacted both energetically and imaginatively to exploit the opportunities that had presented themselves and to stave off the growing threat of competitive products. Connoisseurs are agreed that the later seventeenth century and the opening decades of the eighteenth comprise the finest period of English pewter in terms of both design and workmanship.[3] It was the period when an enormous amount of the most attractive pewter was made and when pewterers strove to drum up business by many rapid changes in style and by displaying a much greater freedom of design than hitherto. Although English pewterware is generally notable for the absence of the purely ornamental decoration so common to continental pewterware, in this period innumerable pieces were produced with engraved 'wriggled-work' designs, and punched

[1] *Ibid.*
[2] E. B. Schumpeter, *English Overseas Trade Statistics, 1697–1808* (Oxford, 1960), p. 23.
[3] See, in particular, Peal, *British Pewter*, p. 97 ff.

and cast ornamentation also became fashionable.[1] As the pewter market in the seventeenth century, unlike that of earlier times, was composed primarily of replacement demand rather than of original demand from that part of the population which had not previously possessed it, the 'velocity of circulation' of the country's stock of pewter was of fundamental importance to the level of activity in the industry. The strict control which pewterers' gilds, and the London Company in particular, exercised over the size, design, composition, and range of articles fashioned of pewter, essential though it was to the maintenance of high standards of production and the elimination of fraud, had hitherto almost certainly restricted the turnover of old pewter.[2] But in the later seventeenth century pewterers, liberated by the waning of gild authority, used frequent changes in designs to induce consumers to tire of their old-fashioned wares and trade them in for those made in the latest style.

But advances were not restricted to fashion and style alone, and a major technological improvement took place with the production of 'Hard Metal', which was probably introduced into England in the 1650s by James Taudin, a French Protestant refugee. A detailed discussion of this form of pewter is contained in Chapter 5, and it will suffice to state here that it was extremely durable and ideally suited to the manufacture of plates and dishes. Although 'Hard Metal' was considerably more expensive than fine pewter (in the 1690s it was 1s2d to 1s6d a pound compared with less than a shilling) it rapidly achieved great popularity, and by the close of the seventeenth century a multitude of pewterers were proclaiming their ability to manufacture it.

The effects of the stimuli provided by the developments outlined above can be discovered most readily in the freeman and apprentice data of the London Pewterers' Company. In the 1660s the highest number of apprentices ever, 564, were enrolled, and in the 1670s the highest number of freemen ever, 303, were admitted, and 147 licences to open shop were granted, a total only exceeded in the 1620s. Consequently the number of master pewterers in the capital rose to a new peak, and in the 1680s probably more than 350 were at work—in 1688 Mint officials put the number at 415.[3] The beneficial effects of the Great Fire of

[1] *Ibid.*, pp. 108–10; Michaelis, *Antique Pewter*, pp. 86–94.
[2] See ch. 4.   [3] Appendix A, table 12.

1666, although shortlived, are worthy of notice since much of the pewter destroyed in the Fire was subsequently replaced by its owners, and the supplies of scrap pewter made available were so great that the scheme for the pre-emption of tin production then in force was wrecked.[1] It is, of course, impossible to provide comparable data for the provincial industries. Nevertheless, the remarkable growth of the Wigan industry by 1683 has already been noted, and it is most unlikely that increased vigour on the part of London searchers was alone responsible for a rise of almost a third in the number of pewterers' premises searched in towns that were visited in both 1635–41 and 1669–83.[2]

The English pewter industry thus appears to have reached its maximum size at some point in the closing decades of the seventeenth century, perhaps in the 1680s, and perhaps with a total of between 2,500 and 3,500 masters, journeymen, apprentices and servants. The nation's stock of pewter was almost certainly also at its peak, with more households containing pewter than ever before, due to rising population and wider dissemination. The difficulties caused in mid-century by the shortage of tin and the Civil War had been overcome, and the threat of pottery and tinplate contained. The proud claim of the London Pewterers in 1703 that 'the manufacture of pewter is now and always hath been of great advantage to the nation; great numbers of his majesty's subjects being constantly employed therein' was fully justified.[3] Yet the foundations of this prosperity were far less secure than ever before, and within a matter of decades cheap home produced pottery, tinplate and, at a later date, Britannia metal were to throw abruptly into reverse over four centuries of almost uninterrupted growth.

[1] State Papers Domestic, Chas. II, ccxxx, 75 (quoted, Lewis, p. 52n).
[2] There were, in the thirty-five towns visited at both dates, a maximum of eighty-one pewterers searched on any one occasion between 1635 and 1641 and of 109 between 1669 and 1683.
[3] Guildhall MS 7090/8, 18 Nov.

4 Pewterers' gilds and the regulation of the industry

The greater part of industrial activity in pre-industrial Europe was organized on a gild basis. Craft gilds, which may be defined briefly as associations of skilled workers following the same industrial occupation within the same town, pursued policies designed to achieve as complete a control as possible over the manufacture and distribution of the commodities produced by their members.[1] Their power stemmed in the main from monopolies granted by municipal governments, although certain leading craft gilds, especially those of London, had their powers reinforced and extended by royal charters. Attempting to measure the success with which statutes, laws, ordinances etc. were enforced is a perennial bugbear of the historian, and it is invariably far easier to discover what restrictions and regulations the gilds wished to enforce, than whether they were able to enforce them effectively, or whether such enforcement had the desired effect. It is essential, therefore, to distinguish as far as possible between real and illusory authority; and to judge from recent work, opinion appears to be shifting towards allowing gilds only a limited degree of effectiveness in the enforcement of their ordinances.[2]

The effectiveness of gild control over an industry depended upon a wide range of factors in addition to the attitude of local and central governments, including the degree of solidarity amongst members, the ability of sanctions to dissuade defaulters, the degree of skill and the amount of capital needed to set up as

[1] Among the standard works on English craft gilds are: E. Lipson, *The Economic History of England: the Middle Ages* (10th edn, 1949), pp. 308–439; G. Unwin, *The Gilds and Companies of London* (4th edn, 1963) and *Industrial Organization in the Sixteenth and Seventeenth Centuries* (2nd edn, 1957); S. Kramer, *The English Craft Gilds* (New York, 1927).
[2] For example, S. L. Thrupp, 'Medieval gilds reconsidered', *Journal of Economic History*, ii (1942).

a producer, the ease with which raw materials could be obtained and their cost, the nature of consumer demand for the finished product, and the extent to which acceptable substitutes were available. If one constructs a league table on the basis of the powers enjoyed by the various craft gilds it is usual to place goldsmiths at the top. Goldsmiths' gilds were often controlled by extremely rich merchants endowed with substantial capital and extensive political influence, they were able to impose a rigid discipline on members, entry was automatically restricted by the high degree of expertise required to work in gold and silver and, of course, supplies of these metals were limited and extremely costly; moreover there were no adequate substitutes, and the clientele for gold and silverware were wealthy enough to tolerate generous profit margins. The base metal gilds are thought to have enjoyed substantially less power, and to have ranked towards the middle of the league, above workers in wood, for example, but below those in leather.[1] Yet such broad generalisations as these are of limited utility, since influence varied from town to town, time to time, and from one branch of the trade to another, and a detailed study of pewterers' gilds reveals that their powers were generally greater and persisted far longer than those of gilds specialising in other base metals.

In our industry the most comprehensive authority was inevitably enjoyed by the London Pewterers, but a clear uniformity of purpose can be detected not only between London and provincial pewterers' gilds, but also between pewterers' and other craft gilds. The corpus of law relating both to the administration of individual pewterers' gilds and to the manufacture and sale of pewter was an amalgam of edicts, some common to many crafts and some unique. Such edicts as those concerned with admissions, apprenticeship, the limitation of competition amongst members, discrimination against non-members, and the maintenance of uniformly high standards of workmanship in association with a pricing policy, were the common currency of craft gilds. Others were less general, as for example those concerning the compulsory marking of wares with the touch of the maker, or the hiring of wares, while those concerning such matters as precise techniques of manufacture, the size and weight of the various

---

[1] For example, S. L. Thrupp, 'The gilds', *Cambridge Economic History of Europe*, iii (Cambridge, 1963).

articles made of pewter, and the purchase of tin or scrap pewter, were obviously unique to pewterers' gilds.

Before studying the specific areas of control in detail it is essential to provide an outline of the chronological development of the regulations adopted by pewterers' gilds. It would be grossly misleading to lump together ordinances promulgated at widely differing points in time, since their evolution was, in large measure, a cumulative process. Furthermore gild policy was flexible and changed with the needs of the moment and the attitudes of town and central authorities, and although ordinances were rarely formally discarded their importance waxed and waned along with the enthusiasm and success with which they were enforced. What is more, it is manifest that the most comprehensive lists of ordinances were compiled in the eighteenth century when the power of enforcement was far weaker than it had been in earlier centuries. It is also essential to note that gilds were not free to pass whatever rules they saw fit, even when those rules related exclusively to internal matters. Ultimate authority resided with municipal governments, or even Parliament, and ordinances had to be approved and supported in civic courts, and these institutions were bound to pay attention to public welfare. Gild ordinances were frequently annulled by municipal governments, largely on the grounds that they were not in the public interest, and from time to time the state also saw fit to attempt to curb gild powers.[1] Ordinances and by-laws therefore to a large extent, merely reflect the public attitudes of the gilds, and it is imperative to search for the clandestine rules that were made and enforced privately at meetings of members or in gild courts, which frequently secured widespread obedience out of self-interest. The fixing of minimum prices, often declared illegal by municipal and state authorities, comes into this category.[2]

It is fitting that the ordinances and by-laws of the London Pewterers should command the centre of our discussion: the London industry was far larger at all times than any in the provinces and the records it has left are unparalleled in their detail and continuity, but of even greater significance is the fact that London legislation invariably provided a model for that introduced by the provincial gilds.

[1] For example in 1437 and 1504 (Lipson, *Economic History*, i, 418–22).
[2] For illicit price fixing by the London Pewterers' Company see below pp. 179-82.

The earliest record of rules governing the manufacture and sale of pewter in Britain dates from the ratification of a series of ordinances by the mayor and aldermen of London in 1348.[1] At the heart of these ordinances lay the desire of a rapidly expanding group of London metalworkers specialising in the manufacture of pewter to organise themselves into a craft, on the pattern of many others which had long existed in the City, with control over admission to the practice of the trade and the quality of wares produced and sold in London. It was necessary for the pewterers to demonstrate that they did not seek such powers out of self interest, but 'for the common profit', as the preamble to the ordinances shows:

> seeing that the trade of pewtery is founded upon certain matters and metals, such as copper, tin and lead, in due proportions; of which three metals they make vessels, that is to say, pots, salts, dishes, platters, and other things by good folks bespoken; which works demand certain mixtures and certain alloys, according to the manner of vessel so bespoken; the which things cannot be made without good knowledge of a pewterer, well taught and well informed in the trade; seeing that many persons, not knowing the right alloys, nor yet the mixtures or the right rules of the trade, do work and make vessels and other things not in due manner, to the damage of the people, and to the scandal of the trade; and the good folks of the trade do pray therefore, that it may be ordained that three or four of the most lawful and most skilful in the trade may be chosen to oversee the alloys and the workmanship aforesaid; and that by their examination and assay, amendment may speedily be made where default has been committed.[2]

Accordingly the first ordinance stipulated the constituents of the alloys to be used in the manufacture of the various types of pewterware, and subsequent ordinances provided for the examination and testing of all pewterware offered for sale in the City and made in the City and sent for sale 'to fairs, or to markets, or

---

[1] The original enrolment of these ordinances was made in Letter Book F, fol. clv, and is translated in *Memorials of London Life*, ed. H. T. Riley (1868), pp. 241–4. A translation, probably made in the late fifteenth century, is contained in the records of the Pewterers' Company and is transcribed in Welch, i, 2–5.
[2] *Memorials of London Life*, pp. 241–2.

elsewhere in the kingdom'. Of scarcely less significance was the second ordinance which stated that 'no person shall intermeddle with the trade aforesaid, if he be not sworn before the good folks of the trade, lawfully to work according to the points ordained', by which the craft sought a monopoly of production in London. Later in this ordinance, and in subsequent ordinances, it was specified that only those who had been apprenticed 'or otherwise a lawful workman known and tried among them' should be admitted as a master or employed by another master. Additional clauses forbade night work 'seeing that ... the sight is not so profitable by night, or so certain as by day, to the profit, that is, of the community', and the taking away of the journeyman of another master without his agreement. Penalties for breach of these ordinances, and also for thefts perpetrated by apprentices or journeymen against their masters, ranged from fines of 40d and the forfeiture of 'false' wares to expulsion on the third offence.

Although the enrolment of these ordinances was an event of immense importance in the history of the craft, it should be noted that they were to be enforced at the discretion of the City council, a body which, in common with those of other towns, was dominated by merchants rather than industrialists.[1] The privilege of trying offenders in the Pewterers' own court was not to be granted until incorporation in 1474; furthermore only half of every fine levied and half of the false metal seized was retained by the craft. This procedure can be seen at work in the following entry in the City records, which is of particular interest because it illustrates the ordinances relating to standards of manufacture being enforced within two years of their ratification:

> On Monday next after the Feast of the Apostles Peter and Paul in the 24th year of the reign of King Edward III (29 June 1350), 23 measures called 'potels',[2] and 20 saltcellars, of pewter, were brought before Walter Turk the Mayor, and the Aldermen, by the men of the trade of Pewterers; who said that the potels and saltcellars aforesaid were false, and made of false metal by John de Hiltone, *peautrer*, here present in Court, in deceit of the people, and to the disgrace of the whole trade. And the said John de Hiltone acknow-

[1] See, for example, Thrupp, *Merchant Class of Medieval London*, Appendix A.
[2] A pottle was of four pints capacity.

ledged that he had made the vessels aforesaid: and so that
might be known whether the same vessels were of good and
befitting metal or not, order was given to William de
Greyngham, serjeant, to summon forthwith before the Mayor
and Aldermen, Arnold de Shypwaysshe, Nicholas de Ludgate,
John Syward, William de Uptone, John de Arlicheseye,
and William de Greschirche, Wardens of the Articles of the
trade of Pewterers, that they might certify the Mayor and
Aldermen, as to the genuineness or falsity of the make of
the vessels aforesaid. Who, being sworn, after viewing and
examining the vessels aforesaid, said upon oath, that the
greater part of the metal of which the aforesaid potels and
saltcellars were made was lead; whereas to one hundredweight
of 112 pounds of tin there ought to be added no more than
16 pounds of lead. It was therefore adjudged that the said
vessels should be forfeited to the use of the Commonalty.[1]

The sources for the study of constitutional developments in this early but critical period in the craft's history are extremely scanty, and the next mention of significance does not occur until 1438. In November of this year the leading members of the craft, having been brought before the mayor and aldermen, confessed to having made ordinances without the authority of the mayor. The offending ordinances were carefully examined by the City council the following February, were deemed to be against the liberties of the City and against the common profit, and were 'adnulled and utterly reicete'.[2] It is probable that this drastic action was taken by the mayor and aldermen under the direct stimulus of the Act of Parliament passed in the previous year, which represented that 'the masters, wardens and people of the gilds... make themselves many unlawful and unreasonable ordinances... for their singular profit and common damage to the people' and ordered that all gild ordinances should be submitted to civic authorities in cities and towns or justices of the peace in counties.[3] Reconciliation was close at hand, however, and in March 1439 new ordinances were approved by the mayor and aldermen 'after diligent examinacion'. Nevertheless it is clear that the Pewterers had thereby suffered a serious reversal, for the new ordinances constituted only a slight extension of the

[1] *Memorials of London Life*, pp. 259-60.   [2] Welch, i, 8-9.
[3] Lipson, *Economic History*, i, 418; Unwin, *Gilds and Companies of London*, pp. 161-2.

authority enjoyed since 1348, and were not at all commensurate with the spectacular increase which had undoubtedly taken place in the scale of the London pewter industry since that date. One result was that, according to municipal law at least, the powers of the London Pewterers were inferior to those of York. Yet, paradoxically, the comprehensive *Ordinaciones pewderariorum* accepted by the York city council in 1416 were modelled on those of London, as the preamble explicity states: 'Ceux sont les articles de lez pewderers de Lounders, les queux les genz de mesme lartifice dyceste citee Deverwyk ount agrees pur agarder et ordeiner entre eux par deux ans passez, devant Johan Moreton, maire'.[1]

The York ordinances provided penalties for workmen who made sadware with metal of less than fine standard, whose holloware did not come up to the assize of lay metal, who soldered with an alloy worse than pale,[2] and who sold vessels that were badly wrought. Furthermore there were widereaching edicts concerning conditions of service and setting up in business: apprentices had to serve a minimum of seven years and were not to leave their masters during this term or steal from them, no alien or bondman could be apprenticed, no man was to employ a servant who had not been released by his previous master or pay him more than 40*s* a year in wages, all masters who had not served an apprenticeship in York had to pay an entry fee of 20*s*, and no one could open shop until he had proved his ability to make good pewterware.[3] By contrast the London ordinances of 1439 were of very limited scope, and apart from allowing the officers of the craft to fine members for non-attendance at meetings and to collect 12*d* per year from shopkeepers, the only new powers related to smelting, the prohibition of competition amongst members for shops and standing places, and the sale of pewter on usurious credit terms. A list of the standard weights of various articles was appended to the ordinances in the craft's Jury Book.[4]

Given that the York ordinances of 1416 were based on London ordinances, yet were far more comprehensive than those of 1348 and 1439, it is permissible to assume that they had something in

[1] *York Memorandum Book*, i, 211.
[2] A mixture of tin and lead in approved proportions.
[3] *York Memorandum Book*, i, 212–13.   [4] Welch, i, 9–12.

common with those rejected by the mayor and aldermen in 1438. But there is little in the York ordinances which, in the economic philosophy of the times, could be interpreted as pernicious: the insistence on a seven year apprenticeship, the exclusion of the alien and the unfree, the restriction of competition for labour, and the maintenance of standards of manufacture are to be found in the ordinances of most gilds of that time. It is possible, therefore, that the London Pewterers were punished because between 1416 and 1438 they had made further secret and less acceptable rules among themselves, which perhaps related, among other things, to prices. Notwithstanding, it would be unrealistic to assume that the new ordinances of 1439, together with those in existence since 1348, constituted the sole basis of the craft's powers until incorporation, and it can be safely assumed that many other rules, corresponding to those enjoyed by other crafts, were of necessity enforced.[1]

Little more than a decade after the rejection of their ordinances, and immediately on commencement of their records, we find reference to the Pewterers seeking to secure from Parliament the power to search for imperfect wares throughout England.[2] The quest for additional powers and privileges from Parliament rather than the City government was inevitably to develop into a quest for incorporation, an ambition which was finally to be fulfilled on 20 January 1474. Incorporation, which by virtue of a royal charter conferred the immortal collective personality of a corporation with the right to hold property in mortmain, was the aim of most of the leading misteries of London, but it remained a rare and exceptional privilege until the reign of Henry VI, being extended only to the richest and most fortunate, such as the Mercers, Goldsmiths, Tailors, Skinners and Saddlers. Henry VI, however, adopted a more liberal policy towards incorporation, and he granted charters to many of the great trading and manufacturing misteries including the Grocers, Fishmongers, Vintners, Brewers, Drapers, Cordwainers, Leathersellers, Haberdashers and Armourers. The benefits bestowed by incorporation were also enlarged by Henry, and whereas early charters had

---

[1] In 1462, for example, 2s4d was paid 'for makyng of a bille of ordinaunces of the Craft' (Guildhall MS 7086, 1461–2), and at about the same time a member was fined for suing another member without leave of the Master and Wardens (Guildhall MS 7086, 1465–6).
[2] Guildhall MS 7086/1, 1452–3.

emphasised the religious and benevolent aspects of incorporation, by mid-century the legal and economic aspects relating to the government of the mistery and the control of the trade or industry were coming to the fore.[1]

It was fitting, therefore, that the Pewterers should seek to join the expanding ranks of incorporated companies. In particular incorporation would not only give the Pewterers enhanced status and a vital measure of independence from City authority, but also, and perhaps of even greater significance, it would give them a measure of control over the manufacture and sale of pewter outside London. London pewterers who had long since supplied all parts of the realm with pewterware were facing increased rivalry in the later fifteenth century from local producers, many of whom by not adhering to the high standards of manufacture enforced in the capital were able to sell at lower prices. The power to search for and confiscate substandard pewter on sale throughout the country offered an excellent opportunity to reduce competition.[2]

The achievement of corporate status proved to be a long and expensive process, and from extant records it appears to have taken more than twenty years and cost almost £200.[3] In addition to payments for such matters as counsels' opinion, the entertainment of officials of the Cutlers' Company and other learned men, and a variety of other legal fees, the bulk of the recorded cost of securing the charter consisted of £80 paid in 1467–68 to Robert Chamberlain, who had been Master the previous year, 'for the purchase of our lyvelode', and £41.17s8d paid in 1473–74 to William Large 'for the Costs of the Corporacyon'. The Pewterers had not previously possessed a hall of their own, they had hired rooms in the Austin Friars for official meetings and festive gatherings; but enhanced status and the specific right granted in the charter 'of Acquiring and Holding in Fee and Perpetuity Lands, Tenements, Rents, Services, and all other Possessions whatsoever' made such an acquisition a priority of the first order. Within months of incorporation members were examining a number of possible sites, and in 1475 possession of land and buildings in Lime Street was obtained at a rent of 20s

---

[1] For a discussion of incorporation see Unwin, *Gilds and Companies of London*, pp. 158–63.   [2] Above pp. 73–5.
[3] The full cost may well have been substantially higher.

a year, and plans were set in hand for eventual purchase and the building of a hall. Probably because the Company was left with insufficient funds after the expense of procuring its charter, the site and premises in Lime Street were purchased jointly with William Smallwood, Master in 1469, 1477, 1481, and 1486, on the understanding that they would pass to the Company on his death. Smallwood died in May 1492. In 1497, after careful inspection had been made of the style of the halls of other companies and institutions, the building of a great hall for feasts and general assemblies was begun. It was completed within two years.[1]

The London Company was not alone in the extension of its powers and influence. Mention has already been made of the comprehensive ordinances of the York pewterers enrolled in 1416, and in 1457 those of the pewterers of Bristol were written in that city's records, to be followed in 1494 by the enrolment of the Coventry pewterers' ordinances in the Coventry Leet Book.[2] The Bristol and Coventry ordinances were brief compared with those of London and York, but they both contained the essential regulations concerning alloys and workmanship, and the right to search for substandard wares; in addition those of Coventry also stipulated a minimum apprenticeship of seven years, and that pewterers should not sell wholesale to chapmen or any person who had not served as an apprentice in the trade. Many other associations of pewterers existed at this time but they formed part of composite gilds, and their regulations have not survived.

The ability to exercise some control over the rapidly expanding provincial industry was increasingly seen by the London Pewterers as an essential prop to their prosperity. We know that appropriate powers 'to have serche thurgh England' were being sought as early as 1453, and the granting of them in 1474 took up over half the length of the charter. It is difficult to overestimate the importance, in the eyes of the Company, of the right to 'have a search and Government of all manner of Workmanships and Merchandizes belonging or appertaining to the said Mystery wrought or to be wrought and Exposed to Sale within the said City and Suburbs thereof and in any other places whatsoever without the said City throughout... [the] Kingdom of England and... to

---

[1] Welch has extracted from the audit accounts most of the entries of interest concerning incorporation and the acquisition of a hall (i, 18–86 *passim*); an account is also contained in Unwin, *Gilds and Companies of London*, pp. 164–6.
[2] *Little Red Book of Bristol*, ii, 184–5; *Coventry Leet Book*, ii, 554.

Punish and Correct the Defects of the said Workmanships and Merchandizes'.[1] No time was lost in enforcing these rights and also in enrolling country craftsmen into the Company, but the itinerant manufacturers and retailers of pewter posed a particularly formidable problem which the faculties granted in the charter of 1474 were not capable of solving. After much further lobbying a statute quaintly entitled 'Pewtrers Walkyng' was passed in 1504, which imposed London standards of manufacture on hawkers and pedlars, made the marking of all holloware with the maker's touch compulsory, laid down penalties for the use of inaccurate beams and weights, and restricted the points of sale of new pewter and the purchase of old to open fairs, markets, and the dealers' dwelling houses—customers' houses were only to be visited by invitation.[2] The importance of pewter manufacture to the economy at large, and the expertise with which the pewterers' case was put, is further evinced by the prohibition of all pewter imports, the emigration of pewterers, and the employment of aliens, in a statute passed in 1534.[3]

A final important concession granted in the charter of 1474 was that the 'masters, wardens and commonalty and their successors' should have the authority to 'make and Ordain Honest and reasonable Ordinances and Constitutions for the good rule and Government of the said Mistery as often as they shall please and it shall be needfull without any Impeachment, Impediment, or Agreivance of us, our Heirs, the Justices, Mayors, Sheriffs, Escheators, Bailiffs, Constables, or other Officers or Ministers of us or of our said Heirs whatsoever'. Unfortunately, owing to the lack at this early date of records of Company court proceedings or of such ordinances as may have been passed, it is impossible to determine whether this new independence resulted in major changes in internal policy. A study of the occasional recording of fines on the annual financial accounts of the Company suggests that such changes as may have taken place were not fundamental, although attempts to fix prices do appear to have become more explicit.[4]

The substantial degree of freedom to legislate on trade matters

---

[1] The translation of the charter is taken from Company records, and is transcribed in Welch, ii, 199–202.   [2] 19 Henry VII, c. 6.
[3] 25 Henry VIII, c. 9. This Act went through many drafts before it was finally passed (G. R. Elton, *Reform and Renewal: Thomas Cromwell and the Common Weal*, Cambridge, 1973, pp. 80–1).   [4] For example, Guildhall MS 7086/1, 1482–3, 1493–4.

granted to incorporated companies and the increasingly restrictive policies adopted by craft gilds as a whole, posed ever greater threats to the interests of the community at large, and to the authority of civic magistrates in particular. The time was clearly ripe for some form of state intervention, and in 1504 an Act, similar in intention to that of 1437 but somewhat wider in scope, was passed through Parliament for the express reason that gilds 'often times, by colour of rule and governance to them granted and confirmed by charters and letters patent of divers kings, made among themselves many unlawful and unreasonable ordinances as well in prices of wares as other things, for their own singular profit and to the common hurt and damage of the people'.[1] The 1504 Act differed from its predecessor in two major respects. In the first place it provided national as well as municipal machinery for the oversight of gilds, by ordering that their ordinances ought to 'be examined and approved by the Chancellor, Treasurer of England, and Chief Justices of either Bench, or three of them; or before the Justices of Assize in their circuit'. In the second place special attention was directed towards price fixing. Controversy exists as to the effectiveness of this Act,[2] but the Pewterers' Company in 1522 expressed no doubts that it had constituted a severe restraint on its ability to control its members. In the preamble to new ordinances, duly presented to the appropriate royal officers, it was claimed that 'by occasion of whiche restraynte [i.e. 19 Henry VII, c. 7] dyverse and many of the saide crafte or misterye beinge unreasonable parsones have nowe of late fallen in to greate disobedience to the greate hurte and inquietenese of the good and obediente parsones of the same crafte or mysterye'.[3]

It is possible that the Company felt itself unduly inhibited by the need to have its ordinances approved, for those of 1522 contain little that could be construed as offensive, although in three areas a substantial tightening of influence was intended. First, following accepted gild practice within London and other major towns, restrictions were imposed for the first time on the numbers of apprentices each master might have. Second, it was ordered that the wares of members should be searched and tested without hindrance, at least five times a year, and that the marking of all pewterware with the maker's touch should be

[1] 19 Henry VII, c. 7.
[2] For example, Lipson, *Economic History*, i, 420–1.   [3] Welch, i, 106.

compulsory. Third, a number of further measures were introduced with the intention of discriminating against non-members and discouraging freemen from seeking employment outside London.[1]

Two of the most prominent features of the ordinances promulgated by both London and provincial pewterers' gilds in the sixteenth and seventeenth centuries were the desire to restrict the numbers practising the craft and the desire to restrict competition among members. Such aims are exemplified by progressively more severe limitations placed on numbers of apprentices, the need for formal approval before ex-apprentices could set up shop, the forbidding of partnerships without licence, and stringent penalties for advertising or stealing another member's customers. Fortunately the survival from 1551 of a virtually continuous series of remarkably detailed minute books of the court of the London Pewterers' Company adds a further dimension, and enables some of the day-to-day realities behind the official ordinances to be discovered, and previously hidden conflicts of interest to be revealed.

Before examining the various areas of gild policy in detail it is essential to gain some insight into the composition of the policy-making bodies, in order to assess the extent to which they were representative of majority or of merely factional interests. Such a task involves some discussion of the constitutions of pewterers' gilds, and once again our attention is, perforce, centred on the London Pewterers.

It is a commonplace that the government of gilds was rigidly oligarchic. Furthermore, it has frequently been maintained that the industrial gilds increasingly came under the control of rich merchants and that mere manufacturers were bereft of political and economic power and, in many cases, condemned permanently to the subservient status of lesser masters employed at piece rates, or journeymen.[2] But such hypotheses, although providing an indispensable framework for early research on gilds and industrial organisation, can no longer be accepted without

[1] Welch, i, 107–15.
[2] Unwin in particular tended to overstate the success of merchants in their attempts to control industrial gilds; for a more balanced view of this question see Kramer, *English Craft Gilds*; F. J. Fisher, 'The influence and Development of the Industrial Gilds in the Larger Provincial Towns under James I and Charles I' (London M.A. thesis, 1931), pp. 70 ff.

question; in general they mask a miscellany of different experiences in a multitude of gilds, and in particular they tend to confuse developments in the gild with developments in the industry. Even a superficial investigation of pewterers' gilds and the pewter industry reveals that although there were obvious strong sympathetic links between the two, the domination of much of the industry by rich merchants did not inevitably lead to a similar domination of the gild. On the contrary the gild and the leading merchant industrialists were often in conflict, and it is possible to find examples of many gild policies which were expressly formulated to protect the interests of the lesser masters and journeymen and counter the tendencies towards the growth of large units of production. Some discussion of these matters is contained in the following sections and the next chapter, our main concern at this point is to sketch the evolution of the constitutions of pewterers' gilds.

Despite the lack of information concerning the London craft in the first half of the fourteenth century, it would not be naïve or rash to assume that major policy decisions, such as the framing of the 1348 ordinances, were made with the approval of the great majority of members. The numbers in the craft at this time were small enough to permit an easy democracy bred of informality, and the overwhelming desire was to create an effective organisation consisting of as many practitioners as possible, which could only be achieved by making membership attractive. Inevitably the membership contained a number of persons with wealth or skill far above the average, and it was doubtless that from among these the two, and later six, Wardens were chosen; but there is no reason to deny that the prime function of the Wardens was to implement the will of the majority. Wardens were still the governors of the craft in the fourth and fifth decades of the fifteenth century, as we learn from the ordinances of 1439 and the two regulations concerning the tin trade made by the City council in 1444.[1] It is not until 1450 that we have evidence of the craft being governed by a Master, with two Wardens as assistants, an arrangement which was given perpetual status in the charter of 1474.[2] The oath these officers took on assuming their positions,

[1] Welch, i, 12–14.
[2] The earliest audit account, that of 1451–52, gives the names of the retiring Master and Wardens (Guildhall MS 7086/1).

devised in 1463, provides an interesting insight into the way in which members at large conceived of their functions:

> Ye shall swere that you shall be faythefull to oure soverayne lorde the kynge and to his ayris kyngs, and you shall well and onestly Inret your felyschepe, and Ryght do as well to the poure as to the ryche, and the profett of the felyschyp in that that you is, to youre power laufully and ryghtuously you shall mayntayne and incresse, and a trewe accounte thereof make. An Just Jugys you shalbe upon the complaynt of youre felyschep as well to the poure, as to the ryche. And no syngular profett do to youre owne parsons where thorowe the common profytt of the felyschep may be harmed or hurte, and all the good laufull ordenauncys and Rulys of the said ffelyschep that nowe be made or in tyme to come shall be made, yow shall kepe and mayntayne to your powre. Nor no man receyve in to the said felyschep withoute the assent of the felyschep of the more parte of them. In these and all other thyngs that pertayneth to your office to do, you shall well and trewly be have you. So god be youre helpe and all sayntts.[1]

The enhanced status of the craft subsequent to incorporation led immediately to further moves towards a more formal constitution. It was seen as both impractical and undesirable that sole power should be vested in the hands of only three persons, but similarly it was felt unwise to entrust major decisions to general meetings of the 'comynaltie', as had hitherto been the practice. Accordingly on 1 October after incorporation it was decided:

> for the greate weale tranquillytie good rule and reste to be had in the saide Crafte, and to put awaie and amove debate, rancor, dissention and discorde hereafter happelye to be moved and had which god forbitt, do make and ordeyne by vertue and aucthoritie of the said lettres pattentes: That the maister and wardens of the saide fraternitie or gilde for the tyme beinge and other tenne parsons of the worshipfulleste discreteste wisest and unwilfulleste fremen of the saide crafte chosen by us ... have full power and aucthoritie to make all statutes ordinaunces and constitucions frome

[1] Guildhall MS 7114.

henceforthe concerninge the weale prosperitie and good rule and governaunce of the saide crafte, and to adde and demynishe in that behalfe after there wisdomes and discretions.[1]

It was further specified that these men were appointed for life and had the right to nominate persons to fill vacancies caused through death. Furthermore if a Master or Warden was chosen from amongst the thirteen, as was likely, then his predecessor in that office was to remain one of the thirteen. This surely was a Court of Assistants in all but name, and when some nine years later the names of the members of this body were recorded we can see that they were all Pastmasters and Wardens.[2] The concept of a permanent self-perpetuating ruling clique, offensive as it is to the twentieth-century mind reared on the sanctity of universal suffrage and frequent elections, was nevertheless in keeping with the accepted doctrines of the age and can be seen in operation in municipal government as well as in the universities and inns of court.

Other indications of an emergent hierachy within the London Pewterers are discernible in the later fifteenth century. Distinctions between 'bretheren' and small numbers of householders (shopkeepers) 'that be no bretheren' were made in the earliest extant Company records of the 1450s,[3] and as early as 1466 we find the following entry: 'These be the names that beth taken in to the lyvery this seid yere by the mayster and wardeyns and the thryfty men of the crafte.'[4] The counterpart of a livery composed of the richer and more influential masters was a yeomanry. From as early as 1473 an organised body of yeoman pewterers was in existence, with independent though subservient status[5]; its master and wardens were liverymen appointed by the livery. By the 1520s there were more yeomen in the Company than liverymen.[6] The yeomanry was composed of lesser freemen, some of whom were journeymen working for wages, and some of whom were small independent masters who possessed an apprentice or journeyman or two.[7]

[1] Guildhall MS 7086/1, f. 3.   [2] Guildhall MS 7086/1, 1481–2.
[3] For example, Guildhall MS 7086/1, 1456–7; MS 7086/1, 1458–9.
[4] Guildhall MS 7086/1, 1465–6.   [5] Guildhall MS 7086/1, 1472–3.
[6] Audit accounts (Guildhall MS, 7086/1–2).
[7] This information can be obtained from the lists of masters, journeymen and apprentices continued in Guildhall MS 7086/1, 1456–7 and 1458–9.

Thereby the Pewterers' Company gradually adopted the archetypal administrative and political framework of the larger livery company, with an annually elected Master and two Wardens and a small select permanent body of senior advisers at its head, followed by liverymen, yeomen, and apprentices, and unfree wage labourers at the bottom.[1] Yet it would be naïve to leap to the convenient conclusion that the system was one of blatant and unbridled exploitation, since by far the greatest expenditure of energy was devoted towards the exploitation of non-gild producers and consumers for the benefit of all members. In the first place many gild members who may have suffered discrimination were comforted by the knowledge that their status as apprentice or journeyman was transitory, and that with good fortune and the passage of time they would come to enjoy positions of greater privilege and power. It was only the unfree labourers, a body we know little about, who were permanently condemned by the laws of the gild to remain wage-earners. In the second place, the exercise of power within the gild was rarely arbitrary, being usually tempered by an intricate system of checks and balances and, in the last resort, subject to the acquiescence of the majority of masters. Furthermore, although the Court of Assistants conducted the day-to-day business of the Company, important matters were often referred to committees which frequently contained yeomen as well as liverymen, and the most vital decisions were frequently taken by the 'whole house' or the 'whole company'.[2]

There was a tendency in the course of the sixteenth century for the governing body of the Company to consult widely amongst liverymen and even yeomen. In 1561, for example, arrangements for the purchase of tin were agreed to 'by the master, wardens and assystaunce and the most part of the whole company'.[3] Similarly, we find in 1583 that a committee set up to 'syt and determyne as well of pryces of ware as also any other matter which they shall find necessary and Good for the company' was composed of twelve members of the Court of Assistants, four liverymen, and four yeomen,[4] and in 1593 a committee of six

---

[1] For the organization of the London livery companies see Unwin, *Gilds and Companies of London*, esp. chapters 11–14.
[2] Court Minute Books, *passim* (Guildhall MSS 7090/1–8).
[3] Guildhall MS 7090/1, 18 Jan.
[4] Guildhall MS 7090/2, 12 Dec.

liverymen and two yeomen was appointed to reply to Sir Walter Raleigh's letter on the proposed restriction of the tin trade and to negotiate with Mr Giffard on the same matter.[1] Interested parties were often given leave to determine their own policies, and when in 1615 it was decided to fix the 'sales and rate of Tryffles' the matter was referred to six 'Sadwaremen' and six 'Triffelers'.[2] It is also evident that changes in policy could often be successfully initiated by yeomen; the regulation passed in 1564 that any master with three apprentices should 'be Bound in an obligacon of xli to set ij Jornymen on worck' seems a clear result of lobbying by journeymen.[3] It is also more than probable that the strict enforcement of limitations upon the numbers of apprentices a master might keep, and upon the ease with which apprentices might set-up in business on obtaining their freedom, which feature so prominently in sixteenth and seventeenth century gild policy, owed much to the pressure of journeymen and lesser masters.[4]

Yet it would also be patently false to suggest that relations within the craft were always cordial. On the contrary settlements were sometimes reached only after conflict, and occasionally aggrieved sections of the craft found it necessary to appeal to the mayor and the Court of Aldermen, much to the chagrin of the Court of Assistants.[5] Nevertheless, most of the more serious conflicts can be traced, directly or indirectly, to the pre-emption of tin output by farmers operating under royal patents which persisted for more than a century.[6] The climax of discontent was reached in the first half of the seventeenth century and had two major sources. In the first place a number of Company members who were leading tin dealers attempted to ensure that the interests of raw tin exporters triumphed over those of pewter manufacturers. In the ensuing power struggles the government of the Company became so remote and oligarchical that a large number of the 'genneralletie' attended a court meeting on 6

[1] Guildhall MS 7090/3, 5 July.
[2] Guildhall MS 7090/4, 29 Mar.
[3] Guildhall MS 7090/2, 21 Sept.
[4] See below, pp. 194–7.
[5] In 1535, for example, the yeomanry successfully petitioned the Court of Aldermen and obtained a guarantee that journeymen would be granted work on acceptable terms whenever possible (Welch, i, 135); and in 1631 a petition signed by sixty freemen complaining about the distribution of tin allocated to the Company was presented to the Lord Treasurer and Chancellor of the Exchequer, 'without any aucthority from the Master and Wardens' (Guildhall MS 7090/4, 19 Apr.).
[6] Discussed below, pp. 234–7.

September 1641 and claimed, through the charter of 1474, that 'there is power given to the whole Commonaltie to rule and govern the brothers and members of this Company'; when pressed by the court to make specific charges they refused and demanded the right to present their case before the Court of Aldermen.[1] Unfortunately the outcome of this episode is not known, but in the ensuing years the ambitions of the tin dealers were thwarted. In the second place justifiably bitter feelings were aroused by the manner in which the tin obtained by the Company on favourable terms from the tin farmers was distributed amongst freemen. This problem was never satisfactorily resolved but temporary solutions were sought through committees of distributors composed of equal numbers of liverymen and yeomen elected by the livery and yeomanry respectively.[2]

In the second half of the seventeenth century, in the face of mounting competition from country pewterers and rival products, the government of the Company became more representative. By 1702 the Court of Assistants, excluding the Master and Wardens, had expanded to a minimum of twenty-four and a maximum of forty. The Master and Wardens came to be elected by the livery, although nominated by the Court of Assistants, and the power to make ordinances was vested in the livery as well as the Assistants.[3] In the day-to-day administration of Company affairs a far greater degree of participation by the membership in general is in evidence, and in addition to court meetings of the Assistants, we find that other court meetings frequently included the livery, and that the quarterly courts admitted the yeomanry also. General courts were also held from time to time and all members attending—Assistants, liverymen and yeomen alike—appear to have had equal voting rights.[4] In the later seventeenth century the admission of freemen to the livery became largely an exercise in fund-raising, and it is possible that the greater political power given to yeomen contributed to the difficulty encountered in persuading members to take up the livery.

This outline of the growth of the powers of the Company and of the exercise of power within the Company has necessarily been superficial, but it is hoped that further light will be shed on

[1] Guildhall MS 7090/4.   [2] *Ibid.*, 19 Apr. 1631, 21 Feb. 1639.
[3] A very comprehensive list of by-laws was enrolled in 1702 (Guildhall MS 7116).
[4] Guildhall MSS 7090/3–5, *passim*. An example of equal voting rights, on the question of a clause in a petition to Parliament, is given in Welch, ii, 169.

these topics by the more detailed discussions of the particular branches of policy adopted by pewterers' gilds which will now be undertaken.

The achievement of uniformly high standards of production was invariably the ambition of craft gilds, and for pewterers' gilds it remained perhaps the foremost objective throughout their history. As we have seen, the first article in the earliest London ordinances laid down the composition of the alloys that were to be used in the manufacture of various types of pewterware, and similar mandatory specifications also held premier position in the ordinances of York, Bristol and Coventry pewterers, and indeed of pewterers' gilds throughout Europe.[1] In addition to regulations concerning alloys, high standards of workmanship were enforced. The acquisition of the requisite skills was facilitated from an early date by compulsory apprenticeship, and many detailed rules sought to ensure that these skills were practised. But the control of the quality of workmanship and metal was only part of the regulation of production, and uniformity in the size and style of wares was also stipulated. Consequently specifications of the weight, size, and shape of a wide range of articles made of pewter are frequently encountered in craft records, and were an essential prerequisite of the common policy of price fixing. The regulation of all aspects of the quality and type of production was pursued relentlessly throughout the medieval and early modern eras, and was felt to be indispensable to the proper conduct of the industry; as late as 1683 Wigan pewterers were seeking a royal charter to enable them to protect local pewter output more effectively 'from being abused by that which is too much allayd, ill tempered, or not truely wrought'.[2] Furthermore, a number of other common regulations, such as those relating to apprenticeship, night work, the marking of wares with the maker's touch, and, of course, the right of search, were in whole or in part designed to facilitate conformity to standards.

The motives which lay behind policies such as these have been the subject of considerable controversy amongst gild historians. Opinions range from an almost complete acceptance of even the

---
[1] *Memorials of London Life*, pp. 241–4; *York Memorandum Book* i, 211–13; *Little Red Book of Bristol*, ii, 184–5; *Coventry Leet Book*, ii, 554; for continental standards see Massé, *Pewter Plate*, pp. 152–4; Bell, *Old Pewter*, p. 13.
[2] Shelley, *Wigan and Liverpool Pewterers*, p. 10.

most florid professions of good faith and concern for consumer interests contained in the preambles to gild enactments, to a thoroughgoing disbelief that craftsmen were guided by any motives other than blind self-seeking and the exploitation of the consumer. As is usually the case in such controversies neither extreme is tenable, indeed it is as well to be reminded that some general good often comes from even the most blatantly selfish policies. Moreover, the motives which fostered the control of standards of production were extremely complex, and all the results of such policies were not clearly discerned even by their proponents.

Professions of concern for the 'common profit' and the need to rectify abuses in the public interest were often indispensable aids to the achievement of gild status and, *a fortiori*, incorporated status (the preamble to the ordinances of 1348 quoted above is an excellent example of a universal phenomenon). Yet it would be too cynical to dismiss all such professions of concern as pure public relations propaganda. From the records of the London Pewterers, for example, it is possible to discern that an awareness of the benefits stemming from a reputation for high quality often went hand in hand with a genuine pride in workmanship.

One of the most crucial issues, as far as the consumer was concerned, was whether prices generally took account of variations in quality, or whether widespread frauds were perpetrated. The detection of false alloys required considerable skill, and it was relatively easy to defraud the consumer by adding too much cheap lead to too little dear tin, with the result that the finished product, being much softer than if made of the correct alloy, would quickly lose shape and wear out. Before 1700 the price of tin was usually between five and seven times greater than that of lead, so the advantages accruing to the deceitful pewterer were substantial.[1] On the other hand it is difficult to avoid the conclusion that if gild policies striving for first class pewterware at high prices had been successfully enforced throughout the country, the poorer consumer would have been driven from the market.

It would, of course, be ingenuous to suggest that the considerable attention devoted by gilds to the enforcement of standards was solely, or even predominantly, motivated by altruism. On the contrary, a wide range of benefits accrued to the practitioners.

[1] Rogers, i, 605; iv, 488; v, 504.

In the first place a well-earned reputation for quality was of inestimable value to the members of a gild, especially when goods were sold far distant from the point of manufacture and in an age when frauds were common. The excellence of London pewter, for example, which from the fourteenth century was renowned throughout Europe, enabled distant markets to be penetrated in the face of formidable competition and difficult trading conditions. To a remote consumer or retailer, for whom redress against an individual manufacturer was likely to prove an extremely difficult task, the knowledge that the gild to which he belonged was energetically enforcing standards might well prove an incentive to purchase. In the second place, it was in the spirit of the gild system that competition between members should be kept at a minimum, and if uniformly high standards could be exacted from all and price competition could be eliminated, then the ultimate goal of homogeneous products at uniform prices might well be attainable. In the third place, the stamping out of both price and quality competition within the gild's own town, in which an effective monopoly of the production of pewter for sale might be held, would result in enhanced profits by ensuring that the market for expensive first-rate pewter was not spoiled by the presence of cheap second-rate pewter. In the fourth place, the higher the standards applied by the skilled workers of the gild, the less likely it was that country pewterers could match them, and therefore the easier it would be for their products to be identified and confiscated when searches were conducted. In the fifth place, high standards of manufacture meant that members would be less likely to suffer losses through the purchase or exchange of substandard scrap pewter. A succession of Acts of Parliament made it illegal for pewterware of less than the London standard to be offered for sale, and gave the London Company the authority to undertake searches throughout the realm, with the assistance of civic and county officials.

There was a distinct correspondence between the alloys adopted by European pewterers' gilds and, as we have seen, those of London became the standard for the whole of England. The alloys specified in the London ordinances of 1348 were undoubtedly based on traditional mixtures, and bore a close resemblance to those stipulated in early thirteenth-century Paris.[1]

[1] Massé, *Pewter Collector*, p. 31.

A fundamental distinction, of enduring significance, was made between fine pewter, which was to be used primarily in the manufacture of flatware or sadware such as dishes, plates, porringers and saucers, consisting of pure tin tempered with as much copper 'as of its own nature, it will take', and lay pewter, which was to be used for holloware such as pots, cruets, and candlesticks, consisting of tin and lead alloyed 'in reasonable proportions' but generally not less than 4 : 1.[1] Individual pewterers were doubtless permitted to adopt slight variations of these mixtures, and the Company itself modified its standards from time to time, but on the whole there was relatively little change before the eighteenth century. Among the most important advances in formulae were the addition of bismuth and later antimony to tin to make fine pewter, and the adoption in the sixteenth century of a third standard for 'trifling ware'—tavern pots, candle moulds, stills, toys, buttons and such like. It was, of course, essential that precise rules were also adopted as to which articles should be made of fine, lay or trifling pewter.[2] Standards were also laid down for the quality of solder used in the manufacture of pewterware. Since much of the metal used by pewterers was derived from scrap pewter, sometimes no doubt of dubious quality, considerable skill was required in the mixing of true alloys, and it is probable that many false alloys were the result of negligence rather than deceit.

In order to enforce these standards effectively it was necessary first to be able to conduct an accurate test of the quality of alloys, and second to discover who had produced them. The first criterion was achieved by a variety of methods, the most accurate being assaying by the weight, while the second was achieved by the compulsory marking of wares. With practice it is possible to acquire the skill with which to make a number of rudimentary tests of the quality of pewter which do not involve melting. Colour and texture often provide a guide to the amount of lead and, as the Company laid down the weights of most articles,

[1] It is clear that the composition of lay metal was not yet fixed: when the ordinances of 1348 were enrolled in City records 22 lb of lead to 112 lb of tin were specified, when the craft copied those ordinances into its own records, in the late fifteenth century, 26 lb of lead to 112 lb of tin were specified and, as we have seen (p. 147 above), the officers of the craft accusing John de Hiltone in 1350 of making substandard holloware claimed that no more than 16 lb of lead ought to be added to 112 lb of tin.
[2] These technical matters are dealt with in more detail in Chapter 5 below.

substandard alloys could be detected by weighing suspected pieces against the standard. Additional tests could be made by scraping the metal with a knife, the greater the lead content the deeper the cut and the softer the sound emitted, or touching it with a hot soldering bit, the quality being ascertained by the appearance of the streak produced by the bit.[1] All these crude methods, and no doubt others, were used to distinguish possible frauds from true pieces, but as prosecutions with fines and forfeiture often followed from the detection of substandard pewter, final judgment had to rest on a more exact assay. This was provided by taking a sample of the suspect pewter and comparing its weight with that of a standard piece of pure tin or pewter of the same size. Tin being lighter than lead, the heavier the sample the worse the alloy. The precise method used was to take a small mould, similar to that used for casting lead shot, and cast balls of both the standard and suspect pewter in it;[2] to this end pieces of pure tin, and standard fine and lay metal were kept at the hall. Thus we can understand the frequent entries in the court minute books which refer to metal being so many grains worse (i.e. heavier) than assay. Sadly, craft records contain few mentions of the precise alloys that were adopted as standards. Ordinances, with the exception of those of 1348, were invariably vague on this point, perhaps deliberately so in order to allow amendments to be adopted as the course of trade and the price of tin dictated; they contain instead such phrases as 'truly and substantially mixed ware' or, in the case of some provincial gilds, merely a reference to the assay of London.

Fortunately, London Company records contain a number of detailed lists of the standard weights and sizes of articles commonly made of pewter. The earliest list, which relates only to sadware, was appended to the ordinances of 1439 because 'divers artificers of the craft of peautrers hidir unto have do to be forged and made vessel weinge lighter or hevier than thei out to wey, therefore that in every sorte of vessels to be made a comen certainte shalbe had in tyme comynge thece quantitees of weghtes ben limited and assigned in alle assises of the vessel undirstond undirwriten'. In this list the precise weights of chargers, platters, dishes, saucers, 'Galey' dishes and saucers, and square pots and salts were

---

[1] See, for example, Massé, *Pewter Plate*, pp. 26–8, and *Pewter Collector*, pp. 51–4.
[2] For a photograph of an assay tool used by the Company and dated 1728 see below pl. 24.

specified, which ranged downwards from seven pounds for the largest charger to $5\frac{1}{4}$ ounces for the smallest saucer.[1] That Company control in this area was considerably extended as time passed is exemplified by the astonishingly comprehensive list of over 100 separate types of 'trifles' drawn up in 1613, ranging from 'Great duble bells with peper boxes and baules, the halfe dozen to weighe 9 lb' through salts, beakers, bowls, cupps, candelsticks, spirit pots, ewers, saucers, tankard pots, porringers and cruets, to stool-pans of various sizes from $5\frac{1}{2}$ lb to 3 lb each.[2] These specifications, it must be stressed, were not merely for guidance, they were mandatory, and it was ordered that 'everie brother of this Companie useinge to worke the lyke wates before rectyted, shall make noe other for sale'. Nor had the degree of restriction the Company attempted to impose lessened by the late seventeenth century, for in 1674 the most comprehensive list yet of sadware and holloware specifications was proclaimed containing, *inter alia*, fifteen sizes of dishes, six sizes of Guinea basins, four types of candlesticks and five types of porringers;[3] it is clear, however, that by this time the power of enforcement was waning.

Strict supervision was exercised over the frequent changes in fashion and the ever widening range of articles produced by pewterers, and rules were made to cover most eventualities. We find, for example, that in 1572 the manufacture of 'pettie sawcers' was forbidden and that none weighing less than 4 lb a dozen were permitted.[4] The growing use of commodes induced the Company to rule that no 'close stole pans' should be made of less than 5 lb weight,[5] and we learn that in 1591 two such pans were kept in the hall 'for samples of workmanship'.[6] The Company's eagerness to keep up to date is illustrated by the accusation made in 1704 that William Hur had made watches of 'bad Mettle'.[7] It is clear, however, that in this instance it was uncertain what constituted good metal, for although Hur admitted that the watch-case should be fine, he claimed, successfully it seems, that the 'Dyall Plate could not be made so well of any other Mettle' than '19 grains worse than Lay'. In the following year it was ordered that 'all Bedd Pann Handles shall be made of Plate Mettle', and that the pans should be assembled with true solder.[8]

[1] Guildhall MS 7114, ff. 31–2.
[2] Guildhall MS 7090/4, 27 Feb.
[3] Guildhall MS 7090/6, 14 Apr.
[4] Welch, i, 247.
[5] Guildhall MS 7090/2, 17 Mar. 1581.
[6] Guildhall MS 7086/3.
[7] Guildhall MS 7090/8, 22 June.
[8] Guildhall MS 7090/8, 22 Mar.

Regulation was also extended to the workmanship of pewterware, thereby completing the control of all aspects of the quality of production. Consequently we find that from the commencement of records penalties were imposed for bad workmanship, and rules were enforced specifying the classes of ware that ought to be beaten as well as turned, those that should be burnished, the parts that could be soldered on and those that had to be cast on, and so forth. The meticulous scrutiny of journeymen wishing to open workshops and start up their own business included an examination of their skills in the pewterers' craft. In York a prospective master had to 'worke his ablinge ware in one of the Searchers shoppes, before he shall sett up or be received into the Company as heretofore custom hath been',[1] and in London he had to 'bringe in a sample of his worke and so to be sene, vewed, and adjudged by the master, wardens and assystaunce'.[2]

In provincial cities and towns offenders against these and similar by-laws would normally be brought by the officials of the gild before civic courts, but in London the Pewterers' Company possessed the right to hold its own courts from the date of its incorporation. Offences relating to the quality of production were brought to the attention of gild officials in a variety of ways, the most important of which was probably the periodic inspections or searches undertaken by the officials themselves or their deputies, but complaints made by customers, frequently fellow pewterers purchasing stock for their shops or for sale outside the city, were also common. Officials were invariably under strict instructions to administer the ordinances of the gild stringently and without favour, and many successful cases were brought against prominent members of the London Company including members of the Court of Assistants and even Pastmasters and Wardens.[3] Punishments were clearly dependent on a multitude of factors including the seriousness of the offence, the record of

[1] University of York Library, MS E.54.
[2] Welch, i, 201. This rule was reiterated in 1620 when it was ordered that no one should set up as an independent workman before submitting 'a proofe pece of his owne makinge' (Guildhall MS 7090/4, 6 Mar.).
[3] Peter Broklesbury, Warden in 1616/17 and Master in 1628/9, was ordered to have only one touch to mark his wares in 1618 (Welch, ii, 75); Henry Deuxell, a prominent member of the Assistants was fined £3 in 1601 for warning his chapmen at Wigan of a coming search, and was expelled from the Assistants and livery in 1629 (Welch, ii, 32, 86); and in 1618 Ralph Powell, Warden in 1612/13, was fined £10 for warning a pewterer of the coming of the Company searchers (Welch, ii, 75). A case brought against John Catcher a former Master is discussed below.

the offender, and the harshness of the court. The ultimate sanctions of expulsion and imprisonment were rarely resorted to, and even when imposed were invariably of short duration. Fines and the confiscation of substandard goods were the usual penalties, although the courts had a wide range of alternative measures at their disposal, to compel obedience. The following examples are drawn from the voluminous minutes which were kept of the London Company's court proceedings, which stretch in almost unbroken sequence from the mid-sixteenth century. It would be unwise to draw firm conclusions from isolated cases, and the reasons which lay behind the wide variations in punishment inflicted upon the offenders in the examples below are not always easily discernible.

Thus, Thomas Norfolke was fined 40s in 1518 for making holloware worse than the lay metal standard,[1] whereas in 1556 George Hudson was sent to prison for an apparently similar offence, and on his release had to provide sureties to his future good conduct guarantee to rectify any faults in his wares found in the hands of Company members, and suffer relegation to journeyman status if he offended again.[2] Fines were frequently heavy, and we find that in 1606 Edward Hewtrell was fined £4 for making lay metal 12 grains worse than assay,[3] and in 1612 Edward Benson was fined no less than £30 when a large quantity of substandard lay and fine was found in his house, the false metal was also forfeited.[4] In 1613 William Lobb was sent to the Compter for making beer bowls 3 grains worse than fine in the body and no less than 30 grains worse than fine in the foot.[5] Prosecution was not always so simple a matter, however, since many leading dealers frequently put out unfashioned pewter to be worked up into wares by lesser masters, while others produced items to order for fellow pewterers who then retailed them. An interesting example of the former practice appeared before the court of 19 October 1599 when John Catcher, a Pastmaster and Warden, was found guilty and fined £6.13s4d for casting approximately fifty 4 lb pewter platters which he gave to workmen to be wrought into basins for ewers; the workmen suspecting them of being substandard refused to work them and the matter subse-

---

[1] Guildhall MS 7086/1.
[2] Guildhall MS 7090/1, 17 Jan.
[3] Guildhall MS 7086/3.
[4] Guildhall MS 7090/4, 30 Apr.
[5] Guildhall MS 7090/4, 11 Mar.

quently came to the notice of the Master and Wardens.[1] In order to circumvent the complications caused by subcontracting and by sales between pewterers, it was ordered in 1618 that when sub-standard lay metal was found 'all the losse of the wares shalbe borne by the party and parties wher the same wares shalbe taken'.[2]

The administration of precise standards for individual types of pewterware can also be seen from court proceedings. Thus, in 1557 it was recorded: 'Be yt Remembered that all manner of Lymbeckes (alembics) is made of ffyne and the burnyng ys of leye and the knop of the stills is fyllyd with lead'. In the same year Lord Burgaveny secured through the court a replacement for a faulty still,[3] and in 1613 William Dixson, having sold a still of base metal weighing $13\frac{1}{4}$ lb to the Earl of Worcester, was ordered to make a new one weighing $3\frac{1}{4}$ lb more and also pay 18s towards its workmanship.[4] It is interesting to note that in 1673 Jonathan Ingles was fined 5s for making square candlesticks of poor quality 'considering that in regard of the great price which is paid for workmanship of that sort of ware, they used and ought to be made as good as Plate mettle', and that a few months later the court ruled that 'all planished ware and square-work which is wrought by the hand and all round Fyne Chamber-potts and new ffash-ioned spoones shall henceforward be made of good ffyne plate mettle'.[5]

The hammering of most forms of sadware was an essential, though time consuming, process to ensure maximum strength and durability, and pewterers' gilds were most careful to insist that it should be performed at all times.[6] The 1457 ordinances of the Bristol pewterers, for example, state that 'all maner of such vessell that ought to be bete aftur the reule of the craft of old tyme used, that hit have his sufficient beting, and nott to be sold otherwise upon payn of 20s'.[7] In the course of time, however, exceptions came to be made, as the following case illustrates: in 1674 Daniell Mason, on being called before the Company court for 'makeing Plates unbeaten in the Pitch or booge, aleadged that they was

---

[1] Guildhall MS 7090/3, 19 Oct.
[2] Guildhall MS 7090/4, 30 Mar.
[3] Guildhall MS 7090/1, 14 May, 10 Dec.
[4] Guildhall MS 7090/4, 19 Aug.
[5] Guildhall MS 7090/7, 21 June, 13 Dec.
[6] The marks of the hammer were frequently deliberately not obliterated so that it was evident this process had been performed.
[7] *Little Red Book of Bristol*, ii, 184.

Spanish Plates and they are usually soe alowed'. His plea was not accepted because he had struck a 'fillett' upon them, and it was felt by the court 'that under such pretences they might be sold for new fashioned Plates by retaile, which requires much more and better workmanship, and so the strikeing of the ffillett would be but a Couler of Cheat'; Mason was therefore fined 20s.[1] A further example of the determination of the Company to retain control of the trade, as well as valuable information on techniques and exports, is furnished by the case of John Elderton, who on 20 March 1699 presented to the Court of Assistants 'a dozen of Two sorts of Trencher Plates unbeat in the Pitch of which sort he designed to send a quantity of to Russia if the Court please to approve thereof'; after several debates and careful measuring and weighing it was 'agreed by vote that the said Plates may be sent to Russia tho unbeat in the Booge'. A complaint by two sadware men 'of a decay of theire work of Sadware by sending Plates to Russia and Spain unbeat in the Pitch', was not accepted. But the matter was not allowed to rest there and later the same day at a general court a 'generall complaint against Mr Eldertons Plates' was made and Elderton dutifully 'promised to desist from sending the Plates debated on this day in the Court of Assistants notwithstanding any order or leave for the same'.[2]

In order that offenders against the standards imposed by the gilds might readily be identified it was essential that all wares carried the personal mark of their maker. The marking of wares by reputable producers probably became common in the fourteenth century, but it was not made compulsory for all until the sixteenth. The Act of 1504, which sought to control the purchase and sale of pewter by hawkers, contained the earliest surviving regulations on marks, yet its provisions were more limited in scope than many previous historians of pewter have assumed, and specified only that makers of holloware 'that is to say salts and pots made of pewter called lay metal . . . shall mark the same wares with several marks of their own with the intent that the makers of such wares shall avowe the same wares'.[3] The limitation of compulsory marking to holloware is probably connected with the necessity for liquid measures to be made of true capacity in

---

[1] Guildhall MS 7090/6, 27 May. A fillett was probably a rim with a thin beading round the edge on the underside (Michaelis, *Antique Pewter*, p. 18).
[2] Guildhall MS 7090/8, 20 Mar.   [3] 19 Henry VII, c. 6.

order to combat fraudulent retailers of wine and ale. The London ordinances of 1522, however, extended the requirement to 'eny maner vessell or other stuff of pewter' made by Company members,[1] and in 1527 we have the earliest record of fines for producing unmarked wares.[2] A systematic record of the touches of freemen of the Company was obviously kept in a very similar form to the touchplates of later centuries, for in an inventory of goods in Pewterers' Hall in 1550 we find mention of 'a Table of Pewter with every mans Marke therein'.[3] The ordinances of York pewterers, collected together in 1602, also specified that every master should have his own mark and should put it upon every vessel he produced, and it is likely that by this time almost all provincial associations of pewterers were enforcing similar rules.[4]

Nevertheless it was not until 1639, after sustained pressure from the London Pewterers, that the production of unmarked pewterware anywhere in the realm was made illegal.[5] But this tardy prohibition appears to have had little effect, and the large number of unmarked pieces that have survived into our own age suggests that the law was frequently evaded, even by the producers of first class holloware.[6]

One of the severest penalties which could be inflicted by gilds on the producers of substandard pewter was the loss of the right to strike a touch, or its compulsory substitution by a double 'F' to denote falsity; as in the following case which is quoted in full because of the interesting light it throws upon so many matters:

> At this Court (15 July 1596) hemfry weetwood havyng byne found in conferacy with thomas cowes to make eare dyshes, beakers and godderdes of gobbetes of false metall iiij graynes worse then laye, the which wares have byne sold unto the countery not only unto the dyscredyt of us all workemen in London but also agreat wronge and lose unto those which shall herafter melt those agayne, tuchynge forfaytur of those dyshes we leve them to the quene and the taker and humfrey weetwood and thomas cowes to make

[1] Guildhall MS 7114.   [2] Guildhall MS 7086/1.
[3] Welch, i, 165. The oldest surviving touchplate dates from 1667–68.
[4] Univ. of York Library, MS E.54. For compulsory marking in Scotland, for example, see H. Lumsden and P. H. Aitken, *History of the Hammermen of Glasgow* (Paisley, 1912), p. 140; Wood, pp. 31, 75, 150–1.
[5] Welch, ii, 98–9; Guildhall MS 7090/4, 19 Jul.
[6] Michaelis, *Antique Pewter*, pp. 102–3.

satysfaction unto the pewterers in the countery which bought them of eather of them, And farther they being ponyshed by Imprysonment, we farther order that humfrey weetwood shall submyt hyme selfe unto all the company and confese his fawlt and to desyer to thynke of hyme and to accept of hyme agayne as abrother of the company, which he dyd in the presence of the whole company, being farther Inyoyned to brynge in his tuch and that for knolege herafter of his falshood he shall have for his tuch a duble ff, and also that he shall put in shurtes (sureties) for his true and honest dealynge in his trad.[1]

No doubt Weetwood was forced to give up independent production, and work instead as a subcontractor or even as a journeyman. A similar case occurred in 1557 and concerned Robert West, who was imprisoned and banished from the Company for a short while after making pots of false measure; on his return the Master and Wardens devised a new mark for him consisting of 'W.F.', but 'he denyed yt and wold not have yt'.[2]

As we have seen in previous chapters the manufacture of measures and pots for use in hostelries and ale-houses was a flourishing branch of the pewterer's trade. It was also one in which honesty was of prime importance, and in which the authority of pewterers' gilds was frequently superseded by that of civic and state authorities anxious that all measures should be of full capacity. Consequently the control exercised over this branch of the trade was the most stringent of all and the punishments for the casting of deceitful measures were amongst the most severe to be inflicted upon pewterers. Thus in 1557 it was ordered by the London Court of Assistants:

> That if any man of the felowship do from hensforthe make or cause to be made prevely or aperte (openly) any measure pottes comonly called taverne pottes of any lease measure then by the standard apoynted for the same pottes that then the person so making such pottes lesse than measure shall paye for making defalt thereof to the crafts boxe Tenne pounds, And if the person so making Defalt be not able to paye the sayd fyne of xli then the master, wardens and assystaunce shall so Sue the same person that he shall stand

[1] Guildhall MS 7090/3.   [2] Guildhall MS 7090/1, 14 June, 21 Oct.

on the pillarye thre lawfull market dayes according to the order of the Cytie for suche ofenders without any favor therein to be shewed.[1]

That this was not an empty threat is proven by the treatment meted out to Robert West later in the year. It is also significant that the standard weights of tavern pots and measures were promulgated more frequently than those of other wares, and that even their shape was sometimes specified. In 1563, for example, City authorities decreed that 'no pewterer from hensforthe make eny other barred pottes of pewter but only thirdendales and half thirdendales',[2] and in 1575 Roger Hawksford was forbidden by the Court of Assistants to make any more of his special wine pots 'for that by their greate breadethe in the mouthe, and shortenes throughoute, there appearethe a manifeste deceite in measure to all other qweenes maiesties subiectes receyving wyne'.[3]

Thus it is evident that determined efforts were made to achieve high and uniform standards of production in the major centres of pewter manufacture throughout much of the medieval and early modern eras, yet the benefits accruing to gild members from the successful prosecution of these policies in their own towns could be severely diminished if large quantities of cheap substandard wares were easily obtainable elsewhere in the country. Due to persistent effective lobbying by the major pewterers' gilds an extremely comprehensive system of restraints was imposed upon country producers by a succession of royal charters and parliamentary statutes.[4] In effect, from the early sixteenth century it was illegal for any pewter not up to the London standard to be produced for sale anywhere in the realm, or for pewter to be sold or bought on a door-to-door basis. Nevertheless, although these measures were given the force of law by Parliament, they were not an integral part of state policy and, as a result, their enforcement was left primarily in the hands of interested parties.[5]

[1] Guildhall MS 7090/1, 30 Jan.   [2] Welch, i, 234.
[3] Guildhall MS 7090/2, 5 Aug.
[4] For example, it is clear from the preamble that the pewterers and braziers of London and York had combined to procure the Act of 1504 (19 Henry VII, c. 6).
[5] The problem of enforcement in general is still largely unresolved, even with respect to statutes central to government policy (Elton, pp. 162–6).

By virtue of their charter the jurisdiction of the London Pewterers over standards of production was extended throughout the realm. In practice, at least in the sixteenth century, the Company relied on the major provincial gilds to enforce standards within their respective towns, and was therefore free to concentrate its energies largely upon non-gild producers and rural fairs and markets. Even so the task of exercising a strict oversight was found to be impracticable in terms of the time and money that it would have consumed. In the years immediately following incorporation many members expended much energy in conducting a series of intensive searches in various parts of the country, but it soon proved impossible to maintain this level of activity without serious harm to members' own businesses and the efficiency with which other Company affairs were administered.[1] A more effective use of the limited resources that could be devoted to country searches had to be devised.

The granting of associate membership to provincial pewterers in the hope that they would more readily conform to Company rules was partially successful, but the initial impetus was soon lost and from the mid-sixteenth century 'country' freemen were mostly located in the suburbs of the capital.[2] Informers played an important part in law enforcement in Tudor and early Stuart times—indeed they have been called 'the chief instrument for the enforcement of economic legislation'—and as statutes relating to pewter positively encouraged private initiative by offering as a reward half the fines imposed on offenders and half the wares that were confiscated, it is likely that informers had some deterrent effect.[3] But of greater significance was the delegation of the Company's powers of search, both by the action of the Company itself and by statute. In 1556–57, for example, five prominent freemen of the Company were given the right to 'Searche through-

---

[1] Above, pp. 69, 73-4.
[2] In contrast to the late fifteenth and early sixteenth centuries when provincial pewterers were actively recruited, by the 1550s the onus appears to have been on non-Londoners to apply for membership (see, for example, the admission of a Newcastle pewterer in 1567: Guildhall MS 7090/2, 18 June). By the early eighteenth century an inquiry revealed that it had long been the invariable practice to grant freedom only to persons who had served an apprenticeship in London (Guildhall MS 7090/9, 21 Mar. 1723).
[3] For the role of the informer see M. W. Beresford, 'The common informer, the penal statutes, and economic regulation', *Economic History Review*, new ser., x (1957); M. G. Davies, *The Enforcement of English Apprenticeship 1563–1642: A Study in Applied Mercantilism* (Cambridge, Mass. 1956), I.

out all this Realme of Englande (London and gravisende and tenne mylles about London only except)' on the understanding that they 'paye Clerelye to the hall the Sum of Twelve pounds' and 'one half of the wrytting and sealing of another Reading patent'.[1] In 1567 the practice was extended and a licence was given without charge to 'William marshall, Robert hewet and John Thomas of madystone pewterers for the Execucons and disabolishing all hawkers for any manner of mettall within kent and Sussex and elles wheare as they shall have occasion' on the understanding 'that they be bounde unto the companye in one hundrethe poundes that they shall not doo anything contrary to the lawes and Statutes of this Realme, nor doo any other act whereby it might be hurtfull unto the Companye',[2] and in 1570 a similar agreement was reached with Humphrey Francis an Abingdon pewterer who undertook to 'dele with Hawkers according to the lawes of this realme' in Berkshire, Oxfordshire, Wiltshire and Gloucestershire.[3]

One should not expect Tudor and Stuart statute law to follow a completely coherent policy, nor to run absolutely parallel with common law, and it therefore comes as little surprise to learn that the Act of 1504 contradicted the charter of 1474 without consciously amending it, by urging civic authorities and justices of the peace to appoint local searchers for substandard pewter, without reference to the London Company. Doubtless any assistance in the suppression of hawkers and the manufacturers of substandard pewter was welcomed, and in subsequent statutes the Company appeared willing to sacrifice its autonomy in favour of effective enforcement. Much local research will have to be undertaken before it is known whether independent enforcement was attempted on a significant scale outside the large towns, but evidence from late seventeenth-century Warwickshire suggests that at this date there was considerable confusion among justices as to their authority in this matter. Consequently we find that in September 1664 'Upon perusal of several statutes and Acts of Parliament made in the several reigns of king Henry the seventh and king Henry the eighth' the justices of the peace of Warwickshire granted a licence to John Scruby and William Brookes 'to enter into and make search in the day-time in the house, shop,

---

[1] Guildhall MSS 7090/1, 18 Sept. 1556; 7086/2, 1556–7.
[2] Guildhall MS 7090/2, 18 June.   [3] Guildhall MS 7090/2, 14 July.

cellar, warehouse or other places of or belonging to any pewterer or brazier inhabiting any borough, town or village within the said county of Warwick', saving only those cities and towns which had their own searchers; only to revoke it shortly afterwards. A similar licence was, however, granted to six other pewterers a year later.[1] We also learn that in 1636 Sir Selwyne Parker and others petitioned the king for the right to search for substandard pewter, and early in 1637 the Company was asked to concur; but nothing appears to have come of the project.[2]

The Company saw its powers of search as an essential instrument of policy and continued to undertake regular excursions into the country until the eighteenth century. Indeed, even in the later seventeenth century, far from viewing the country search as the tiresome burden it had become to many other livery companies, the London Pewterers persistently and successfully lobbied Parliament for an extension of its powers over the provincial trade. In 1639, for example, a petition was made to Parliament for the 'power and Authoretie to search and sease all falce mettle and wares in Ireland and Scotland, according as in England is Provided by Statute',[3] and as late as 1674 a further charter was granted which provided a few additional measures to facilitate searches.[4]

Company records contain a multitude of references to the frequent country searches conducted from 1474 onwards, but the pride of place must be given to three books of country searches covering the years 1635-41, 1669-83, and 1689-91.[5] From these books it is possible to glean precise details of the towns that were visited, the shops that were entered, the wares that were analysed, and frequently also the names of the makers. It would appear that very serious attempts were being made by the Company at this time to enforce standards in many parts of England. To this end between 1635 and 1641 two or even three parties of searchers were sent out from London each year to conduct substantial and doubtless arduous searches, usually lasting at

---

[1] For example, the 1534 Act, of which the London Pewterers were the prime movers, contained much encouragement for local initiative in the searching for substandard pewterware (25 Henry VIII, c. 9). [2] Guildhall MS 7090/4, 16 Mar.
[3] Guildhall MS 7090/4, 12 Dec. This privilege was not granted, but a new charter granted in March 1639 had given the Company the right of search in England over all workmen in the pewter trade, even if they belonged to other misteries (Welch, ii, 99). [4] This charter cost the Company £150 (Welch, ii, 149).
[5] Guildhall MSS 7105, 7105/1, 7106.

least a month and sometimes far longer. Later in the century it was usual to conduct only one search each year, but this was generally ambitious in scope and frequently involved the inspection of more than fifty pewterers' shops and sometimes almost a hundred. The financial success of these searches is attested by a regular surplus of income over expenditure, a feat achieved only rarely by other London livery companies.[1] The searches were well organised and appear to have been planned according to information received by the Company concerning regions where standards of production were low. But searchers were also allowed to exercise their discretion and to alter plans as circumstances demanded, and it is interesting to find that the names of the makers of substandard wares which were found in a number of shops or towns were noted, and a detour subsequently made in order to fine them 'for badware found in several places'.

The search books have already been used in the previous chapter to throw light on the numbers and distribution of provincial pewterers, and are analysed in the next chapter for information on the distribution and marketing of pewter, but it will be profitable at this point to look more closely at two particular searches in order to reinforce impressions of their scale at this time. The searches of 1636 provide good examples as they are typical of their period, both in respect of duration and itinerary. On 6 May Robert Butcher, Warden, led a party consisting of Thomas Butcher, William Hatfield and Edward Gibbons northwards to Cambridge. From Cambridge the searchers proceeded in a broad north-westward sweep through Northampton, Leicester, Coventry, Lichfield and Derby, with Ashbourne the most northerly town visited. The homeward itinerary included Worcester, Gloucester, Bristol, Bath, Devizes, Salisbury and Blandford Forum, the last search being conducted in Winchester on 1 June. In all twenty-nine towns were visited and fifty separate pewterers' premises inspected. On 25 July, Thomas Butcher, William Hatfield and Edward Gibbons set off again, this time westwards to conduct searches at Reading, Marlborough, Bristol, Exeter, Bridgwater, Gloucester, Worcester, Oxford, Abingdon and Witney. They returned to London

[1] Notes of expenses and receipts from searches are contained in the audit accounts; see also J. R. Kellett, 'The breakdown of gild and corporation control over the handicraft and retail trade in London', *Economic History Review*, 2nd ser., x (1958), 386–7.

on 11 August having visited fourteen towns and the fairs of Tan Hill (Wilts), Trowbridge and Exeter, and having inspected the wares of over forty pewterers.[1]

It is evident that the Company was no longer relying on local gilds to enforce standards; on the contrary, whereas in the later fifteenth and early sixteenth centuries the independence of the local jurisdiction of the major provincial gilds had been scrupulously observed by the Company, in the seventeenth century the major centres of manufacture were subjected to special attention by London searchers.[2] Bristol, for example, was visited five times between May 1636 and September 1638 and fifty individual searches of pewterers' wares were carried out in the city.

Between 1635 and 1647, although occasionally penetrating as far west as Cornwall, London searchers went no further north than Derbyshire and appeared to have deliberately avoided the important manufacturing centre of Walsall. The most northerly search of which we have record is that of 10 April to 11 May 1676, which proceeded via Lincolnshire to Doncaster, Pontefract, Tadcaster, York, Northallerton, Newcastle and Durham, before returning to London via Wigan, Walsall, Birmingham, Warwick, Banbury, Aylesbury, and Watford.[3] The complaint of the Wigan pewterers in 1683 that local production was suffering from a lack of supervision on the part of the London Pewterers 'who yett by reason of their remoteness from these Northerne parts, and the great trouble and charge in travelling soe farr, come seldome on this account, and then are in too much hast to rectifye those abuses',[4] is hard to reconcile with the note appended to the London Company's Wigan search of 1676 which recorded 'that the towne of Waggen haveinge advice of the Master and Wardens being at York and other places Northward and of their being at Kendall and Blackbourn faire had removed the greatest part of their goods'.

Despite the considerable endeavours of the London Pewterers, however, it is difficult to avoid the conclusion that the seventeenth-century searches were little more than a periodic inconvenience to provincial pewterers and retailers of pewterware.

[1] Guildhall MS 7105/1.
[2] There is widespread evidence to suggest that provincial gilds in general were not rigorously enforcing their rights of search (Fisher, 'Industrial Gilds', pp. 57-8).
[3] Guildhall MS 7105.
[4] Shelley, Wigan and Liverpool Pewterers, p. 10.

Sometimes the fines were heavy—Richard Tonges of Warwick, for example, was fined 58*s* in 1640—and the breaking of faulty wares was no doubt irksome, but in the face of a general decline in the willingness or ability of provincial gilds to enforce standards as the seventeenth century progressed it is likely that the successes of the London Pewterers were small in scale and temporary in duration.

Important though they were regulations concerning standards of alloys and workmanship comprised only part of an extensive and exhaustive system of controls exercised over the sale of pewter. Naturally most of the regulations relating to the sale of pewter were designed to further the gild philosophy of mutual cooperation and the limitation of competition between members, and to achieve a collective monopoly with the power to discriminate against outsiders, be they consumers or producers. Consequently we find, *inter alia*, gild rules stipulating selling prices, the prohibition of competition for customers, and the forbidding of the sale of pewter to persons who planned to resell it. Of these rules those relating to prices were of the most consequence, being second only to the maintenance of standards of production.

From the fifteenth century to the eighteenth the London Pewterers' Company prescribed uniform prices for both the new pewterware sold by its members and the old pewterware that was bought or accepted in part-exchange. In this it may well have been acting untypically, and it was certainly, for the most part, acting illegally. It is generally assumed that attempts by gilds to manipulate the prices of their products were intermittent and usually unsuccessful: first, because competition from outsiders invariably thwarted attempts to gain monopoly power, and second, because the attitude of both civic and national governments to price manipulation was implacably hostile.[1] Whereas before the later sixteenth century most gild policies were regarded as acceptable, if not always commendable, price-fixing was widely interpreted as too blatant an exploitation of the consumer, and from as early as the turn of the thirteenth century the interests of the community were defended by the fining and imprisonment of ringleaders.[2] The attitude of civic authorities was supported by Acts of

[1] This is the general conclusion reached by both S. Kramer (*The English Craft Gilds and the Government*, New York, 1968, p. 99 ff.) and S. L. Thrupp (*Cambridge Economic History of Europe*, iii, 246 ff.). [2] Lipson, *Economic History*, i, 338–9.

Parliament passed in 1437 and 1504, with the latter laying great stress on the harm done to the public interest by gilds which attempted to fix prices.[1] Consequently, gild policies in this area were rarely made public and the right to make regulations affecting prices was never claimed in ordinances. The role of the gild in the determination of prices is therefore an extremely hazardous field of study for the historian.

Fortunately the survival of both audit accounts and court minute books means that we do not have to rely solely upon ordinances for our knowledge of the London Pewterers' policies. From these sources we can learn much that was never revealed to the world at large, since it was considered a serious offence for members to disclose any details of the Company's business which might bring discredit.[2] The regulation of prices was not something imposed by the ruling oligarchy upon the freeman, on the contrary it was one of the most democratically determined policies of the Company, and decisions were frequently taken in general assembly after the hearing of a committee report. The earliest regulation of which we have record, dating from 1482–83, was agreed to by all householders, and later regulations were often made with the agreement of 'the whole howse', or by 'Erection of Hands', and some were signed by large numbers of freemen.[3] Policies based upon such general approval were likely to have commanded widespread conformity, but some undercutting inevitably came to the attention of the court, and offenders were duly fined.[4]

The regulation of prices was a complex procedure as account had to be taken of a multitude of products made of divers alloys and requiring variable amounts of labour to fabricate, as well as of frequent fluctuations in the price of tin. Consequently, in addition to setting general prices for broad categories of ware, such as sadware and holloware, specific prices had also to be set for particular items. In 1674, for example, prices ranging from

[1] 15 Henry VI, c. 6; 19 Henry VII, c. 7.
[2] Clauses to this effect were contained in the ordinances of 1564 (Welch, i, 240) and 1760 (Guildhall MS 7117/1).
[3] For example: Guildhall MSS 7086/1, 1482–3; *ibid.* 1493–4; 7090/1, 18 Sept. 1560; 7090/2, 8 May 1562; 7086/3, 1572-3; 7090/2, 15 Mar. 1582; *ibid.* 12 Dec. 1583; 7090/4, 29 Mar., 24 April 1615; *ibid.*, 10 Dec. 1629; *ibid.*; 13 Dec. 1632; 7090/5, 22 Mar. 1655; 7086/3, 1654–5; 7090/6, 19 June 1666; *ibid.*, 21 Mar. 1667; *ibid.*, 14 Apr. 1674; 7090/7, 18 Mar. 1680. It is clear that many price regulations have not survived.
[4] For example, Guildhall MSS 7090/1, 1 Apr. 1560; 7086/3, 1614–15; 7090/4, 3 Oct. 1639.

12d to 14d per pound were set for eight sorts of sadware, each made of the same alloy, yet each requiring different amounts of labour to produce.[1] Furthermore, it was not sufficient merely to specify selling prices, since a great part of the pewterer's business was conducted on a part exchange basis, and effective price-cutting could be practised simply by offering higher rates for the scrap pewter which was traded in. The maximum prices which could be paid for old pewterware had therefore also to be specified. In 1674 it was ordered that no more than 9d per pound should be paid for old sadware, of whatever category. Discounts were allowed to large-scale purchasers, but these were also strictly controlled; and again in 1674 freemen were permitted to sell sadware to merchants for export at 1d per pound below the retail price, and to sell them holloware at 1$\frac{1}{2}d$ in the pound profit instead of 2d. The directive of 1562 that 'no money be abated neither to chapmen nor others' was not typical Company policy,[2] and chapmen were generally also allowed special terms; as in 1615 when they could buy 'Triffles' at 10 per cent discount, and in 1655 when it was 'ordered and voted by a generall Consent that the sadware shall be Sould at 15d per lb and for change take 3d per lb this of retaile Customers, and to Chapmen in the Country 14d per lb and Change 2d per lb'.[3] Freemen were allowed to trade amongst themselves at lower prices; in 1562, for example, the retail price of lay was set at 9d to 9$\frac{1}{2}d$ per lb as against a trade price of 8d.[4] Occasional attempts were also made to impose a minimum charge for the hire of pewter, and in 1616 it was set at not less than 2s per garnish of rough vessels.[5] Small wonder then that the task of regulating prices was frequently delegated to specialist committees composed of representatives of the makers of the classes of ware under scrutiny, or that substantial payments were made to the draughtsmen of price regulations.

The fact that price-fixing was illegal seems to have caused the Company surprisingly little discomfort. One of the most disturbing incidents occurred in 1567 when the City authorities demanded that 'the hole company and incorporacion of the pewterers of this Cyttye shall enter into bonde to the Chamberlyn of this Cyttye in the some of D li under ther Comen Seale', which was to be made

[1] Guildhall MS 7090/6, 14 Apr.   [2] Welch, i, 225.
[3] Guildhall MSS 7090/4, 24 Apr.; 7090/5, 22 Mar.
[4] Welch, i, 225; see also Guildhall MS 7090/4, 13 Dec. 1632.
[5] Guildhall MS 7090/4, 29 June, 15 Oct. 1616.

null and void only if the Company permitted 'everie person and persons of ther said Companie at his and ther freewill and libertie to utter and sell his goods and wares as he and they biers thereof can reasonablie agree among themselves'.[1] The threat had remarkably little impact, however, and we learn that only six years later Nicholas Boddam, the beadle, was paid 10*s* 'as for his paynes ... in travaylinge about the prizes of wares, to be reduced into one rate'.[2] By the close of the seventeenth century the desire to regulate prices had not lessened, indeed to judge from the many injunctions promulgated in these years it may well have increased.[3]

The explanation of the remarkably untrammelled supervision of pewter prices enjoyed by the Company for more than two centuries may lie in the probability that the primary motive was not the exploitation of the consumer but the provision of an adequate livelihood for all members through the elimination of harmful price competition. The levels of prices that were set do not appear to have been immoderately high, indeed to judge from fairly widespread data drawn from a number of towns they were usually no higher, and often somewhat lower, than those ruling in the provinces. In this connection it is interesting to note that in 1560 it was agreed that London pewterers at markets and fairs should sell for no less than a halfpenny per pound *more* than the London price 'unles that there be in the same markyt or ffayre any Countreemen that sellith for lyke pryce as is at london'.[4] Given the strength of competition from provincial pewterers, the opposition of civic and national authorities to price-fixing, and the fact that the Company contained well over 300 masters by the mid-seventeenth century, it is difficult to see how exorbitantly high prices could have been maintained in the capital for any length of time. Furthermore much of the trade of London pewterers was with distant markets where competitive pricing was essential. Thus while there is a distinct possibility that those London pewterers in receipt of cut-price tin from the tin farmers of the seventeenth century, enjoyed enhanced profits by not passing the benefit on to the consumers in the form of lower pewter prices, it is likely that the opportunities for such excess profits were severely limited.

[1] City of London Letter Book V, f. 113 (quoted Welch, i, 255–6).
[2] Guildhall MS 7086/3, 1572–3.   [3] Guildhall MSS 7090/6–8, *passim*.
[4] Guildhall MS 7090/1, 18 Sept.

The same desire to restrict competition among freemen is reflected in the prohibitions placed upon any attempt to capture the customers or shop of a fellow pewterer. From as early as 1439 it was stipulated 'that no persone of the said craft hire, procure, ne put othir persone of the same craft out of his hous, shop or stonding place in the cite of london nor in faires, markettes, nor in othir places out of this Citee . . . on lesse than the person that hathe ocupied it byfore tyme be dede or ells wol it yeld up and leve it bi his fre wyl', and similar rules found a place in both London and York ordinances of the late sixteenth and early seventeenth centuries.[1] Rules against the stealing of customers and any form of advertising were clearly of greater significance and although they did not make a formal appearance until the mid-sixteenth century they were speedily applied to the sale, hire and repair of pewterware.[2] The 'boasting' of wares was specifically precluded, and in 1560 'yt was agreed by the master, wardens and assystaunce and the most part of all the whole ffelowship, as well of the yemandry as of the Clothing, that no person doo ffrom hensforth in his shop or in any other place eyther in selling or Chepnyng of his ware do saye that his ware is better then any others of the company' upon pain of 20s fine.[3] The principal of fair dealing between members was so ardently espoused that the lesser masters who wrought pewter for leading manufacturers and dealers were governed by similar rules. In 1615, for example, it was agreed

> for preventinge of thingrossinge of the best customers into some few mens handes, the said lea men have eich of them made choyce of 3 men, whose names are underwritten, whome they desyre and Conscent to serve, leaveing the rest of the whole Companie att libertie to take and themselves to serve them lea at theire pleasures, yf therefore anie of them shall serve either directlie or indirectlie anie of thotheres Customers here under written shall forfeit and paye as aforesaid.[4]

The maker's mark which had to be stamped upon pewterware was an unavoidable breach in the anonymous uniformity of wares

[1] Guildhall MSS 7117, 7117/1; Univ. of York Lib. MS E.54.
[2] The ordinances of 1564 are the earliest to contain these restrictions (Guildhall MS 7115, c. 15, 18).
[3] Guildhall MS 7090/1, 19 June.   [4] Guildhall MS 7090/4, 2 May.

which pewterers' gilds appear to have sought. Steps were duly taken to restrict the potential value of the mark as an advertising medium, but pewterers were remarkably assiduous in devising methods to circumvent them. We find that in 1564 the Rose and Crown was an additional mark used by the London Company to denote ware of exceptional quality, and that the right to strike it was, at this time, a jealously guarded privilege awarded by the fellowship to a limited number of deserving manufacturers.[1] The Scottish equivalent was the Thistle and the Deacon's mark.[2] But the restriction of the use of the Rose and Crown was an extremely difficult task and by the later seventeenth century not only were London pewterers using it indiscriminately, but also it was being widely used by provincial and even foreign manufacturers to impart to their wares a false seal of quality.[3] A similar history attaches to the striking of 'London', and whereas even as late as 1677 the Company were forbidding its own members to strike it, by the mid-eighteenth century it was admitted that nothing could be done to prevent its use by country pewterers.[4]

The growing unwillingness of many freemen to accept limitations on advertising and competition in general, combined with the declining powers of the Company to produce a rapid change in conventions in the later seventeenth and early eighteenth centuries. Attempts to prevent the striking of the maker's full name and address, an 'X' on wares not of extraordinary quality, and slogans such as 'étain sonnant', 'E.S.', 'Superfine Hard Metal', and even 'Nephew of Taudin' were eventually doomed to failure.[5] At the same time pewterers began to use trade cards or bills to advertise their products. One of the earliest complaints concerning the use of such blatant advertising material was made in 1690 against Robert Lock of Newgate Street, whose 'Tickets' had been spotted as far afield as Stamford.[6] But once again by the early eighteenth century many pewterers were distributing trade cards and headed bills which claimed that they were makers of 'the best fine White Hard Metal called French Pewter' and wholesalers

---

[1] Welch, i, 240. [2] Michaelis, *Antique Pewter*, 97–8.
[3] Massé, *Pewter Collector* (rev. edn), pp. 100–1; Hedges, *Tin in . . . History*, pp. 82, 86–7.
[4] Guildhall MSS 7090/7, 13 Dec.; 7090/10, 24 Sept.
[5] Much evidence is contained in the court minutes of the later seventeenth and early eighteenth centuries (Guildhall MSS 7090/6–9); a number of excerpts are quoted in Welch, ii, 163 ff. James Taudin was a famous pewterer (below, pp. 225–7).
[6] Guildhall MS 7090/7, 9 Oct.

and retailers of 'all sorts of Pewter Wares in a curious manner' at 'reasonable rates' and even 'at the Lowest Prices'.[1]

Although, we have seen, the hawking and peddling of pewter was made illegal in the statute of 1504, it is clear that a substantial proportion of the retail trade remained in the hands of itinerant dealers throughout the medieval and early modern eras. The hawking of pewter was undoubtedly considered subversive to the interests of the gilds and yet their attitude to it was understandably ambivalent, since although in part hawkers and petty chapmen were competitors who produced simple articles, repaired those that were damaged and carried on a thriving business in second-hand pewter, they also constituted an important channel for the distribution of gild products, and many leading freemen relied upon them for the disposal of a sizeable part of their output. Thus although we find some regulations forbidding freemen to serve hawkers or 'mayntaners of hawkers' with pewter, especially on credit terms,[2] and the persistent lobbying of Parliament to curb the hawkers' trade in old pewter,[3] we also find that the importance of hawkers and chapmen was generally appreciated and that freemen were allowed to grant discounts to them and to maintain networks of them without hindrance.[4]

There was no such equivocation as far as unfree hawkers in the gilds' own towns were concerned, or in the disapprobation of hawking by freemen. The former was a threat to the wholesale and retail monopoly which the gild sought to preserve, and the latter involved the soliciting of customers and made it much more difficult to supervise the quality of wares offered for sale. The desire of pewterers' gilds to create and preserve a monopoly of the sale of pewter in their home towns necessitated constant vigilance, and the struggle became more and more desperate as the seventeenth century wore on. In London the position was more complex as the Pewterers' Company never enjoyed the

---

[1] H. H. Cotterell and A. Heal, 'Pewterers' trade-cards', *The Connoisseur* (December 1926), 221–6.
[2] Guildhall MSS 7090/2, 4 Sept. 1560; 7090/3, 30 Apr. 1593. Regulations forbidding the sale of pewter by 'chevisaunce' are found in the London ordinances of 1439 and 1522 (Welch, i, 10, 107–8); those of York of the early seventeenth century forbid the sale of tin or wrought wares, new or old to 'hawkers of the country... without redye money' (Univ. of York Library MS E.54).
[3] For example, it was proposed in 1621 to introduce a bill into Parliament for suppressing hawkers and the buying and selling of old pewter by persons who were not pewterers (Guildhall MS 7090/4, 21 Mar.).
[4] Below p. 254.

benefits of a legally enforceable monopoly of the sale of pewter within the city, since it was customary to allow all London freemen to follow all 'lawful trades' and to engage in the buying and selling of all commodities.[1] Nevertheless, despite the severe limitations of the evidence, it appears that in practice the specialist knowledge required in the trade and the considerable advantages to be derived from membership of the Pewterers' Company, were sufficient to ensure that the vast bulk of the lawful retailing of pewter was in the hands of Company freemen. Haberdashers appear to have provided the only significant legal competition, but even they appeared to have sold only small items such as salts, spoons, buttons and the like.[2]

It is extremely difficult to assess the amount of the London retail trade in the hands of unfree hawkers and chapmen, some of whom appear to have been supplied illicitly by Company members.[3] This was a problem common to many trades, and in 1592 joint action was taken to curb hawking by the Pewterers, Armorers, Cutlers, Blacksmiths, Plumbers, Founders, and Spurriers.[4] With the mounting diffidence of civic authorities the onus of prosecution fell increasingly upon the gilds themselves, and it was surely an indication of weakness that the Pewterers' Company sometimes found it necessary to temper coercion with bribery, even from as early as 1592, as the following case demonstrates:

> Wheras John backhouse hath byne alonge tyme acommon hawker about london, not only to forstall the brethrene of the company, but also a decypt unto the quenes subiectes, the sayed John bachouse uppon consyderation of vs. of money geven hyme at this court to buy hyme tooles to work to get his lyvyng with all, the sayed John backhouse and also John boswell, cytozen and carpenter of london, do stand bound in tenne poundes unto our soveraygne lady the quene

---

[1] Lipson, *Economic History*, i, 358; Power and Postan, ed., *Studies in English Trade*, pp. 261, 286.
[2] Welch, i, 137, 146. Any pewter offered for sale by non-pewterers was, of course, subject to Company searches.
[3] For an interesting case of a freeman encouraging the hawking of his wares in London see Guildhall MS 7090/2, 18 Mar. 1568. It is also interesting to note that in 1552 a Newcastle pewterer, Edward Watson, felt that the London Company's powers were sufficiently extensive to warrant making a complaint at its court against a painter-stainer and a goldsmith of Newcastle who, he alleged, were selling licences to hawkers at 6d a day (Guildhall MS 7090/1, 21 June).
[4] Welch, ii, 7.

upon this condition that the sayed John backhouse shall never hereafter use the trad of hawkynge.¹

As time passed disregard for the Company's rules against hawking by members became prevalent, and in the ordinances of 1702 it was stated that 'some lewd and idle persons of the said Company and Mistery doe go about from house to house in and about the said Citty and suburbs thereof under pretence of mending or sowdering of pots and other pewter vessels ... and do frequently mix bad and corrupt mettle' and that others 'doe also goe about from house to house to hawk and expose to sale certaine corrupt wares for good pewter and thereby avoid search and inspection of the said wares'. The Company's solution, which bore a close resemblance to that adopted two hundred years earlier in the statute of 1504, was to allow repairs to be conducted only in the house or shop of the pewterer, and pewterware to be carried to the house of the customer only upon his request.² Insistence upon the use of the pewterer's own permanent premises was extended in 1654 to a prohibition upon freemen keeping stalls or booths at any market or fair within seven miles of the City,³ and it is amusing to discover that William Archer was fined £10 in 1670 for keeping a stall at Bow Fair, since he had been Master at the time the by-law was passed.⁴

Complementing the control exercised over standards of manufacture and the sale of pewter was a framework of policies, no less comprehensive and no less important, designed to regulate the numbers practising the craft and the level of output. At the heart of these policies lay the system of apprenticeship; indeed apprenticeship has a claim to be the most typical feature of the European craft gild, and compulsory training in the occupation later to be followed as a livelihood was adopted by Tudor and Stuart governments as a major plank in their industrial programmes.⁵

Consequently apprenticeship was one of the first institutions to be adopted by pewterers' gilds. In the early fourteenth century, which was the formative era of the London craft, it was not

[1] Guildhall MS 7090/3, 5 Oct.   [2] Guildhall MS 7116.
[3] Guildhall MS 7090/5, 17 Aug.
[4] Guildhall MS 7090/6, 28 Apr. The fine was subsequently reduced.
[5] See, in particular, Davies, *The Enforcement of English Apprenticeship*.

possible to insist on masterships being restricted to those who had served an apprenticeship in pewtering, and the qualifications for admission were deemed in 1348 to be either completion of apprenticeship or acceptance as a 'true workman, known and tried'.[1] Such flexibility was essential in these times when recruitment of practising pewterers was the first priority, and apprenticeship to the craft was still not common.[2] But freedom without apprenticeship was considered unacceptable in the long term and as soon as was practical it was limited to those who had served an apprenticeship. By the early fifteenth century, if we may judge from the ordinances of York pewterers, apprenticeship involved a minimum of seven years' service and was not open to aliens or bondmen.[3] By the later fifteenth century apprenticeship was almost certainly the normal method of entry into all provincial pewterers' crafts; we know it to have been so in Bristol and Coventry as well as York.[4]

The institution of apprenticeship was far from being simply the means of acquiring the skills with which to practise a craft or trade in an expert manner. On the one hand it also played an important role in the maintenance of codes of morality and social order by assigning adolescents to the charge of masters who acted *in loco parentis*, and on the other it provided a source of cheap skilled labour and an effective method of restricting entry, and thereby output and competition. Apprenticeship fitted in well with the widely practised custom of sending children away from the parental home when they reached their early teens. The average apprentice's period of service lasted from the age of thirteen or fourteen until his early twenties, during which time he received no wages, only clothes, board and lodging, and experienced a strict code of discipline which entailed almost complete subservience to his master and mistress. The master's authority, which was supported by social conventions in general and the officials of the gild in particular, extended to most aspects of the apprentice's working and private life including his leisure activities, sexual morality, and attire. An indication of the meti-

[1] *Memorials of London Life*, p. 242.
[2] Between 1309 and 1312 not a single pewterer had been made free in London by apprenticeship, and not a single apprentice pewterer had been enrolled (above, p. 39).
[3] *York Memorandum Book*, i, 212.
[4] *Calendar of the Bristol Apprentice Book 1532–65*, ed. D. Hollis (Bristol Record Society Publications, xiv, 1949), i, 3–13; *Coventry Leet Book*, i, 554.

culous discipline that was imposed was provided in 1629, when widow Boulton's apprentice was brought before the Company's Court 'with unseemly haire not befitting an apprentice, which they caused to be cut off'.[1] It was ordered that all serious disputes between a master and his apprentice, journeyman or servant, should be referred to the craft court and settled by the Master and Wardens; punishments were frequently severe and incorrigible apprentices could be whipped, imprisoned, or expelled.[2]

The behaviour expected of an apprentice varied according to the moral climate of the age in which he lived as well as the character of his master, but the rules laid down for apprentices in 1702 demonstrate clearly that severity and exemplary standards of probity were not restricted to the Middle Ages or the harsh days of the Commonwealth:

> if any Apprentice shall in the time of his Apprenticeship Marry or contract himself in Marriage to any Woman, or shall misbehave himselfe towards his Master or Mistress, or shall be of so rude behaviour that the persuasion or lawfull correction of his Master or Mistress will not cause him to reforme his misbehaviour, Or if he shall wilfully waste or consume his Masters Goods, or if he shall be a drunkard, haunter of Taverns, Ale houses, Bowling Allies, Gameing houses, or other lewd or suspected places of evill Company, Gameth, Dyceth, Runneth away or shall lye out of his Master or Mistresses house without his or her privity, or shall be an Inciter of other mens Servants to evill manners, and shall be brought to the Hall of the said Company by his said Master or Mistress and there these or such like offences proved against him at a Court of Assistants of the said

---

[1] Guildhall MS 7090/4, 19 Nov. It is also interesting to note that in 1573 the Company had paid 2*d* for 'a proclamacion, tending to the reformacion, of the greate abuse, latelie practized by Apprentizes, in excesse of apparraile' (Guildhall MS 7086/3, 1572–3).

[2] For example: in 1560 John Smythe was incarcerated in Bridewell prison for running away to work with a Maidstone tinker and for 'beinge Suspected to come and Entice mens servauntes and prentices to be obstynate agaynst there maisters as before tyme he hath donne' (Guildhall MS 7090/1, 12 Jan.); in 1566 two apprentices were imprisoned 'for that they consettered to gether to have Ronne away, and had Enbeaseled certayne patrons and Tooles of their maisters goodes' (Guildhall MS 7090/2, 12 Dec.); in 1569 Francis Bawdwyn, who had several times robbed his master of goods and money was whipped in open court (Guildhall MS 7090/2, 30 Dec.); and in 1579 Thomas hyxson was whipped in the Hall for 'dysobedyence and unduetyfulness' to his master and mistress and for being unreverent before the court (Guildhall MS 7090/2, 3 Oct.).

Company, the party so offending in all or any the causes or matters aforesaid shall loose the benefit of the time and Service past before such offence or offences committed, and shall either become new bound to his Master for Seaven yeares or else make his Master such recompence as the Master and Wardens of the said Company for the time being or any two of them shall think fit.[1]

The subjection of the apprentice did not cease here, however, for he was in a real sense the chattel of his master and could be 'turned over' to a new master at the discretion of the officers of the Company if his master died or ceased working, and he could even be sold to repay debts.[2] The turning over of apprentices who had served only part of their term was a frequent occurrence, and one in which the apprentice was apparently given little choice. We learn, for example, that in 1666 an apprentice who had formerly been bound to a Mr Dod, but refused to serve Mr Gabriell Redhead his successor, was deemed by the Company court to be 'mr Redheads Chattle' and all freemen were forbidden to provide him with work 'as they will answer it at their utmost peril.'[3] Yet it is distorting to dwell only on rules and on the occasions when relations between masters and apprentices reached breaking point, since most apprentices managed to complete their service without being hauled before the gild court for misbehaviour. Furthermore, the apprenticeship, although overlong, did succeed in equipping recruits with expertise in the trade, which in turn permitted pewterers' gilds to insist on high standards of manufacture.

Nevertheless, the personal reflections of the successful pewterer and Lord Mayor of London, Sir John Fryer, leave us in no doubt as to the harshness of his own apprenticeship. This unique autobiography provides so many precious insights into the pewterers' trade and London life at the turn of the seventeenth century that it must be quoted at length.[4] Fryer, the son of a modest Buckinghamshire farmer, recounts how he was brought to London early in 1685, aged fourteen,

[1] Guildhall MS 7116, c. 39.
[2] The value of an apprentice doubtless varied according to the number of years he had served and the skills he had acquired; we learn that an apprentice was sold for 20 lb of metal in 1560 (Guildhall MS 7090/1, 18 Mar.), another for more than 20*s* in 1570 (Guildhall MS 7090/2, 14 Nov.), and another for 53*s*4*d* in 1593 (Guildhall MS 7090/3, 15 Aug.).
[3] Guildhall MS 7090/6, 13 Dec.   [4] Guildhall MS 12017.

to be improved in writeing and accompts that I might be
fitted to go Aprentice to some Trade. . . . I haveing continued
at the Writeing School till the Christmas, and my Relations
haveing heard of one Mr. Harford a Peuterer in
Bishopsgate street (the next house to the corner house of
Cornhill) who wanted an Aprentice, it was soon agreed I
should go on trial to him, which I did about the 16th of
January, and on the 1st day of March I was bound to him
for 7 years according to the Custom of the citty of London:
my Honoured Uncle Edmund Boulter [a maltster of Abingdon,
Fryer's father having died in 1676 leaving only a house and
land and £85.14s6d in goods] discharged what was necessary
on my account: £10 in money and a New suit of Clothe's
was the condition on which I was bound. . . . I must also
observe that he [Harford] had not been long sett up for himself,
so that his Trade was but small, and that not being suficient
to keep himself and me in full work he contrived to take
in work from other men, which in that buisness is called
Trucking, but properly it is working of Journy work to
other men, when I had been with him some time and was
capable of finishing work, he began to be tired of working
so hard as we generaly did (and most young beginners do
at first) so the work fell the heavier upon me; and which
added to my labour the goods which I finish'd, I carry'd
on my back into Southwark where the owner dwelt, and I
brought more back to work, this was my custom 3 or 4
times weekly if not ofter; I had just reason to be very
unease under this servitude for I was naturaly of a Weak
constitution, and being the only surviving child, my Dear
Mother had not inured me to any hard labour; and which
was worse in my infancy I had been cured of a Rupture,
and I found such carrying of burthens strained that part
and did me much hurt; my Master being of a very near
temper in his house and put me upon doing the servile part
of the trade, such as turning the Wheel, Oileing, and cleaning
the Ware when finishd, carrying of Basketts of goods to the
Inns and other such like things not commonly done by other
aprentices and some other things which I forbear to relate;
these things as well as my severe confinement were irksome
to me: especially when I observed the pleasant and easie

Trades that most of my School fellows were put to, it did oft make me repine, butt under all these things the goodness of my god supported me; I had some thotts of quitting such servitude but then I considered my Mother haveing only me should I ruine my self it would be a sore afliction to her. . . . I had other trialls and temptations dureing that seven years servitude; such as the loose carriage of my Master, who when he found himself to prosper in the World took more liberty to keep company and led a more dissolute life then when I first went to him. . . . His company keeping brought him to such a sottish temper that his cheif delight was in Alehouses and Taverns and by furnishing of them he seems to gett his cheif buisness to this day, and by this sottish way he supports himself, makeing of them pay an extravagant rate for goods, and by this course of life gained the name of Drunken Harry:—but to return to the account of my self; when my time was expired, 1st March 1692/3, I workt a little while with him, was made free of the Company of Peuterers about the 21st of this month, and soon after of the Citty of London; and one of the Trade being ill and desirous of leaving of his buisness: I waited on my Honoured Uncle Edmund Boulter, and desired him to assist me to take the said Shop etc., which request of mine he considered of and granted: he lent me the Money that the goods came to, which I think was about £300, I gave him Bond and paid him intrest.

Thus, although suffering adversity while an apprentice, Fryer was able to start his own business immediately after gaining his freedom. Many were less fortunate, however, and lacking the means with which to acquire premises, tools, equipment, and raw materials, were forced to work for wages as journeymen in the hope of eventually accumulating sufficient capital with which to achieve independence.[1] There can be no doubt that the formal restraints which were from time to time imposed on progress from apprentice to master were of far less consequence than simple lack of capital on the part of the would-be master.[2]

Journeyman status, although obviously providing more in-

---

[1] In the later sixteenth century, for example, there were years when the yeomanry of the London Company contained almost as many journeymen as masters (Appendix A).

[2] This also appears to have been true in the provincial gilds (Fisher, Industrial Gilds, pp. 35–6).

dependence than that of apprentice, was nevertheless still one of irksome restriction and even subjection. Journeymen were frequently required to live in, keep reasonable hours, attend church, show deference to their masters, and refrain from improper behaviour.[1] The terms of journeymen's contracts were also controlled. There is evidence to suggest that masters frequently operated policies of wage restraint, which were often justified as being in accordance with state directives, although those practised in London appear never to have been as blatant as those of York.[2] Completion of the full period of service that had been undertaken was strictly enforced, with severe penalties imposed on any who dared to give work to a journeyman who had not been discharged by his former employer.[3] In 1561 a London journeyman who departed from his employer's service before the agreed date was ordered to 'serve one Sevennight more for the tyme he hath bynne absent' and to 'lye within his masters howse and be there every night by ix of the Clock at the farthest'; furthermore if he ran away again it was agreed that his employer should set him 'ffast by the heeles'.[4] Masters were also expressly forbidden to entice workmen from other masters, or openly compete for their labour; these were not only some of the earliest but also some of the most frequently reiterated regulations, and it is likely that they served to inhibit journeymen from obtaining the true reward for their labour, especially in times of labour shortage.[5] Journeymen, like apprentices, were also prohibited from buying and selling pewter on their own account.[6]

[1] For example, we find that journeymen of the London Company in the later sixteenth century were expected to wait upon the Masters and Wardens of the yeomanry at all offerings, and were forbidden to go to 'any Taverne, ale house or such lyke unsemely places' (Guildhall MS 7115, 1564 ordinances).
[2] For example, in 1554 the London Pewterers' court appears to have determined the wages of journeymen at from 4d to 5d per day, plus food and drink, and one journeyman's contract forbade him to indulge in 'dising, bowling, and Carding or any other such unlawfull games' but allowed that 'upon the sondayes and other holly dayes after devyne service ys done [he] shall take his pastyme in the ffeildes with his bowe' (Guildhall MS 7090/1, 7 May, 16 Nov.). None of the surviving London ordinances mention journeymen's wages, but those of York of 1416 and 1602 set maxima, and forbade the providing of gifts or additional rewards of any kind (*York Memorandum Book*, i, 213; Univ. of York Library MS E.54).
[3] In 1560 the London Pewterers' Company specified that journeymen on annual contracts should give six months notice, those on half-yearly contracts three months, and those on weekly contracts a week (Guildhall MS 7090/1, 19 June).
[4] Guildhall MS 7090/1, 9 May.
[5] See, for example, the London ordinances of 1348 (*Memorials of London Life*, pp. 243-4) and those of York of 1416 (*York Memorandum Book*, i, 212).
[6] Guildhall MS 7115, 1564 ordinances.

Yet on certain issues journeymen were able to exercise considerable influence, and it appears to have been largely due to their efforts that most English gilds steadfastly adopted strict limits on the numbers of apprentices that masters were permitted to enrol.[1] On this matter there was a direct conflict of interest between the master who saw apprentices as a cheap form of labour, and journeymen who saw them as rivals for employment and also potential rivals for premises. Whereas the established master seeking to expand his business was usually willing to face the distant threat of greater competition from uncontrolled entry into apprenticeships, the journeyman seeking work and perhaps hoping to set up shop could not afford to. In the event the tenacity, and at times ferocity, with which the journeymen fought their case, supported no doubt by the innate conservatism of many senior members, secured a complete and lasting victory. The need for restrictions upon the numbers of apprentices clearly varied according to the prosperity of the industry, but, given the fluctuating nature of demand in pre-industrial England, even cycles of rapid growth were frequently interspersed with bouts of severe depression.

In the later fifteenth century, when no restrictions were in force, a few leading London pewterers accumulated as many as six to eleven apprentices each, and the industry as a whole had almost three times as many apprentices as journeymen.[2] By the third decade of the sixteenth century the consequences of such freedom were being reconsidered and it was claimed that

> dyvers persones of the saide crafte Peauterers of theyr coveteus myndys not regardying the goode and honeste contynuaunce of the same crafte, not regardinge the preferment and honestye lyvinges of the poore apprentices comynge out of their apprentyshoddes, but rather woll doo thoose actes that shall brynge them to extreme povertye or elles to use soome other vyle and laboriouse occupacyons after they have sarved their termes of apprentyshodes, have of late dayes for their syngular profyttes and advauntages

[1] Restrictions upon the numbers of apprentices a master might employ were amongst the most common of gild by-laws: Lipson, *Economic History*, i, 316–22; Fisher, 'Industrial Gilds', pp. 31–4; Unwin, *Gilds and Companies of London*, pp. 264–5. For seventeenth-century restrictions, and the decline in their enforcement, see Kramer, *English Craft Gilds*, p. 160 ff.
[2] Below, pp. 241–3.

taken in to theyr sarvyce soo many apprentices that the nowmber of the said crafte is soo encreased that oon of theym is not able honestlye to lyve by a nother.

The result was that liverymen were to be allowed three apprentices each, and non-liverymen two, with a fine of £10 for breaking the ordinance.[1]

Restrictions on the numbers of apprentices were so widespread, and fears for employment so prevalent in London and the provinces in later sixteenth-century England that it is possible that pewterers' gilds at first adopted restrictive policies more out of deference to pressures from civic authorities and other gilds than out of pure necessity, since pewter industries appear to have experienced fewer economic problems than most other urban industries at this time. Certainly the batch of further restrictions imposed in London in the late 1550s owed less to the initiative of pewterers than to that of other misteries. In 1555 an Act of Common Council provided that no person should be admitted to the freedom of the City, and so enabled to set up in business, before attaining the age of twenty-four, nor should apprentices be taken for fewer years than such as would bring them to that age on completion of their service; as a result apprenticeships of eight, nine or even ten years became common.[2] A year later an order limiting the numbers of apprentices was assented to by seventeen of the lesser companies, including the Pewterers.[3] Within two months of this last order the Court of Assistants of the Company ruled that the numbers of apprentices allowed to liverymen should be reduced from three to two, and to yeomen from two to one;[4] a subsequent amendment allowed members of the Court of Assistants to keep three apprentices as long as they also employed two journeymen.[5] Still greater concern was displayed in 1559 when a committee was elected 'to way Indifferently the state of the whole companye who is able to mayntayne and kepe prentices and who is not', and the power to grant leave to set up shop was taken from the Master and Wardens and given to the Court of Assistants.[6] The importance that the limitations upon

[1] Welch, i, 110–11 (1522 ordinances).
[2] Welch, i, 195; Guildhall MSS 7086/2, 3 *passim*. The average term of the fifteen apprentices bound to pewterers in Bristol between 1532 and 1542 was nine years (*Calendar of the Bristol Apprentice Book*, i).
[3] Welch, i, 194–5. [4] Guildhall MS 7090/1, 12 Nov.
[5] Guildhall MS 7090/2, 21 Sept. 1564. [6] Guildhall MS 7090/1, 7 July, 4 Aug.

numbers of apprentices speedily attained is exemplified by an agreement made in 1564 'that if any parson what so ever he be that shall heare after move any matter which might sound to the breache and undoynge' of the ordinances on this subject he was to forfeit £10.¹

These policies, formulated in what was probably a period of urban industrial crisis in England, were retained with relatively few amendments until the eighteenth century. Some concessions were made to ensure that masters were not left without skilled assistance by permitting them to enrol new apprentices as existing apprentices approached the end of their service, and from time to time masters were permitted to purchase the right to take an apprentice in excess of the stated number.² But far from allowing the conditions of the later fifteenth century to return, the Company's policy hardened as the seventeenth century progressed. By 1702 past and present Masters, including those who had paid to be excused office, were allowed two apprentices, with another when either had served half his time; past and present Wardens were allowed two apprentices, with another when either had served all but two years of his time; stewards were allowed one apprentice, and another when he had served half his time; liverymen were allowed one apprentice, and another when he had served all but two years of his time; and other master pewterers were allowed to take an apprentice only after they had been in business for a year, with another when he was within six months of finishing. Additional apprentices were only to be allowed upon payment of no less than 20s per month.³ In seventeenth-century York no master was permitted to take more than one apprentice until his first had served four years, and any additional apprentice had to be a freeman's son.⁴ Nevertheless, it must not be forgotten that the most effective obstacle to a too rapid expansion of the numbers of masters was the extremely high proportion of apprentices, probably between 40 and 60 per cent, who failed to complete their service, primarily through death or disillusionment.⁵

A similar concern for employment and an acute fear of over-

¹ Guildhall MS 7115, c. 19.
² During the first half of the seventeenth century, for example, fines for additional apprentices were generally within the £1–2 range, although one fine as high as £10 is recorded. Two or three such licences were granted each year on average (Guildhall MSS 7086/4, 5 *passim*.).
³ Guildhall MS 7116, 1702 ordinances.
⁴ Univ. of York Library MS E.54.   ⁵ Appendix A.

expansion is also displayed in a series of additional measures widely adopted by pewterers' gilds. The prohibitions placed on the sale of secondhand pewter and of rough pewter clearly fall into this category; and both measures were firmly supported by journeymen.[1] In 1663 a petition from London journeymen sought to extend these provisions by seeking to redress 'the abuses of letting [hiring] or serving the Maiors and Sheriffs as others with ould pewter or vessell at the second hand to the great loss of there imployment'.[2] The prohibitions placed on working at night and on the Sabbath and other holy days stemmed in part from similar motives, but were much less strictly enforced.[3]

Journeymen doubtless also played a part in ensuring that few formal restrictions were placed on aspiring masters: we have seen that from the mid-sixteenth century they had to present a masterpiece, convince a committee of their competence, and pay a small entrance fee, but the only restriction of significance appears to have been that relating to partnerships. The London Company first became concerned about partnerships in the early seventeenth century, probably as a result of pressure from senior freemen, and it was decided that all prospective partnerships had to be licensed by the Court of Assistants.[4] This was clearly a device to discourage journeymen with insufficient capital from joining together in order to start a business, and the attitude of the Court of Assistants is made clear in its exhortation to young men to be 'put to some good service and so work as a Journeyman untill such time as it may please God to enable him to take a masters charge upon him'.[5] In York, by contrast, prospective masters were forbidden only from entering into partnerships with persons who were not 'free brothers' of the craft, and freemen of modest wealth were also greatly helped by being able to borrow moulds from the large stocks which the craft held for this purpose.[6]

[1] Guildhall MSS 7090/3, 23 Dec. 1591; 7115, c. 24; 7117/1, c. 29; Welch, i, 196.
[2] Guildhall MS 7090/6, 17 Aug.
[3] The prohibitions remained in force until the early seventeenth century (Guildhall MS 7117/1, c. 10), but they appear to have been enforced stringently only in the late fifteenth and early sixteenth centuries (for examples of enforcement in 1478 and 1483 see Guildhall MS 7086/1).
[4] Guildhall MS 7117/1, c. 15.   [5] Guildhall MS 7116, 1702 ordinances c. 31.
[6] Univ. of York Library MS E.54. Upon admission to the freedom in the later seventeenth century York pewterers had to pay £4, 'towards the maintaining of the moulds'. A number of York ordinances were concerned with the use of the craft's moulds (see below p. 221).

The primary aim of securing as great a share of pewter production as possible for their members led pewterers' gilds to impose still more legislative measures, this time with the object of preserving trade secrets, restricting the employment of non-gild labour, and penalising members who left the town to practise in the country or even abroad.

Concern with the leaking of trade secrets, especially to foreigners, might well appear to have reached almost paranoiac proportions in periods of severe slump. Mention has already been made of the commencement of restrictionist policies in the export slump of the late fifteenth and early sixteenth centuries, when embargoes upon the importation of foreign pewter, the emigration of English pewterers, and the employment of immigrants were enshrined in statute law.[1] The fear that foreigners were being taught 'not only the Cunning of mixing and forging of all manner of Pewter Vessels, but also . . . all Things belonging to the said Craft of Pewterers' by unscrupulous Englishmen,[2] is understandable at this time since the export trade was of the utmost importance to London craftsmen, and since it is probable that the techniques of English pewterers were more advanced than those of pewterers in many other countries. One historian of early modern technology has gone so far as to claim that before the mid-sixteenth century 'Englishmen had almost nothing to teach foreigners in the way of practical mechanical knowledge except in connection with the production of tin and the manufacture of pewter'.[3]

Although these anti-alien measures remained on the statute book and were constantly reiterated in gild ordinances it appears that native pewterers suffered far less from the competition of immigrants than many other crafts. The influx of large numbers of Dutch and French Protestant refugees from the interminable continental wars of religion created serious problems for many London companies, but the lists which were regularly compiled of alien craftsmen resident in England reveal scarcely a single pewterer.[4] In the later seventeenth century, however, the London Pewterers were forced to face up to the problem of skilled immigrants for the first time, and records reveal that a number of

[1] Above, p. 77. [2] 25 Henry VIII, c. 9.
[3] Nef, 'The progress of technology...', p. 23.
[4] Archer, p. 190 ff; *Lists of Foreign Protestants, and Aliens, Resident in England 1618–88*, ed. W. D. Cooper (Camden Society, old. ser., lxxxii, 1862).

French pewterers who had fled from Catholic persecution set up in business in London. At first the attitude of the Company was implacably hostile. In 1656, for example, James Taudin was prosecuted at great expense and trouble before the Court of Aldermen and in the Exchequer.[1] Owing to government support for Protestant refugees the Company was forced to base its case upon the dubious grounds of bad workmanship, and in 1658 it admitted defeat and granted Taudin the status of freeman and liveryman upon payment of £50 and a bond for a further £10, and on condition that he sacked all his foreign workmen and employed only freemen of the Company as journeymen.[2] Although the Company's powers to stamp out competition from non-gildsmen within London were waning, the granting of admission to the freedom by redemption was viewed unfavourably and was accepted as a solution only if all else failed. Thus in 1689 Mark Henry Shabroles, another French Protestant refugee, was granted only temporary leave to continue working as a pewterer, Daniel Taudin, brother of James, was allowed only to work privately 'in his owne Chamber', and a free pewterer of Cork named Geffers who had been forced to flee from persecution and prayed leave to work was instead granted 20s in relief.[3] But such reluctance could no longer be defended on the grounds that trade secrets might be at risk; on the contrary there is clear evidence that the influx of French pewterers, in particular the Taudins, resulted in substantial technical advances in the London industry.[4]

But aliens constituted only a small part of the competition facing gildsmen. The role of the hawker and the country pewterer and the control exercised over the quality of their products has already been discussed, yet mention must be made here of the additional restraints which gilds tried to impose on them, once again largely as a result of pressure from journeymen and from masters who earned their living by working for others. For example, gildsmen were discouraged from dealing with non-members, either by selling them tin or by putting out pewter to be worked by them. In London these rules appear to have applied both to pewterers who were freemen of other companies and to the unfree craftsmen who dwelt in the suburbs and beyond.[5] The suburbs of

[1] Guildhall MS 7086/4, 1655–6.   [2] Guildhall MS 7090/5, 21 Jan.
[3] Guildhall MS 7090/7, 7 May, 20 June.   [4] Below, pp. 225-7.
[5] See the ordinances of 1522, 1564 and 1607 (Guildhall MSS 7114, 7115, 7117/1).

London provided a potential source of cheap labour for unscrupulous gildsmen[1] but the relatively expensive capital equipment and the skill required to make pewter ensured that the Pewterers' Company suffered less than many other companies from such competition. Unfree labourers could be employed directly, although they were only to be used upon simple and menial tasks such as carrying, oiling and polishing, and turning the wheel to drive the lathe. As late as 1673 a master was accused of setting his 'Turn wheel to work on the mistery' by using him to cast sadware.[2] We know that unfree workmen were employed in significant numbers—presumably most of the larger workshops possessed at least one—but Company records are silent on their exact numbers or their conditions of service.[3]

The final restraint that could be imposed on the provincial and country industry by the London Pewterers was to deter its own freemen from leaving the capital. Journeymen were forbidden to leave London if 'suffycient servyce and reasonable wadges' could be found for them within the City,[4] and those who left were not permitted to be subsequently re-employed without licence.[5] But it was not merely journeymen who left London, on the contrary the attractions of lower costs and greater opportunities in the provinces, combined with less risk of contracting plague, lured many pewterers of all ranks away from the capital, and it is interesting to note that some emigrated to Virginia in the early seventeenth century.[6] Indeed it is probable that London trained pewterers constituted a significant proportion of the workforce of provincial industries. We even learn that in 1596 a substantial number of members of the Court of Assistants had 'drawen them selves to dwell in the country', but in this instance we can be sure that their decision owed more to fear of the plague than the promise of economic advance.[7] In practice the Company could do little to discourage mobility; it was felt to be unwise to impose severe penalties upon returning freemen since it was

[1] Archer, *passim*.
[2] Guildhall MS 7090/6, 19 June; see also Guildhall MS 7090/4, 5 Oct. 1615.
[3] The ordinances of 1702, for example, distinguish between apprentices, journeymen and servants.
[4] Welch, i, 110; Guildhall MS 7117/1, c. 8.
[5] For example, Guildhall MS 7090/1, 22 Feb. 1553.
[6] Guildhall MS 7095/1, 1619.
[7] Guildhall MS 7090/8, 15 Aug. London experienced an outbreak of plague in 1592–93 (C. Creighton, *A History of Epidemics in Britain* (1965 ed.), pp. 351–6).

preferable to grant re-admission rather than suffer their competition. Consequently punishments were usually modest: in 1558 John Sawnderson was re-admitted upon a token payment of a dozen spoons, and John Taylor was merely warned that 'if ever he goo owt in to the Countree to worke agayne he shalbe clene dismyssed and never be Receyved agayne',[1] while in 1594 Robert Bullardyne was re-admitted after spending seventeen years in the country upon payment of a fine of 10*s* and 8*s*6*d* for arrears of quarterage to the yeomany.[2]

The waning of gild control over the nation's handicraft industries and retail trades in the seventeenth and eighteenth centuries is a commonplace of economic history,[3] yet relatively few attempts have been made to advance beyond generalisation to a detailed examination of the experience of individual gilds or industries. Nevertheless, it seems certain that the powers of pewterers' gilds, especially those of the London Pewterers' Company, were both more extensive and more durable than those of many other gilds. We have seen how the pewter industry lent itself more readily than most to precise controls over standards of production, which were in turn supported by state legislation, and how the twin requirements of relatively expensive capital equipment and not inconsiderable skill exercised a significant restraint on the numbers capable of producing high quality wares. Also of importance is the fact that the industry expanded and prospered as the sixteenth and seventeenth centuries progressed, and remained, for the most part, located in the older urban centres. Additionally, and one must stress paradoxically, the London Pewterers' Company as an institution derived substantial support from the hated pre-emption of tin production by Crown patentees, which persisted with few major interruptions from the opening years of the seventeenth century until 1717.[4] The selling of the right to pre-empt tin output was consistently and strenuously opposed by the Company because it forced up the price of tin and frequently made supplies difficult to obtain, even at inflated prices. Yet

[1] Guildhall MS 7090/1, 18 June, 5 Aug.
[2] Guildhall MS 7090/3, 10 May.
[3] It is surely an overstatement, however, to suggest, that 'the functions of craft gilds were being undermined even as early as 1500 and their history during the sixteenth and seventeenth centuries is one of continuous decline' (Clarkson, p. 104).
[4] See below pp. 234-6.

although the Company was unable to secure the cessation of the practice, the concerted actions of its members managed to wring a number of valuable concessions from the Crown as compensation for the damage inflicted upon the industry. The most important concession, and the one which tended to benefit the richest members of the Company the most, was the right to purchase an agreed supply of tin, on occasion as much as 500 thousandweight but more often 100–200 thousandweight, at a reduced price. The other concessions were the granting to the Company of a monopoly of casting into bars all the tin which was exported in this form, and occasional cash subsidies from the Crown, often of the order of £100 or more, which were distributed to poor freemen.[1]

If the specific benefits of cheap tin, the profitable monopoly of the casting of the bars, and poor relief, are added to the many other advantages accruing to members which have been discussed earlier in this chapter, it becomes apparent why the Pewterers' Company retained such a firm grip on the London industry for so long. Even as late as the closing decades of the seventeenth century, not only did the vast majority of London pewter manufacturers belong to the Company, but also the membership of the Company was overwhelmingly composed of practising pewterers. Between 1621 and 1700 an average of nine out of every ten new freemen had served as an apprentice pewterer in London, and what is more the proportion of freedoms granted by servitude rather than by patrimony or redemption showed no tendency to decline as the seventeenth century progressed.[2] The predominance at all levels of the Company of practising members of the trade meant that policies connected with the manufacture of pewter were implementated with rare vigour. In trades which were declining the proportion of members following the nominal trade of that company was, by contrast, invariably extremely low: in 1756, for example, only five members out of eighty-six in the Girdlers' Company were practising girdlers, while only seventeen out of 214 in the Glovers' Company made gloves.[3]

It must be stressed once more, however, that the most successful

---

[1] For example £100 was distributed to almost 150 poor freemen and freemen's widows in 1616, in amounts which ranged from 2s6d to £5 (Guildhall MS 7090/4, 24 Dec.). In 1618 well over £200, including arrears, was received by the Company to be distributed to its poor (Guildhall MS 7090/4, 1618 *passim*).
[2] Appendix A.   [3] Kellett, p. 390, n.3.

areas of legislation for pewterers' gilds were those which commanded the support of the majority of members. The strength of the London Company lay in its cohesion, and in its ability to convince pewterers to remain within its fold. In order to evince this cohesion the enforcement of legislation required a thoughtful compromise between rigour and discretion. An errant colleague was wisely preferred to a bitter competitor, which meant that few members suffered the ultimate sanction of permanent expulsion. These important points have been made before, yet examples drawn from periods when the Company was enjoying great power provide welcome confirmation. At the court held on 20 June 1562 two members of the yeomanry were disenfranchised at the wish of the whole Company. The first, Nicholas Rodes, was expelled because

> he contrary to his othe and lyke no trewe pewterer which was never heretofore sene did in the sight of straungers myxed tynne and leade together, and made of good Tynne ffalse tynne to the great decyving of the Quens majestes people as well in this Realme as other fforen parties to the great slaunder of all the pewterers in London.

The second, Robert Somers, because he had contrived to break a truly prodigious number of craft rules, as his indictment shows:

> ffirst for going abowt lyke a hawker and prowling others mens bargaynes of the Company owt of their handes.
> Item for procuring away the customers from mr. daye who was his master.
> Item for keeping a boye contrary to the orders of the howse and agaynst the maisters comaundement and for mocking the master when he sent for hym saing he had put him awaye and kept hym still.
> Item for procuring awaye a shoppe from Browne our Clark.
> Item for fforstawling of a Brother of the company John chester and taking a lease of the howse of the same chester over his hed.
> Item for bying of old mettall and selling it old as it was.
> Item for discrying the previties of the Company saying he wolde geve more for olde mettall by $\frac{1}{2}$d in a pound for that it was all Redy tempored with tynne glasse.[1]

[1] Guildhall MS 7090/2, 20 June.

Notwithstanding the gravity of Rodes's and Somers's offences we find that on 10 August following it was agreed that Rodes should be re-admitted on payment of a £5 fine by instalments and an additional 4d per quarter, and that exactly four months later the whole Company agreed that Somers after paying a 30s fine 'shoulde be taken in agayne to the Company uppon Condicion that he never doo any such acte as before he hath done but become a new man'.[1] It is interesting to note that Somers subsequently became a liveryman.

That reconciliation of this sort was common is evident from many other comparable examples contained in Company records. Furthermore, even the most junior members were frequently treated with generosity. For example, on 22 March 1597 John North, who was only months out of his apprenticeship, was found guilty of taking an apprentice without licence and making 'large bowe pottes, 50 graynes worse than the say', and imprisoned and banished from the Company, only to be freed and readmitted three days later on payment of a £3 fine.[2] Finally, the case of Nicholas Jurdeine is of particular interest since it embodies many matters of relevance. In 1574, Jurdeine, a wealthy Merchant Taylor who had married the widow of a leading pewterer and gained admission to the livery of the Pewterers' Company by redemption in 1573, was discovered attempting to send 18 cwt of pewter from London which had not been inspected by the Company searchers, in contravention of the ordinances.[3] When also challenged by the Master and Wardens for illegally striking a touch reserved for royal pewter, namely a crowned bell, 'He skoffingelie answered them that whatsoever ordynaunces they had for that matter, he cared not a Rushe, for as he did use yt so would he do still, and do they what they liste' and accused the Master himself of using an illegal touch. Further attempts to calm Jurdeine succeeded only in rousing him to greater anger and he answered:

> Seinge you do thus abuse me, I will laie downe my hoode and from hensfurthe never come emoungeste you, and yet will I keep open shoppe, and give the Crowned bell, in spite of you all, and doo the best and wourste you can, and therewith verie unreverentlie before them all, did put on his

[1] *Ibid.*, 10 Aug., 10 Dec.   [2] Guildhall MS 7090/4.
[3] Guildhall MSS 7086/3; 7090/2, 10 Sept.

cappe, flange away, as one that had bene madd, and in such manner departed he.

Fascinating though it is to have such an unusually lively account painted by an exceedingly conscientious clerk, the true value of this story lies in the fact that exclusion from the benefits of membership of the Pewterers' Company eventually proved too great a sacrifice, even for one so haughty as Jurdeine, and he subsequently apologised and, on payment of a 10s fine, was welcomed once more into the livery.[1]

Yet, in the course of time it was inevitable that the many strengths of the Company should serve only to delay rather than to reverse the powerful forces of economic, social, and legal change which were undermining the whole gild system. As has already been indicated the ebbing of the London Pewterers' authority over the provincial industry was precipitated by the decline of the provincial gilds themselves, which in turn owed much to the harmful effects of a series of unfavourable legal decisions in common law courts and, in some cases, the growth of competition from newer and less strictly regulated centres of manufacture.[2] The legal position regarding many of the most typical powers claimed by gilds became increasingly confused as the seventeenth century progressed. Basically there was a conflict between central common law, which invariably championed complete freedom of trade, and municipal and gild courts, which attempted to retain as many of the old restrictions as possible. Nevertheless, although no individual legal judgment can be singled out as having had a decisive influence, there can be no doubt that the succession of prejudicial judgments made in common law courts in the seventeenth century resulted in a serious debilitation of gild powers in general.[3]

Consequently it was inevitable that by the early eighteenth century signs of growing weakness were discernible in a number of key areas of Company jurisdiction. Perhaps one of the most striking features of court minutes at this time is the combination

---

[1] Guildhall MS 7086/3, 1574-5. It is interesting to discover that three years later Jurdeine, who was the Queen's pewterer, unsuccessfully attempted to gain the exclusive right of making all measures used in selling wine, ale, and beer by retail (*C.S.P.D. 1547-80*, p. 556).
[2] For example, the rise of the Walsall and Wigan pewter industries in the seventeenth century seriously affected the prosperity of the York pewterers.
[3] Kramer, *English Craft Gilds*, p. 139 ff.; Lipson, *Economic History*, iii, 344-51; Kellett.

of, on the one hand, an earnest determination to enforce rules and, on the other, a growing proclivity among members to circumvent them. Attention has already been drawn to the blatant contravention of by-laws relating to advertising and hawking, but perhaps the greatest deterioration was experienced in the powers of search. By the closing decades of the seventeenth century a number of test cases based on pleas of trespass had persuaded the Company drastically to curtail its country searches, and by 1700 it was proving difficult to search the premises of non-members in London, owing to the fear of prosecution for trespass.[1] By 1741 a committee of the Company virtually admitted defeat on the question of fraudulent marks when it reported that nothing could be done to prevent country pewterers from striking 'London' and 'Made in London' on their wares, unless further authority could be obtained from Parliament.[2] A fuller discussion of the decline of the Company's power over the pewter industry in the eighteenth century must be postponed to a later chapter.

One of the cardinal sins of the historian is to interpret the past solely in terms of the values of the present. Viewed in this way gild philosophy assumes irredeemably sinister proportions, espousing monopoly rather than competition, stagnation rather than growth, and tradition rather than progress, and most gild ordinances appear to modern eyes to be either self-seeking or as fussily irrelevant as the wilder flights of eighteenth-century rococo architecture. Yet to take only this view is to ignore the economic and social forces which helped to mould the gilds. Without doubt the most powerful formative influence on the small artisan-industrialist in pre-industrial society was the discontinuous nature of the demand for his products. The overwhelming dependence of society on agriculture and, in turn, on the weather, was the root cause of these oscillations in demand with, in simple terms, a good harvest tending to result in greater purchases of manufactures and luxuries, and a poor harvest in reduced purchases. Furthermore it is likely that the pewter industry was especially vulnerable to this inevitable cycle, for although pewter was used by a very large section of the population it was a durable product and old wares could be made to last another year or two in times of economic retrenchment. In addition, demand for all products was frequently disrupted by plague and foreign wars, and a further

[1] Guildhall MS 7090/8, 24 June.   [2] Guildhall MS 7090/10, 24 Sept.

source of uncertainty for pewterers was the fluctuating nature of tin output, the effects of which were compounded by the machinations of the tin farmers. All in all long-term planning was an extremely hazardous undertaking and it was always possible that any expansion of production could lead to increased unemployment at some future date. The pewterers of Wigan succinctly expressed their appreciation of this basic instability in 1683 when they argued that 'London probably takes of about 200 tun [of tin] a yeare and Wigan about 40 or 50 tun yearly, lesse or more according to the cheapness or dearness of the Tine, or dearth of corne, for if either bee verry deare out comes the old pewter apace, and soe the lesse Tin is used'.[1]

It was perhaps inevitable that extreme uncertainty should beget excessive caution. Small masters and journeymen having served a long and exacting apprenticeship, and possessing no alternative skills and only scant capital resources, understandably viewed with hostility any intemperate expansion of production and with approval any measure designed to protect their employment. Hence the stringent limitations on the numbers of apprentices, the prohibition of the employment of non-gild labour, and of the sale of secondhand pewter and pewter that had not been fully wrought. Fear of the effects of unbridled competition in difficult trading conditions doubtless lay behind the stress laid on co-operation, the attempts to improve profit margins by the fixing of selling prices, and the cultivation of goodwill amongst customers by insistance on high standards of production.

Nevertheless even the most sympathetic appreciation of the motives which fashioned gild policies must stop short of condoning all the consequences that followed from them. On the credit side one can see that the system did much to ensure that high skills were transmitted from one generation to another, that high standards of production were successfully encouraged, and that industries achieved a considerable measure of stability and continuity. But the catalogue of harmful consequences on the debit side is also long and weighty, and what is more it tended to grow as time passed. The maintenance of excellence in production and the persecution of non-gild producers inevitably restricted supply to the detriment of consumers; the intricate system of controls on entry to the craft and the widespread fear of expansion

[1] Shelley, 'Wigan and Liverpool Pewterers', p. 11.

inevitably resulted in a sluggish response to increased demand and a failure to exploit to the full the opportunities for growth that presented themselves; and conservatism and the stifling of competition inevitably provided a favourable breeding ground for inefficiency and backward technology.

It is at present impossible to draw up an exact balance sheet of the advantages and disadvantages of gild organisation to the pewter industry, far less to the nation as a whole, but it is conceivable that whereas advantages predominated in the Middle Ages disadvantages came increasingly to the fore as the sixteenth and seventeenth centuries wore on, and that eventually the strength of the gild was to contribute to the weakness of the industry. Disapprobation was the automatic response to changes in techniques and the development of new products and alloys. Within the London Company the painting or gilding of pewter was forbidden, engraving was strictly controlled, and mechanical improvements were regarded with suspicion. The insularity bred by gild values resulted inevitably in attempts to stamp out promising technological developments both within and outside the Company, on the grounds that they posed threats to the livelihood of members. Thus the Company in the seventeenth century set its face firmly against the manufacturers of 'silvorum', 'white plate' and 'Crooked Lane ware', and consequently failed to seize the opportunities for diversification that these new alloys presented. In later years the slowness of pewterers to experiment and diversify, particularly with spinning and stamping rather than casting, was to prove a fatal error of judgment, and the blame for this must lie to a large extent with the attitudes fostered by a gild mentality.

5 Manufacturing and marketing

In this chapter the opportunity has been taken of providing a more detailed and systematic treatment of a number of topics central to the history of pewter which have received only passing attention in preceding chapters. This approach will inevitably involve some repetition, but a considerable body of new material will also be presented.

THE TECHNIQUES OF MANUFACTURE

The low melting point of tin, the ease with which it fuses with many other metals, and the softness of the resultant alloys meant that the manufacture of many pewter utensils was a relatively simple procedure. Nevertheless, although crude wares could be produced with little expertise or equipment the production of high quality pewterware demanded a considerable knowledge of metallurgy, exacting standards of craftsmanship, and a range of expensive tools. The basic processes of manufacture were casting, soldering, turning, and hammering, and the basic equipment consisted of ladles, moulds, soldering irons, a lathe with a selection of turning tools, and a variety of hammers and mallets. Sadware was usually cast in moulds, then hammered to provide greater strength, before being skimmed, burnished, and polished on a lathe. Holloware was also cast, sometimes in several separate parts which were subsequently soldered together, then finished off by hand and by lathe. In addition a range of sadware articles, including some large chargers and certain types of basin, were sometimes wrought by hand from cast flat discs of pewter.

The rudimentary nature of the three distinct stages of manufacture ensured that they underwent little fundamental change in over one and a half millennia of British history. A number of Romano-British pewterers' dish moulds have been found, many surviving pieces display clear evidence of having been turned on the lathe, and hammering was doubtless a common practice in pewtering as it was in other branches of metalwork.[1] The moulds were made of stone rather than bronze, and the rough finish of much extant Romano-British sadware proves that the turning apparatus was frequently extremely crude, but a close similarity to the techniques of successive pewterers up to the eighteenth century cannot be denied.

Within these broad limits, however, a substantial amount of improvement was accomplished. The progress of technology was not always a smooth cumulative process, and in earlier centuries in particular hard won advances often vanished in the frequent periods of war and upheaval, and had to be rediscovered by later craftsmen. Our knowledge of the technology of pewtering between the fifth century and the fourteenth is extremely sparse, because both pewter and written records were rare. We are therefore extremely fortunate to possess Theophilus Presbyter's unique detailed descriptions of various manufacturing processes at the beginning of the twelfth century, an age in which mere handicrafts were usually deemed unworthy of committing to writing. We are even more fortunate that Theophilus, who was probably a German monk, chose to concern himself with the method of making a pewter cruet. His account is of such value and from so early a date that it must be quoted in full:[2]

> Make yourself two iron spindles, the length of a hand and slightly thinner than the little finger; they should be thicker at one end and taper gradually to the other end, so that they can be drawn out of the core. At the thicker end they should have flat tangs so that they can be fixed into round pulleys which should have short, round pins on their other ends on which they can be turned. Put clay round the spindles, at first a little, then more, according to the size you wish. When the clay is dry, set up your lathe in the same way as the one on which platters and other wooden vessels

---

[1] Liversidge, 'Romano-British Pewter from Icklingham', 1; Peal, Romano-British pewter plates and dishes', 24.
[2] The following translation is largely taken from the Hawthorne and Smith edition of *The Treatise of Theophilus*, pp. 181–3.

are turned with one post fixed firmly and the other movable. When the latter is in place, it should be secured by a flat key [wedge] at the bottom.

Set a core between posts [i.e. the headstock and the tailstock] and the pins in their holes and put a strap around the wooden pulley. Seat a boy to pull it [to and fro] and turn as you please; then cover it with wax. When the wax has been similarly turned, withdraw the mould with the spindle from the pulley, attach the vents [and a gate], put clay over it, and let it dry; remove the wax [by melting] and put the mould into the furnace to bake it. . . . When it is completely red-hot inside, take it off the fire and let it lie until it is cool enough to be held for a short time in your hand. Immediately melt some tin in an iron pan or in a dish and when it is time for casting add a little mercury to it in such proportions that if there is a pound of tin, there should be a farthingweight of mercury.

Pour it into the mould without delay. When the mould is entirely cold, break the clay off the outside and when the pulley has been replaced mount the work on the lathe and turn it evenly all over. Finally polish it with shave-grass. After this take some of the scrapings of the tin, mix a little mercury with them, and rub them together with your fingers until they become completely liquid. Then, with a small cloth, smear this around the cruet while turning it until it is left dry and shining. Now extract the spindle and the clay inside and dig a small groove in the centre of the [thickness of the] tin around the hole at the bottom where the spindle has been, and fit into it a small piece of the same tin slightly thicker than the cruet is to be. Put inside [the cruet] a round piece of wood to support the tin so that it will not be bent, and hammer it on the outside with a medium-size hammer until the tin is forced into the groove and stays firmly there. You can also seal up the hole in another way. Put a piece of wood inside the cruet, as above, with its end wrapped in a cloth; now scrape the hole and smear it with wax, melt some plain lead and pour it in and then quickly even it out with a small hammer.

How tin should be soldered

Hammer out of tin two matching cups and fit them together in the middle so that the rim of one goes inside the other. Put the one which holds the other in hot ashes. Then hammer very thin a piece of the same tin, mixed with a third part of lead, and cut it up in little pieces. Place these around [the joint], apply a few lighted coals and as soon as [the work] warms up, smear it around with resin from a fir tree and immediately you will see the pieces melt and flow about. Take away the coals at once and when it is cool it will be firm. Any kind of work in straight tin can be soldered by this method, namely, spouts and handles on pots and the hinges for lids; also any hole that occurs in a cast pot as a result of negligence.

Casting the spout

The spout can be easily made also in this way. Cut a piece of cleavable wood to a round shape and make a longitudinal hole in it with a drill but not right to the end. Split it down the middle and make a hole in the end that has not been drilled. Through this hole fit into place a round piece of iron [to form the core], thinly coated with clay, to correspond to the inside dimensions of the spout. Then bind the mould firmly around on the outside, warm it, and pour in the tin. When it is cold, loosen the wood, take out the piece of iron, file the spout, finish it off smoothly, and solder it to the vessel in the way described above.

The method of casting holloware described by Theophilus, the lost-wax (*cire-perdue*) process, in which molten metal was poured into the space previously occupied by wax, had been practised since the Bronze Age, if not earlier. It was obviously suited only to the production of small quantities of articles, and furthermore the resultant castings would of necessity differ slightly from each other and have a very rough finish. The process was not as simple as Theophilus makes it appear, for the two parts of the clay mould had to be kept absolutely steady once the wax had melted. The composition of the metal is most interesting, comprising pure tin with the addition of a tiny quantity of mercury. Unfortunately the original text is ambiguous for it reads: '*Si est libra stagni, quadrans sit vivi argenti*', which can mean either a fourth part, four per cent, or a farthingweight of mercury per pound of tin. Nevertheless, guided by the previous sentence, which speaks of 'a little mercury' and discounting alloys containing 3.9 per cent and 20 per cent mercury respectively, which would be useless, we are left with an alloy of 1 part of mercury to 960 parts of tin, in which the mercury would produce a significant hardening effect on the tin.

The only other descriptive account of the pewterer's craft written before 1700 is contained in the *Pirotechnia* of Vannoccio Biringuccio, which was first published in 1540. Unfortunately for our purposes Biringuccio, who was himself an expert metalworker, adopted a dismissive attitude towards pewter, and he introduced his short chapter, entitled 'Concerning the art of the pewterer', in the following manner:

> Having told you of the practices of the arts involving other metals, I wish to tell you also of the practice of that of tin. Indeed since this is an easily melted metal, in common use for the utensils which are made for human needs, it is an art known not only to skilled men but also almost to children, wherefore I could proceed without telling of it. However, besides the production of plates and bowls and many other dishes for eating from and keeping things in, this embraces two other arts, both of which you should know about because they are useful and beautiful. One of these is the art of making the letters with which books are printed, and the other is that of making the sheets from which organ pipes are built.[1]

Biringuccio relented, however, but only to provide two brief and barely adequate descriptions of the manufacture of sadware and holloware:

> The vessels, as perhaps you have seen, are cast one by one in moulds made of white tuff. Several pieces fastened together are then put on the iron axle of a wheel rotated by hand, and they are turned with a slightly bent tool which has a cutting edge. In this way they are made thin and of a good shape. Then they are polished with a piece of linen cloth

[1] Biringuccio, p. 374.

and a little powdered tripoli, and thus they are finished. . . .
Other vessels, besides round [flat] ones, are made of pewter,
such as flasks, containers for preserves, and saltcellars. These
are cast in halves in moulds made of white tuff, and then
fitted together and soldered. With rasps and scrapers and
other cutting tools they are smoothed, polished, and made
more beautiful.[1]

As Biringuccio's account appears to be based on the practices of Italian pewterers, who were few in number and probably inferior in technique to those in some other parts of Europe, we should not pay too much attention to the fact that he has them using stone moulds, even though bronze moulds had long since been introduced elsewhere. Indeed by this date it is possible to piece together from other sources a far more detailed picture of the pewterer's craft. Inventories are the most informative source for the tools of the pewterer, and one of the fullest from an early date provides us with the equipment of a Rouen pewterer who died in 1402:[2]

A lathe
A pair of tongs (*fourquettes*)
14 turning tools
2 square turning tools
2 soldering irons
An iron auger (*tort*)
4 brushes
A burnisher for two hands
2 hooks and 1 rasp
2 files
A pair of pincers
7 cores or mandrels (3 large and 4 small)
A drill (*chinole à tourner*)
Small moulds
3 iron casting-ladles
3 small hammers
A pair of shears
1 small chisel
A small mould for low salt-cellars with lid, embossed
A mould for salt-cellars on a foot, with lid, embossed

[1] *Ibid.*, pp. 374, 377.   [2] Bapst, pp. 156–7.

A mould for salt-cellars *en façon de gallice* with lid, embossed
A mould for lead beakers
2 moulds for acorn hinges (one large, one small)
2 moulds for knobs for salt-cellar lids
A pair of small scales
A pair of small compasses
A little bunch of iron wire
2 pairs of wooden scales
A borer for boring pots (*un percheur à perchier poz*)
2 pairs of old bellows
A whetstone or hone

Unfortunately, the vast majority of inventories are far less informative than this. But the inventory of Henry Grene (d. 1569), a wealthy pewterer and bell-founder of Worcester, is valuable not only for details of equipment, but also for the arrangement of his premises into six separate chambers:[1]

The ware howse	£. s. d.
Item in new pewter 2 cwt 8 lb	7. 0. 0
Item in new ley 53 lb	1. 6. 8
Item in old ley 84 lb	1. 6. 8
Item 2 drincking pottes, 16 saltes and 6 dossen of spones and fyve bottells	1. 0. 0
Item fyve chawfing dishes, one morter, one greate pare of candlestickes, 2 pare of yallowe playtes, 18 musyn candlestickes	1.10. 0
Item 90 lb of old kettels	3.13. 4
Item 90 lb of newe brasse pottes	1.13. 4
Item 120 lb of old brasse	2. 0. 0
Item 140 lb of leade	10. 0
Item 187 lb of bell mettell	3. 0. 0
Item brasse mowlds 290 lb	7. 5. 0
Item weightes of leade, an yron beame and skales	1. 3. 0
Item in odd yron and tooles 4 cwt, with other implementes	2. 0. 0
Som	33. 8. 0

[1] 'Probate inventories of Worcester tradesmen 1545–1614', *Miscellany II*, ed. A. D. Dyer (Worcestershire Historical Society, new ser. v (1967), pp. 27–8.

The sadware shoppe

	£.	s.	d.
Item an yron whele, 6 hambers, 6 hookes, 3 anvildes and 4 swayges, 2 rapes, on smalle hamber, a byckorne, with other ymplementes	3.	0.	0
Som	3.	0.	0

The casting shope

	£.	s.	d.
Item 4 pare of clames, 2 pare of lyftinge tonges, fyve soldring yrons, 2 pare of sheres, 2 pare of plyers, 1 casting ladle, 4 spindles and a hollowe ware whele, with other ymplementes	1.	4.	0
Som	1.	4.	0

The working chamber

	£.	s.	d.
Item one greate whele with 3 spindles, 32 hookes, 2 planes, 3 rapes, 2 haunce mowldes, 1 tancket mowlde, 1 present quart mowlde, a playne quarte mowlde, a playne pynte mowlde, 1 flowre cup mowlde, 2 salte mowldes, 3 vyses with that as belonges to the same, with other ymplementes and one turnynge lathe	3.	0.	0
Som	3.	0.	0

The potte howse

	£.	s.	d.
Item one pare of bellis, 2 ponnes, a loche yron, a colrake, an old ladle, 2 hookes, 2 spades, with other ymplementes	3.	13.	4
Som	3.	13.	4

The bell howse

	£.	s.	d.
Item a greate yron beame, 7 bell mowldes, the bell furnesse, 4 pare of bellis, 300 (sic) potte mowldes, with other ymplementes	7.	0.	0
Som	7.	0.	0

Two detailed inventories of the equipment, raw materials, and sales stock of seventeenth-century Cornish pewterers are appended as further examples of the larger-scale producer:[1]

	£. s. d.
Peter Towsen, Liskeard, d. 1667	
the sad moulds	18. 4. 0
hollo moulds	5. 5. 0
the wheeles	3. 0. 0
the spoone hamer and stampe	13. 4
3 smaule hamers	10. 0
hollo ware hookes and floots	9. 4
a set of letters	3. 3
3? and 1 pair clains [clamps]	2. 0
in rufe ware	8. 0. 0
in nue sad ware	10. 0
in nue hollo ware	1.10. 0
in new layer ware	7. 0
in tinn	1. 0. 0
in new kittells and old brass	10. 0
in ould layd	5. 0
in holla ware blocks	4. 0

Martin Williams, Bodmin, d. 1695
goods in the shopp
   3 platter moulds, on porrenger mould, 2 flagon
   moulds, on salt mould, 2 tumbler moulds, on
   blod dish mould, 3 spoon moulds, on scrue mould 4. 0. 0
in the workshop
   on handveell [anvil], 5 hammers, 2 flots, 2 rasps,
   2 sadware huckes, on sadware wheele, on
   hollow ware wheele, 20 hollow ware huckes,
   4 burnishers, 3 sodering irons, 2 kettles, on
   paire of claimes, 2 ladles, a sett of letters,
   on vise, 3 metle moulds, on pair of sheares,
   on paire of bellows and the horsse, 2 beames
   and scales and wights   2.10. 0
  5 brasse potts, 3 litle kettles, 2 stilles, 22 pewter
   dishes, on pastie pann, on cheese plate, 3 pie
   panns, 2 dozen and 4 plates, 3 dozen and halfe

[1] Douch, pp. 70, 74.

of spoons, 13 chamber potts, 3 porrengers,
on stoole pan, 1 dozen and halfe of tynn
tumblers, 4 coverd flaggons, 3 plaine flagons,
3 tankards not finisht, 5 quart tankards, 6 halfe
pint tankards, 3 paire of tinn candlesticks,
on dozen sawcers, 2 wine quarts, on pinte and
half pinte, 2 brandie botles, on litle salt,
2 muster potts, on litle brandie bowle   8. 0. 0
ware not finished
15 plates, 47 flaggons, on tankard, 2 dozen and
8 porrengers, 3 dozen and ten blood dishes,
3 dozen and 5 cupps, 3 wine quarts, 21 blockes,
on platter and 100 wight of old brasse,
108 lb of old tyn, 49 lb of shaveings   4.10. 0

Lists such as these which provide the names of the various tools used by pewterers are clearly of great value for an understanding of the craft, but a simple listing can create a false impression of stagnation in techniques. In fact substantial advances were accomplished, particularly with respect to the nature of moulds, the construction of lathes, and the composition of alloys. To begin with moulds. We have already seen that moulds of stone and clay were used in Roman and early medieval times, indeed the very low melting point of pewter even made it possible to cast flat articles in sand. Nevertheless, the primitive nature of these moulds placed severe limitations on the scale and efficiency of production in these early times, especially as lathes also were rudimentary. The production of sadware was clearly far easier than the production of holloware: the stone sadware mould was relatively easy to fashion, and it could turn out appreciable quantities of castings, albeit with a rough finish. It was the casting of holloware which presented the most difficult problems, and as long as craftsmen depended upon the *cire-perdue* process it was bound to be costly and time consuming. Furthermore from our knowledge of early medieval pewter it is evident that holloware was in far greater demand than sadware; it was not mere chance that led Theophilus to choose a cruet as his example of pewter manufacture.

The development of moulds of bronze, and later gun-metal, was therefore a substantial advance. Metal moulds not only produced better castings, they were also extremely durable. Although stone moulds were apparently used for casting holloware (indeed even as late as the mid-sixteenth century Biringuccio asserts that Italian pewterers were using them) they could not have been satisfactory; the introduction of bronze moulds composed of a series of interlocking parts honed to a fine degree of tolerance, facilitated the efficient production of large quantities of high-quality utensils. It is impossible to put a precise date upon the introduction of metal moulds, but they were clearly in widespread use in fifteenth-century England.[1] Because of very high cost, however, their dissemination through the ranks of small-scale country pewterers must have been a slow process. It was no easy task to make metal moulds, and many days were spent shaping and smoothing the inner surfaces, since it was far better to spend time on the mould and have near perfect castings than to file and polish the imperfections on every piece that was cast. Consequently moulds were greatly prized and among the most expensive items of equipment that the pewterer possessed.

Improvements in the lathe were even more dramatic. The softness of pewter enabled small items to be turned on primitive machines more suited to wood, but heavy items required stronger and more efficient lathes, and the imparting of a smooth finish without undue effort required an advanced form of drive which turned the article continuously in one direction. The lathe described by Theophilus for the finishing of a pewter cruet consisted of a horizontal spindle between two posts, one of which was movable, rotated by means of a strap wound round the spindle and drawn by a seated boy.[2] This lathe would have resulted in an alternating rotation of the cruet, and since the turning tool would cut in only one direction, the craftsmen had to coordinate the action of the tool with the changing direction of rotation of the cruet. Alternating rotation also produces a jerky motion which has to be compensated by great skill on the part of the craftsman.

The next major development was the invention of spring-pole-and-treadle drive at some point in the late twelfth or early thirteenth century. The pole lathe still retained a cord drive, but

[1] Some of the earliest references are contained in the London Pewterers' records: Welch, i, 14–15, 105, 120, 175, 179.
[2] See above, pp. 210–11.

one end of the cord was fastened to the end of a flexible wooden pole secured above the lathe and the other to a treadle hinged to the floor. When the craftsman stepped on the treadle the work was rotated rapidly in one direction, and when his foot was lifted the elasticity of the pole pulled back the cord and rotated the work in the opposite direction.[1] Thus alternating rotation was still retained, but the available power was probably somewhat greater, and the craftsman could more easily coordinate tool and rotation. From a series of contemporary illustrations of the pole lathe it is clear that secondary, but nevertheless significant, advances were also achieved. In particular the lathe bed and the head and tailstocks were constructed of heavy timbers, and the whole structure was made more rigid and therefore more suitable for turning weighty articles.

Nevertheless the pole lathe still remained far more suitable for working in wood than in metal. The cutting force required in metalwork was such that the craftsman had to concentrate his energies on guiding his tool accurately and with sufficient force, and alternating rotation and the need to provide power with his foot were considerable inconveniences. Continuous drive provided by an assistant using a cranked flywheel was the solution. Once again precise dating is impossible, but it is evident that the principles of cranked wheel and cord drive were known in the second half of the fifteenth century. The application of this important discovery to the pewterer's lathe may well have taken some time, but it was certainly in use well before 1568, the date of the earliest illustration.[2] Coincidentally Henry Grene's inventory quoted above dates from the following year, and by referring to an 'yron whele' and a 'greate whele' suggests that this form of powered lathe was then in use in Worcester. But once again dissemination was a slow process, and one which was deliberately hindered by craftsmen anxious to preserve an advantage, and it is interesting to note that in 1602 the London Pewterers Company

> ordred uppon the abuse of dyvers of the company who worketh openly in the shopes with ther grete wheles, which is ane occasion that pewterers of the country and others shall come to great lyght of farther knowleg to the great hindraunce of the company as well at this present as here-

[1] See pl. 21. See also R. S. Woodbury, *History of the Lathe to 1850* (Ohio, 1961), pp. 38–44. [2] See pl. 22 and Woodbury, pp. 44–9.

after, now ther is comaundment that presently before bartelmew day they do reforme it.[1]

Continuous drive was a technological advance of far reaching proportions: the speed of rotation of the workpiece could be substantially increased and also varied by the use of pulleys to suit the needs of the work, and the introduction of a tool-holder and slide rest, which resulted in greater ease of working as well as greater precision, was facilitated. By the later sixteenth century, therefore, pewterers casting from bronze moulds and turning on powerful high speed lathes using long-handled tools which rested on the machine, were not only capable of producing a wide range of fine quality articles, including many of prodigious proportions and complex designs, but also of producing them with far greater speed than their predecessors.

Having dwelt on the equipment of a pewterer it would be useful to look briefly at how it would have been used in the manufacture of specimens of sadware and holloware in the seventeenth century.[2] For casting, the constituents of the intended alloy, having first been carefully weighed, would be melted and mixed in an iron pot or kettle over a forge fire. The fire needed to be only a simple affair, and wood was often used as a fuel,[3] although in the course of the sixteenth century the increased supplies of coal available in London and elsewhere were almost certainly used. Increased heat could easily be generated by the use of hand bellows. In preparation for receiving the molten metal the appropriate moulds were heated on the outside (to avoid damage),[4] and brushed on the inside with one of a variety of concoctions ranging from powdered pumice-stone to egg-white and red ochre, to facilitate smooth castings and prevent striations. If a plate were to be cast the hinged mould would be snapped tightly closed, and possibly also held in a clamp or a vice, to make it perfectly tight. An appropriate quantity of molten metal would then be scooped into a ladle and poured slowly

[1] Guildhall MS 7090/3, 13 Aug.
[2] The following works have been particularly useful in compiling these descriptions: H. J. Kauffman, *The American Pewterer; his techniques and his products* (New Jersey, 1970); Massé, *Pewter Plate;* Massé, *Chats on Old Pewter.*
[3] A number of pewterers' inventories contain stocks of wood; see, for example, that of J. Baron (Douch, p. 75).
[4] On 18 April 1684 the York pewterers passed a rule stipulating that all moulds were to be heated on the backside and not on the right side (Univ. of York Library MS E.54).

into the tedge, or gate, of the mould, with great care exercised to ensure that none of the scum of the melting pot got into the mould. The temperature of the metal and the mould had to be carefully married, and it was usually essential to make a number of trial castings in order to reach the desired level. A reserve of metal would be left in the tedge in order to keep the mould full as the cooling metal contracted. On removal from the mould the pewter would always have a white and frosted appearance, but the amount of repair and finishing it required would depend on the condition of the mould and the skill with which the casting had been made.

The first task after casting was to remove the excess metal from the rim which, depending on the quantity, would be accomplished by melting with a soldering iron or snipping with pincers. Small holes would be filled with melted scraps of pewter, then scraped smooth. The plate should then have been placed on a narrow anvil or swage, and hammered in the booge (the rounded portion between the rim and the well) and sometimes all over, in order to perfect the shape and compact the metal, thereby strengthening it. For this task the pewterer used a wide variety of short-handled hammers with long heads; the pane of the hammers also varied both in size and section, some being almost flat and others steeply convex. Hammers and anvils, and indeed all pewterers' tools, had to be kept undamaged, spotlessly clean, and very brightly polished in order to avoid marking the pewter.

After hammering the plate was transferred to the lathe; sometimes separate sadware and holloware lathes were provided, but many lathes could be adapted to take both sorts of ware. The plate was then attached by wire or a metal band to a revolving chuck of wood. The first operation was usually to skim and eliminate the unevenness resulting from the casting, using a variety of tools of varying degrees of fineness. After the plate had been skimmed and smoothed it was burnished. Burnishers, which could be made of steel, bloodstone or agate, came in various shapes and sizes, and were frequently used with soap and water as a lubricant. Finally the plate would be polished on the lathe using rags or leathers charged with oil and rottenstone, held in place with tools. The reverse of the plate would then be treated in similar fashion, although care would be taken not to obliterate the marks of the hammer on the booge.

Holloware usually consisted of two or more parts, which were cast separately and then soldered together. A simple lidless tankard or tavern pot, for example, might be cast in three sections— body, base, and handle;[1] more complex articles could consist of many more sections. The mould for each section might in turn consist of as many as four separate parts: for the body an inner core which provided the hollow interior of the pot, two outer parts which confined the molten metal to the desired shape and size, and perhaps a cap to complete the boundary of the molten metal and hold the outer parts together. The whole would then be compressed with clamps in a vice. When cast the body and base would be roughly finished by hand, fitted together with the aid of wire or a special tool, then soldered. Good soldering required not only skilful workmanship but also high-quality solder. The Pewterers' Company records contain frequent injunctions forbidding the use of 'soft pale', which probably contained more lead than tin and was not as durable as a tin-rich solder. The tankard was then finished on the lathe in much the same way as sadware, but using a holloware lathe and special holloware tools.[2] The handle which had been cast, was trimmed and polished by hand, and then soldered or burnt on to the body.

The series of distinct processes involved in the manufacture of pewterware facilitated the adoption of the division of labour. In the larger workshops productivity could be increased by allocating specific tasks to each craftsman, and it must be assumed that only in the smallest businesses did one man normally perform all the operations described above. Certain tasks 'such as turning the Wheel, Oileing and cleaning the Ware when finished' were considered the most menial parts of the trade, and were usually reserved for unfree labourers or apprentices in the early stages of their apprenticeship.[3] But more than this, a clear distinction appears to have grown up between hammering on the one hand, and lathe-work and casting on the other. As early as 1486 we find that a Scots journeyman was allowed to be employed in London 'To carste, To sowde, to fflote, to shave, To wype, To

---

[1] It is clear this practice was followed in London in the mid-sixteenth century, for in 1558 'yt was agreed that no personne from hensforth shall make any tankerd pottes or hoped pottes but they shall sother the same with fyne mettall in all places saving only the setting in of the bottam' (Guildhall MS 7090/1, 18 June).
[2] The hammering of holloware appears to have been an infrequent practice.
[3] Guildhall MS 12017, fol. 19.

holde the hoke, to rowe or to plane', but no mention was made of hammering.[1] By the early eighteenth century the two branches of the craft were considered to be quite separate, at least among London pewterers, and a handbook of London trades states: 'Making of Pewter consists chiefly of two Parts; 1. Melting, Casting, and Turning, which is one Persons's Business, the harder Work, and not so healthy; 2. Hammering or planishing, which is another's; one Workman but seldom doing all the Operations'.[2]

Finally we turn to the composition of the alloys that were used to manufacture pewterware. The range of alloys which can be classified as pewter is truly vast, but most are of far greater interest to the metallurgist than to the historian, and we shall concentrate on those that were widely used by English pewterers. A number of such alloys have already been noted in earlier chapters, but by reconsidering them and placing them in a chronological sequence it is possible to discern a course of development. In Roman Britain there were clearly no firm opinions on the most suitable alloy, or at least no attempt at conformity. Analyses of pewter finds reveal alloys ranging from pure tin to more than 50 per cent lead, although the majority lie within the limits of two to three parts of tin to one of lead. What is also clear is that no temper or hardening agent was used, and that the lead content was far higher than was to be permitted in subsequent centuries.[3] In the early Middle Ages it is possible that pure tin, sometimes alloyed with a hardening agent such as mercury, was the common form of pewter. Such a conclusion is in accordance with Theophilus and the fact that pewter was confined almost exclusively to ecclesiastical usage, which would result in stress being placed upon expensive tin rather than cheap lead; but it is also probable that tin–lead alloys were well known.

In the London ordinances of 1348 a fundamental distinction was made between pure tin alloyed with as much copper 'as of its own nature it will take' called fine pewter, used for the manufacture of sadware, and tin mixed with lead in proportions of not less than four to one, used for the manufacture of holloware.[4] In the sixteenth century a third, and lower, standard of pewter was permitted for the making of trifles—toys, buttons, salts, candlesticks etc. By the later sixteenth century English pewterers

[1] Guildhall MS 7086/1, 1485–6.
[2] T. Waller, *A General Description of All Trades* (1747), pp. 164–5.
[3] Above, pp. 16–18.   [4] *Memorials of London Life*, p. 242.

were adding bismuth (tin glass) to fine pewter in order to produce a harder and more durable alloy. Harrison's statement that three or four pounds of bismuth were added to a mixture of 1,000 lb of tin and 30 lb of copper is borne out by the records of the London Company, which contain frequent orders that 2½ to 3 lb of bismuth should be added to each thousandweight of tin; and in 1654 the Company even went so far as to provide a supply of bismuth in the Hall for the use of members.[1] Although pewterers' gilds attempted to enforce uniformly high standards it must be appreciated that both members and non-members frequently used substandard alloys; furthermore it is to be expected that many pewterers evolved their own favourite alloys within the accepted limits.

After a century or so of relative stability in the composition of alloys an advance of considerable significance was achieved by the introduction into England of a new form of pewter. Difficult as it may be for connoisseurs of English pewter to accept, there can be no doubt that a substantial debt is owed to French Protestant refugees, and to James Taudin in particular, for the dissemination of this improved form of fine pewter.[2] Taudin probably came to England and set up business in London in the early 1650s. By 1656 he was causing the Pewterers' Company great concern, and in that year Taudin's wares were seized by a formidable array of persons consisting of the 'Beadle, Souldiers, Carmen and Porters, and other Officers', and substantial sums of money were expended in assaying them and in prosecuting him before the Court of Aldermen and in the Exchequer.[3] It was all to no avail, however, for Taudin secured the support of Cromwell, and moreover the tide of common law was turning against gild law. In January 1658 Taudin was reluctantly admitted to the Company as a freeman and liveryman on payment of £50 and a bond for a further £10, and on condition that he kept only two apprentices and discharged 'all his strangers workmen' and employed only freemen as journeymen.[4] But all did not run

[1] Harrison, *Description of England*, p. 367; Welch, i, 226, 291, ii, 76, 89, 117, 119.
[2] For example, Cotterell noting the frequent references to 'French Pewter' on English pewterers' trade-cards wrote 'It is little short of amazing to find English pewterers desiring any advertisement better than "Made in London"' ('Pewterers' trade-cards', p. 222).
[3] The audit account for this year contains a multitude of references to his prosecution, with the sums expended in each instance: Guildhall MS 7086/3.
[4] Guildhall MS 7090/5.

smoothly between the Company and Taudin thereafter, and in the following decade a series of prosecutions were brought against him in the Company's court for breach of by-laws.[1] But over the same period Taudin had managed to build up a considerable reputation in London,[2] and he even prevailed on Charles II to write to the Company on his behalf.[3] Eventually, generous gifts from Taudin on the one hand and a grudging acceptance of his value to the Company on the other ensured a more amicable relationship.

Taudin's contribution to English pewtering in the later seventeenth century should not be underestimated by the historian, for it was fully appreciated by contemporaries. In 1677 Houghton published a defence of immigration entitled *Englands Great Happiness: or a Dialogue between Content and Complaint*, in which in order to rebut arguments hostile to the influx of aliens he wrote of the benefits that English industry had derived from them in the following terms:

> Would they not bring several new trades with them or help to increase those we have? Witness the Flemings in the time of Edward the Third, the colonies of Colchester, Canterbury and Norwich, the silk trade in Spitalfields, the tapestry-makers in Hatton Garden, Clerkenwell, and elsewhere, Mr Todin, the rare pewterer in St Martin's Lane, the husbandmen in the Fens, and divers others.[4]

Praise indeed to be numbered amongst such enterprising company!

It is at present impossible to be certain of the precise nature of the alloy or process of manufacture introduced by Taudin. The major technical advances of the later seventeenth century have so far received scant attention from connoisseurs of pewter, and Company records are unrevealing. We know that the resultant pewter was for a time called *étain sonnant*, for Taudin incorporated this phrase into his touch, as did his son and nephew in theirs.[5] But from various sources it is apparent that the alloy used in the

---

[1] Guildhall MSS 7090/5–6.
[2] It is probable that Taudin was 'the French pewterer' who sold Pepys pewter in March 1668 (*The Diary of Samuel Pepys, M.A., F.R.S.*, ed. H. B. Wheatley, 10 vols (1912–18), vii, 362).
[3] Charles II's letter is reproduced in full in the court minutes of 3 December 1668 (Guildhall MS 7090/6).
[4] Quoted in Lipson, *Economic History*, iii, 59.   [5] Cotterell, *Old Pewter*.

production of *étain sonnant* in France was unremarkable, consisting simply of 100 parts of tin to five parts of copper or one to three parts of copper and one of bismuth[1]—in other words the recipe which had been in general usage for fine pewter in England for well over a century. It is likely, therefore, that the special qualities of *étain sonnant*, as produced by Taudin, came as much from the process of manufacture as from the constituents of the alloy. Such a hypothesis is borne out by the charge brought against Taudin in 1667 'for makeing distinction between fyne and double refyne, and that his Costomers as well as others may know his fyne by his single touch and his double refyne by his double touch', to which Taudin answered 'the reason why he made such distinction was for that he gave servants double wages for that which he called double refyned'.[2]

It may well be a false trail but it is tempting to see some connection between Taudin and the Parisian pewterer of the mid-seventeenth century who claimed that he could make pewter of such excellent quality that it would serve as melting-pots for other makers' silver, and which was also light, brilliant and silverlike in appearance.[3] But the trail is unlikely to be false which connects Taudin's pewter with the 'Hard Metal' pewter that assumed such widespread popularity in the closing years of the seventeenth century. We know from pewterers' trade cards and bill heads that Hard Metal was also known as French Pewter,[4] and William Sandys, who gained his freedom in 1681, went so far as to proclaim that 'William Sandys who wrought with Mr James Taudin deceas'd makes that Fine White Metal call'd French Pewter. He having exactly the same art of Refining, Tempering, Casting and Working it up as Mr Taudin had in his lifetime'.[5]

It is possible that Hard Metal contained antimony, and was therefore similar in composition to Britannia metal. Indeed it would be strange if antimony were found not to have been included in the formulae for English pewter before the discovery of 'White Metal', later to be known as Britannia metal, about 1770.[6] Regulus of antimony, the metal as opposed to the sulphide,

[1] For example, Massé, *Pewter Plate*, p. 20; Hedges, *Tin in . . . History*, p. 71; Haedeke, *Metalwork*, p. 207; Bell, *Old Pewter*, p. 13.
[2] Guildhall MS 7090/6, 18 June.
[3] Massé, *Chats on Old Pewter*, p. 37 (quoting *Journal d'un Voyage à Paris*, 1657).
[4] Cotterell and Heal, 'Pewterers' trade cards' and 'About pewterers' trade-cards etc.' [5] *Ibid.*, 2.   [6] See below, pp. 287–8.

had been known since Chaldean times and we have clear evidence that it was being produced in Germany, Italy and elsewhere in the sixteenth century.[1] It was also well known that antimony was a powerful hardening agent in tin and bronze alloys, and Biringuccio claims that it was being used in early sixteenth-century Venice not only in the manufacture of type metal and bells but also by pewterers.[2] Furthermore we know that antimony was available in late seventeenth-century London.[3]

Yet, if one assumes that Hard Metal is simply fine pewter with the addition of antimony a number of difficult problems remain to be solved, in particular the major price differential between Hard Metal and ordinary fine pewter. In the 1690s, for example, Hard Metal plates were sold at between 1s6d and 1s2d per pound, while fine pewter plates fetched only 11d or 1s per pound.[4] The cost of antimony was not the cause of this difference; on the contrary at about 24s a hundredweight antimony was far cheaper than tin and barely a tenth of the price of copper.[5] Whereas it is just possible that for a time the price differential could have been accounted for by high profits accruing to a select body of manufacturers, it is inconceivable that it could have been maintained in the face of the extremely widespread manufacture of Hard Metal which took place from the early eighteenth century. It is probable therefore that the workmanship involved in the production of Hard Metal was substantially greater than that involved in the production of fine pewter (and here Taudin's 'double refyne' is perhaps suggestive). But a final solution to the composition of Hard Metal, and perhaps also to its process of manufacture, is much more likely to lie in the chemical analysis of surviving examples of late seventeenth-century wares than in inspired guesswork based upon inadequate written evidence.[6]

THE SUPPLY OF RAW MATERIALS

From what we know of the alloys, and of the relative proportions of the sadware, holloware, and trifles that were produced, it would appear that tin accounted for approximately 90 per cent

---

[1] G. Agricola, *De Re Metalliva*, ed. H. C. and L. H. Hoover (New York, 1950), pp. 400, 428; Biringuccio, p. 92.
[2] *Ibid.*, pp. 91–2, 374. [3] Rogers, vi, 469.
[4] *Ibid.*, v, 492, vi, 470–1. [5] *Ibid.*, v, 496, vi, 469.
[6] Such analyses are now being conducted by the Research Laboratory of the National Museum of Antiquities of Scotland, Edinburgh.

Plate 19   Lidless tavern mugs. From left to right, *c.* 1680–90, *c.* 1760–70, *c.* 1710–20.

Plate 20   A selection of seventeenth-century candlesticks, measures, and capstan salts. The dishes are considerably earlier.

Plate 21 A turner using a pole lathe, 1395 (*Zwölfbrüderbuch*, Mendelschen Stiftung, Nürnberg).

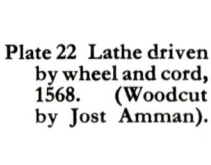Plate 22 Lathe driven by wheel and cord, 1568. (Woodcut by Jost Amman).

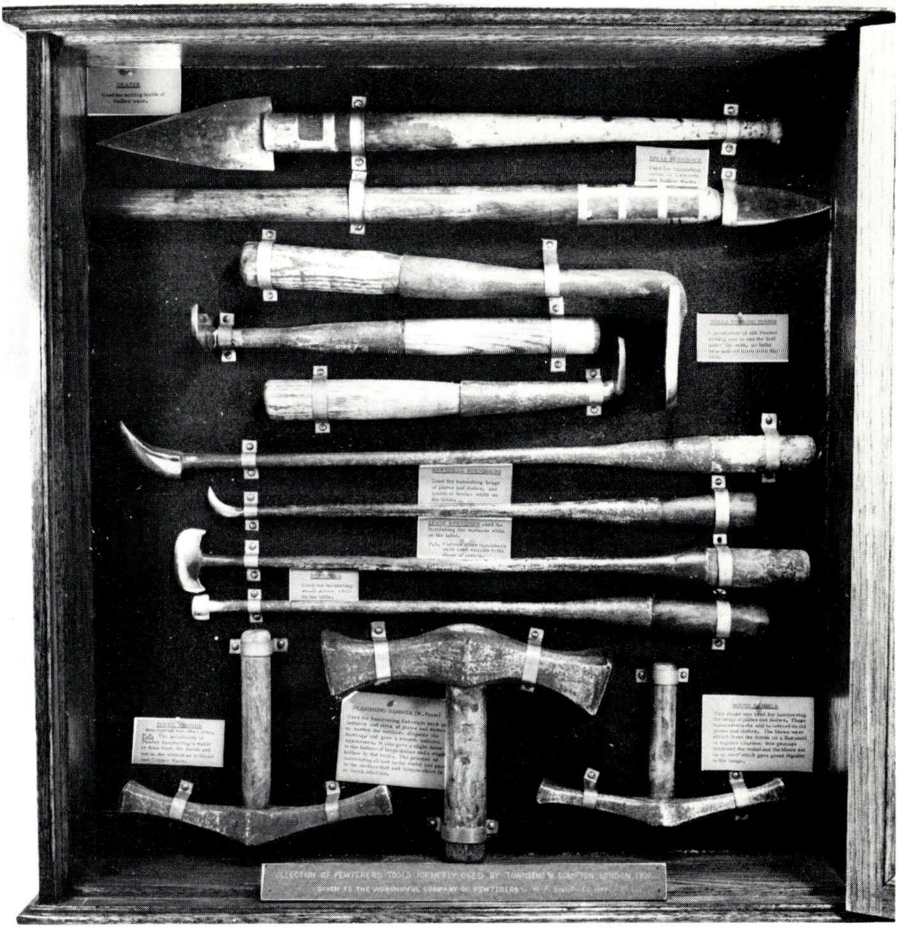

Plate 23   Selection of pewtering tools, formerly owned and used by members of the Townsend and Compton families, dating from the early eighteenth century.

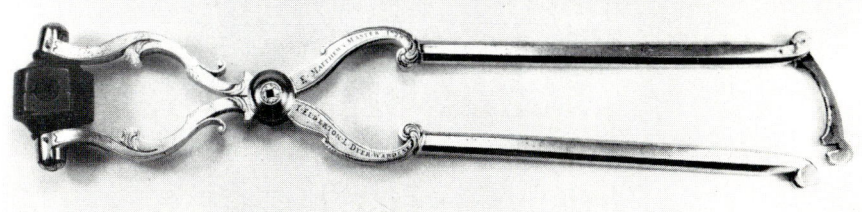

Plate 24   Steel assaying tool, inscribed with the names of the Master and Wardens of the Worshipful Company of Pewterers, dated 1728.

Plate 25　A pewterer casting from an old mould.

of the raw materials that went into pewter, lead for approximately 8 per cent, and copper and bismuth for the remaining 2 per cent. It must not be assumed, however, that all or (by the seventeenth century) even the major part of these materials consisted of virgin metal; scrap metal was always an important source of supply, and as the stock of pewter in the country grew it came to assume pre-eminent status. Nevertheless, the rapid rate of growth experienced by the industry over much of the period between 1300 and 1700 meant that the supply of new tin was invariably of great importance.

The tin trade had many unique features: most notably tin was produced only in Cornwall and west Devon, none was imported, and the production was put up for sale, after tax had been paid upon it, in a small number of coinage towns on only two to four occasions in the year.[1] The supply of tin was therefore peculiarly susceptible to the machinations of monopolists seeking to manipulate the market; moreover, stannary charters specifically reserved the right of the lord of the stannaries to pre-empt the whole output. In these circumstances it was essential for the major pewterers to safeguard their interests by involving themselves directly in the tin trade.

The tin trade involved at least three major interest groups, which were often in conflict: the tinners who sought to obtain the highest possible prices for their tin, be they labourers or merchant tinners; tin dealers, usually Londoners or foreigners, who sought to supply the most profitable markets, usually overseas; and pewterers, who were concerned to obtain secure and ample supplies of tin at low prices. The intervention of the Crown, or patentees who had purchased the right of pre-emption from the Crown, created yet another source of conflict. The right of pre-emption was exercised only rarely before 1600. Intermittent, and frequently unsuccessful, attempts were made by Richard I, John, Edward II and the Black Prince to profit from purchasing the whole output of the stannaries. For two hundred years after 1368, however, the tin trade was completely free of royal interference, only for pre-emption to be reintroduced on an almost continuous basis from the close of the sixteenth century until it was finally abandoned in 1717.[2]

---

[1] Hatcher, pp. 77–9; R. R. Pennington, *Stannary Law: a history of the mining law of Cornwall and Devon* (Newton Abbot, 1973), p. 140.   [2] Lewis, pp. 142–4.

The bulk of the tin that was not exported direct from south-western ports was shipped along the coast to Southampton and London. And again, of the tin sent to Southampton the bulk of that which was not exported went overland by cart to London, for Southampton's pewter industry was of modest proportions. London as a leading port, the centre of both the manufacture and export of pewter, the hub of the internal commodity distribution network, and the major source of finance for the tin mining industry, thus received massive quantities of tin each year.

Because of the central role played by the capital and the exceptional scale of its pewter industry, the involvement of London pewterers in the tin trade was far greater than that of provincial pewterers. As early as 1360 we find Nicholas 'Le Peudrer' (probably the same man as the Nicholas de Ludgate who was entrusted to supervise the articles of 1348) writing to the Black Prince and offering to 'come to the next coinage after Easter to buy a great part of the tin and pay promptly for the coinage thereof if the prince would assist him with boats for carrying the tin to Hampton [Southampton]'.[1] Unfortunately no local customs records for the port of London have survived, but we are fortunate in having a unique series of local port books and brokage books for Southampton, and for a century or more after 1430 it is possible to study the shipment of tin from the south-west to this port and its subsequent overland transportation to London, in gratifying detail. We must be careful, however, not to let the chance survival of records blind us to the continuing importance of tin shipments sent direct to London.

In the 1430s the role of London pewterers in the shipment of tin to London via Southampton does not appear to have been substantial; at this time the most prominent figure was a Cornish-man called John Dogowe, who was the owner of almost 30 tons of tin unloaded at Southampton in 1435-36, and of about 20 tons unloaded in 1439-40.[2] The dangers of this detachment were manifested in 1441, when an association of seven leading tin dealers, comprising two grocers, two drapers, a fishmonger, a salter, and a pewterer, was accused of attempting to buy up all the tin coming into the capital, no doubt to force up the

[1] *Registers of the Black Prince*, ii, 170.
[2] *The Local Port Book of Southampton, 1435-36*, ed. B. Foster (Southampton, 1963), p. 44; *The Local Port Book of Southampton for 1439-40*, ed. H. S. Cobb (Southampton, 1961), p. 52.

price.¹ In order to combat such malpractices and to safeguard the interests of the London Pewterers a City ordinance was promulgated in 1444 reserving for the Pewterers' craft, at the prevailing free market price, a quarter of all the tin brought to the capital.²

Wisely the Pewterers decided not to place all their trust in the law. In 1451 John Dogowe was admitted to the freedom of the craft, and on his death a special relationship was established with Thomas Butsyd, another leading Cornish tin dealer.³ Moreover, in succeeding years we find pewterers taking a substantial interest not only in purchasing tin in Southampton to be carted to London, but also in purchasing tin at source in Cornwall. In 1469–70, for example, 348 of the 1058 pieces⁴ of tin discharged at Southampton were owned by two prominent pewterers, Thomas Goodluck and John Paris; while in the following year the same pair held 380 of the 980 pieces that were unloaded.⁵ It seems likely from the scale of their activities that Goodluck and Paris were acting on behalf of a syndicate, perhaps consisting in part at least of London pewterers, for the tin in their hands in each of these years weighed around 40 tons and was worth in excess of £1,000—far more than could possibly have been used in their own workshops. These two pewterers appear also to have attended coinage sessions in Cornwall, for they feature on the coinage rolls of 1466–67 invoiced for the duty on a total of some 13 tons at Lostwithiel on 1 June.⁶ Pewterers are also represented in subsequent port books, and in 1499–1500 we find that Thomas Alexander and Laurence Astlyn, who had both held the office of Master of the Pewterers' Company, owned tin brought to Southampton from Cornwall.⁷

Nevertheless, pewterers never constituted a majority in the relatively small groups of merchants that controlled the tin trade in the fifteenth and sixteenth centuries, and furthermore they do

---

[1] E. Power and M. M. Postan, eds., *Studies in English Trade in the Fifteenth Century* (1933), p. 269.
[2] *Calendar of Letter Books, Book K*, p. 219.
[3] Welch, i, 39, 45. The desire of the Company to maintain good relations with tin dealers is further exemplified by an entry in the audit account of 1490–91 'paide for Ale whanne the Cornysshe men were at our halle iiid' (*ibid.* 77).
[4] A piece of tin weighed approximately 250 lb.
[5] *The Port Books of Southampton for the Reign of Edward IV*, ed. D. B. Quinn and A. A. Ruddock, 2 vols (Southampton, 1937–38).
[6] PRO E.101.266/13.
[7] Southampton Corporation MSS, Port Book for 14–15 Henry VII.

not appear to have played a significant part in the export of unwrought tin. Tin dealers were drawn from a wide range of London companies: in the 1440s they included Stephen Forster, fishmonger; Philip Malpas, draper; Thomas Boston, brasier; John Crowe, girdler and haberdasher, Richard Lee, grocer, and Bartholomew Stratton, Richard Riche, and Thomas Cantelowe, mercers;[1] and in the 1470s they included William Hampton, fishmonger; John Lewis, tailor; Geoffrey Kidwelly, horner; John Browne, mercer; Robert Billesdon, haberdasher; and William Yonge, grocer.[2] It is interesting to note that most of these men attained the office of Alderman of London, a sure sign of great wealth.[3]

There is no evidence to suggest that the Pewterers' Company engaged in the collective purchase of raw materials on a significant scale before the mid-sixteenth century. From time to time small reserves of cash accumulated by the Company were invested in tin, which was subsequently resold to members at a profit; but such dealings were on a modest scale, involving only a few hundredweight, and no attempt was made to offer an alternative to the normal channels of supply.[4] Consequently, London pewterers relied for their tin supplies upon close relationships with Cornish merchants, occasional associations of enterprising members, and the London tin market in general.

One of the first indications of the Company wishing to move towards collective purchase comes in 1561 when it was agreed by

> the master, wardens, and assystaunce, and the most part of all the whole company that foure honest men of the Company shall have the bying of all such bargaynes of tynne as hereafter shalbe by any manner of meanes come to any of the company by Brokership or any other shift, and the partie shall send the broker or other partie to one of the said foure and they by theire good advise shall make bargayne for the same in the name of the whole Company and that the same tynne so by them bargayned shalbe brought to the hall to thentent that every man that will

[1] PRO E.122.128/30, 128/31; E.122.73/23, 73/25, 77/4.
[2] Quinn and Ruddock (eds.), *Port Books, passim.*
[3] Thrupp, *Merchant Class of Medieval London*, Appendix A.
[4] For example, eleven pieces of tin were sold at a profit of £4.1s1d in 1481–82, five pieces of tin were sold at a profit of 30s in 1493–94, and eleven slabs of Devon tin in 1502–3 at a profit of 20s (Guildhall MS 7086/1).

have any thereof shall have suche porcion as shalbe thought by the master, wardens and assystaunce, Provided alwayes that none of the said iiij men shall do no manner of act or actes that shalbe preiudiciall to the said bargaynes or otherwise for theire owne lucer or gayne shall take the bargayne into their owne handes, upon payne of fforfayture of tenne poundes for every suche offens. And also it is agreed that if any suche tynne shall happen to be bought by the iiij men in manner aforesaid that no person of the said Company shall bye no pece of tynne but of the same tynne so bought, untill that be all gone upon forfayture of xls for every pece so bought.[1]

Two years later we learn that the Company agreed to purchase 500 pieces of tin (*c*. 55 tons) in Cornwall, thereby providing evidence of the first attempt at collective purchasing.[2] But such measures appear to have been of limited duration and may have resulted from short-term difficulties encountered in obtaining adequate supplies from the normal channels; they could scarcely have been welcomed by those richer freemen who engaged in tin dealing.

Doubtless some rich London pewterers played a part in the provision of the credit on which the stannaries depended. In simple outline the financing of tin production consisted of three tiers, each linked to the other by a chain of credit: tin dealers, for the most part Londoners and alien merchants, advanced money to merchant or master tinners, for the most part men of substance native to the south-west, who in turn loaned this money together with funds of their own, to labouring tinners. The security for these advances was invariably tin: the merchant tinners usually pledged delivery to the tin dealers of white, pure smelted tin upon which coinage duty had been paid, and labouring tinners usually pledged delivery of black tin ore, dressed and pulverised, but not smelted, to the merchant tinner. With each of these transactions there was ample scope for usury, and the value of the tin that was pledged generally far exceeded the amount of the loan.[3] Tin dealers and merchant tinners alike were subjected to much criticism from contemporary commentators, amongst

[1] Welch, i, 217–18.
[2] Guildhall MS 7090/2, 26 Feb. 1563.
[3] Hatcher, pp. 51–9.

which that from Richard Carew, writing at the end of the sixteenth century, was perhaps the most virulent:

> When any Western Gent. or person of accompt, wanteth money to defray his expences at London, he resorteth to one of the Tynne Marchants of his acquaintance, to borrow some: but they shall as soone wrest the Clubbe out of Hercules fist, as one penie out of their fingers, unlesse they give bond for everie twentie pound so taken in lone, to deliver a thousand pound waight of Tyn at the next Coynage, which shal be within two or three months, or at farthest within half a yeere after. At which time the price of everie thousand, will not faile to be at least twentie three, perhaps twentie five pound. . . . In this sort, some one Marchant will have 5 hundred pound out beforehand, reaping thereby a double commoditie, both of excessive gaine for his lone, and of assurance to be served with Tynne for his money . . . this in truth can be none other, then cutthroate and abominable dealing.[1]

The stannaries in the second half of the sixteenth century were beset by many problems. Output was falling in the face of the necessity to construct deeper mines as surface deposits were being exhausted, and the prevailing price levels were insufficient to provide adequate incomes for the tinners, many of whom turned to husbandry.[2] Small wonder then that the Tudors began to consider applying their favourite remedy for industrial ills—monopoly. In the closing months of Edward IV's reign Gilbert Brokehouse secured the right, in consideration of an annual rent of 3,000 marks, to purchase at the ordinary market rate all the tin coined. The difficulties of arriving at a 'market price' with only one purchaser were not elaborated on, but in all events Brokehouse's lack of capital and business acumen led swiftly to bankruptcy and the revocation of his patent by Queen Mary.[3] For nearly fifty years after this fiasco the question of a tin monopoly was repeatedly discussed, but it was never put into practice. Conditions in the stannaries continued to worsen, and with tin prices stagnating in the face of a rampant inflation of the prices

[1] R. Carew, *The Survey of Cornwall* (1769 edn), p. 15.
[2] Lewis, p. 41; Hatcher, pp. 46–7; Carew, p. 19.
[3] British Museum, Harleian MS 6380 fol. 5; Lewis, p. 145.

of foodstuffs, the opposition of the tinners weakened and made further attempts at monopolies inevitable.[1]

A series of short-lived pre-emptions were exercised by Queen Elizabeth, Bevis Bulmer, Sir Walter Raleigh, and Brigham and Wemmes, within the space of the four years 1599 to 1603; but each was thwarted by the concerted opposition of the leading tin dealers, led by two brothers, Richard and Roger Glover, and the Levant Company, which played a major role in the exporting of tin.[2] The Glovers were pewterers, and succeeded, with the support of other leading pewterers including Thomas Smith and Nicholas Collier, in turning the Pewterers' Company against pre-emption. No doubt the membership of the Company in general was alarmed at the prospect of being forced to pay higher prices for its tin, but the Glovers had much more to lose and it is difficult not to give some weight to the charges of the patentees that the policies pursued by the Glovers were not always in the Company's best interests. Upon the accession of James I the Company petitioned for the revocation of the monopoly held by Brigham and Wemmes, and the king acceded, but only to proceed immediately to exercise it on his own behalf. Once again the Glovers and others resorted to policies aimed at distorting the tin market, and through a lack of funds the king was forced to abandon the project. Whereupon the Glovers were brought before the Star Chamber, fined and imprisoned. The pre-emption then passed to a new syndicate headed by Sir Thomas Bludder, and although this too was quickly ruined, succeeding syndicates generally managed to operate the monopoly at a profit.

The drastic measures taken by the Glovers had at least managed to persuade the Crown of the necessity to avert the outright hostility of the London Pewterers to the monopoly. Furthermore the Pewterers' Company managed to play on mercantilist sympathies by stressing that whereas the patentees sought to export merely a raw material, pewterers conducted an export trade in a manufactured product which not only added to the wealth of the nation, but also provided employment for large numbers of

---

[1] For signs of intense activity concerning possible pre-emptions in the 1590s see *HMC Salisbury MSS*, v, *passim*; *CSPD, 1591–4*, p. 556; *ibid., 1595–7*, pp. 48, 57, 58, 75, 81, 331.
[2] The following account is based primarily upon: Guildhall MSS 7090/3–7; 7086/3–4; Welch, ii, *passim*; Lewis, pp. 48–53, 145–9; Unwin, *Industrial Organization*, 153–6; *CSPD, 1603–10*, pp. 13, 84, 157, 334.

craftsmen in England. The result was that subsequent grants contained many valuable concessions to the Company, including a monopoly of the casting of tin into bars for export, occasional grants of £200 'bar money' for the hammermen of the craft, and most important of all the right to purchase substantial quantities of tin from the patentees at rates below the market price. For example, in 1608 the Company secured no less than 500 thousandweight (over 200 tons), later reduced to 300 thousandweight, for supplying the home pewter market; in 1612 the Company was allowed all the tin its members could use at the reduced price of £4.5s per hundredweight, provided that none was exported unwrought; and in 1615 the Company was granted the right to share in the pre-emption for five years, to the extent of no less than 500 thousandweight—almost half the total output.

It would be unrewarding to relate in detail the complicated story of successive tin farms, but it should be noted that the special provisions made for the Company gradually became less generous. The patent held by Sir John Catcher and William Cockayne, for example, allowed '300 thousandweights at £4.7s the hundredweight for the service of the kingdom, and 100 thousandweights at £5 for transportation [as pewter]'; whilst that of Sir John Harby and partners allowed only 100 thousandweight at £4.10s, and more as requested at £5, and later at £5.12s. During the Commonwealth the tin farm fell into disuse, but on its resurrection after the Restoration no provision at all was made for the Company, although by 1665 a maximum of 200 thousandweight of cheap tin was granted. But by this time the tin farm was proving more difficult to operate at a profit, and after a series of failures it was allowed to lapse for the rest of the century.

Another plank in the Company's platform to secure abundant supplies of tin at low prices for the home market, was to lobby in support of high duties on the export of raw tin, and at times, quite unrealistically, even to press for a complete prohibition of the export of tin in blocks.[1] These policies were pursued with patient dedication but a notable lack of success, in the face of concerted opposition from tinners and tin merchants and the prudence of government ministers.

[1] For example, Welch, ii, 12, 14–15, 21–2, 109, 113, 115, 118.

Company records contain much information on how the cheap tin was distributed to members. In the unusual circumstances of the pre-emption of 500 thousandweight granted to the Company in 1615 we find that the tin was purchased by subscription, with the Company 'adventuring' £800, and individual members sums ranging upwards to £1,600.[1] But the resale of the tin allocated to the Company by the patentees was the normal procedure, and we can trace how it was accomplished from a series of Tin Ledgers which run from 1633 to 1638. As might be expected it was the richest and most powerful members who benefited most. In 1634, for example, the 100 thousandweight received by the Company was sold to between fifty and sixty members at an increment of 6d per hundredweight, with the largest quantities going to prominent members of the Court of Assistants such as John Fulham, Henry Cowes, John Robins, Thomas Smith, William Hurdman, Peter Brocklesby, and John Child. In addition the recipients of the tin were allowed up to six months' credit: the accounts for the tin sold in March or April were often not settled until the autumn. From entries in the margins of the ledgers it is clear that the recipients subsequently sold some of the tin to other members, but we are given no indication of the prices that they charged.[2]

It is probable that the allocation of tin had been even less equitable in earlier years, since in 1630–31 a petition signed by sixty members of the Company 'complaining against the distribution of the Tynn which the Company have from the ffermours at an under rate' had been delivered to the Lord Treasurer and Chancellor of the Exchequer 'unknowne and without any authority from the Master and Wardens', from whence it was referred to the tin farmers. Eventually a representative of the farmers concurred with the decision of the Pewterers' court that distributors should be elected in equal proportion by and from the livery and yeomanry.[3] Further friction over this matter was inevitable, and in 1639 another request for a more equal distribution of cheap tin was met by delegating the task to a committee to consist of the Master and Wardens, three other liverymen, and six representatives of the yeomanry to be appointed by themselves.[4]

[1] Guildhall MS 7090/4, 14 Feb.
[2] Guildhall MSS 7107/1, 2. The increment was subsequently raised to 1s and then to 2s to provide funds for the Company.
[3] Guildhall MS 7090/4, 19 and 28 April 1631.   [4] *Ibid.*, 21 Feb. 1639.

The Company also appreciated the need to supervise the quality of tin bought by its members, whether from the farmers or from private dealers. The frauds practised in the tin trade were many and various: heavy stones were sometimes placed in the centre of a block of tin, a thin coating of tin might be placed over a core of lead, and inferior grades such as 'hard tin', 'pilion tin', 'cinder tin', and 'relistian tin' might be passed off as tin of the best quality. Stannary officials exercised a close supervision of quality, and at the coinage ceremony each block was graded and stamped accordingly; furthermore there was machinery for investigating complaints in the stannary courts if they were accompanied by the marks of identification which the smelter and original owner had to stamp on each block.[1] But the resourcefulness of dishonest dealers made Company intervention a necessity. As early as 1444 the wardens had been granted authority to search for and assay all tin smelted within London because 'in these dayes grete multitude of Tynne which is untrewe and deceyvable is brought to this Citee and here is solde as dere as the best Tynne',[2] and subsequent action took the form of vigorous protests to the Crown and stannary authorities,[3] requests for expert assayers to be present at the coinages, and ultimately the appointment of a Company assayer to work in Cornwall.[4] In addition boycotts were imposed on dealers who sold substandard tin or lead to members,[5] and frauds perpetrated by Company members were met by severe punishments.[6] Another aspect of Company policy was to insist that members obtained due allowance for waste matter (cloff) when purchasing tin.[7] It is interesting to note that ready mixed but unwrought pewter was sold in the form of strakes or griddles, and that these were subjected to the same controls as those exercised over pewterware.[8]

Little is known in detail of the supply of new tin to provincial pewterers, but it is clear that most were dependent on the London

[1] Carew, p. 14; Lewis, pp. 172–3; Pennington, pp. 132–6.
[2] Welch, i, 13–14. [3] Ibid., ii, 66, 141, 151–6.
[4] Ibid., 9, 92–3, 94, 99–100, 105, 120, 129.
[5] For example, on 7 May 1559 the court agreed 'that no man sholde by any Tynne of Allyn the Taylor in bucklers bury after this daye' (Guildhall MS 7090/1). See also the case regarding lead purchased from 'ffrank the glassyer' (Guildhall MS 7090/1, 17 Jan. 1556).
[6] In 1562 Nicholas Rodes was banished from the Company because he 'in the sight of straungers myxed tynne and leade together, and made of good Tynne ffalse tynne' (Guildhall MS 7090/1, 20 June 1562).
[7] Welch, i, 185, 212, 268, 288; ii, 131. [8] Ibid., i, 280.

tin market and were served by London dealers. The exceptions were pewterers in towns in the west of England, such as Bristol, Gloucester, Chester, Liverpool and Wigan, who received some supplies direct from Cornwall and Devon.[1] Provincial pewterers no doubt smarted at the injustice of being excluded from allowances of cheap tin, and the Wigan pewterer's gild for one argued a case for sharing the Londoners' privilege.[2]

Attention has already been drawn to the importance of scrap pewter in providing raw materials for the production of new wares, which is the major cause of the scarcity of early specimens of pewterware today. The regularity with which old or damaged pewter was traded in for new is exemplified in the price ordinances of the London Company, which specified not only the permitted rates at which new pewter could be sold but also those at which old pewter could be purchased,[3] and in the surviving records of retail transactions. It would be tedious to provide many examples of such a universal occurrence, but the following drawn from different types of customer in different centuries may be of interest:

> Item, the ferst day of Septembre [1464], my mastyr [Sir John Howard] bowt of the pewtrer of Colchester di. a garnyshe of counterfet vessellys, conteynynge xxixli., prise the li., iiijd.; j and a di a garnyshe of playne vessellys, conteynenge xliiij li., prise the li., iiijd.; and ther of my mastyr payd hym in old vessellys c. li., prise the pownd, iid; and the same tyme my mastyr toke hym in mony, iiis. vjd.
> And so he is content ffore the sayd vessellys.[4]

> 1655/6, paide to Thomas Banckes for exchanging the church flagine: 3s. 0d.
> 1661/2, paid for 2 plates for the comunion table in exchange of the Chrisning bason: 2s. 8d.
> 1666, paid in exchange of the pewter bowle for a flagon for the communion: 3.s 2d.[5]

[1] Carus-Wilson, *Medieval Merchant Venturers* (1967 edn), pp. 7, 11; T. S. Willan, *The English Coasting Trade, 1600–1750* (Manchester, 1938), pp. 74, 92, 173, 185, 186.
[2] Shelley, 'Wigan and Liverpool Pewterers', pp. 10–11.
[3] Above, p. 181.   [4] *Manners and Household Expenses*, p. 279.
[5] Drawn from the Wigan Parish Churchwardens' Accounts to and the Childwall Registers (Shelley, 'Wigan and Liverpool Pewterers', p. 15).

The Whorsh: Co. Clothworkers   London: Nov. 27, 1714
Bought of John Shorey and Son

	£.	s.	d.
Hardmettle Dishes and 1 Plate of the superfine hardmettle: 64 lb. att 15d. per lb.	4	0	0
4 Hardmettle Porringers		4	8
To Ingraving 9 pieces		2	3
	4	6	11
Recd. old Mettle: 62 lb. at 9d. per lb.	2	6	6
	£2	0	5[1]

It is also of interest to note that old pewter was regularly sent from Ireland to Chester, Milford and Cardiff for reworking; during the first six months of 1585, for example, about 2,300 lb of old pewter and brass were sent to Chester, mainly from Dublin.[2] Owing to the fact that the British government forbade the export of raw tin to the American colonies, pewterers there had to rely exclusively on scrap for their raw materials.[3]

Naturally supplies of scrap pewter from customers did not always balance exactly with requirements, and pewterers frequently bought and sold scrap amongst themselves.[4] Hawkers and chapmen were also an important source of scrap, and statutes and ordinances seeking to control their activities invariably depicted them as both buyers and sellers of pewter; no doubt they found the purchasing of old pewter for resale to pewterers a welcome source of profit.[5] It was also frequently alleged that hawkers and chapmen dealt in stolen goods, as in 1592 when joint action was taken by a number of London companies, including the Pewterers, against the great 'number of "yale persones lewdlye disposed" who under colour of selling old iron, lead, tin, brass, "male", harness, swords, daggers, hair

[1] See note p. 113, above.
[2] A. K. Longfield, *Anglo-Irish Trade in the Sixteenth Century* (1929), pp. 126-7.
[3] Kauffman, p. 14.
[4] A number of such transactions are given in Shelley, *Brief Notes*, pp. 11, 13. For debts involving new and old metal see Welch, i, 228, 232, 287.
[5] For example, Statute 19 Henry VI, c. 6. In 1621 the Company decided to introduce another Bill into Parliament for suppressing hawkers and the 'buying of tynn and old Pewter by brokers and others not Pewterers, selling of old pewter and transporting and uttering it' (Welch, ii, 78).

and wool, and such like things, were no better than common receivers, pilfering Servants and others and purloining and stealing other men's goods'.[1] An earlier ordinance in a similar vein drew attention to the common practice of casual purchases of lead from 'Tylers, Labourers, Masons, boyes' and such like.[2]

The small quantities of copper used by pewterers were doubtless obtained from craftsmen such as coppersmiths and brasiers who consumed large quantities.[3] Bismuth probably gave rise to greater problems, and it may have been purchased by a few pewterers for resale to their fellows;[4] the decision to keep a supply in Pewterers' Hall is perhaps an indication of its scarcity.[5]

INDUSTRIAL STRUCTURE

With the pewter industry, as with so many industries, the earliest records reveal a marked degree of economic stratification among producers, with a wealthy élite at the top and sizeable groups of masters of dependent status and wage labourers at the bottom. If a 'golden age' ever existed when the industry was composed of small independent craftsmen of roughly comparable wealth, which must be extremely doubtful, then it had long been passed by the mid-fifteenth century. The founders of the London gild in the early fourteenth century, Stephen Le Straunge, John Syward, Ernald Schipwaysshe, and Nicholas de Ludgate, were in relative terms almost certainly as wealthy as their successors in the sixteenth and seventeenth centuries—indeed in view of Ludgate's claim to be able to take a great part of the Cornish tin production in 1360, he deserves to be ranked with the leading pewterer tin dealers of the seventeenth century.

The shortage of records of the fourteenth century renders analysis difficult, but we know that a body of journeymen and wage labourers was in existence before 1348 in London, and before 1416 in York.[6] In 1457 and 1459 the London Pewterers

[1] City Ordinance, 4 March 33 Elizabeth (quoted Welch, ii, 7–8).
[2] Guildhall MS 7090/1, 1 July 1555.
[3] Coppersmiths were included in the membership of the Pewterers' Company, and many provincial pewterers also worked in brass and bronze.
[4] For example, Baptyst Hassell purchased 1¾ cwt of 'tyne glasse' from Nicolas Collier at 19d per pound in 1583–84 (Guildhall MS 7090/2, 21 Feb. 1584).
[5] Guildhall MS 7090/4, 16 Mar. 1654.
[6] Ordinances of these dates refer to the employment of journeymen (*Memorials of London Life*, pp. 243–4; *York Memorandum Book*, i, 213).

Table 9

London pewterers and staff in 1457 and 1459

Masters	Apprentices per master	1457 Journeymen per master	Total Employees per master
1	11	7	18
1	8	4	12
1	6	3	9
1	5	2	7
1	4	1	5
2	3	1	4
1	2	2	4
4	3	0	3
6	2	1	3
1	1	2	3
9	2	0	2
3	1	1	2
9	1	0	1
3	0	1	1
43	97	35	—

Approximate number of masters working alone: 10–20

		1459	
1	8	5	13
1	6	3	9
1	6	1	7
1	4	2	6
2	4	1	5
1	4	0	4
1	2	2	4
3	3	0	3
6	2	1	3
5	1	1	2
2	2	0	2
11	1	0	1
2	0	1	1
37	79	28	—

Approximate number of masters working alone: 10–20

Source. Guildhall MS 7086/1.

conducted a unique survey of the numbers of apprentices and journeymen employed by each master; the results of which have been presented in Table 9.

Although it is clear that these surveys were not comprehensive, they do provide a remarkable insight into the structure of the London industry at a very early date, and one which was never to be repeated. From them we learn that although the average unit of production was typically small, some were extremely large for the times. Thomas Dounton's workforce of eleven apprentices and seven journeymen, with no account taken of unfree workmen, is the largest to appear in the records of any London craft of the period.[1] In both surveys approximately a fifth of the masters employed four or more assistants, and one in ten employed six or more. Account must also be taken of masters who worked alone, and at both dates it is probable that between ten and twenty persons fell into this category. On this assumption the average workshop consisted of a master, somewhat less than two apprentices, and about half a journeyman; but it must be stressed that the surveys took no account of unfree workmen.

Yet even such matchless records provide only a partial account of the scale of pewterers' activities. The largest employer, Thomas Dounton, was also a mercer[2] who dealt on an exceptional scale in a wide range of commodities with merchants from Danzig and the Low Countries.[3] And we learn that John Paris, who employed five and six assistants respectively in 1457 and 1459, was dealing in tin on a grand scale in the later 'sixties;[4] his contribution of £1,112 to the loans which Edward IV raised in the first half of his reign is also a measure of his great wealth, since the largest amount raised by a single person was £2,850 from a London goldsmith.[5] But even with respect to the pewter industry the members of workers directly employed can give a misleading impression since much production was organised on a 'putting out' or 'domestic' basis.

It is probable that the scale of the workshops of the leading mid-fifteenth-century pewterers was not greatly surpassed in the

[1] Thrupp, *Merchant Class*, p. 9. [2] *Ibid.*
[3] See, for example, the scrivener's book of 1457–58 (PRO E.101.128/37) in which the deals recorded by Dounton far outweigh those of any other merchant.
[4] Above, p. 231.
[5] A. Steel, *The Receipt of the Exchequer, 1377–1485* (Cambridge, 1954) pp. 345–6. For loans from other tin dealers, including Thomas Goodluck, pewterer, see *ibid.*, p. 354.

ensuing 250 years. Fears for employment voiced by journeymen, and a general concern for the effects of overhasty expansion, led to strict controls on the numbers of apprentices that each master might enrol being continuously imposed in London from 1522. By the mid-sixteenth century members of the Court of Assistants were permitted to keep three apprentices only if they also employed two journeymen, while liverymen and yeomen were permitted two and one apprentices respectively.[1] Even though some members doubtless evaded these regulations and others were permitted to enrol additional apprentices upon payment of a fine, these restrictions were a major part of gild policies throughout England and must have served to restrict the size of workshops. Moreover, the pewter industry, in common with all industries of the time, was subject to powerful economic and technical forces which combined against any form of factory production. Demand was notoriously unstable, and consequently the risks involved in purchasing and installing large quantities of expensive capital equipment were inordinately high. Furthermore there was no capital equipment available to the pewter industry which was capable of producing economies of scale substantial enough to offset these risks and reverse the process which inexorably gave greater profits to merchants than to industrialists.

Rather than attempt to produce large quantities of wares by the direct employment of labour, leading pewterers therefore supplied lesser masters with unwrought or partially wrought pewter which was finished as required at an agreed rate of remuneration. The lesser masters were thus in some sense the employees of the greater, but their contracts were temporary and they invariably owned their own equipment and worked in their own premises. Just as this arrangement benefited the richer pewterers, who could concentrate their investment on raw materials rather than equipment, it also had advantages for impecunious masters who could secure employment without the complete loss of their independence, and without the need to purchase an extensive range of tools and equipment or raw materials, or secure premises suitable to serve as a retail establishment. In practice neither the richer nor the poorer pewterers tended to specialise completely and become exclusively tradesmen or craftsmen. In the majority of cases both functions were com-

[1] Above, pp. 194-6.

bined in varying proportions: the entrepreneur retained his own workshop with apprentices and journeymen, and the craftsman was usually keen to purchase raw materials with which to manufacture pewter for sale if the opportunity presented itself.

Putting out was so prevalent that ordinances had to be passed to take account of the special problems that it created. One of the earliest such ordinances dates from 1483 when agreed rates of pay for the making of several kinds of pots and tankards were promulgated, with provisions for fines both upon those who offered and those who accepted higher rates.[1] In subsequent years the rates were amended to take account of changing conditions.[2] In 1522 members were prohibited from giving out 'any maner of pewter to any parsone or parsones to be wrought, but only to a freman or brother of the same crafte', and similar restraints were frequently reiterated in subsequent years.[3] Subcontracting also gave rise to particular problems when the metal employed was substandard, and in 1552 it was agreed that 'Certayne Saltes which were made of laye mettall of dyverse mens, which ought to have byne of fyne mettall [are] to be broken forthwith, and the owners to have theyre mettall agayne and the makers thereof to beare the one half of the losse of workmanship and the owners thereof that bought them to beare the other half of the workmanship'.[4] If it could be proven that the workmaster, as he was termed, was solely to blame then he alone was liable to prosecution; thus John Catcher was fined 20 nobles (£6.6s8d) for putting out about one and a half hundredweight of 4 lb platters of 'false' metal to be wrought by workmen into basins,[5] and Bartholomew Humber was fined 'for delivering of deceipfull mettalls two severall tymes to workmen, putting in plomers Soder that he bought at Markatts'.[6] It is also of interest to note that when Matthew Pellytory, a yeoman, was fined 20s for making lay 16 grains worse than assay, two wealthy liverymen, Henry Duxell and Richard Staple gave 'ther wordes to paye it by xs. apeece at michaelmas next'.[7] But if the workman was deemed to be at fault then he had to make recompense, and when 'my lorde of Burgaveny' complained about a faulty limbeck which had been sold to him, the

[1] Guildhall MS 7086/1.
[2] See, for example, Guildhall MSS 7090/1, 4 May 1560; 7090/4, 2 May 1615.
[3] Welch, i, 111; Guildhall MSS 7116, c. 41, 42; 7117, c. 14.
[4] Guildhall MS 7090/1, 13 Aug.   [5] Guildhall MS 7090/3, 19 Oct. 1599.
[6] Guildhall MS 7090/4, 4 Nov. 1618.   [7] Guildhall MS 7090/3, 2 July 1607.

9

workman who had made it, John Bowlting, was ordered to 'content his master, master baker, for one newe Lymbeck, and he shall make another substancially and delyver hit to his said master and so to be marked with the mark of master Baker and then delyvered by master baker to my lord'.[1]

It appears that some of the allotments of cheap tin to members of the Company during periods when pre-emption was being exercised were made on condition that those who so benefited should use part of it to provide employment for poorer members. In 1611 five leading liverymen 'mr. ducsell, mr. Roger glover, mr. staple, Robert burton and John child were found in fault' and it was decided 'that at the next allotment we shall make to the poores use such abatement of ther porcyon as wyll countervayle ther fynes'.[2] The following year a meeting was held 'for the eleccion of workmen for transportacion worke', and the names of thirty-three workmen were placed alongside those of eighteen liverymen, who shared an allocation of 20 thousandweight of tin; Henry Duxell, Roger Glover, Richard Staple, Robert Burton, and John Child were amongst the eighteen.[3] Competition for employment was clearly intense at this time and in 1615 in order 'for preventinge of thingrossinge of the best customers into some few mens handes' the producers of lay pewterware 'eich...made choyce of 3 men...whome they desyre and Conscent to serve'; from the appended list we can again identify John Child, Roger Glover and Robert Burton amongst the twenty-one 'workmasters'.[4]

Thus we see that the membership of the Company can be divided into four major groups: first, the merchant pewterers who supplied large numbers of customers in England and overseas on a predominantly wholesale basis, and who produced only a fraction of the pewter that they dealt in; second, the retailer-producers of modest scale, some of whom might either put out work or take it in according to circumstances; third, masters who derived the bulk of their income from manufacturing rather than selling, most of whom were dependent on merchant pewterers and retailers for contracts and materials; and fourth, journeymen who were directly employed by members of the other three groups on a wage basis. Each of the three categories of master

[1] Guildhall MS 7090/1, 10 Dec. 1557. [2] Guildhall MS 7090/3, 14 March.
[3] Guildhall MS 7090/4, 15 July 1612. [4] *Ibid.*, 2 May 1615.

naturally included pewterers of widely differing wealth, and furthermore their status was fluid. We know from John Fryer's recollections that young masters had to work very hard and commonly 'contrived to take in work from other men, which in that business is called Trucking, but properly it is working of Journey work to other men', in the hope of building up a business of their own.[1] Other distinctions are also apparent: sadwaremen were generally more wealthy than hollowaremen or laymen, then came the manufacturers of pots and trifles, with spoonmakers at the bottom.

It is interesting to note that many of the cases involving debt which were brought before Company courts were settled by the debtor undertaking to work an agreed quantity of pewter for the benefit of the creditor. Just one example of many occurred in 1566 when John Mearse confessed a debt of 20s, and it was agreed that he 'shall worke unto the said parties so muche in workmanshipp of ware as their monie shall amount unto at the will and pleasuer of the said parties'.[2]

To set up in business, even on a modest scale, the pewterer required substantial resources, but there are indications that in return he stood a good chance of securing an above average income. The most direct evidence we have comes from two books containing descriptions of various London trades, written in the mid-eighteenth century to advise parents on where to apprentice their sons. That written by Campbell describes pewtering as 'an ingenious business and abundantly profitable',[3] while that of Waller states of London pewterers that 'most of them are large Shop-keepers and very considerable Dealers'.[4] These statements are borne out by estimates of the cost of being bound as an apprentice pewterer, which Campbell places at between £20 and £40[5] and Waller at £20,[6] both far above that demanded in the majority of trades. Furthermore, the amounts of capital which they estimated a pewterer needed to set up as a master also placed the trade amongst the most exclusive: Waller asserted that 'it requires £500 to set one up handsomely',[7] while Campbell felt that £300 was a minimum figure and that £1,000 could be

[1] Guildhall MS 12017, f. 19.
[2] Guildhall MS 7090/1, 10 Oct. 1566. See also Welch, i, 196, 228, 232, 287.
[3] R. Campbell, *The London Tradesman* (1747; repr. Newton Abbot, 1969), p. 320.
[4] Waller, p. 165.   [5] Campbell, p. 338.
[6] Waller, p. 165.   [7] *Ibid.*

expended.¹ Amongst the other major metal trades we find that brasiers would require £20 to £100, smiths of most types less than £500, and even goldsmiths only £500 to £1,000.² Alongside these estimates we can place the experience of John Fryer, who with an investment of £300 in 1693 was able to purchase and run only a small business, and whose trade began to increase substantially only after a further £500 had been forthcoming from his father-in-law.³

These sums were far in excess of those possessed by most freemen who were granted licence to open shop in London in the mid-sixteenth century, which usually ranged between £10 and £30.⁴ Much of the difference was accounted for by the depreciation in the value of the pound between the two dates and a substantial rise in London rents and property values, but some also by the fact that many young masters were forced to set up on a very modest scale indeed. Whereas Fryer had purchased an established shop, most young men could probably afford to rent only a single room in an unfashionable quarter, and acquire secondhand a limited range of basic equipment. The high cost of London property and the intense competition from established pewterers were reasons why so many young freemen left the capital to work in the provinces.⁵

Unfortunately, the values put on pewterers' tools and equipment by the appraisers of inventories were invariably gross underestimates. Presented with a range of metal moulds the appraisers usually simply weighed them and valued them according to the prevailing price of scrap, and not their worth to another pewterer. Thus in Jonathan Baron's inventory compiled in 1713, we find 'old brasse and shruffe' at 6d per pound, and over 5 hundredweight of new and old moulds also valued at 6d per pound.⁶ But even at these absurdly deflated valuations moulds could account for considerable sums: Baron's were valued at £15.3s0d, while those of Robert Banks of Wigan were appraised in 1626 at almost £50.⁷ Similar distortions occurred with the appraisers' valuations of other tools and equipment, and we can obtain

---

[1] Campbell, p. 338. [2] *Ibid.*, pp. 331–40.
[3] Guildhall MS 12017, ff. 22–3.
[4] These figures are based upon a limited number of reports by masters on the substance of their apprentices who were about to be granted licences to set up shop in 1568 (Guildhall MS 7090/1).
[5] Above, p. 200. [6] Douch, p. 75.
[7] Shelley, 'Wigan and Liverpool Pewterers', p. 6.

scarcely a clue from inventories as to the true value of wheels, lathes, hammers, turning tools and so on. The 50*s* put on an anvil, three dozen assorted tools, two lathes, soldering irons, kettles, ladles, moulds, a vice, sheares, bellows, and scales belonging to Martin Williams is by no means an extreme example.[1]

Pewterers naturally sought to spread the costs involved in setting up shop. Partnerships of working pewterers are often encountered, although they were discouraged in London.[2] The sharing of equipment, particularly moulds, was widely practised. The high cost of moulds and the large quantities required to produce an adequate range of wares was a major problem for the pewterer of modest means, which joint purchase went some way towards alleviating. In 1428, for example, two London pewterers in partnership had tools and equipment valued at £19.16*s*5*d*, of which half belonged to one of the partners; and the heavier moulds were shared by as many as six other pewterers.[3] The York pewterers' gild kept a stock of moulds for the use of members, and each new freeman was required to pay £4 (£7.10*s* from 1674) 'towards the maintaining of the moulds' and also to undertake to treat them well; while for their part the officials of the craft swore to 'serve each of the craft indifferently with the mulds'.[4] Further economies could be achieved by using interchangeable parts: a tankard body mould could also be made to serve as a mould for the central casting of a flagon and so on. Nevertheless, such measures served only to ease rather than solve the problem, and many pewterers were forced to specialise in the production of a limited range of wares, and were inhibited from initiating changes in style which would necessitate the use of new moulds.

Moreover the pewterer who wished to trade on his own account had also to invest in raw materials, and the cost of the raw materials constituted a very high proportion indeed of the selling price of pewterware. In the mid-seventeenth century, for example, according to the rates stipulated by the London Pewterers' Company the cost of the metal accounted for 80 per cent of the retail price and 85 per cent of the wholesale price of sadware.[5] The stocking of a small shop with perhaps 5 hundredweight of

[1] Above, p. 217. [2] Above, p. 197.
[3] Thrupp, *Merchant Class*, p. 111.
[4] University of York Library, MS E.54.
[5] In 1655 it was stipulated that sadware should be sold retail at 15*d* per lb and wholesale at 14*d* per lb, with 12*d* allowed for old metal (Guildhall MS 7090/5, 22 Mar.).

pewterware, would thus have involved the shopkeeper in an investment of almost £30 in metal alone, a greater sum than a skilled craftsman could earn for eighteen months' work. Small wonder, then, that many young pewterers were forced to labour at piecework with materials they did not own.

Yet despite the substantial costs of setting up, especially in London, it appears that relatively few freemen spent their whole working lives as journeymen. Tables 12 and 14 in Appendix A below suggest that there were often two or even three times as many masters as journeymen in London. The rapid rate of growth achieved by the industry, coupled with high mortality rates in the capital, doubtless created opportunities for ambitious and able journeymen. It should also be noted that most apprentices were drawn from middle-class homes, and that many must have received gifts or loans to help them set up in business, while a few benefited from the legacies which freemen occasionally made 'to be lent unto yonge men of our company'.[1] It should not be surprising therefore to find abundant evidence of frequent shortages of skilled labour in the industry, which restrictions on the enrolment of apprentices served to exacerbate. We have already noted in an earlier chapter that apprentices were sometimes sold, that wage restraint was frequently practised, that journeymen were required to give lengthy notice of their departure from service, and that one of the most frequently reiterated ordinances was that which forbade the enticing of workmen from their masters and open competition for their labour.[2] Moreover, disputes between masters concerning the right to a journeyman's labour were sometimes brought before the Company's court, as was the 'certayne varyaunce betwene Thomas fisher and William Jones for the service of Richard bigg whiche was hyred by fisher to serve wekely with hym one weke and anither weke with Jones',[3] while 'Jhon Robbardys' was ordered 'note ffor love nor ffor ffavour to o [one] man more than to anothir of the sayde Craffete' to be willing to work for all masters.[4] All of which stresses the indispensability of the putting out system.

Once more, because of the excellence of the records, we have perhaps dwelt overlong on London's pewter industry. But it is

---

[1] See, for example, Welch, i, 298, for two such bequests totalling £70.
[2] Above, pp. 190–3.
[3] Guildhall MS 7090/1, 1 July 1558.
[4] Guildhall MS 7086/1, 1485–6.

clear that although many provincial pewterers operated on a small scale—like John Launder of Leicester (d. 1625) who had only £4.10s invested in pewtering,[1] or William Sandys of Liskeard (d. 1701) whose 'goods in the trade' amounted to only £4.5s[2]— some were responsible for the production and sale of large quantities of pewterware and thereby accumulated considerable wealth. It is impossible at present to provide an adequate sample of the scale of activities and wealth of provincial pewterers, and much local research remains to be done. But from inventories we can select prominent figures such as Henry Grene, pewterer and bell-founder of Worcester (d. 1569), whose five workshops and a 'ware-house' all apparently in full use, and an estate valued at over £100, made him by Worcester standards a very substantial industrialist,[3] Robert Banks of Wigan (d. 1626) who left moulds valued at almost £50 and scrap metal worth over £100,[4] and Digory Tonkin of St Blazey (d. 1684), one of the most prosperous of seventeenth-century Cornish merchants who, in an estate valued at £2,298, left in a warehouse at Parr new pewterware worth almost £50 and 'pewter moulds, tooles and other implements thereto belonging' valued at £22.10s.[5] Perhaps even more informative of the scale of production of leading pewterers is the evidence provided by surviving pieces, and by the contents of shops selling pewter throughout England in the seventeenth century, which is examined below.

INTERNAL TRADE

Throughout the medieval and early modern periods the retail distribution of pewter, in common with that of a wide range of products, was effected through a variety of channels including the permanent shop, the stall at market and fair, and the itinerant petty dealer. With each of these methods some of the wares sold by the retailer might be of his own making and some not. The traditional assumption that before the later seventeenth century the producer-retailer in the durable goods trades and elsewhere manufactured most, if not all, of the products he sold does not apply to the pewter trade. Each pewterer's shop sought to offer a

[1] *Victoria County History: Leicestershire*, iv, 97.   [2] Douch, p. 74.
[3] A. D. Dyer, 'The City of Worcester in the Sixteenth Century' (Birmingham Ph.D. thesis, 1966), pp. 202–5.
[4] Shelley, Wigan and Liverpool Pewterers, p. 6.   [5] Douch, p. 69.

representative selection of the vast range of articles which were produced in pewter; it would have been not only uneconomic but also quite impossible for the shopkeeper to have manufactured them all. Consequently he stocked the wares of other pewterers, some of which were perhaps obtained by putting out quantities of pewter in a raw or unfinished state to be worked up by craftsmen who lacked the resources to trade on their own account, while others were acquired by straightforward purchase. This was true even of the leading London pewterers, and when in 1557 Robert West was convicted of making pots of false measure it was discovered that eleven liverymen and yeomen had bought some from him for resale.[1]

Established pewterers sold their wares by all available methods: they kept retail establishments, sold at fairs and markets, either in person or through employees or middlemen, and also dealt with or employed chapmen and hawkers.[2] What is thought of as the typical pewterer's shop consisted of premises which combined living accommodation for family and employees, a workshop, and a room or area where goods could be displayed and retail sales conducted. Lock-up shops were extremely rare, if they existed at all. The more prosperous pewterers doubtless obtained premises in the most fashionable districts, improved the appearance of their sales areas, and insulated them from the noise and fumes of the workshop, but even in seventeenth-century London there were many premises in which workshop and retail shop were divided only by a flimsy partition.[3]

The importance of fairs and markets for the distribution of goods in this period is well known, and pewter was no exception.[4] A statute of the late fifteenth century reports 'There be many fairs for the common weal of your people' who resort to them

> to buy and purvey many things that be good and profitable, as ornaments of Holy Church, chalices, books, vestments, ... and also for household, as victuals for the time of Lent

[1] Guildhall MS 7090/1, 14 June.
[2] It is notable that the leading merchant pewterers and tin dealers in the Company tended to keep apprentices and journeymen.
[3] See, for example, Welch, ii, 34, 84.
[4] For the importance of fairs and markets see D. Davis, *A History of Shopping* (1966), pp. 25–48; D. Alexander, *Retailing in England During the Industrial Revolution* (1970), pp. 29–60.

and other stuff as linen cloth, woollen cloth, brass, pewter, bedding, osmund, iron, flax and wax and many other necessary things, the which might not be forborne.[1]

A poem of about the same date suggests that much of London's retail trade was conducted from market stalls, with Eastcheap specialising in pewter.[2] Gild ordinances provide further evidence, and in the early fifteenth century members were forbidden to secure the eviction of their brethren from their shops, booths or standing places within the City or in fairs, markets and other places outside.[3] In the early sixteenth century it was ordained that consignments of more than one hundredweight of pewterware, whether it was to be delivered direct to a customer or sent for sale in fairs or markets, had to be searched by gild officials before despatch.[4] From cases brought against offenders we learn of such a consignment totalling 18 hundredweight,[5] and of one of 7 hundredweight of assorted wares sent by a member of the yeomanry to Stourbridge fair.[6] From Company search records of the seventeenth century it is evident that fairs attracted pewterers from considerable distances. The evidence presented in a case concerning a pasture dispute in York in 1494–95 is also of interest, since it relates that in Michaelmas 1485 the two partners in a York pewtering business, John Tanfeld and Robert Wylkynson, both rode off to fairs, one to Barnsley and the other to Bedale.[7]

Fairs and markets continued to contribute a significant volume of sales until well into the eighteenth century. Some fairs such as Stourbridge, the most famous in England, contained an important wholesale element, and provided country shopkeepers with the opportunity to restock their shops, and London dealers to meet with their chapmen and discuss business affairs.[8] But there are signs that in the later seventeenth century the leading London pewterers were anxious to put an end to the traditional practice of selling pewter from stalls at fairs and markets within the City, and to restrict sales to shops; and in 1654

> It was generally conceaved that the kepinge of boothes in Smithfield or ther abouts at Barthollmetide or in Southwarke

[1] Quoted Lipson, *Economic History*, i, 248–9.
[2] 'London Lykpenny', *Minor Poems of Lydgate*, ed. J. O. Halliwell (1840), p. 105.
[3] Above, p. 148.   [4] Ordinances of 1522 (Welch, i, 108–9).
[5] Guildhall MS 7090/2, 10 Sept. 1574.   [6] Guildhall MS 7086/2, 1570–1.
[7] York Cathedral, Dean and Chapter Archives, v, *Book XII*, I am indebted to Dr D. M. Palliser for this reference.   [8] Alexander, p. 37.

was very preiudiciall to the publicke good of this Companye. And therfore Concluded and soe ordred that from henceforth this yeare excepted, that Noe free brother shall keep any faire or market within 7 myles of this Cittie.[1]

A similar motive may well have inspired York pewterers to resolve in 1702 'that none shall henceforth keep Stanford Bridge fair', but we cannot be sure.[2]

The obsessive concern displayed by pewterers' gilds towards hawkers and chapmen must be taken as an indication of their importance in the distribution of pewter. The strenuous attempts to stamp out hawking in towns where a pewterers' gild enjoyed monopoly rights, and door-to-door sales throughout the country have already been examined,[3] but it must be stressed that they were only partially successful and that the attitude of some gildsmen towards itinerant traders was understandably equivocal. Country people in particular were accustomed to buying from such traders, and it is clear that they performed a valuable function by delivering goods in small quantities to consumers who lacked easy access to markets or shops. Furthermore, there was never any question of banning the itinerant trader from fairs or the markets of country towns. Not surprisingly perhaps, gild records are relatively uninformative about the relationship between pewterers and hawkers and chapmen. We know that pewter was frequently sold to them at a discount, and from occasional references we can discover that the relationship was sometimes far closer than this. Not only did some poorer members resort to hawking themselves, but also leading pewterers used bands of retainers to distribute their wares on both a wholesale and a retail basis throughout the country.[4] One of the most revealing illustrations of this practice occurred in 1600 when a country search was being planned by the London Company, and 'Mr Deuxell to prevent ther procedynges dyd make it knowen to dyvers of his chapmen by a letter At wyggen, wherby ther procedyngs was greatly hyndred, and upon master deuxells confessyon he did that his chapmen should not be hindred to his hurt'.[5]

[1] Guildhall MS 7090/5, 17 Aug.
[2] Univ. of York Library MS E.54.
[3] Above, pp. 115–2, 173–5.
[4] Above, pp. 181, 185.
[5] Guildhall MS 7090/3, 11 Aug.

Manufacturing and marketing 255

By far the most valuable information of all concerning the marketing of pewter at this time is contained in the Company Search Books.[1] These records have already been used to plot the distribution of provincial pewterers, they can now be used to reveal the contents of their shops. Reports of searches conducted in 1635, 1636, 1637, 1640, 1641, 1669, 1673, 1674, 1675, 1676, 1677 and 1683 are contained in the books, and occasional reference is made to the makers of the substandard pewter that was discovered. Pride of place must go, however, to the searchers' reports of 1640 and 1641 which contain not only a systematic record of all makers' names but also of the town in which they practised. It is possible, therefore, to reconstruct from these reports a unique picture of the distribution of pewter by maker. The data contained in the report of the four searches conducted in 1640 is presented in full in Table 10.

Table 10

The London Company's country search of 1640

Date visited	Name of shopkeeper	Town	Substandard stock: maker's name	Maker's address
27 March	Stevenes	Northampton	Own Making	
			Lovell Smith	Longford
27 March	Robert Berey	Northampton	Own making	
			William Nicholas	Walsall
			Lovell Smith	Longford
28 March	Christopher Robey	Market Harborough	Lovell Smith	Longford
			George Gesonn	Walsall
28 March	Landere	Leicester	George Gesonn	Walsall
28 March	Burros	Leicester	George Gesonn	Walsall
28 March	Pilkinton	Leicester	George Gesonn	Walsall
			Humphrey Tedman	Walsall
31 March	Smith	Coventry	Thomas Wilkes	Walsall
			William Nicholas	Walsall
			Lovell Smith	Longford
31 March	Knowles	Coventry	Thomas Wilkes	Walsall
			Thomas Cheshire	Walsall
31 March	Widow Poultney	Coventry	Thomas Wilkes	Walsall
			William Nicholas	Walsall
32 March [sic]	Lovell Smith	Longford	Own making	

continued overleaf

[1] Guildhall MSS 7105, 7105/1; MS 7106 contains rough notes of little value on searches conducted between 1689 and 1691.

Table 10 *continued*

Date visited	Name of shopkeeper	Town	Substandard stock: makers' name	Maker's address
1 April	Richard Tonges	Warwick	Thomas Wilkes	Walsall
			Richard Nicholas	Walsall
			Philip Cave	Chipping Norton
			Richard Seynerdy	Walsall
			Lovell Smith	Longford
			Own making	
2 April	Philip Cave	Chipping Norton (at Banbury Fair)	John Fox	Woodstock
			William Nicholas	Walsall
			Thomas Wilkes	Walsall
13 April	Henry Frewin	Reading	Robert Gibbins	Reading
13 April	Walker	Reading	Robert Gibbins	Reading
13 April	Robert Gibbins	Reading	Own making	
14 April	Arthur Robins	Abingdon	John Fox	Woodstock
			William Nicholas	Walsall
14 April	Greene	Abingdon	Henry Frewin	Reading
15 April	Anthony Carter	Oxford	Own making	
			William Nicholas	Walsall
			John Fox	Woodstock
16 April	Philip Cave	Chipping Norton	John Fox	Woodstock
			Thomas Wilkes	Walsall
			William Nicholas	Walsall
			Blansone	Walsall
17 April	Walter	At Bicester Market	John Fox	Woodstock
17 April	Burges	Thame (at Bicester market)	Own making	
			John Fox	Woodstock
18 April	Alexander	Aylesbury	Burges	Thame
22 July	Antony Carter	Oxford (at Wallingford fair)	John Fox	Woodstock
			William Nicholas	Walsall
22 July	Antony Carter	Oxford	John Fox	Woodstock
			William Nicholas	Walsall
22 July	Cardy	Oxford	John Fox	Woodstock
24 July	Samson Bourne	Worcester	Own making	
			William Senere	Walsall
			Robert Roberts	Gloucester
24 July	Ten	Worcester	Own making	

Table 10 continued

Date visited	Name of shopkeeper	Town	Substandard stock: maker's name	Maker's address
24 July	Nicholas	Worcester	Own making	
			Thomas Cheshire	Walsall
			William Synaky	Walsall
24 July	Greenebanke	Worcester	William Sinay	Walsall
27 July	William Lea	Hereford	William Nicholas	Walsall
27 July	Thomas Arindall	Ross	Own making	
			Robert Roberts	Gloucester
28 July	Knowles	Gloucester	Robert Plumer	Gloucester
			Nicholas	Worcester
			Christopher Bradshawe	London
			Christopher Dutton	London
			Own making	
28 July	Browne	Gloucester	Robert Plomer	Gloucester
			Robert Roberts	Gloucester
			Samson Bourne	Worcester
28 July	Robert Prise	Gloucester	Samson Bourne	Worcester
28 July	Robert Plomer	Gloucester	Own making	
30 July	Browne	Cricklade	Robert Plomer	Gloucester
30 July	Tayler	Chippenham	Pascoll	Bristol
31 July	Read	Bath	Pascall	Bristol
			John Goldsmith	Bath
31 July	John Goldsmith	Bath	Own making	
1 August	Thomas Bulorke	Monkton-Farley	Own making	
1 August	Robert Carrier	Bruton	Own making	
			Henry Gibson	Marlborough
1 August	Richard Turke	Bruton	Henry Gibson	Marlborough
			Own making	
3 August	Randall Coupy	Sherborne	Clothere	
			James Gibson	Marlborough
			Robert Childe	Marlborough
			Own making	
3 August	Taylore	Dorchester	Own making	
			Henry Andrees	Marlborough
3 August	John Samwayes	Dorchester	Own making	
			Robert Childe	Marlborough
			Henry Gibson	Marlborough
4 August	Antony Parsoy	Blandford Forum	Edward Haukins	Salisbury

continued overleaf

Table 10 continued

Date visited	Name of shopkeeper	Town	Substandard stock: maker's name	Maker's address
5 August	Nicholas Peeke	Shaftesbury	Henry Gibson	Marlborough
			Widow Burte	Salisbury
			Goldsmith	Bath
			Own making	
			James Gibson	Marlborough
			Edward Hawkins	Salisbury
5 August	Edward Hawkins	Salisbury	Fined by not searched	
2 September	John Smith	Coventry	Own making	
			Thomas Cheshire	Walsall
			Thomas Wilkes	Walsall
			Lovell Smith	Longford
			William Nicholas	Walsall
3 September	Nicholas Kirkon	Lichfield	George Gesson	Walsall
			Thomas Cheshire	Walsall
			Thomas Seneres	Walsall
			Thomas Gesson	Walsall
			Christopher Nicholas	Walsall
			Robert Senores	Walsall
5 September	George Nortonn	Ashbourne	George Gesson	Walsall
			Robert More	Derby
			Thomas Wilkes	Walsall
5 September	John Sharpe	Derby	Robert More	Derby
			Thomas Gesson	Walsall
5 September	Robert More	Derby	Own making	
7 September	George Briges	Burton	Own making	
7 September	William Hilles	Burton	George Gesonn	Walsall
			Robert Seney	Walsall
			Thomas Cheshire	Walsall
			Robert More	Derby
			Blonsone	Walsall
8 September	Thomas Gesonn	Walsall (at Atherstone fair)	Own making	
8 September	Lovell Smith	Longford (at Atherstone fair)	Own making	
8 September	John Wood	Atherstone	George Gesson	Walsall
			Thomas Cheshire	Walsall
8 September	Humphrey Tedman	Walsall (at Atherstone fair)	Own making	
			Robert Seney Senior	Walsall
			Robert Seney Junior	Walsall

Manufacturing and marketing 259

Fig. 5.1. Distribution of substandard Walsall pewter in 1640, by maker

It should be noted that reference is made only to substandard stock discovered by the searchers; pewterware tested and found to be good is scarcely ever mentioned. Also of importance is the almost complete absence of London pewterware; this is almost certainly misleading, however, and due either to its high quality or to the reluctance of the searchers to test it, since there can be little doubt that it was present in many of the shops that were visited. Nevertheless, despite these limitations a clear picture of the extensive distribution of the products of a number of large-scale manufacturers emerges, along with the universal practice of shopkeepers stocking the products of a wide range of makers in addition to those from their own workshops. The distribution

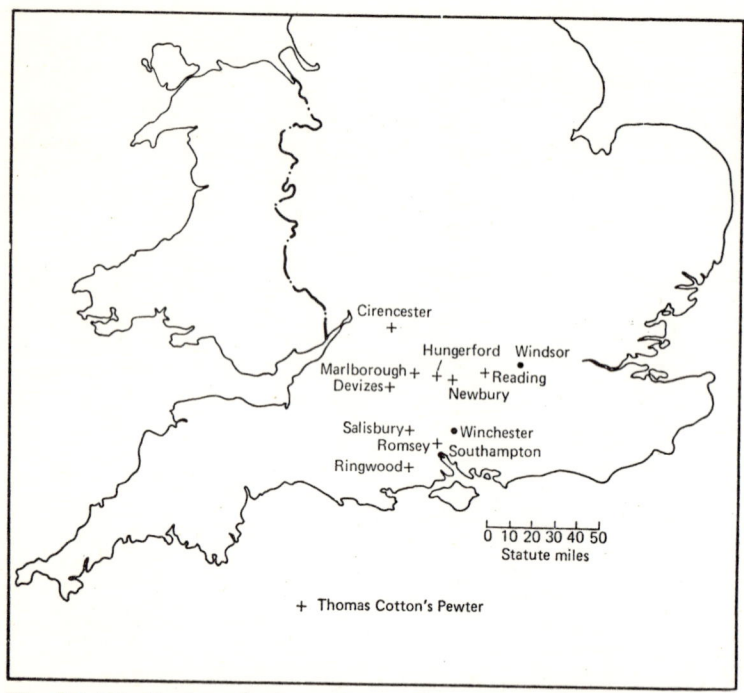

Fig. 5.2. Distribution of substandard pewter made by Thomas Cotton of Marlborough, 1676 and 1677

of the wares of a relatively small group of Walsall pewterers is perhaps most striking, with substandard Walsall pewter found in virtually every shop that was visited as far south, Abingdon, as far west, Hereford, and as far north, Ashbourne, as the searchers ventured—a radius of well over fifty miles. The scale of both the manufacturing and marketing operations of pewterers such as George Gesonn, William Nicholas, Thomas Wilkes and Thomas Cheshire were clearly very substantial. We can also discern a series of manufacturers who achieved an intensive distribution of their products over more limited areas, such as Lovell Smith in Warwickshire and Northamptonshire, John Fox in Oxfordshire and Berkshire, Henry Gibson in Wiltshire, Somerset and Dorset, and John Harris in Devon and Cornwall.

In the 1660s and '70s the searchers, as well as revisiting many towns, ventured into new regions. But although we naturally encounter the names of many additional manufacturers and detect a few shifts in the centres of manufacture the pattern of distribution remains essentially the same. At this later date the dissemination of Wigan pewter was perhaps the most striking of all, since it was found not only throughout the north and west, even in York, but also as far afield as Salisbury and Southampton.

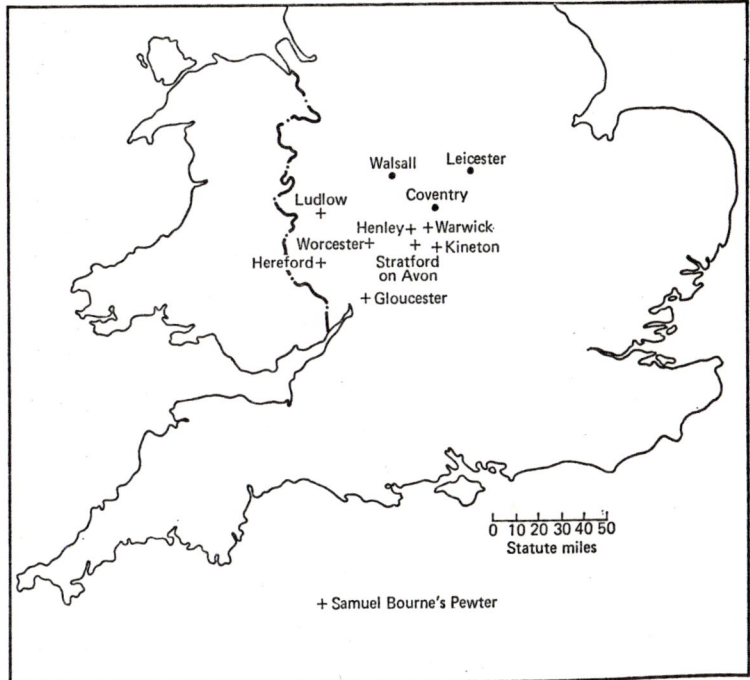

Fig. 5.3. Distribution of substandard pewter made by Samuel Bourne of Worcester, 1676 and 1677

Walsall pewter, by contrast, was of much less importance than it had been a generation before. Once again we can see the regional markets carved out by enterprising manufacturers: the searchers found pewter made by Samuel Bourne of Worcester in Warwick, Henley, Stratford-on-Avon, Ludlow, Kineton, Hereford and Gloucester, and that of Thomas Cotton of Marlborough in Cirencester, Newbury, Reading, Hungerford, Devizes, Salisbury, Ringwood and Romsey.

Turning to the stocks held by individual shops we find that

although the evidence suggests that the great majority of shop-keepers made pewterware, if only spoons in some cases, it was exceedingly rare for the wares of other makers not to be stocked. Remembering that our sources refer only to pewter found to be substandard, it is surely significant frequently to find the wares of three or four pewterers in a single shop and, by the 1670s, sometimes even as many as six or seven. In Stephen Cumberlidg's shop in Warwick in 1676, for example, the searchers found substandard pewter made by Cave of Banbury, Bourne of Worcester, Smith of Coventry, Nicholls of Worcester, Smith of Rugby, Ling of Longford, and one Billing of unknown address; while the two other Warwick shops which were searched contained in addition the products of Gorton of Birmingham, Heal of Coventry, and Seely whose address is not given. The wares of a comparably divers range of makers were discovered in William Mountfort's shop in Kidderminster in 1677, and included those of Nicholls of Worcester, Nicholls of Walsall, Gorton of Birmingham, Banks of Wigan, Biggs of Bromsgrove, and James of Bristol. Bristol pewter at this date appears to have been largely confined to the mid-west of England. Thus pewter, although produced locally throughout the realm, was clearly also an article of long-distance trade and large-scale production.

But the excellence of the records of the distribution of provincial pewter must not be permitted to lead to the neglect of the pre-eminent role enjoyed by London pewter. Although detailed evidence of the distribution of the products of the London industry is meagre, and therefore any estimate of scale and extent must be largely based on conjecture, there can be little doubt that it far exceeded that of even the most successful provincial industry. We learn from London Company records that much pewter was dispatched inland as well as overseas, but destinations are rarely given. Coastal vessels were often used for transportation, but London port books are also sadly deficient, and we can do little more than highlight the odd shipment, such as that to King's Lynn in 1621 or that to Faversham in 1628.[1] Occasionally, too, we find that specific attention is drawn in inventories to pewter of London manufacture, as at Speke Hall,

[1] Willan, *English Coasting Trade*, pp. 97, 127 n; see also *ibid.*, pp. 126, 148, for shipments of pewter from King's Lynn to Hull and from Chichester to London; and p. 112 for a 'wheel and some other utensils for a Pewterer' sent from London to Newcastle in 1732.

Liverpool, in 1624. But in the last resort we are forced to claim that the trade from the capital was infinitely greater than our record of it would suggest.

OVERSEAS TRADE

Many proud claims were made concerning the reputation, scale and widespread distribution of exports of pewter, the vast bulk of which was made in London. Pewterers themselves asserted in 1533 that 'the Commodity of Pewter Vessel [is] much to be had in Reputation in all strange Regions and Countries',[1] and later in the century two eminent commentators, Harrison and Camden, proclaimed that English pewter was valued almost as highly as silver in certain parts of Europe and that vessels made from English tin 'not inferior to silver in brightness ... are carry'd for table-use to all parts of Europe'.[2] By the close of the seventeenth century the development of trade with regions outside Europe led the London Pewterers to boast that 'the greatest part of the world [is] being served with pewter from this Kingdom'.[3] That pewter attracted so much favourable comment is partly due to the fact that it was one of a tiny range of manufactured goods exported from England—indeed in this respect it was second only to cloth. In *A Discourse of the Common Weal of this Realm of England*, an anonymous mid-sixteenth century author spelt out the reasons why pewterers were so valuable to the nation:

> As ye must consider iij sortes of occupacions: one that bringes owt the treasure: the second sort, that as it bringes none forth out of the countrey, so it bringes none in, but that it gites it spendes in the countrey; the iij bringes in treasure into the countrey. Of the first sort ar vintoners, milners, haberdashers, the gally men, mercers, fustian sellers, grocers, poticaries, that selles as anie ware made beyond the sea; for they do but exhause the treasour out of the Realme. Of the seconde sort ar vitaylers, inholders, bochers, bakers, brewers, taylors, cordewayners, sadlers, ioyners, masons, blacksmithes, turners, cowpers; which like as convey no

[1] Statute 25 Henry VIII, c. 9.
[2] Harrison, *Description of England*, p. 367; W. Camden, *Britannia* (1965 edn), p. 2.
[3] Guildhall MS 7090/8, 18 Nov. 1703 (petition addressed to the Lord Treasurer).

money owt of the countrey, so they bringe none in, but where they get it they spend it. Of the third sort be these: clothers, cappers, worsted makers, pewterers, tanners, which be all that we have of anie arte, which I can nowe reken, that bringes into the Realme anie Treasour. Therfore these artes ar to be cherishede wheras they be used; and wheare they be not, they would be set up'.[1]

But whereas the high quality of most pewter exports cannot be disputed, an examination of customs accounts reveals that for much of our period not only were exports generally small in scale they were also restricted in distribution.

In general pewter exports fell into two categories: those that were dispatched in relatively large quantities to serve countries whose native industries had insufficient capacity to satisfy the demands of their inhabitants, and those of the best quality, dispatched in small quantities, to discerning consumers in a wider range of countries. The relative ease with which pewter could be manufactured, and the energetic salesmanship of both English and German tin merchants, meant a constant search for new markets, as successive new industries arose and flourished. That these markets were not always forthcoming is evident from the severe export depression which persisted throughout most of the period from the last quarter of the fifteenth century to the last quarter of the seventeenth.

Medieval customs accounts rarely give the nationality of merchants or the destinations of vessels; they do, however, distinguish between natives and aliens, an exercise rendered necessary by differential rates of duty. But this does not mean that our analysis of exports need be limited to a division of trade between denizens and aliens; on the contrary a careful use of the names of both merchants and vessels enables the ownership and destination of much pewter to be determined. By these means four major branches can be discerned in the thriving export trade of the first seventy-five years of the fifteenth century, three to north-west Europe and one to the Mediterranean.

By the fifteenth century it seems probable that the mines of central Europe, situated primarily in Bohemia and Saxony, were producing enough tin to satisfy demand in neighbouring coun-

[1] *A Discourse of the Common Weal of this Realm of England*, ed. E. Lamond (1893), p. 127.

tries, and possibly also to permit a small export trade to Baltic regions. Nevertheless, despite having easy access to tin supplies and despite possessing many substantial centres of pewter manufacture, including Cologne, Nüremberg, Augsburg, Lübeck, Liège and Dinant, we find that the merchants from the leading Hanse towns of the Netherlands, north Germany and the Baltic regularly purchased pewter in London. Hanseatic exports appear to have averaged between 5 and 10 tons per annum at this time and were valued at between £150 and £250; in other words they constituted approximately 15 to 20 per cent of total pewter exports. This trade was thus not great when compared with total Anglo-Hanseatic trade, but it was significant, particularly in view of the flourishing production of pewter in many Hanse towns. One can only conclude that the pewter purchased in England by Hanseatic merchants was destined for wealthy consumers and was made by leading English craftsmen with the finest alloys, and consequently deemed superior to that produced abroad.[1]

The second major branch of the fifteenth-century export trade was in the hands of merchants from the Burgundian provinces of Holland and Zeeland. In the London customs accounts a multitude of small vessels from the many ports of Holland and Zeeland, as well as from Flanders and Brabant, can be traced returning home with cargoes of cloth and pewter. By midcentury pewter exports by merchants of the Low Countries exceeded those by Hansards.[2]

Relatively few customs accounts of the period record pewter exports by English merchants, but from those that survive it appears that they were generally smaller than those in the hands of foreigners, and as with most other exports, tended to be destined for ports across the Channel. It is possible to identify most of the exporters, and they were drawn from a wide range of London companies. Included amongst English merchants exporting pewter in 1442–43 and 1448–49, for example, we find a fishmonger, a shipwright, a draper, a cutler, a girdler, a number of mercers, and a single pewterer, John Coldham.[3]

In contrast with these short-distance trades the pewter shipped aboard Italian vessels was often bound for exotic destinations.

[1] Hatcher, p. 104.   [2] *Ibid.*, pp. 105–6.
[3] PRO E.122. 77/4, 73/23, 73/25. John Coldham can also be traced as the owner of tin shipped from Cornwall to Southampton (*The Brokage Book of Southampton, 1443–1444*, vol. i, p. xxii).

Although trade was conducted in the many intermediate ports which lay along the return routes, and the cities and hinterlands of Genoa, Florence, and Venice provided ready markets, some pewter eventually found its way into the east Mediterranean and Asia Minor. Italian merchants were primarily interested in cloth, wool and tin, but their combined exports of pewter generally compared favourably with those of the merchants of north-west Europe.[1] In addition a small but steady trade in pewter was also conducted with the Iberian peninsula, largely in Spanish and Portuguese vessels.[2]

Although few pewterers appear to have engaged in the export of pewter, some leading members of the London craft dealt directly with foreign exporters in England. In the hosting accounts of 1441–43, for example, the sales of pewter to merchants of the Hanse and the Low Countries, which were worth almost £400, lay almost exclusively in the hands of William Dere.[3] There can be little doubt that Dere was one of the wealthiest pewterers of his day, and in 1451 he achieved the unusual distinction for a member of an artisan gild of attaining the office of Alderman of the City of London.[4] In the same accounts we discover lesser quantities of pewter sold to Genoese and Venetian merchants by John Gugge, Richard Lumney and Thomas Grey. The unique survival of a scrivener's book for 1457–58 provides us with details of many transactions between merchants from Danzig and the Low Countries and English dealers.[5] Unfortunately, the products which changed hands are not specified, but pewterers occur frequently, including Peter Bishop, John Kendale, John Paris, and Richard Chamberlayne. The transactions of Thomas Dounton are by far the most substantial of all, and although the greater part no doubt involved cloth, it is likely that pewter also featured prominently.

[1] Hatcher, pp. 98–103.
[2] For Portuguese exports of pewter from London see, e.g., PRO E.122. 73/12 (3 cwt); 72/23 (12 cwt); 73/25 (1 cwt); for exports from Southampton see PRO E.122. 141/21 (2 cwt); *The Port Books of Southampton, 1427–30*, ed. P. Studer (Southampton, 1913), p. 126; *Local Port Book, 1435–6*, pp. 30, 62; *Local Port Book, 1439–40*, p. 16; for exports from Bristol and London see V. M. Shillington and A. B. W. Chapman, *The Commercial Relations of England and Portugal* (New York, 1907), pp. 60, 106. For exports of pewter in Spanish vessels see *CCR 1409–13*, p. 167. Although pewter manufacture was established in Barcelona by 1406 it was small in scale (Bell, p. 63).   [3] PRO E.101. 128/30, 31.
[4] Thrupp, *Merchant Class*, p. 336. See also M. R. Thielemans, *Bourgogne et Angleterre, relations politiques et économiques entre les pay—bas bourgignons et l'angleterre, 1435–1467* (Brussels, 1966), p. 304 n.   [5] PRO E.101. 128/37.

The onset of a pewter export slump in the last quarter of the fifteenth century, caused by the spread of production on the Continent and aggravated by the difficulties encountered in Anglo-Italian trade, necessitated a concentration of effort on those markets that remained, and a search for new. It soon became apparent, however, that a full recovery was impossible and the most that could be accomplished was the preservation of a residual trade of somewhat less than 50 tons per annum. Fortunately the growing wealth of Spain enabled her greatly to expand her imports of pewter, and English exporters gratefully turned their attention increasingly towards this market. As early as 1554 the Venetian ambassador in England reported that the greater part of English pewter exports was sent to Spain.[1] Small quantities of pewter were also supplied to Russia, but for the time being this market offered little prospect of growth.[2] Doubtless war in the 1580s seriously hindered Anglo-Spanish trade, but by the return of normal trading conditions in the reign of James I half of English pewter exports were being sent to Spain. The Low Countries continued to provide an outlet for a few tons of pewter each year, but exports to Germany, France, and Italy were now averaging little more than a ton each.[3]

The settlement of Ireland under the early Stuarts and Cromwell provided a temporary minor growth point, and in 1639–40 about four tons of pewter were exported from London to Dublin, Coleraine and Galway, the bulk of it in the name of James Symkin; a little more probably left for Ireland from Bristol.[4] A steady demand for English pewter emanated from Scotland, but it never amounted to much more than a ton or two, and alternative supplies were obtained from Europe.[5] Trade with Russia was also expanding, and in 1639–40 she imported about six tons from London. But once again growth was matched by decline, the latter manifested in the form of falling sales to Spain and the Low Countries, precipitated by the renewal of hostilities. The New World

[1] *CSP Venetian, 1534–54*, p. 543.
[2] T. S. Willan, *The Early History of the Russia Company, 1553–1603* (Manchester, 1956), pp. 53, 136, 266.
[3] See, for example, PRO E.190. 16/2, 16/8; See also T. S. Willan, *Studies in Elizabethan Foreign Trade* (Manchester, 1959), p. 46; G. D. Ramsay, *English Overseas Trade during the Centuries of Emergence* (1957), p. 11. The figures are inevitably minima.
[4] PRO E.190. 43/1; Ramsay, *English Overseas Trade*, p. 143.
[5] Port Books, *passim*; T. C. Smout, *Scottish Trade on the Eve of the Union, 1660–1707* (1963), p. 199 f.; A. Halyburton, *The Ledger of Andrew Halyburton* (Edinburgh, 1867), p. 87.

continued to offer promise rather than opportunity, and by the mid-seventeenth century New England and Guinea together accounted for less than a ton of pewter a year. Even by the early 1670s this dismal picture was little, if any, brighter: exports to Sweden had grown markedly to reach almost 10 tons per annum, and some pewter was being sent to Turkey, but scant progress had been achieved with the level of exports to the Americas and Africa.[1]

Attention has already been briefly drawn to the upsurge of pewter exports in the closing years of the seventeenth century, based primarily on the rapid expansion of English trade with America, the British West Indies and West Africa. Some detail can now be added. The formation of the Royal African Company in 1674 led to a shortlived boom in trade with West Africa, and although the company's aim of exporting from England goods to the value of about £100,000 a year was never achieved, in a number of years this figure was approached. The exports were miscellaneous, consisting of cloth, weapons of all sorts, spirits and metal goods. Table 11 gives the weight and value of pewter shipments to West Africa made by the Royal African Company, to be exchanged for local produce, including slaves.[2]

British economic policy was designed to make her colonies fulfil the dual function of consuming her manufactures and supplying

Table 11

Exports of pewter to West Africa, 1673–1704

Year	Weight (tons)	Value (£)	Year	Weight (tons)	Value (£)	Year	Weight (tons)	Value (£)
1673 (from 15 Nov.)	1·2	137	1683	14·7	1718	1694	4·5	466
			1684	16·8	1807	1695	8·5	944
1674	2·7	380	1685	22·7	2383	1696	7·6	737
1675	1·2	161	1688	18·5	1969	1697	4·2	477
1676 (from 15 Nov.)	1·5	211	1689	10·4	1049	1698	13·6	1433
			1690	3·7	352	1701	17·5	1765
1680	3·7	502	1691	2·7	346	1702	4·2	420
1681	9·3	1254	1692	6·4	768	1703	0·75	67
1682	12·6	1569	1693	14·6	1404	1704	0·1	12

[1] For example, PRO E.190. 59/1, 66/3.
[2] K. G. Davies, *The Royal African Company* (1957), pp. 45, 165–79, 351.

her raw materials. In consequence the Americas and the West Indies were allowed to purchase only British pewterware, and the importation by them of unwrought pewter or tin was forbidden. Thus as soon as these colonies began to prosper and expand on the basis of tobacco and sugar production the way was open for massive pewter exports. By 1700 it is estimated that America, excluding Georgia, consumed almost a fifth of total pewter exports, amounting to some 50 tons valued conservatively at £4,000.[1] Nor did the attractions of the colonial markets lead to the neglect of Europe; Russia in particular offered attractive prospects, and in 1699 pewterers secured admission to the Russia Company.[2]

In keeping with the general policy of the Pewterers' Company, price discounts were allowed to merchants engaged in the export trade,[3] and we learn that the agents of the African Company, for example, negotiated contracts in 1685 for the supply of pewter at $2\frac{1}{4}d$ per lb below current prices.[4] Whereas the American markets sought a range of pewterware similar to that sold in Britain, other regions had specialist demands. In Africa, for example, although jugs and tankards were popular, the most highly prized article was the basin, called the Guinea basin. These were manufactured in London in six sizes ranging from four pounds to one pound.[5] Special wares were also produced for Russian consumers and, as with Spanish consumers some time before, these included trenchers of distinctive style. Such concern for the requirements of overseas consumers became a necessity as the export trade increasingly assumed a more important role in determining the prosperity of the English pewter industry.

[1] Kauffman, p. 14.
[2] HMC, *The Manuscripts of the House of Lords, 1697–9*, p. 295.
[3] See, for example, the rates agreed in 1674—Guildhall MS 7090/6, 14 Apr.
[4] Davies, *Royal African Company*, p. 178.
[5] Guildhall MS 7090/6, 14 Apr. 1674.

Appendix A

Data extracted from London Company records: 1451–1700

It is hoped that the accompanying tables will prove a valuable guide to the fortunes of the London pewter industry and, as London was by far the most important centre, also throw some light on the English pewter industry. The assessment of the utility of the data is an extremely complex task, and in this connection readers are recommended to refer to the discussions of the powers of the Company and related matters contained in Chapter 4 above. In general the evidence suggests that the Pewterers' Company retained an exceptionally strong hold over the London pewter industry until the eighteenth century, and although the membership of the London Company and the London pewter industry were not identical (some pewterers were not freemen of the Company and some freemen were not pewterers) there was a considerable degree of coincidence. It would appear, therefore, that the data presented here can be used with rare confidence. It must be borne in mind, however, that short-term fluctuations in numbers could owe more to demographic factors than to factors affecting the prosperity of the industry; plague was endemic in London until 1665, and severe outbreaks occurred in 1479, 1499–1500, 1535, 1563, 1603, 1625, and 1665.[1] The specific points made below must also be taken into account.

THE NUMBER OF SHOPKEEPERS AND MASTER PEWTERERS

The data on the numbers of shopkeepers and the numbers of licences granted to open shop have been compiled from the

---
[1] See, for example, Creighton, *passim*.

annual lists of freemen liable to pay quarterage and the numbers of licencees recorded in the audit accounts. In the words of the ordinances of 1522:

> every housholder within the saide crafte that is a freman or a broder of the same crafte shall pay for hys quarterage as hathe been accustomed, that is to say xvj d. every yere. Also that every parsone of the saide crafte that woll kepe house and open his shoppe for hym selfe shall paye for his openynge of his Shoppe as hathe bene accustomed tyme oute of mynde, that is to say vjs viijd.[1]

The amounts payable were varied in subsequent years, but the principles on which they were exacted remained unchanged throughout the period. It should be noted that 'shop' referred primarily to a workshop, although the same premises usually served for both the production and the sale of goods. At the least the licencee was granted master status, permitted to strike his touch, and produce pewter on his own account, but he may have worked in a single rented room on materials supplied to him by another pewterer. Widows who paid quarterage have been included as they can be assumed to have carried on their former husbands' businesses.

Table 12 uses italics in column one post-1611, because thereafter the data have been extracted from the yeomanry accounts and from lists of freemen instead of from the audit accounts; the audit accounts cease to provide quarterage details at this time as the receipts were farmed by the bailiff. Masters were still liable to pay quarterage to the yeomanry, however, and relevant details are recorded therein until the series of yeomanry accounts ceases in 1635; from this date periodic lists of freemen have been used to provide the number of masters. The consequence of these changes in source is to move from modest understatement to modest overstatement. Masters who were members of the yeomanry were not always fully recorded on the audit accounts, while the yeomanry accounts and freemen lists, besides being more comprehensive, each cover two years, and thus include some masters who were not alive in the second year.

A number of further factors also lead to a measure of distortion. On the side of overstatement: firstly, a small group of

[1] Welch, i, 114.

Table 12
London Company shop and apprentice data

Decade	Average annual number of shopkeepers and master pewterers in Company	Average annual number of licences granted to open shops	Average annual enrolment of apprentices
1451–60	—	2·3	—
1461–70	54	1·8	—
1471–80	53	—	—
1481–90	50	2·9	5
1491–1500	58	2·4	10
1501–10	51	3·8	13
1511–20	63	3·7	14
1521–30	57	4·7	16
1531–40	87	5·5	18
1541–50	99	6·0	24
1551–60	128	6·2	22
1561–70	139	8·4	25
1571–80	149	10·5	24
1581–90	153	10·9	33
1591–1600	143	11·3	28
1601–10	—	11·9	37
1611–20	*266*	14·1	39
1621–30	*317*	15·2	41
1631–40	*339*	13·5	35
1641–50	*346*	10·7	40
1651–60	*257*	13·4	48
1661–70	*324*	14·0	56
1671–80	*319*	14·7	42
1681–90	*363*	12·8	47
1691–1700	*334*	9·7	37

Sources. Guildhall MSS 7086/1–4, 7094, 7095/1–2.

coppersmiths were freemen of the Company, and although it is impossible to discover their exact number they probably never exceeded a dozen[1]; and secondly, owing to the London custom of allowing freemen to follow any craft or trade regardless of company affiliation, the Pewterers' Company contained some freemen who were not pewterers, although Table 13 proves that their numbers were small. Tending to understate the numbers of

[1] For example, nine master coppersmiths signed an important petition relating to apprenticeship restrictions in 1615 (Guildhall MS 7090/4, 14 Feb.).

master pewterers in London is the fact that some pewterers were members of other companies, and others were unfree and practising illicitly. On balance it appears that Company data tends more towards under- than overstatement. In 1618 an enquiry into the number of London master pewterers, conducted by officers of the Mint and based upon Company records, reported that there were about 350 in 1664 and 415 in 1688.[1] Freemen residing outside London (country members) were liable to pay yeomanry quarterage only and have not been included in Table 12.

Table 13
Average annual admissions to the freedom of the London Company

Decade	Total	By servitude	By patrimony and redemption
1611–20	19·2	—	—
1621–30	15·6	13·8	1·8
1631–40	21·8	19·6	2·2
1641–50	17·8	16·7	1·1
1651–60	21·5	18·6	2·9
1661–70	28·0	25·3	2·7
1671–80	30·3	27·7	2·6
1681–90	22·0	19·9	2·1
1691–1700	22·8	20·1	2·7

Sources. Guildhall MSS 7086/3–4.

APPRENTICESHIP DATA

The figures in Table 12, column three, include apprentices who were 'turned over' from one master to another during the term of their apprenticeship; they do not include, of course, those pewterers who were to be made free by patrimony. A rough guide to the proportion of apprentices who became freemen of the Company can be obtained by comparing the figures in this column with the figures for the subsequent decade in column two of Table 13. Such a comparison suggests that less than half the apprentices successfully completed their term: high death rates, high drop-out rates, and the attraction of provincial pewtering, are some of the factors responsible.

[1] The report is entered in the Company's records: Guildhall MS 7090/6, 1687–88.

YEOMANRY DATA

It was felt useful to present the data contained in Table 14, despite the fact that it is by far the least reliable. Yeomen masters, journeymen, and country freemen were all required to pay quarterage to the yeomanry, but in practice there were many defaulters and the officers found it an impossible task to trace all those who were liable to pay. The figures in this table therefore reflect, to a greater extent than any others, the efficiency of recording as well as actual changes in the membership.

Table 14

Yeomanry data in annual averages

Period	Shop-keepers	Journey-men	Country members	Spoon-makers	Pensioners	Total
1551–53	—	—	—	—	—	140
1553–55	92	78	—	—	8	178
1555–57	100	88	—	—	—	188
1557–59	86	89	—	—	—	175
1559–61	110	57	21	4	—	192
1561–63	121	74	23	4	—	222
1563–65	132	49	29	4	—	214
1565–67	100	51	25	4	—	180
1569–71	100	100	20	4	—	224
1571–73	109	101	39	5	—	254
1573–75	125	78	32	5	—	240
1577–79	160	65	—	7	—	232
1581–90	—	—	—	—	—	228
1591–1600	—	—	—	—	—	227
1601–10	—	—	—	—	—	224
1611–21	—	—	—	—	—	314
1621–23	252	53	32	—	10	347
1623–25	205	49	44	—	—	298
1625–27	229	44	33	—	—	306
1627–29	222	59	33	—	—	314
1629–31	283	38	28	—	9	358
1631–33	268	12	27	—	—	307
1633–35	—	—	—	—	—	380

Sources. Guildhall MS 7094.

Appendix B

The retail price of pewterware before 1700

There was no single price for pewterware. Different prices were charged according to the composition of the alloy and the amount of workmanship involved. Thus we find that in 1615 the London Company specified that sadware (fine) should be sold retail at $10\frac{1}{2}d$ per lb and lay (holloware) at $9d$ per lb.[1] But these were only general guidelines, and in 1674 a further ordinance specified in detail prices ranging from $12d$ to $14d$ per lb for various types of dishes and plates, each made of the same alloy but each requiring a different amount of workmanship; and in 1560 the workmanship allowed for tavern pots ranged from $9s$ to $11s$ per 100 according to style.[2] Unfortunately our two main price series do not afford sufficient detail to enable us to distinguish variations dependent upon type or quality. Column (*a*) is based exclusively on purchases made by Winchester College, whereas column (*b*) is based on prices drawn from a wide range of sources, among which purchases made by Oxford and Cambridge Colleges predominate.

[1] Guildhall MS 7090/4, 29 Mar.
[2] Guildhall MSS 7090/6, 14 Apr.; 7090/1, 4 May.

Table 15

The retail price of new pewterware

Decade	Per dozen pounds: (a) s d	(b) s d	As an Index (1451–75 = 100)	Price of a sample of industrial products (c) (1451–75 = 100)
1411–20	4	4	120	107
1421–30	3 3	3 3	98	108
1431–40	3	3	90	106
1441–50	3	3	90	101
1451–60	3	3	90	99
1461–70	3 6	3 6	105	103
1471–80	3 6	4 3	115	100
1481–90	3 9	3 6	108	103
1491–1500	4	4 3	125	97
1501–10	4 3	4 6	131	98
1511–20	5	5 3	154	102
1521–30	4 9	5 3	150	110
1531–40	5	5	150	110
1541–50	5 3	5 9	165	127
1551–60	8	8 6	248	186
1561–70	8 3	7 6	236	218
1571–80	8	7 6	233	223
1581–90	8	7 6	233	230
1591–1600	8 6	7 9	244	238
1601–10	9 6	9	278	256
1611–20	12	11	345	274
1621–30	12 6	12	368	264
1631–40	13 3	13 3	398	281
1641–50	14	14 6	428	306
1651–60	14 6	15	443	327
1661–70	14	14 6	428	343
1671–80	—	13	390	351
1681–90	—	11	330	310
1691–1700	—	10 6	315	331

Sources
(a) Beveridge, pp. 85–90.
(b) Rogers, iv, 488; v, 501–4.
(c) E. H. Phelps Brown and S. V. Hopkins, 'Wage rates and prices: evidence for population pressure in the sixteenth century', *Economica*, xxiv (1957), 306. This column comprises an unweighted index of the prices of charcoal, candles, oil, canvas, shirting, woollen cloth, building materials, lead and solder.

Part Two

❀ *Pewter in
modern Britain*

6   The decline of pewter

The pewterers, who had ably exploited the possibilities of a growing home market during the sixteenth and seventeenth centuries, failed to follow up this earlier success and take advantage of its even greater growth after 1700. Indeed, British pewtering seems to have reached its zenith in the later seventeenth century and, after resting on a plateau of prosperity in the early eighteenth century, actually started to go into decline from the 1740s onwards, just when both population and purchasing power started to increase more rapidly. The population of England and Wales, as we have seen, probably rose from 2·5 to 3 million in 1500 to approximately 5·5 million in 1700. There were then probably a further million people living in Scotland. By the time the first census was taken, in 1801, Great Britain had a population of 10·5 million and by 1851 this figure had been doubled. Estimates suggest that the nation's wealth was growing more rapidly than its population, certainly in the eighteenth century and to a smaller amount in the first half of the nineteenth. National income per head may have increased from about £10 at the end of the seventeenth century to about £21 at the beginning of the nineteenth and perhaps to about £24 around 1850.[1] There is much debate about how this increase was distributed, particularly in the first half of the nineteenth century, and the extent to which it went to the better-off rather than to the poorer sections of society.[2] Over the period as a whole, however, there were many

[1] B. R. Mitchell and Phyllis Deane, *Abstract of British Historical Statistics* (Cambridge 1962), pp. 6, 366; Phyllis Deane, 'Contemporary estimates of national income in the first half of the nineteenth century', *Economic History Review*, 2nd ser. ix (1956–7), 353.
[2] E. J. Hobsbawm and R. M. Hartwell, 'The standard of living during the Industrial Revolution', *Economic History Review*, 2nd ser. xvi (1963–4), A. J. Taylor 'Poverty and progress in Britain: a reappraisal', *History*, xlv (1960).

more households to be supplied, and possibly even during the contentious first half of the nineteenth century the overwhelming majority enjoyed more purchasing power. Why, then, was less pewter being sold on the home market?

Pewter had had much to commend it during the sixteenth and seventeenth centuries. Bright in appearance, it was an admirable substitute for the less attractive eating utensils and drinking vessels previously used. It was readily transportable over considerable distances, being unbreakable; and it was durable. It maintained a high secondhand value and it could be easily recast or repaired when required. Its attraction, both as a good to be used and as a modest investment, was such that it found its way eventually into most households. From a national point of view it was wholly advantageous, for it was made almost entirely of tin produced within the country and value was added to it by employing English labour, thereby encouraging home industry and avoiding foreign imports. Indeed, pewter was a significant English export. Its technology was fairly simple and straightforward, appropriate in fact to an economy at that particular stage in its development.

The pewterers' high degree of success in getting their product into so many households before 1700 explains to some extent why they found it difficult to exploit the market still further. They might have continued to sell the same kind of articles to the additional households as the population grew, and the market might have been penetrated more fully at its social base. But such was the durability of pewter that there was only a limited replacement demand, though there was undoubtedly employment to be had in remaking worn items and perhaps in producing pieces of more modern design. But there was nothing basically new and fashionable about pewter; and there was limited scope for pewterers to make their product more fashionable merely by changes in design.

It was when the pewter industry was in this rather unpromising stage in its history that a very important change occurred in the drinking habits of the British people. They turned increasingly to warm beverages, particularly tea. Although eighteenth-century trade statistics are notoriously unreliable, especially when highly taxed and therefore much-smuggled goods such as tea are concerned, they do nevertheless give a fairly good guide to general trends. Retained imports of tea into England and Wales, only a mere 26,000 lb per year during the first decade of the eighteenth century, rose to about 1 million lb per year in the 1730s, exceeded 3 million per year in the 1750s and reached 5 million lb per year in the 1770s. By the later 1780s, after the duty on tea had been greatly reduced, retained tea imports regularly exceeded 15 million lb and in the early nineteenth century retained imports for the whole of Britain were often in excess of 20 million lb per year.[1] Beer consumption, on the other hand, rose very slowly. The best estimate suggests that total sales grew from 6,100,000 barrels in 1722 to only 7,350,000 barrels over a century later, in 1833. This represented a reduction in consumption per head of over 50 per cent. During the same period, by contrast, the consumption of tea had grown from 1 oz per head to 2·3 lb.[2] This change in drinking habits favoured the potter, not the pewterer, and, having sold the cups, the potter also supplied the matching saucers, plates and other dishes as well. It was the potter, in fact, who seized his opportunity to exploit the growing market in the eighteenth century as the pewterer had done in the earlier, though less spectacular, period of growth during the previous two centuries.

Although many books have been written about British pottery and almost as many about British potters, a systematic study of the growth of the British pottery industry has yet to appear.[3] It seems clear, however, that attempts were already being made in Britain before the end of the seventeenth century to supplement expensive imported porcelain by an improved home-produced product. The manufacture of delftware was the earliest of these attempts, with production increasing throughout the seventeenth and early eighteenth centuries, particularly in London but also in Bristol and Liverpool which both developed a healthy export trade in it. This earthenware was bulky and glazed with tin oxide, giving a white surface on which were painted a variety of designs,

[1] Schumpeter, pp. 60–1.
[2] Peter Mathias, *The Brewing Industry in England* (Cambridge 1959), p. 375.
[3] There is, however, a valuable chapter dealing with pottery by R. G. Haggar in *VCH, Staffordshire*, vol. ii (1967). Useful material will also be found in Weatherill, *The Pottery Trade of North Staffordshire* and in N. McKendrick, 'Josiah Wedgwood: an eighteenth-century entrepreneur in salesmanship and marketing techniques' *Economic History Review*, 2nd ser. xii (1960–1). Mrs Weatherill is now extending her work into a national study, and she has kindly supplied us with material arising out of this further research. We gratefully acknowledge her assistance.

predominantly blue, yellow and orange in colour. Its disadvantage was that it was not hard-wearing; nor was it really suitable for hot drinks.

Stoneware did not have this disadvantage, although its early production in London was of heavy vessels and bottles of many types. The largest and earliest factory was that at Fulham, founded about 1672. At the end of the seventeenth century this manufacture had spread to Nottingham and North Staffordshire where alehouse and other drinking vessels were of particular importance. Tea pots and cups were made at this time, but in small quantities. Two Dutch immigrants, the Elers brothers, were responsible for a pottery in North Staffordshire which worked for a few years in the 1690s. It was here that Celia Fiennes mentions her attempt, in 1698, 'to see them making the fine tea-pots cups and saucers of the fine red earth, in imitation and as curious as that which comes from China'.[1]

Important changes took place in North Staffordshire from the 1720s onwards when West Country white-firing clays and calcined crushed flints began to be used as an ingredient in stoneware bodies, and from about 1725 this harder and more durable white variety, which showed off the transparent salt-glaze to better advantage, replaced the existing kinds and came to be used increasingly for domestic purposes.

The manufacture of coarse earthenware—heavy, red pottery— was located in a number of centres and it seems to have been in demand for general purposes in farming. Efforts were made to improve its method of manufacture so as to make it more acceptable for domestic use, the first serious attempt dating from the 1720s alongside the development of white stoneware. This marked the beginning of further experiment and improvement and to greater production of finer pottery culminating, in the 1760s, in the production of cream-coloured earthenware which carried all before it not only in Britain but also abroad. Thanks to the scientific and business enterprise of a number of entrepreneurs, among whom Josiah Wedgwood was outstanding, North Staffordshire established itself as the national centre of production. This rise of the Potteries was assisted in no small degree by improvements in transport arrangements which made it easier and cheaper to carry white clays into the area and the fragile

[1] *The Journeys of Celia Fiennes*, ed. Christopher Morris (1947), p. 177.

finished product away from it. North Staffordshire also participated to a small extent in the expansion of high quality porcelain production. London and several other centres were, however, of greater importance in this branch of manufacture and Britain continued to be an importer of porcelain.

The remarkable rise of the pottery industry during the eighteenth century and the growing ascendancy of the thrusting businessmen of North Staffordshire who developed the trade specialisms there and the necessary ancillary crafts, is most conveniently summarised by the best estimate for the numbers employed in the industry during these years. These figures suggest a fivefold increase in the labour force; and no doubt, the greater efficiency in methods of working, the application of power to some of the processes and the economics of scale associated with concentration in one particular area meant that output grew at a much faster rate than this.

Unfortunately, because the inventories peter out by the middle of the eighteenth century, it is not possible to trace this greatly increased pottery output to the customer and relate it to his personal possessions of pottery on the one hand and pewter on the other. We cannot, therefore, use this source to show just when pottery was supplementing pewter in various sections of society and when it was replacing it. The inventories down to the 1740s, however, do make it quite clear that in the earlier part of the century, as we would expect, there can have been little replacement. Pewter ownership remained very widespread indeed. These inventories show, too—as we would also expect to find—that domestic earthenware and china were already spreading in better-off households and had made quite a deep penetration in those of the gentry[1] and tradesmen.

The sample is too small to tell us much about the penetration of the other sections of society, though the limited amount of pottery possessed by the yeoman class would suggest that there

[1] The very full, interesting and well edited journal of Nicholas Blundell, squire of Little Crosby to the north of Liverpool, may indicate what was happening among the squirearchy. In the first two decades of the century he bought mugs on various occasions and (in 1712) some delftware coffee cups. Two years before this he had bought two china dishes and two china bowls and in 1719 he bought six china coffee cups and dishes. But throughout this period there is no reference to his purchasing any pewter even though the important provincial pewtering centre of Wigan was close by. He also had as an acquaintance a 'Mr. Ford the Putarar' (15 June 1713): *The Great Diurnal of Nicholas Blundell*, ed. Frank Tyrer, 2 vols (Liverpool 1968, 1970), Vol. i, *1702-1711*, pp. 19, 188, 262 n., 268; vol. ii, *1712-1719*, pp. 30, 65, 260.

Table 16.
Estimates of employment in the pottery trades of England and Wales, 1680–1770

Type of pottery		1680	1690	1700	1710	1720	1730	1740	1750	1760	1770
Course earthenware	North Staffs	180	200	225	225	250	250	250	250	250	250
	Elsewhere	422	414	380	325	318	284	271	266	240	250
	Total	602	614	605	550	668	534	521	516	480	500
Delft ware	(never made in North Staffs)										
	Total	380	445	420	475	480	560	550	665	490	425
Stoneware	North Staffs	24	48	77	115	150	200	250	300	350	350
	Elsewhere	80	85	180	195	195	195	165	165	145	150
	Total	104	133	257	310	345	395	415	465	495	400
Fine earthenware	North Staffs					50	150	500	900	1,300	2,400
	Elsewhere					50	65	130	205	350	395
	Total					100	215	630	1,105	1,650	2,795
Porcelain	North Staffs								20	40	
	Elsewhere								130	440	480
	Total								150	490	480
Totals	North Staffs	204	248	302	340	450	600	1,000	1,470	1,940	3,000
	Elsewhere	882	944	980	995	1,043	1,104	1,116	1,581	2,145	2,179
Grand Total		1,088	1,192	1,282	1,335	1,493	1,704	2,116	3,051	4,085	5,179

Source. Information from Mrs. Lorna M. Weatherill.

Table 17.

Domestic earthenware and china in samples of inventories between the 1680s and the 1730s

Owner's status	1680s T	1680s E	1700s T	1700s E	1720s T	1720s E	1730s T	1730s E
Gentry	9	3	11	4	3	1	2	2
Tradesmen	41	10	49	28	35	28	16	13
Yeomen	109	35	40	17	30	12	16	3
Labourers and others (occupations unspecified) worth under £20 in value	13	4	6	2	1	0	1	0

T — total.
E — number of inventories containing references to domestic earthenware and china.
Source. Information from Mrs Lorna M. Weatherill.

was still a vast market to be supplied. The onslaught upon this was to come from the 1740s onwards and it is significant that in urban markets, of growing importance and the main buying centres for people of modest means, pottery stalls predominated among those selling household goods.[1]

There can be no doubt that the top end of the pewterers' main market—for tableware of all kinds—was under increasing challenge in the first half of the eighteenth century and particularly from about 1720 onwards. By the middle of the century this market as a whole, for rich and poor, was in jeopardy. And the pewterers' competitive position was soon to be made worse by the rise in price of their main raw material.

From the ending of tin pre-emption by Crown patentees in 1717, down to about 1780, the Cornish price of tin was usually below, and often well below, the £3.10s per cwt at which it had been fixed in the last seven-year contract in Anne's reign. The market was clearly dominated not by the West Country tin producers but by the London merchants. Indeed, in some years between 1717 and 1740 the price went down so low as £2.15s.[2] The next three decades saw no basic change in the position; but then a chain of events was begun which was soon to tip the scales decisively in favour of Cornwall.

[1] Dr David Alexander has drawn attention to this in the mid-nineteenth century (*Retailing in England*, pp. 43-4); elsewhere in his book he notes the continued importance of itinerant retailing despite the spread of shops.
[2] John Rowe, *Cornwall in the Age of the Industrial Revolution* (Liverpool, 1953), p. 42.

In the early 1770s a wave of speculation in tin mining and improvement in mining technology caused the price to plummet to £2.14s and, though it recovered soon afterwards to about £3, this recovery was short-lived.[1] The tin trade blamed the spread of pottery for its troubles and it was fortunate for Josiah Wedgwood that a visit he made to Cornwall in 1775 happened to coincide with this temporary price recovery. He noted in his diary on 5 June 1775:

> Truro . . . I was glad . . . to hear that the price of tin was got up from 50 to 60sh per cwt. for I had been seriously advised by some of my friends before I left London not to trust myself among the miners of Cornwall, the tin trade being then low, and they, being persuaded that the use of Queen's ware was the cause of it, had already shewn some instances of their displeasure at that manufacture. However, we found them all very civil.[2]

Tin prices were soon falling again and an Exeter paper reported on 4 April 1776:

> Last week the tinners in Cornwall rose in consequence of the introduction into that country of large quantities of Staffordshire and other earthenware. About a hundred in a body went to Redruth, on the market day, and broke all the wares they could meet with, the sale of which had been intended in that town. From thence they went to Falmouth for the same purpose, and because they could not force their way into the Town Hall, where a large parcel of Staffordshire and other wares were lodged, they were about to set fire to it, had not Mr. Allison, the printer and alderman of that town, with another gentleman, pacified them, by promising to discourage the sale and use of these wares by every means in their power, and by going to a pewterer's and bespeaking a quantity of pewter dishes and plates to evince their readiness to serve them, on which they happily dispersed.[3]

These lower tin prices were, of course, wholly to the pewterers' advantage; but the new mood among the Cornish producers led,

[1] *Ibid.*, pp. 43, 57.
[2] 'Josiah Wedgwood's journal of his journey into Cornwall with Mr. Turner', *Proceedings of the Wedgwood Society*, no. 2 (1957), p. 83.
[3] Quoted in Peter C. D. Brears, *The English Country Pottery: its history and techniques* (Newton Abbot, 1971), p. 56.

after a further difficult period during the bad wartime depression years of the later 1770s, to the combination of the tin-mining interests in 1780.¹ This marked the end of London's dominance of the trade. The price was up again to £3.10s by 1782 and was maintained at this higher rate with only occasional falls from then onwards. The tin producers later made advantageous contracts with the East India Company for the export of their tin, and during the Revolutionary and Napoleonic Wars the price rose to £6, £7 and even £8 per cwt.² It fell again afterwards, but from 1817, when it had been restored to peacetime levels, until 1831 it varied upwards from £3.15s to £4.15s.³ From 1780 onwards, therefore, the age of low-priced tin had come to an end. To the extent that the pewterers depended on new tin for their products⁴ they were being obliged to pay more for it when they could least afford to do so.

They were also by then confronted with a new competitor which was able, by adopting a different technology, to use tin more efficiently. This new product, first known as white metal, was later given the patriotic name of Britannia metal and, so far as is known, it was first manufactured commercially in Sheffield after about 1770. It was, in fact, a successor to Sheffield Plate which had been developed about a quarter of a century before that. 'What plated ware did for those not wealthy enough to furnish their tables with sterling silver', the historian of Sheffield Plate has noted, 'Britannia metal did for the classes unable to afford silvered copper'.⁵ Like the best pewter, it consisted of

¹ Rowe, p. 166.   ² *Ibid.*, pp. 171 ff.
³ *Ibid.*, p. 188.   ⁴ See below p. 292.
⁵ Frederick Bradbury, *History of Old Sheffield Plate* (1912), p. 494. The origins of Britannia metal have yet to be explored; but it should perhaps be noted that from quite early in its production those who advertised themselves as Britannia metal manufacturers were already concerned with the making of plated goods. A Sheffield Directory of 1797 (copied by *The Universal British Directory*, vol. iv, 1798) lists five Britannic-metal [sic] makers. One of these, Froggatt, Coldwell and Lean, was described as 'Britannic-metal and Plated Manufacturers' and a partner in a second (Hancock & Jessop) may have been connected with the introduction of metal plating to Sheffield. *The Universal British Directory* noted: 'Buttons of plated metal had been made by Mr. Bo[u]lsover for a considerable time; but about 1758 a manufactory of this material was begun by Mr. Joseph Hancock, an ingenious mechanic, comprehending a great variety of articles, such as saucepans, tea urns, coffee pots, cups, tankards, candlesticks, etc.'. Hancock later concentrated on rolling the metal and selling it to others for the manufacture of Sheffield Plate (Bradbury, p. 15). The other Britannia metal manufacturers listed in 1797 were: Vickers and Son, Richard Constantine, and Broadhead, Gurney, Spark & Co., the last-named firm being also scissors and knife makers. Most writers have followed the reminiscences of Charles Dixon (1776-1852), a candlestick maker, and credited James Vickers

90 per cent tin but it was alloyed with antimony.[1] This made a strong and hard product which could be made thinner, so effecting a considerable economy in the use of costly tin. As an alloy, Britannia metal was a form of pewter, but it was processed in a completely different way, and it is the method of fabrication which distinguished it clearly from pewter. It was not cast, like pewter, but was prepared in sheets and then either roughly shaped and spun on a lathe or pressed out in a stamping press. Not only did the new product economise in raw material and in moulds and lend itself to more modern production methods; it also possessed a very attractive appearance much more akin to the fine lines of silverware. Britannia metal spoons, pepper and mustard pots, teapots and other hollow tableware soon gained favour, seizing a share of what was left of the pewterers' dwindling market.

The pewterers suffered more competition, too, from their old rivals the manufacturers of 'Crooked Lane Wares' who made articles from tinplate. These men no longer had to rely upon imported German tinplate, for the British industry, dating from about 1720, could boast four or five producers half a century later. They developed a method of rolling the iron sheets from which the tinplate was made and so were able to supply these more cheaply to the tinplate workers.[2] As with Britannia metal, technical change favoured the pewterers' rivals and, again, competition came in an area which the pewterers could least afford to lose, for it included the manufacture of candlesticks which were relatively free from pottery competition though not from that of brassware. The other products which the Tin Plate Alias Wire Workers' Company was still claiming to control included (to quote from

---

with the introduction of white metal manufacture to Sheffield. He was certainly exploiting it successfully by the 1780s and Bradbury (p. 498) includes an illustration of one of his tea caddies made in 1787. The *Sheffield Mercury*, however, in its obituary of Nathan Gower, on 30 September 1813, called Gower 'the Father of the White Metal Trade'; for extracts from Dixon's MS and this newspaper reference, see Bradbury, particularly p. 494.

[1] In an article in *Collectors' Guide*, soon to appear, Mr C. A. Peal has argued that pewter made before 1770, perhaps about 1700 and even earlier, can be shown to contain some antimony. He also believes that after 1770 tin alloyed with antimony was widely used in the casting of pewter. It produced a harder-wearing metal and looked more like silver. That is to say, in response to increased competition—including competition from Britannia metal—the pewterers concentrated to a greater extent upon a higher quality and more attractive product.

[2] Minchinton, p. 15.

one of its lists, dated 1767) 'Coffee pots, porringers, pint pots, quart pots, pudding pots, pots to spit in'.[1]

The British pewter industry was only saved from rapid collapse by the continued sale of beer pots to public houses (which increased considerably in number with the switch from home to public brewing from about 1780 onwards[2]) and by the growth of pewter exports. The many specimens of surviving beer pots, from 1770 usually without lids, testify to the importance of this remaining major outlet on the home market. Pewter pots, being cast, could be made more accurately to approved sealed measures than could earthenware mugs, as a deprived drinker had been at pains to point out to the Treasury early in the eighteenth century.[3] They were also much less liable to damage than pottery or glass and could stand up to heavy wear. Indeed, the publicans' most frequent complaint was that so durable were they that customers often stole them, particularly when beer was sent out for consumption off the premises. In 1812 the licensed victuallers and publicans of London even went so far as to petition Parliament for legal protection against these thefts by making it a punishable offence for publicans to send out 'any pewter or other pots' and to confine the use of pewter pots 'for the purpose of measuring their beer to their customers'. They claimed that pewter comprised 'a considerable portion of their Property' and were prepared to produce evidence which would show that thefts were then costing them £70,000 to £80,000 per year. Parliament, however, went no further than ordering a return to be produced giving details of the numbers convicted of stealing these pots.[4] So the pewterers retained this market, which became even more valuable to them after 1830, for in that year the duty on beer was removed and anyone was allowed to sell it to the public merely on payment of an excise licence fee. This attempt to establish free trade in beer in an attempt to discriminate against spirit drinking succeeded in

[1] Oliver Warner, *A History of the Tin Plate Alias Wire Workers Company of the City of London* (1964), p. 25. [2] Mathias, p. 377.
[3] PRO, T1/136, Petition of R. Pilkington, 14 August 1711. The problem of earthenware mugs had been discussed by the Court of the Pewterers Company on two occasions before this (Guildhall MS 7090/8, 23 September 1703; 15 December 1709).
[4] *Journals of the House of Commons*, lxvii, 24 January, 1812; Account of all persons tried and convicted at the several sessions of the Peace holden for the County of Middlesex between October 1811 and May 1813 for stealing pewter pots, 1812/3 [219] XIII. 19 had been convicted during this period plus four more in Surrey, 10 in Westminster and 34 at the Old Bailey.

encouraging the British public to drink more beer even if it was less successful in its attempts to discourage the consumption of spirits. The breweries' output nearly quadrupled over the next half century and beer consumption per head in Britain seems to have reached an all-time peak (34·4 gallons per head) in 1876.[1] The demand for pewter pots obviously grew at a far more rapid rate in the vastly increased number of public houses after 1830 than it had done in the century before then.

The eighteenth-century trade statistics show that exports of pewter, despite quite severe fluctuations from year to year, were on a strong upward trend, particularly in the first half of the century.[2] In 1700–9 they were running at about 150 tons per year. By the 1790s they had risen to 1,000 tons or more and around 1800 they touched 1,500 tons for a year or two. But then they fell back again. (The years 1807 and 1808 were particularly bad, indicating the importance of the American market, a fact which is also to be seen from the big cutback in exports in the later 1770s and beginning of the 1780s, during the American War of Independence.) The annual value of these exports at their peak, c. 1800, was about £100,000. By the middle of the nineteenth century, when pewter is no longer separately listed in the returns but appears as 'tin and pewter wares' (which, however, excluded tinplate), the total value under this combined head was only £30,000 or so.[3] Australia had by then become the main market; about one-third of these exports went there. The rest was sent to British possessions in South Africa, the British East Indies and the British West Indies.

Having lost most of its home market (apart from the trade in pewter pots), the pewter industry managed to stagger on for a time by shipping its goods abroad to people with less sophisticated tastes. Just how much of the exports categorised as 'tin and pewter wares' were pewter it is impossible to say. Thomas Yates, who reported on the trade for the 1865 meeting of the British Association in Birmingham, emphasised the importance of the discovery of gold in Australia in encouraging pewter exports. 'From the substantial character of its manufactures', he wrote, 'they were suited to the requirements of the colony, and a

---

[1] Mitchell and Deane, pp. 252–3; Brian Harrison, *Drink and the Victorians* (1971), ch. 3; John Burnett, *Plenty and Want* (1966), p. 11. [2] Schumpeter.
[3] Trade and Navigation Returns, published in *Parliamentary Papers* from 1853 onwards.

considerable trade was at once commenced. The demand is still steady and increasing, especially as regards ale and wine measures, drinking cups, etc.'[1] The trade statistics, however, suggest that by then pewter exports had dwindled into insignificance. The category 'tin and pewter wares' was replaced from 1862 onwards by the much drearier-sounding bureaucratic creation of 'tin and tinned wares unenumerated (British)'.[2]

Since we know the total amount of white tin produced (from the coinage figures) and since we also possess statistics of tin exported both in the form of tin blocks and as pewter, it is possible to arrive at a rough idea of the total amount of tin left over for manufacture into pewter for sale in the home market and for other purposes.

Table 18.

Estimates of annual tin production and annual exports of tin in tin blocks and in pewter in the early, mid, and later eighteenth century (tons)

Decade	Tin production	Tin exports	Pewter exports	Tin content of exported pewter containing		Tin remaining for home market	
				(a) 90% tin	(b) 80% tin	if (a)	if (b)
1700–09	1,400	1,100	150	135	120	165	180
1750–59	2,700	1,700	775	700	620	300	380
1790–99	3,200	2,300	1,200	1,080	960	—180	—60

Sources. Rowe, p. 58; Schumpeter, Tables VIII and IX.

These figures are puzzling and difficult to interpret, for there were no other major sources of tin at that time—any imports were not of significance—and there were, of course, other uses for tin within Britain apart from pewter destined for the home market. A petition in 1707, for instance, referred to its use by 'scarlet dyers, tin foil workers, potters of all white ware [i.e. delftware], pinmakers, founders, plumbers and glaziers',[3] to which should be added, from about 1720 onwards, the tinplate makers. It seems difficult to believe that they could all be sustained by the tiny surplus which remained after export needs had been

[1] Samuel Timmins, ed., *Birmingham and the Midland Hardware District* (1866; repr. 1967), p. 618.
[2] Trade and Navigation Return for 1862, 1863 [3218] lxv.
[3] *Calendar of Treasury Books*, xxi, pt 2 (1706/7) (1952), p. 516.

met, though the Company's complaint in 1785 of a dire shortage[1] seems to suggest that the figures may not be completely wide of the mark. But the negative surplus in the 1790s seems to make complete nonsense of them. The simplest explanation is that the statistics are wholly or partly unreliable. There is, however, another possible explanation which may explain to some extent the small home market residuum.

It has been calculated that at the end of the seventeenth century the national stock of pewter probably totalled somewhere between 30,000 and 50,000 tons.[2] Because of its high tin content and because it could be remelted, old pewter fetched a good price, usually not very much below its new price. During the eighteenth century, for instance, Oxford and Cambridge colleges were paying out about 11d per lb for new pewter and selling their old for 9d early in the century, and for 7d or 8d in the 1760s and 1770s.[3] It is possible, therefore, that so far as pewter production was concerned, much of the manufacture consisted of melting down and remaking old stock, and perhaps, as the eighteenth century progressed and more people switched to pottery, they were prepared to part with much of their pewter for a good, though falling, price. This, when remade (often with a higher lead content), was either shipped abroad or used mainly for alehouse pots at home. If the industry could have survived in this way on the large national stock of scrap pewter which we know existed, it would not have needed to make any substantial calls on new supplies of tin; and if this were the case, the small surplus remaining for the other tin users would appear much less improbable than the figures in the above table would suggest. The pewterers would also in this way have been able to cushion themselves against rising tin prices later in the eighteenth century.

London remained the most important centre of pewtering during its years of decline as it had done during its heyday. Since the Company abandoned its country searches (the detailed records of these end in 1691) it is no longer possible in this period to use search lists as an indication of the whereabouts and numbers of provincial pewterers. New sources become available, however, notably lists of freemen in provincial towns which were drawn up

[1] Below, p. 305.
[2] Above, p. 130.
[3] Rogers, vii, pp. 396, 397, 400.

Plate 26   A French pewter workshop, c. 1750. (Diderot, *Encyclopaedia of Trades and Industry*).

Plate 27   A selection of fine Georgian pewter, including pieces made for the coronation banquet of George IV.

Plate 28 A long range of bulbous, lidless tavern measurers of Imperial measure. Ranging from the half-gallon to one thirty-second of a pint, c. 1826–60.

Plate 29 A range of eighteenth- and nineteenth-century tankards, mostly quarts.

Plate 30 Fine tableware made by Thomas Chamberlain, London, *c.* 1760.

Plate 31 A selection of contemporary pewter.

Plate 32 A selection of representative pieces of Britannia metal.

for electoral purposes during the eighteenth century, and published directories which named those who lived and worked in these places as well as in London. In the nineteenth century the national census supplements this information; but only the 1841 census provides us with a satisfactory survey of the whereabouts of pewterers at that time.[1] The Company's freedom lists continue to indicate the numbers of pewterers joining the trade in London.

These freedom lists, being compiled on an annual basis, are the best single guide to the dwindling size of the trade in the eighteenth century, for most pewterers worked in London and we know from the 1841 census that this was still the case when the decline was nearing its end. There is no question, that is to say, of the London evidence being misleading because pewtering had moved elsewhere. The evidence of the freedom lists is, however, not beyond dispute, for it can be argued that the reduction in the totals enrolled may have been caused not by any real fall in the numbers entering the trade but by the Company's failing to keep a firm hold on the craft and neglecting to enforce enrolment on all practising pewterers. There was certainly growing laxity in this respect among the City companies generally: the number of freemen recruited to them all declined from 2,100 per year in the late 1670s to 1,700 between 1710 and 1720 and 1,250 by 1745.[2] The continued strength of the craft within the Pewterers Company will be discussed in our last chapter; for our present purposes it is sufficient to note that even in the 1790s at least one-third of the livery consisted of practising craftsmen, a higher proportion than was then usual in other London companies. Moreover, appreciable numbers of apprentices were still being admitted to the freedom when they had served their time, and in 1774 the Company had secured an Act of Common Council reasserting its rights over practising pewterers within the City of London and its liberties and obliging them to become freemen of the Company.[3] It seems reasonable to argue, therefore, that the freedom lists probably are a fairly reliable indicator of the rate at which the trade was declining. It is certainly the only one we possess.

[1] The 1831 census overlooks many pewterers. It enumerates only about 100 altogether, all of them in the London area. The 1851 census does not list pewterers as a separate category. [2] Kellett, p. 389.
[3] Guildhall MS 7090/11, 20 Oct. 1774. For other companies which took this course between 1750 and 1778, see Kellett, p. 390.

Table 19.

Number of enrolments to the freedom of the Pewterers' Company by apprenticeship and by patrimony, 1700–09 to 1790–99

Decade	By apprenticeship	By patrimony
1700–09	165	28
1710–19	139	39
1720–29	169	45
1730–39	133	42
1740–49	118	34
1750–59	120	32
1760–69	74	25
1770–79	69	18
1780–89	52	16
1790–99	35	16

Source. Guildhall MS 7086/4,5 and 6, Wardens' Account Books.

Already, by the first decade of the eighteenth century admissions were well below the totals of the later seventeenth century[1] and those entering by patrimony were higher than they had previously been, though some of these entrants were, in fact, practising pewterers. As Table 19 shows, their proportion continued to rise, from about 16 per cent of those admitted by apprenticeship in the first decade to 25 per cent by mid-century and to nearly 50 per cent by the 1790s.

Of greater interest is the timing of the fall in the numbers enrolled by apprenticeship. If we can discount the unusual decade 1710–19 (the reduced returns for which are to be explained by very low enrolments in a single year, 1716–17), there would seem to be a noticeable step downwards in the 1730s to a lower level of recruitment in the 1740s and 1750s. It was after this that the really dramatic collapse came, the 1760s marking an even bigger step down from previous levels and inaugurating a further decline which became steeper in the 1780s and 1790s. This would accord well with the spread of creamware pottery from the 1760s and the increased competition from this quarter, and from Britannia metal and tinplate manufactures, later in the century. When the increasing amount of employment provided by the continued and considerable rise in pewter exports is borne in mind, the collapse

[1] Above, p. 273.

of home demand for pewter other than alehouse pots must have been very considerable indeed.

That the occupation of pewterer was still one of considerable standing and profitability in the 1740s, is clear from a book on the London trades published in 1747, though the writer goes on to stress that it was not without its hazards: 'It is an ingenious Business and abundantly profitable, but very unhealthful, because of the Fume of the Metal, which soon renders them Paralytic; Journeymen earn from Fifteen Shillings to a Guinea a Week.'[1]

The price of being bound apprentice was £20 to £40, almost on a par with the £20 to £50 demanded for training as a goldsmith; and to set up as a master required £300 to £1,000 (£500 to £1,000 for a master goldsmith).[2] But these days of prosperity for the trade were not to last much longer, and the increased number of trade cards advertising the pewterers' wares, which have survived from the mid and later eighteenth century, may indicate a greater need to keep pewter before the fashionable public.[3]

A later volume on London trades, similar to that of 1747 but published at the beginning of the nineteenth century (and reprinted several times), omitted pewterers altogether, though it devoted some space to tinplate workers.[4] Another such book, published in Glasgow in the mid-1830s, mentioned pewter in the course of a chapter on tin, but dismissed it in a sentence just as an alloy 'made into vessels of all sorts, particularly into measures for beer and other liquors'.[5]

The directory evidence is incomplete and seems to be concerned only with the most important pewtering businesses. *The Universal British Directory*, for instance, which devoted its first volume to London in 1791, could find only twenty-one pewtering concerns among some 17,000 names listed altogether. Not all of these were entirely devoted to pewtering. They included a tinplate worker and pewterer, a pewterer and worm maker[6] and a

---

[1] R. Campbell, *The London Tradesman*, p. 320. [2] *Ibid.*, pp. 335, 338.
[3] Cotterell and Heal, 'Pewterers' trade-cards', 'About pewterers' trade-cards etc.'. We do not think that the evidence supports Dr R. Burt's unsubstantiated contention that home demand for pewter was increasing down to 1770 ('Lead production in England and Wales, 1700–1770', *Economic History Review*, 2nd ser. xxii (1969), 260–1).
[4] *The Book of Trades* (3 parts, 1805–06).
[5] *The Book of Trades* (Glasgow, 2nd edn, 1837), p. 81.
[6] The worm was the spiral pipe in distilling apparatus in which the vapour was cooled and condensed.

pewterer and brazier. Robert Piercy Hodge, to be Master of the Company in 1802, appeared in the list as a pewterer and manufacturer of pewter and leaden toys. Some diversification had obviously developed, though how long it had existed or whether it antedated the pewterers' more difficult times, it is not possible to say. In two later London directories, *Pigot's* for 1822-23 and 1826-27, each trade is listed separately, but the reader who wishes to refer to the list of pewterers is advised to 'see also Beer Engine Makers'. The combination of pewterer and worm maker still survived and there was also one pewterer who was a distillers' apparatus manufacturer. These lists of the 1820s are fuller than those of 1791. They include thirty-eight pewterers for 1822-23 and thirty-nine for 1826-27.

That these totals relate to leading businesses rather than to working pewterers, is evident from the larger numbers given in the 1841 census, though here we are confronted with a problem of interpretation of a different sort. The census recorded everyone whose trade was that of pewterer; but it did not record how many of these were retired men who were no longer practising their craft. If the directories underestimate the total, the census overestimates it. It is nevertheless revealing that, so late as 1841, over 300 people in and about London (including twenty women) should still describe themselves to the census enumerators as pewterers. It is also useful to know in what parts of London they lived. This information is contained in Table 20. The most telling figures in the table are undoubtedly those relating to males under twenty. The trade was recruiting very few apprentices. The Company's freedom lists confirm this. In such a situation a high proportion of the older males listed must have given up the trade.

By this time there were very few people outside the London area who could describe themselves as pewterers, whether they were still actively engaged in the trade or not. The poll books and provincial directories for the eighteenth and early nineteenth centuries suggest that collapse may have come even sooner in the provinces than in London (London, presumably, was better placed than many of these provincial towns to take advantage of the export and pewter tankard trades.) No pewterers, for instance, are listed in the poll books for Derby in 1741, Chester in 1747 and 1748, Colchester in 1768, Southampton in 1774 or Maidstone

Table 20.

Location of those who described themselves as pewterers and were living in the London area at the census of 1841

Location	Males Over 20	Males Under 20	Females Over 20	Females Under 20
London City within the Walls	4			
London City without the Walls	19	1	5	
Westminster City	21		1	
Finsbury Division	30	3	2	
Holborn Division	25		1	
Kensingston Division	2			
Tower Division	74	4	2	
St Botolph, Bishopsgate Without, Christchurch, Spitalfields, St Luke's Old Street and St Matthew, Bethnal Green Parishes	43	6	5	
Clerkenwell	14	1	1	
Bermondsey Parish	8	1		
Lambeth Church District	1			
Rotherhithe Parish			1	
Southwark Borough	18	3	2	
Surrey County [but presumably mostly in the London area]	14			
TOTAL	312 : 273	19	20	

Source. Census of 1841, 1844 [587] XXVII.

in 1780.[1] Later volumes of *The Universal British Directory*, which cover provincial towns between 1793 and 1798, list surprisingly few pewterers. Even a place like Bath is not recorded as possessing one; and Birmingham could boast only one woman pewterer (who made spoons) out of some 2,400 trade entries.[2] Liverpool is credited with none out of 4,000 and Manchester with none out of 5,500. York, where a poll book of 1758 listed four pewterers, is given none by this *Directory*. Wigan is given three out of about 300 entries and Bristol, which had ten in a poll book of 1734 and

[1] Copies of these are to be found at the Institute of Historical Research.
[2] There must certainly have been omissions here for Birmingham was one of the two provincial centres (the other was Bristol) which was specifically mentioned in the Pewterers Company's report of 1799. (See below, p. 310). For the dating of the various volumes of *The Universal British Directory* see Jane E. Norton, *Guide to the National and Provincial Directories of England and Wales, excluding London, published before 1856* (1950), pp. 32–9.

ten again in another of 1784, earns only one entry. The association formed in 1536 by the goldsmiths, plumbers, glaziers, pewterers and painters of Newcastle-upon-Tyne was broken in 1716 when the goldsmiths withdrew; but the pewterers, plumbers and painters of that town were still linked together in 1776 and had their own hall.[1] But the *Directory* does not list any pewterers there. According to it, Sheffield had no pewterers either, though, as we have seen, it possessed five firms which were described as 'Britannic-metal Manufacturers'.[2] The research which has been done on the Wigan and Liverpool pewterers[3] and on nineteenth-century Birmingham directories[4] would suggest that this early list of the 1790s concentrated in the provinces as in London upon a few of the more important businesses and missed a number of others. But not necessarily many of them: we know that of 363 Wigan pewterers identified altogether from the sixteenth century onwards, only about twenty were active in the later eighteenth century and only five for much of the nineteenth,[5] and in Birmingham during the first half of the nineteenth century there were many more manufacturers of Britannia metal (or tutania, another tin alloy) than pewterers, and many of those described as pewterers also had other interests as well. No doubt there were other manufacturing centres about 1800—Bewdley is one which is sometimes mentioned[6]—but it seems extremely unlikely that they were producing pewter on any sizeable scale.

The 1841 census provides the only complete countrywide summary of the situation, again (as in London) erring on the side of generosity because of the inclusion of retired craftsmen. Provincial pewtering had by this time become concentrated in Birmingham, the nation's metal-working capital. Yet it is worth

[1] Howard H. Cotterell, 'The pewterers of Newcastle-upon-Tyne', *The Antique Collector*, November 1935.
[2] Nancy Goyne Evans has listed 124 Britannia craftsmen in Sheffield from directories issued between 1797 and 1860 (*Bulletin of the Pewter Collectors Club of America*, August 1970).
[3] R. J. S. Shelley, 'Wigan and Liverpool pewterers', *Transactions of the Lancashire and Cheshire Historic Society*, xcvii (1946).
[4] Nancy Goyne Evans, 'A Directory survey of pewter and Britannia craftsmen working in Birmingham, England, until 1860', *Bulletin of the Pewter Collectors Club of America*, December 1969.   [5] Shelley, pp. 21-6.
[6] Timmins, p. 617; Massé, *The Pewter Collector* (rev. ed.), pp. 45-6. Production at Bewdley seems to have ceased about 1840. John Caruthers Crane, the main producer there in the 1820s and 1830s, is listed in *Pigot's New Commercial Directory* in 1828-29 and again in 1835 as an ironmonger. By the latter date he was obviously quite well-to-do, for he also appears in the list of local gentry as John C. Crane, Esq., Wribenhall. Neither directory lists any pewterers as such.

Table 21.

Location of men and women outside the London area who described themselves as pewterers at the census of 1841

Location	Males Over 20	Males Under 20	Females Over 20	Females Under 20
Birmingham	17	2	1	1
Bristol	8	2		
Liverpool	6			
Manchester	3			
Cambridgeshire	3	1		
Brighton	2			
Gateshead	2			
Gloucester	2			
Wigan	2			
Cheshire	1			
Dover	1			
Elsewhere in Kent	1			
Exeter	1			
Hampshire	1			
Leeds	1			
Salford	1			
Shrewsbury	1			
Staffordshire	1			
Wakefield	1			
Glasgow City and suburbs	3			
Edinburgh City	2	1		
Edinburgh (suburbs)	2			
Aberdeen	1			
Banffshire	1			
Total	72 : 64	6	1	1

Source. Census of 1841, 1844 [587] XXVII.

noting that the numbers there amounted to only about a third of the total which had been at work in Wigan in the trade's heyday at the end of the seventeenth century.[1] If, however, the thirty-six Britannia metal workers enumerated in Birmingham in 1841 are added to the total, the number becomes roughly the same. According to the census, Sheffield had no pewterers, though

[1] Above, p. 126.

sixty-three people were returned as Britannia metal workers (forty-five males and five females over twenty, and nine males and four females below that age.)[1]

The survival of eight pewterers and two apprentices in Bristol —there were probably about thirty at the end of the seventeenth century—probably reflects the continued existence of some export trade, and the same may be true of Liverpool, though the absence of apprentices there suggests that the trade was on its last legs. The same goes for all the other places where one or two pewterers may still have been practising their craft. The really significant point which emerges from these census figures, however, is the even greater predominance of London as the industry declined. Calculations for the later seventeenth century suggest that there were getting on for twice as many pewterers in the provinces as in London: by 1841 there were four times as many in London as in the provinces and in Scotland together. The loss of the home market for most pewter items hit the hardest those centres and towns which could not take advantage of the continued export, alehouse and industrial equipment demand.

Exports were already waning, as we have seen,[2] and the demand for pewter pots began to fall off, too, when they came to be replaced by pint and half-pint glasses. This change, however, came much later, towards the end of the nineteenth century. Charles Booth, for instance, wrote in the mid-1890s that:

> Until comparatively recently the publican's customers were very particular as to their ale being served in a 'nice bright pewter pot', and the essential virtue in a potman was that he should be a good pewter cleaner; the pot is, however, being now largely supplanted by the glass, and the so-called potman is really a servant who does the general work of a public house.[3]

This change from pewter to glass seems to have been connected not only with cheaper methods of glass production but also with the growing public preference for lighter beers in place of dark porters. People now liked to see the bright, clear contents through the sides of the vessel from which they were drinking and not

[1] A glimpse of juvenile employment in this trade in Sheffield is to be found in J. C. Symons's report on that town in the appendix to the second report of the Children's Employment Commission, 1843 [431] XVI.   [2] Above, p. 290.
[3] Charles Booth, *Life and Labour of the People in London*, vii (1896), p. 236.

just through the glass bottoms which had been put into some pewter tankards.¹ These lighter beers became more fashionable after 1880 and particularly after the later 1880s.²

Pewter continued to be used in public houses in sinks and on bar counters (where it was kind to the glasses which had supplanted it) and it had also been used for many years in the manufacture of beer engines. (Of forty-nine pewterers listed in *Pigot's London Directory* of 1832–34, for instance, eleven were beer engine makers.) But when pewter tankard production eventually fell away, there was little work left for the few craftsmen who remained, though *art nouveau* pewter enjoyed some popularity around 1900 and for several years thereafter, stimulated by a revival of pewter manufacture in Germany.³ The London directories continued to publish lists of pewterers, but most of them seem to have been shopkeepers who merely sold the product; and when Elsie Englefield came to publish her *Treatise on Pewter and Its Manufacture* in 1933, she was able to describe the family business of Brown and Englefield as 'the last of the great pewter manufacturing firms in London'. One of its price lists, issued about that time, included a complete range of bowls, teapots of various sorts, trays, coffee sets, cake and fruit stands, salt cellars, sugar castors, cream jugs, jam dishes, vegetable dishes, sauce boats, beakers and jugs, candlesticks, tobacco jars, biscuit boxes, ash trays, toilet sets and ink stands.⁴ It was an impressive list; but one which could then be issued by only one London concern catering for a very limited market.

[1] Brian Spiller, *Victorian Public Houses* (Newton Abbot, 1972), p. 29.
[2] Evidence to the Departmental Committee on Beer Materials, 1899 [C. 9172] xxx, qq. 339, 2590, 2592; Hurford Janes, *The Red Barrel* (1963), p. 134.
[3] German pewter was, for instance, imported and sold by Liberty & Co. of Regent Street, London. In May 1901 Liberty & Co. (Cymric) Ltd. was established, a joint undertaking of Libertys and W. H. Haseler of Birmingham, whereby the latter was to produce all Liberty's metalware, including the new pewter which began to be made in 1903 and was marketed as 'Tudric' ware. (*Art Nouveau Pewter*, catalogue of a travelling exhibition arranged by the Circulation Dept. of the Victoria and Albert Museum (1973). We are grateful to Major G. S. Johnson for the loan of this catalogue.)
[4] The price list is contained in the Scrapbook of Justus Eck.

7
The Company and the craft

The Pewterers' Company continued to be closely associated with pewtering throughout the eighteenth century. As we have seen,[1] working pewterers were still being enrolled as freemen of the Company and the craft was still well represented upon the Court. The Company, in its turn, did the best it could to maintain a watchful eye upon the quality of pewter produced and the price at which the pewterer could buy his tin.

It is true that, by the eighteenth century, the Company's attempts to control the craft were confined to London. Regular country searches were discontinued and when, in the summer of 1723, the Master and Wardens went on such a search—after having enquired into their rights in this matter following complaints about the quality of Bristol pewter—it was quite an unusual event.[2] Further complaints about Bristol a few years later led to no repeat performance.[3] In 1741 the Company was even advised that it would have to go to Parliament if it was to gain any redress against country pewterers who stamped 'London' on their wares.[4] Within London itself, however, as the Wardens' Accounts show, searches went on throughout the eighteenth century, numbers of Assistants accompanying the Master and Wardens on these occasions and being recompensed for their pains by an allowance and, until the end of the century, a dinner. It is not clear, however, how formal these searches eventually became.

An incident in 1745 reveals that the Company was then still keen to carry out effective searches. It had heard that a cargo of

[1] Above p. 293.
[2] Guildhall MS 7090/9, 21 Mar., 17 July 1722, 20 June, 10 Oct. 1723.
[3] Guildhall MS 7090/9, 17 July 1728, 19 June 1729.
[4] Guildhall MS 7090/10, 13 Aug., 24 Sept. 1741.

pewter made in Cornwall was being shipped to London *en route* to Russia. Did it have the rights of search while the vessel was in the Thames? The Clerk drew up a case for consideration by Counsel.[1] In it he pointed out that the Master, Wardens and Assistants carried out searches regularly in London five times a year, yet

> ... persons at a distance in country places further from observation have been guilty of great abuses both in the baseness of mettals [*sic*] and the imperfect workmanship thereof which is a detriment to the Kingdom in General and to the Trade of this Company in particular as it lessens the Reputation acquired abroad of making the best pewter in the world.

The Clerk went on to note that 'of late years in particular' several pewterers in the outports had been sending abroad these inferior products, some of which were, it was believed, in the vessel they wished to board. The case was considered a few days later by the Attorney-General who agreed that the Company had powers to search ships within the City of London and its suburbs; but he did not consider that these rights extended to the whole of the Port of London. Moreover, the Company had powers of seizure only if the pewter in question was in the possession of the maker or seller, though he agreed that the maker would be liable to forfeit the value of the confiscated wares 'upon information being brought for that purpose against him in the Exchequer'.

On receiving this disappointing verdict at the end of May 1745 the Court decided unanimously that a country search should be made in order to discover to what extent the complaints concerning inferior provincial workmanship were justified. The Master, Wardens and five members of the Court (or any five of them) were deputed to undertake this search.[2] We are not told where they went; but three weeks afterwards the Master reported that they had found the trade 'in pretty good order', the only specific complaint being that some pewterers had been varying their touches.[3] This matter came up again two years later. The main trouble seemed to be that some makers were using touches of small size 'so that it is difficult to discover or distinguish by the

[1] Guildhall MS 7090/10, May 1745.
[2] Guildhall MS 7090/10, 30 May 1745.   [3] Guildhall MS 7090/10, 20 June 1745.

Touch one maker's ware from another'. The Court ordered, therefore,

> that for the future all Dishes, Plates and Basons and other wares capable of a large Touch shall be touched with a large Touch with the Christian name and surname either of the Maker or Vendor at full length in plain Roman Letters. And as to all small wares, the same shall be touched with the Small Touch either of the Maker or Vendor.

Failure to comply made the maker or vendor liable to a penalty of one penny per lb of pewter confiscated.[1]

This evidence from the middle 1740s shows quite clearly that the Company was certainly then still trying, despite its limited powers, to assert its position as upholder of standards within the trade and, in particular, to maintain the reputation of British pewter in foreign markets, now becoming a very important part of the pewterers' trade as was noticed in the previous chapter. The Court order of 1747 is also significant in showing that by this time the maker himself no longer had a monopoly of marking his work. The seller could also do so provided he was prepared to bear responsibility for the quality of the product. There is more than a hint here that the organisation of the pewter trade may have been undergoing change, with production becoming more specialised. Some of the working pewterers were perhaps concentrating increasingly upon particular types of product, and the vendor, possibly a working pewterer by origin, having ordered from them the goods he required, himself concentrated on their marketing and also, perhaps, on the finishing off of the rough pewter items for ultimate display to the customer. As his business grew, he no doubt preferred to sell these manufactures under his own mark, particularly if he was selling wholesale. This kind of organisational development became a feature of other crafts during the eighteenth century. It happened in wholesale filemaking, for instance,[2] and in retail watchmaking where the seller, already known as a watchmaker, often finished off the craftsman's rough work before placing his own name upon the watch face.[3] To what extent the vendors of pewter were perform-

[1] Guildhall MS 7090/10, 25 June 1747.
[2] T. S. Ashton, *An Eighteenth-Century Industrialist* (Manchester, 1939).
[3] F. A. Bailey and T. C. Barker, 'The seventeenth-century origins of watchmaking in south-west Lancashire', in J. R. Harris, ed., *Liverpool amd Merseyside* (1969).

ing a similar function we do not know, for the records are silent upon this matter. Nor do we know whether any shopkeepers were by this time describing themselves as pewterers.

The Company continued to interest itself in tin prices, although between 1717 and the early 1770s, when these were low,[1] the spate of minutes on the subject, which were such a feature of the Company's records at the beginning of the century, comes to an end. The Company did nevertheless keep a particularly vigilant eye on events in foreign markets. In 1754, for instance, a committee was formed to investigate the export of sadware moulds (moulds for large and flat pewter products). Finding no legal means of prohibiting this, and noting that 'several persons, particularly in France and Holland, have of late years decoyed many of his Majesty's subjects who were bred in the Pewterers' Trade into their Service', it advocated once again an increase in the export duty on tin in the hope that a clause could be slipped into the amending legislation prohibiting the export of pewterers' moulds, tools and utensils. The Company pursued these objectives for over a year but without success.[2]

In the early 1770s, following the wave of new investment in Cornish tin-mining, the tin-mining interests attempted to get the export duty on tin removed altogether. The Company opposed this and was pleased to learn that the Bristol pewterers had also persuaded Bristol Corporation to oppose the mine owners' petition to Parliament.[3] The Cornishmen's attempts then came to nothing but, as we have seen,[4] they formed a tin producers' association in 1780 and prices subsequently rose. In 1785, indeed, it was reported to the Court that so much tin was being exported 'that the tin proprietors did not have sufficient for home consumption and that at present business was much at a stand for want of tin'.[5] Again, an increase in the tin export duty was advocated but again without any success; and in 1790, when a Bill to repeal the duty on tin sold east of the Cape of Good Hope was before Parliament—obviously the result of a deal reached between the Cornish tin mining interests and the East India Company—the Pewterers' Company agreed not to oppose it in

[1] Above p. 285.
[2] Guildhall MS 7090/10, 14 Nov. 1745; 10, 25 Feb., 20 Mar. 1755; 8 Jan. 1756.
[3] Guildhall MS 7090/11, 22 Jan., 25 Feb., 19 Mar., 29 June, 7 Sept. 1772; 16 June 1773.
[4] Above p. 287.   [5] Guildhall MS 7090/11, 24 Mar. 1785.

return for a promise from the Privy Council Committee on Trade and Plantations that any representations from them would be seriously considered should a rise in tin prices result. It did, from 72s a cwt at the time of the passing of the Bill, to 81s in the following year. The Company accordingly pointed out that this was a level 'exceeding any price hitherto known and if continued must annihilate the manufacturing of pewter in this Kingdom'.[1] But their cry of anguish fell on unresponsive ears.

By this time the Company had reached the point at which it had to decide how far it was prepared, indeed how far it could afford, to go in support of the pewterers' ailing craft. It had set up a committee in 1787 to consider what was described, rather blandly, as 'the situation in the Pewterers trade'. Two years later this committee said that it had 'examined many books, papers and writing belonging to the company relating to the same'; but it was still in no position to make recommendations and begged for more time to continue its deliberations.[2] It eventually reported in 1791.

The report was a strange document. It did not consider at all the competition which pewter then had to meet, but concerned itself entirely with the result of this competition: the production of more low-quality pewter. Fine metal and ley metal, the committee noted, were regulated in quality by Acts of Parliament dating back to the early sixteenth century. Trifling metal, a quality which came between the two and had been made for more than a hundred years, was not. This, however, had not been a source of trouble

> till of late years when the Adulteration of Metal in various Pewter articles has prevailed to a very great degree especially in the article of Pots which were or ought to have been (under regulation and usage before mentioned) made of Trifling Metal and which Adulteration is greatly to the injury of the fair and honest Trader and is of the more consequence as such Adulterated Wares return in a Manufactured Shape to the Manufacturer and the loss occasioned thereby is greater than at first conceived by persons not acquainted with metals,

---

[1] Guildhall MS 7090/11, 8 Mar. 1790, 15 Dec. 1791. For the passage of the Bill repealing the duty of tin exported beyond the Cape of Good Hope, see *Journal of the House of Commons*, 1, 4, 5, 18, 19, 26 February; 1, 2, 4, 18 March, 1 April 1790.
[2] Guildhall MS 7090/11, 19 Mar. 1789.

a small quantity of bad or adulterated Metal spoiling a large Quantity of good Metal when mixed with the same.

The committee limited its recommendations, therefore, to the need to promote a Bill laying down specifications for a new Middle Metal (its own title) and obliging all pewterers within Britain to put their touch upon all wares. The assay of the proposed Middle Metal was to be 190 grains (to be compared with $183\frac{1}{2}$ grains for fine or plate metal, 182 grains for tin, and 199 grains for ley metal).[1] At a Special Court called on 2 May 1791 the committee was reconstituted to pursue this matter further;[2] but whatever steps it may have taken, they did not result in any Bill being brought into Parliament.

Nothing more is heard of the committee until 1799 when it again met, still referred to as the committee set up by the Court Order of 1787, to consider a petition from Edward Dadley, one of the Wardens and also one of its members. By this time, however, the Company, as well as the craft, found itself in some financial difficulties; and numerically it was certainly much weaker than it had previously been.

By the beginning of the 1790s the numbers of people taking up the freedom had fallen quite dramatically. In the 1720s, the best decade for enrolment during the eighteenth century, 214 new freemen had come in,[3] but from then onwards the total had dropped fairly steadily, to 99 in the 1760s, 87 in the 1770s and 68 in the 1780s. This fall applied to enrolment by patrimony as well as by servitude. Weaker in numbers, the Company did not offset this weakness by the acquisition of valuable new assets of any kind during the eighteenth century. Nor do most of the liverymen give the impression of being men of any substance. A list published in 1792,[4] said to be the first such publication, gave details relating to fifty-seven of them. Of these, the occupations of thirteen were not stated. Of the forty-three which were, eighteen were pewterers by trade. Of the remaining twenty-five, only two were of sufficient status to be described as gentlemen; one lived out in the country at Hornsey and the other at High Wycombe. The Company could also boast a goldsmith, a stockbroker and a collector of taxes (who also lived at High Wycombe). The other

[1] Guildhall MS 7090/11, 24 Mar. 1791.   [2] Guildhall MS 7090/11, 2 May 1791.
[3] See above, p. 294.
[4] *Supplement to The Universal British Directory* (1792).

liverymen, however, all seem to have been a polyglot collection of people engaged in industry and trade, some of them in quite humble capacities. There were three stationers, two coffee-house keepers, two worm makers, a brazier, a founder, a tallow chandler, a white lead worker, an upholder, a woollen draper, a cheese factor, a sail maker and a music seller. One man just had his address, 'India Warehouse', beside his name. The Company even admitted their old rivals the makers of 'Crooked Lane wares': one of the liverymen was a tinplate worker and another worked at (or owned) a lamp warehouse. There were also two tinfoil manufacturers. Here were no great City figures and it is worth noting that, during the eighteenth century up to this time, not one person had joined the Company by redemption. The pewterers, still obviously well represented in the Company, did not have behind them any strong and influential backing in their efforts to mobilise the Company's resources in the defence of their trade.

Much worse, during the 1790s wartime inflation and taxation made the Company cut back on many of its activities. In the financial year 1795–96 its expenditure was £203 above its income of £916 and Bank stock had to be sold to make good the difference.[1] A policy of retrenchment was then urged; but it does not seem to have been pursued at all vigorously and in March 1798, on a day a number of members had assembled to go out on a quarterly search, a Special Court was held to consider the state of the Company's finances.[2] Those present decided that no dinners should in future be held after such searches, that no guests were in future to be invited to Quarter Day dinners and those at Lady Day and Midsummer Day were to be discontinued altogether. The Master, Wardens and other officers were not to be allowed to dine before Court meetings. A further £150 of Bank stock had to be sold,[3] £600 more of it was sold in 1799—this time the principal of a benefaction the interest upon which (£18 per year) was to be paid to the Company's poor members, a responsibility the Company itself then had to assume—in order to redeem land tax payable on the Hall.[4] This recurrent commitment, entered into when the Company was already finding it hard to make ends meet, was undertaken only a few weeks before

[1] Guildhall MS 7090/11, 15 Dec. 1796.
[2] Guildhall MS 7090/11, 19 Mar. 1798.
[3] Guildhall MS 7090/11, 27 Apr. 1798.
[4] Guildhall MS 7090/11, 21 Mar. 20 June 1799.

Edward Dadley reactivated the committee on the state of the pewter trade and asked the Company once again to come to the aid of the craft. This time the response was distinctly chilly.

Pewterers were well represented on the committee. Four of its six members (including the Master) were certainly pewterers by trade and the other two may also have been. Two further pewterers were co-opted. Dadley's petition, 'on behalf of himself and other manufacturers', again concentrated on the high price of tin and asked the Company to petition Parliament in an attempt to bring this down. The committee's report is important, for it marks the real parting of the Company and the trade and it explains why the Company, while continuing to act as 'natural and legitimate Guardians of the manufacture', could no longer be expected to go on playing its active role as the trade's spokesman and protector. This statement of the Company's new position is all the more significant as coming from members who were pewterers, not from the non-trade element. We therefore quote it here in some detail:

> In the Lapse of time this Company as well as most others has become an Association of Persons of Various Trades and Callings, distinct from that of a Pewterer, and there are, Comparatively, but few of the trade amongst its members. Its funds have been become appropriated to various uses—to the support of its poor, to the general purposes of Charity and to the promotion of good Fellowship and social intercourse between its Members.
>
> Under these Circumstances it seems scarce reasonable to expect that the Pewterers Company should engage at their own Costs in any application to Parliament or other proceedings relating to the Trade which must necessarily occasion Expense, for the benefit of the few manufacturers amongst them, and certainly not for the numerous Manufacturers of Pewter or the Consumers of Tin throughout with the Company [*sic*—obviously should read 'throughout the country'].
>
> The Manufacturers of Pewter with the Consumers of Tin should therefore try of themselves by contribution [to] support the Expence of any applications they may think it necessary to make to the Legislature for the support of their

11

own Manufacture, or for the furtherance of their general interest. The Pewterers Company being the natural and legitimate Guardians of the manufacture of this Article, and carrying with them a degree of Weight and Consequence, may be called upon and reasonably expended [*sic*] to stand forward with their name for the furtherance of any object beneficial to the Trade, and the sage and experienced members of that Company many of whom are acquainted with the Policy and Mystery of the Pewter Trade, *though now not engaged in it*,* may be expected and requested to contribute their co-operative advice and assistance.

To this end it seems expedient that the Promoters of, and persons interested in, the proposed Application to the Legislature should form themselves into a Committee for the Conduct of the Business, and that the Pewterers Company should appoint certain of their Members to co-operate with such Committee, to contribute their Advice, Influence and Assistance, and to guard the proper and reasonable Use of the Name and Sanction of the Company.

This arrangement being made, Communication in the name of the Pewterers Company should be immediately opened with the Birmingham and Bristol Manufacturers. Either by correspondence or by Deputations from the London Committee every information and document should be immediately procured. A Petition shall be presented to the House of Commons; a temperate, concise and pointed case or memorial should be drawn up, printed and circulated among the members. The Members for the City of London and the Borough, the Members for Warwickshire and Bristol and such other Members as the parties may be enabled to interest on their behalf should be fully informed and instructed in the business and their strenuous support insured [*sic*] in the House of Commons and to any Committee to which the matter may be referred.[1]

A General Court approved the report on 10 July 1799[2] and the Court was later told that three representatives of the craft (including one from the Company) had attended a general coinage meeting at Truro on 20 July. This deputation had been well

---
* Our italics.
[1] Guildhall MS 7090/11, 2 July 1799.   [2] Guildhall MS 7090/11, 10 July 1799.

received by the tin producers who had promised to reduce the fraction of their output sold to the East India Company to one-sixth not only the following year but also for the two years after that. (It had previously been one-third, two-fifths and even a half of the total output.) With this promise, the trade decided not to make any representations to Parliament.[1]

It is impossible to escape the conclusion that there was an element of special pleading in the report. The Company was in no position to finance any campaign on behalf of the trade; but it explained its reluctance to do so not on grounds of financial stringency but on the more doubtful grounds that it was no longer adequately representative of the trade. Yet pewterers still certainly played a considerable part in its affairs, though these were all London, not provincial, craftsmen. The reference to many retired (or former) pewterers may, however, go some way to explain the Company's contention that it no longer really represented the craft despite the fact that it still included many pewterers among its members. It is possible that the trade's difficulties may have accelerated the normal retirement of some craftsmen. We know of at least one such early retirement, that of Thomas Cotton, a pewterer at London Bridge, who gave up work in 1760 at the age of forty-five. He was then already a member of the Livery and in 1767 he went on to the Court, serving as Master in 1778. In 1801, the old man, then in his eighty-fourth year and living in retirement at Stockwell Green on less than £20 a year, felt obliged to ask the Company for help. The Company agreed on an immediate gift of £10 and a pension of 16 guineas payable quarterly.[2]

The Company's financial condition continued to give cause for concern, especially as the economies ordered in 1798 had not been strictly enforced. Further restrictions were ordered in 1801 and 1802. No dessert, tea or supper, for instance, was to be served at the Company's expense 'on any account whatsoever'.[3] In an attempt to increase revenue, consideration was given to the possibility of permanently letting Pewterers Hall. The East India Company was then advertising for warehouse space and the lease was offered to them; but they were not interested in it. The

[1] Guildhall MS 7090/11, 22 Aug. 1799.
[2] Guildhall MS 7090/11, 19 Mar. 1801.
[3] Guildhall MS 7090/11, 17 Dec. 1801; 11 Mar. 1802.

Company therefore itself advertised the property, on 30 June 1802, and it was let for thirty-one years to John Lodge, a packer of Garlick Hill, for £260 per year, Lodge agreeing to spend £100 at once upon its repair. The original plan was for the Company to retain a few rooms for its own use; but a house in Lime Street adjoining the Hall was acquired instead.[1] The first meeting at the New Court Room took place on 16 December 1802.

The Company was never again to reoccupy this Hall. Its lease in 1802 marked the end of a critical decade in which the working pewterers' growing difficulties, which were not to grow less over time, were matched by the Company's own financial problems, caused by wartime inflation and taxation, which were, however, to resolve themselves in due course when peace returned. But the change in the relationship between the Company and the craft which occurred at this time was irrevocable. Although one member of the Court gave notice in 1812, at the time of the licensed victuallers' attempts to avoid sending out their beer in pewter pots,[2] that he would seek the Company's financial assistance in opposing any Bill which the licensed victuallers might introduce to Parliament,[3] this help was never sought. The Bill never materialised. For the future, and until quite recent times, the Company's links with pewtering were to be confined to its obligations concerning bequests left for its needy members (some of whom were pewterers) and their families and, in a more indirect way, to its educational grants.

During the nineteenth century the Company had very limited resources at its disposal for the relief of its poor members. Unlike other, more fortunate livery companies, very few of its charities derived their income from investment in land and property. This was potentially much more valuable than government securities or Bank stock, for the capital was more likely to increase, especially if the property came to be needed for industrial purposes or if it was situated in or near towns. The Company, in fact, possessed only five endowments the capital of which was in the form of property; but in three of these it had no control over the properties themselves but merely received fixed incomes from them. These incomes were all very small sums, £6 per year in one

[1] Guildhall MS 7090/11, 18 Mar. 15 July, 5 Aug. 1802.
[2] Above, p. 289.
[3] Guildhall MS 7090/12, 19 Mar. 1812.

case and £2 per year in each of the other two.¹ The remaining two such bequests, however, did involve an outright gift of property to the Company. The first was a mid-sixteenth century benefaction from Lawrence Astelyn. This consisted of fifteen small tenements outside Cripplegate and from their rents the Company had to distribute £2 among the poor of St Mary Abchurch parish. By 1830 this payment had been increased to £4.8*s* (and there were between thirty and forty beneficiaries) plus 12*s* to the parish clerk and the sexton. But the property, by then eight houses in 3 Dagger Court and a public house in Fore Street, was producing an annual income of £69 and the balance went straight into the Company's own funds. The other property, a house at 53 Barbican bequeathed by John Robbins in 1648 to provide £2 per year for each of four poor freemen of the Company, brought in £50.²

In the case of the remaining fifteen charitable bequests, most of them of £100 or less, the Company made the mistake of investing the capital in government securities or Bank stock. To some extent this reflected the fact that many of these bequests were made at a late date when such securities were available. Twelve of them were received in the eighteenth century, seven dating from between 1765 and 1784. (Presumably this was an indication of growing need among members of the craft at that time.) Two of these gifts, Thomas Scattergood's in 1776, made immediately after he had served as Master for two years in succession, and John Jones's in 1784—he had also served as Master on two earlier occasions—were exceptional in their size, each being of £600. But, when invested, they each brought in only £20 per year. All the income from Scattergood's benefaction was earmarked for five poor members of the Company and five of their widows, while Jones's was to be spread among nine members and nine widows. *In toto* these two gifts were considerably more valuable than the thirteen others which derived their incomes from government stock and had a capital value of only £950 together. Even with a full 5 per cent yield, all fifteen bequests, worth £2,150, produced little over £100 per year. It was

¹ The benefactors were: Edward Catcher (1562) and the payment in 1830 was made by the Governors of Christ's Hospital, apparently from premises in Broad Street; Ralph Stray (1602) payable on The Saracen's Head, Melton, Suffolk; and Daniel Ingole (1690)—the £6 rent charge—payable on a farm in East Ham (Guildhall MS 7090/13, 23 Sept. 1830; *Report of the Commission on London Livery Companies*, 1884 [C. 4073-II xxxix, pt III, p. 649].
² Guildhall MS 7090/13, 23 Sept. 1830; MS 7086/6, 1830/1.

11*

distributed in individual gifts, usually between 10*s* and £2, to about 100 poor freemen or their widows. This was far from the more adequate provision, often including almshouses, which other companies, deriving their income from land and property, could afford.

The Company did possess property of its own in addition, and total rent income (including that from the Hall and other buildings in Lime Street) added up to just over £1,000 at the end of the 1820s; but most of this was spent on Court meetings and dinner bills. Few practising pewterers participated and by the 1830s their influence at the top of the Company seems to have disappeared. Of nine Masters, for instance, whose occupations can be definitely established in the directories between 1828 and 1844, there were two trunk makers, a coffee roaster, a slopseller, a corn dealer, a tallow chandler, a commercial and general broker, a stationer and a tavern keeper. But no pewterers.

Rent income was built up quite considerably as the nineteenth century proceeded, and a few more benefactions were also forthcoming. By 1869–70, for instance, rent income totalled £2,828— nearly three times what it had been forty years before. Court meetings and dinners then cost nearly £1,900; but there was much more left over than previously for charitable payments of all kinds. These by then included three annuities of £100, £35 and £25 respectively. Small payments of two guineas and £5 were made to a number of charity schools, but as yet nothing towards technical training of any kind.[1] An interest in technical education eventually resulted from pressure which was brought to bear upon all the livery companies during the 1870s, when it was felt that technical education in Britain was falling behind that of its foreign industrial rivals. The City and Guilds of London Institute was formally inaugurated in 1878 and the Pewterers Company was able to tell the Commission which enquired into the London Livery Companies in the early 1880s that it was contributing 100 guineas per year to it. The Company also informed the Commission that, out of a livery of seventy, plus five freemen and five freewomen, only two of its members were, or ever had been, practising pewterers.[2]

Guildhall MS 7086/8, 1869/70.
[2] *Report of the Commission on London Livery Companies*, 1884 [C. 4073–II] xxxix, pt III, pp. 652, 658.

Interest in old pewter happened to revive among a few connoisseurs just when the public house pot was losing its popularity and the trade itself was dwindling into tiny proportions. H. J. L. J. Massé has described how the chance discovery of a round, badly battered pewter dish in Bruges in 1885 first aroused his interest in the subject and eventually led him, in 1904, to publish his *Pewter Plate*. He also organised, in that same year, an exhibition of pewter at Clifford's Inn.[1] (This coincided with the vogue for *art nouveau* pewter.[2]) Another exhibition followed in 1908 and *Chats on Old Pewter* came out in 1911. Meanwhile in Scotland L. Ingleby Wood brought out a book on *Scottish Pewterware and Pewterers* in 1905, and exhibitions followed there in 1909 and 1911. There were other notable publications earlier in the century, too. Charles Welch's rather indigestible but nevertheless informative two-volume *History of the Worshipful Company of Pewterers of the City of London*, based on the Company's records, came out in 1902 and Malcolm Bell's *Old Pewter* in 1905. And in 1913 W. J. Englefield, then the only practising pewterer in the Pewterers Company, struck his touch at Pewterers' Hall, the first working craftsman to do so since 1825. Despite the decline of the trade, appreciation of the product and respect for the old customs were far from dead.

Twelve pewter enthusiasts formed the Pewter Collectors' Society towards the end of 1918. Howard H. Cotterell, one of the most enthusiastic of them and Vice-President of the new Society, had ambitious plans for stirring up the old Pewterers' Company even though he was not a member of it. 'I have great ideas for the Society', he wrote from his home, The Hermitage, Walsall, to another member on 22 October 1918, when the Society was in process of formation:

> I don't see any reason why the Pewterers Company itself should not 'house' us. We are collecting together the work of *its* bygone members, we are making the old Company live again and I suggest we start again at once when the Society is really formed not only a pewter collection which shall develop into the finest in the world but one of the Pewterers' Company's proudest possessions and a national asset. Further, I have in mind that every line written on the

[1] See the preface to Massé, *The Pewter Collector*, published in 1921.
[2] See above, p. 301.

subject shall have a home there, every author shall be bound to present a copy of his work and his original manuscript, if possible. . . . This little band of twelve is going to awaken interest in an old industry in its ancient home, the Pewterers Hall.[1]

Cotterell certainly did not lack vision but he allowed his excitement to run away with him. The Company did not share his enthusiasm and refused to be taken by storm. The Pewter Collectors' Society was obliged to walk much more cautiously. Cotterell himself had, since about 1906, joined the ranks of those working on a book about pewter[2] and the Company had allowed him to copy its five existing touchplates (at his own expense)[3] for inclusion in it. This encouraged him to pursue another line of attack: 'The thought has occurred to me whether there is anything I can do in my book for your Company. . . . If there is anything outside [Welch's] work which I can do, say, or illustrate for you, it will give me very real pleasure to endeavour to meet your wishes in any way I can'. There is more than a hint of an earlier rebuff in the last paragraph of this letter: 'This suggestion is made in no spirit of "pushfulness" but as an act of courtesy to those who have shown much courtesy to me and whatever your reply I shall feel more satisfied that I have not failed in what seems to me a duty.'[4]

The Company agreed to help him with two further illustrations which he had suggested; but its attitude to the craft in general had been made clear in a report to the Court presented by one of its committees (which included W. J. Englefield) a few months before. This contained the unequivocal statement that after due consideration, they had 'come to the conclusions that no opening for furthering the Pewter trade is in our opinion at the present time possible'.[5] The Company confined its support to an annual grant of £250 to the Finsbury Branch of the City & Guilds Institute. It kept in touch with the Pewter Collectors' Society by allowing it to meet occasionally in its Court Room and by

[1] Scrapbook of Justus Eck, Howard Cotterell to Walter Churcher, 22 Oct. 1918.
[2] He informed the Company in 1931 that 'research and investigation, from every aspect, of the Craft of Pewtering and those who practised it, have formed my life work which, for over twenty-five years I have laboured at without a break' (Court Minutes, 26 May 1931). [3] Court Minutes, 22 May 1919.
[4] Court Minutes, 22 April 1920. [5] Court Minutes, 24 July 1919.

inviting one or two of its leading members infrequently to dinner. But that was as far as it was prepared to go.

Eventually, however, the persistent Cotterell did persuade the Company to part with a considerable sum of money. When his long-maturing volume, *Old Pewter, Its Makers and Marks*, eventually appeared in 1929, he presented the Company with a copy. Two years later he was writing, now from Croxley Green (telegraphic address: Pewtercott, London), to say that he had another book in preparation which would open up in the English language 'whole avenues of knowledge which have hitherto been as a sealed book'. But this definitive work, he sadly reported, had come to a halt because he was 'weighed down by an ever-accumulating load of debt and by almost constant ill-health, largely induced by anxiety of my position'. 'To say that I am going through great anxieties', he added, 'is to trifle with words, for I have gone on and on, hoping for some respite until I am at the end of my financial tether.' Would the Company be prepared to act as his patron? It responded at once to this cry for help and sent him £500 with a promise of further assistance a few months later. In this way it eventually supported the pewter collectors' cause to the tune of £1,000, though Cotterell's *magnum opus* never appeared.[1]

By this time the Company was managing its financial affairs much more successfully and was always on the lookout for promising new property in which to invest its accumulating surpluses. Moreover, the whole of the Lime Street site had also been most successfully developed. The initiative in this matter came from Townends, the hatters, who were still leasing the Hall and adjoining buildings over a century after they had first become its tenants. In 1929, having recently been turned into a limited liability company, Thomas Townend & Co. Ltd were anxious to extend their business but were unable to do so in the existing restricted and rundown premises. They enquired whether they could surrender their existing lease, which was due to run until 1942, in return for a building lease which would enable them, in association with others, to develop the whole site.[2] The deal went

---
[1] Court Minutes, 21 May 1931; Scrapbook of Justus Eck, A. Stanley Grant to Eck, 28 April 1936.
[2] Details of these negotiations are to be found in the Court Minutes of 21 Nov. 1929 and 19 May 1932 and the Minutes of the Land and General Purposes Committee, 13 Dec. 1929, 28 April, 22 July 1930, 20 April 1931 and 4 May 1932.

through and by the mid-1930s the Company was drawing a rent of just under £3,000 (after tax had been paid) from the new property. This had meant, of course, the demolition of old Pewterers Hall (then over 260 years old and in a dilapidated state[1]) and the Company's own removal from its premises at 15 Lime Street. The last Court meeting was held there on 4 August 1932 and the Cutlers' Company thereafter provided the Pewterers with paid accommodation at Cutlers Hall in Warwick Lane. After its serious damage in the air raids of 1940, the Company met at Grocers Hall in Princes Street as guests of the Grocers' Company.

Although the Company was temporarily homeless from 1932, it was, largely as a result of its eviction, financially stronger than it had ever been. Its rent income, from property in central London, was now far greater than that from other sources. In the year ended 30 September 1938, for instance, its property produced £6,907 and dividends only £765.[2] It was already toying with the idea of building a new Hall on a site in Queen Victoria Street when its leases there ran out in 1940. But the war put an end to this scheme.

The Company's finances were further strengthened by two bequests. On the death in 1936 of the widow of Harry Carr Gibbs (Master 1912–13), it received a legacy of £1,000 —the income from which was to provide a dinner, every January, for the Master, Wardens and Court—together with share of the residue of his estate which, in 1939, was worth £396 per year. The Company was also responsible for administering a further gift of his amounting to £2,000, the income from which was to provide a scholarship at Dulwich College for the son of a London liveryman, preferably a liveryman of the Company.[3]

The second bequest came from Col. J. W. Pace (Master 1933–34) who died in 1940. His whole estate, including property at Hythe in Kent and freehold licensed premises in Hammersmith, was willed to the Company, though his three elderly sisters were

---

[1] According to the Minutes of the Special Lime Street Committee, 9 Sept. 1932, the ceiling and panelling of the Master's Parlour was offered to the Victoria and Albert Museum but were declined. At the suggestion of the Director of the V and A, however, they were offered to the Geffrye Museum in Kingsland Road where they were re-erected. 117 ft of oak panelling from the Livery Hall itself, described by the architect as 'excellent of the period', was taken down and put into store, together with three brass chandeliers. These were later to be incorporated in the new Hall.
[2] Company Ledger.
[3] Court Minutes, 17 Dec. 1936; 22 July, 21 Oct. 1937; 20 Jan. 1938.

to share its income for the rest of their lives. Its capital value was put at about £22,500 in 1943[1] and the Company was drawing just under £1,000 a year from it by the end of the 1950s.

After the war, with these gifts, war damage insurance in prospect and a healthy surplus on current account being carefully invested in equities, the possibility of a new Hall became much more of a reality. In 1955 the Court learned that the value of its reserve fund was expected to reached £26,000 by 1960 and that two building sites at Queen Victoria Street and Farringdon Avenue would probably bring in another £25,000. By the end of the 1950s its actual annual income from rents and dividends was nearly £11,000.[2] The adaptation of part of Company property at 15 Philpot Lane as a Hall was considered in the mid-1950s;[3] but in the end a completely new building was put up on land in Oat Lane provided by the City Corporation in exchange for the Company's Queen Victoria Street site which was needed as part of the City's development scheme in that area. The new Pewterers Hall was officially opened by the Lord Mayor on 15 May 1961.

The Company's restored status and new prosperity led to a renewal of its interest first with pewter and then with pewtering. The events of about 1800, when the decline of its fortunes and the loss of the use of its Hall were associated with a great weakening of its links with the trade, were repeated; but in reverse. In addition to the greater resources which the Company now had at its disposal, encouraging it to take a more generous and enlightened attitude, this revival of interest can also be attributed partly to a closer connection with the pewter collectors, and with one of them in particular, and partly to a remarkable revival of the trade.

Officers of the Pewter Collectors' Society (in 1968 renamed The Pewter Society) continued to be invited to the Company's functions; but, more important, the Company now numbered among its own members a very keen and knowledgeable collector, Dr Rex Godfrey Blake Marsh, who had come on to the Court in 1948. When he died in 1960, having just completed his term as Renter Warden, he left the Company the whole of his valuable pewter collection. At that time, apart from a few

[1] Court Minutes, 20 June 1940, 24 June 1943.
[2] Court Minutes, 24 March 1955; Company Ledgers.
[3] Minutes of the Committee on the Proposed New Hall, 1954–55.

pieces given in 1928 by Capt. Nelson G. Harries, the Company's own collection was of little worth. There had been nowhere to display it and, therefore, no incentive to build it up or to take an interest in it. The valuable Marsh bequest, however, came just in time for an exhibition to be mounted in the new Hall and it formed the nucleus to which the Company has added since then to form, within little more than a decade, its present magnificent display. This was very much what Cotterell had envisaged in 1918, when such splendid pieces could have been acquired at a tiny fraction of the price which the Company has had eventually to pay for them. In building up this collection, it has been further helped by income from the whole of Marsh's residuary estate which came to the Company, together with his widow's estate, after her death.

The revival of the trade and the Company's renewed connection with it is an even more remarkable story. A considerable export trade, particularly with the United States, was developed after the war and especially after 1960. This was of spun pewterware, particularly drinking vessels—tankards (chiefly) and assorted goblets. By 1970 the trade was reported to have an annual turnover of £1 million.[1] The increase in demand encouraged new manufacturers to set up in business and by 1970 the trade consisted of about thirty separate businesses, six being owned by large producers employing between twenty-five and fifty people and the remaining twenty-four by small makers, often one-man concerns. Twenty-two of these were located in Sheffield, seven in Birmingham and one (Englefields) in London. George Johnson & Co. (Birmingham) Ltd, were the main suppliers of sheet pewter to these manufacturers.

At the end of the 1960s competition within the trade had become very severe and some producers were accepting orders at prices they could only meet at the expense of the quality of their output. In 1969 George Johnson & Co. considered the possibility of forming a British Pewter Guild in an attempt both to reduce undercutting and to maintain standards of workmanship. Mr Ian Wilkie, advertising manager of Associated Lead Manufacturers Ltd, of which Johnsons formed part, approached the Pewterers Company to enquire whether the formation of such a Guild

---

[1] Pewterers Company, Association of British Pewter Craftsmen Ltd. file, Statement to the Company, 16 April 1970; *The Director*, November 1970.

would cut across the Company's own plans in any way. It so happened that his letter arrived very shortly after certain members of the Company had themselves been discussing the possibility of enlarging the Company's links with the trade. An encouraging reply was accordingly sent to Mr Wilkie and a meeting took place at Pewterers Hall on 20 November 1969 to explore the possibilities of forming such an association of craftsmen. To it came Mr G. B. Johnson of George Johnson & Co. and Mr Wilkie. The Company was represented by Mr Kendal Graves (Upper Warden), Mr Cyril Jossé Johnson (Chairman of the Pewter Committee), Mr Richard Ling of Englefields and Mr Charles Grant, the Clerk. The trade's representatives emphasised the need to develop a home market and there was general agreement that, because of the Company's concern with the maintenance of high standards of workmanship, its traditional responsibility, it should also be involved in the proposed association. A working party was accordingly set up. This met for the first time at Pewterers Hall on 19 December 1969. It was then agreed that the aims and objects of the new body, still for the time being to be called The Pewter Guild, should be:

1. To introduce a hallmark.
2. To sponsor the investigation into research and new uses for pewter.
3. To sponsor the development of new designs by competitions, prize awards etc.
4. To award training grants to encourage manufacturers to support apprenticeships for highly skilled hand operations.
5. To consider schemes for stimulating the market for pewter and educating the public about its practical usages and its modern properties.
6. To form an advisory service to help with (*a*) technical problems, (*b*) export difficulties, (*c*) legal aspects and inter-trade relationships and (*d*) finance.

Mr G. B. Johnson was in future to chair the working party which was to have Mr Grant as its secretary and Mr Wilkie as its assistant secretary. The other members of the committee were to be Mr Ling (representing the London area), and Mr Aikin, of the Pewter Manufacturing Company, Sheffield, representing that area.[1]

[1] Pewterers Hall, Notes on Meetings held on 20 Nov. and 19 Dec. 1969 and minutes of meeting held on 20 Nov.

Out of these discussions between the Company and the trade the Association of British Pewter Craftsmen Ltd was created and held its first meeting on 1 October 1970 with the Clerk of the Pewterers Company as its secretary and Pewterers Hall as its registered office. The Company became a corporate member of the Association with the right to nominate three members to its Council. The overwhelming majority of British producers joined. The ABPC mark was launched on 9 October 1972, British Pewter Designs Ltd (a subsidiary of ABPC) having been registered as its proprietor in the previous April.[1] All good quality spun pewterware made by members of the Association had thereafter to be stamped with this mark as well as that of its producer, a control process remarkably like touchmarking in earlier times.

So, after a lapse of nearly two centuries, the Pewterers Company has once more become intimately involved with the craft and with overseeing the quality of its workmanship. And, as it enters the sixth century of its existence as a corporate body, it is also using its increased income to exercise its other traditional function, that of supporting deserving causes and particularly those associated with the trade. At the Institute of Neurology in Queen Square, London, it has founded a fellowship to carry out research into the effect of heavy metals on the brain and nervous system; and at the City University it has endowed a graduate studentship in metals research. It continues to support the City and Guilds of London Institute and the City and Guilds Art School, and, as well as administering the Harry Carr Gibbs scholarship at Dulwich, it has also set up two scholarships of its own, one for boys at the City of London School and the other at the companion City of London School for Girls.

Few London livery companies can point to such a remarkable recovery in recent times. None shows after 500 years a greater sense of its original purpose and history.

[1] Pewterers Hall, Minutes of the Trade Relations Committee, 3 Aug. 1970, 15 Feb. 1971, 9 Oct. 1972.

Bibliography

MANUSCRIPT SOURCES

Guildhall Library

(*a*) Records of the Worshipful Company of Pewterers

Audit Accounts, 10 vols, 1451–1896	MS 7086/1–10
Rough Accounts, 1688–1706	MS 7087
Trust Property Account Book, 1848–88	MS 7088
Rent Ledger, 1838–83	MS 7089
Court Minute Books, Continuous series from 1551	MS 7090
Index to Court Minutes for 1691–1740	MS 7091
Agenda Books, 4 vols, 1891–99	MS 7092
Land Committee Book, 1884–91	MS 7093
Yeomanry Account Book, 1494–1635	MS 7094
Registers of Livery and Yeomanry, 1570–1694	MS 7095
Registers of Freedom Admissions, 1694–1822	MS 7096
Beadle's Lists of Apprentice Presentments and Freedom Admissions, 1734–1843	MS 7097
Rough List of Apprentice Presentments and of Admissions to Freedom and Livery, 1822–62	MS 7098
Alphabetical List of Livery, 1451–1930	MS 7099
Alphabetical List of Members of Company with Record of Service Commissions, 1771–1860	MS 7100
Registers of Presentments of Apprentices, 1694–1860	MS 7101
Register of Apprentice Bindings, 1764–1862	MS 7102
List of All Company Officers, 1450–1860	MS 7103
Record Book of Complaints and Defaults	MS 7104

324 Bibliography

Record Books of Company Searchers, 1635–41 and 1669–83	MS 7105
Rough Notes by Searchers, 1689–91	MS 7106
Tin Ledgers, 1633–37	MS 7107
The King's Tin Farmers' Book, 1633 and 1636	MS 7108
Register of Extracts from Wills, 1561–1642	MS 7109
Book of Inventories and Records, 1490–1756	MS 7110
Reports of a Special Committee on the Company's Trust Property, 1847	MS 7111
Book of Extracts from Legal Instruments relating to Charitable Bequests, 1444–1921	MS 7112
Letter Book, 1838–47	MS 7113
Jury Book	MS 7114
Ordinance Book of 1564, with supplement of 1572	MS 7115
Ordinance Book of 1702	MS 7116
Charter and Ordinance Book	MS 7117
Book of Ordinances of 1761	MS 7118
Charters, Ordinances and Court Orders pertaining thereto, nineteenth century	MS 7119
Collection of Court Orders, 1774–1898	MS 7120
Ordinances of 1766, and Transcript of Charter of 1702	MS 7121
Report of Committee to consider By-laws and Regulations, 1876	MS 7122
Report of Committee to consider By-laws and Regulations, 1899	MS 7123
Promissory Notes, 1666	MS 7124
Account and Note Book of Robert Tarlton, 1675–76	MS 7125
(b) Diary of Sir John Fryer	MS 12017

Public Record Office (PRO)

(a) Customs Accounts

Enrolled (E.356)
Particulars of Account (E.122)
Port Books (E.190)

(*b*) Exchequer Accounts Various

Hosting Accounts and Scrivener's Account (E.101.128/30–8)
Household Accounts (E.101.369/1 ff.)

(*c*) State Papers, Domestic Series, Elizabeth I to James II.

University of York Library

Ordinance Book of the Pewterers of the City
of York   MS E.54

Exeter Cathedral Archives

Visitations of churches in the Diocese of Exeter undertaken in
   1281 and 1301   Dean and Chapter MSS 3672, 3672a

PRINTED PRIMARY SOURCES

In this and the following section the place of publication is London except when stated otherwise.

Accounts of the Executors of Richard Bishop of London 1303, and of the Executors of Thomas Bishop of Exeter 1310, ed. W. H. Hale and H. T. Ellacombe (Camden Society, new ser., x, 1874).

AGRICOLA, GEORGIUS. *De Re Metallica*, ed. H. C. and L. H. Hoover (New York, 1950).

Archdeaconry of Norwich: Inventory of Church Goods, 1368, ed. A. Watkin, 2 vols (Norfolk Record Society, xix, 1947–48).

BIRINGUCCIO, VANNOCCIO. *Pirotechnia*, ed. C. S. Smith and M. T. Gnudi (New York, 1942).

BLUNDELL, NICHOLAS. *The Great Diurnall of Nicholas Blundell*, ed. Frank Tyrer, vol. i, *1702–1711*, vol. ii, *1712–1719* (Liverpool, 1968, 1970).

The Book of Trades (3 parts, 1805–6).

The Book of Trades (Glasgow, 2nd edn, 1837).

The Brokage Book of Southampton, 1443–1444, ed. O. Coleman, 2 vols (Southampton, 1960).

Calendar of the Bristol Apprentice Book, 1532–65, ed. D. Hollis (Bristol Record Society Publications, xiv, 1949).

Calendar of Close Rolls preserved in the Public Record Office (1892, etc.).

Calendar of the Freemen of Norwich from 1317 to 1603, ed. J. L'Estrange and W. Rye (1888).

Calendar of Letter Books preserved among the Archives of the City of London at Guildhall, ed. R. R. Sharpe, 12 vols (1894–1912).

Calendar of Liberate Rolls preserved in the Public Record Office (1916, etc.).

Calendar of Patent Rolls preserved in the Public Record Office (CPR) (1891, etc.).

Calendar of Plea and Memoranda Rolls preserved among the archives of the Corporation of the City of London (1926, etc.).

A Calendar of Southampton Apprenticeship Registers, 1609–1740, ed. A. J. Willis and A. L. Merson (Southampton, 1968).

Calendar of State Papers, Domestic Series, preserved in the Public Record Office etc. (CSPD) (1856, etc.).

Calendar of Wills proved and enrolled in the Court of Hustings, London, 1258–1688, ed. R. R. Sharpe, 2 vols (1889–90).

CAMDEN, WILLIAM. *Britannia* (1695 edn).

CAMPBELL, R. *The London Tradesman* (1747, repr. Newton Abbot, 1969).

CAREW, R. *The Survey of Cornwall* (1769 edn).

Chantry Certificates and Inventories of Church Goods, ed. R. Graham (Oxfordshire Record Series, i, 1919).

Church Plate of the County of Wiltshire, ed. J. E. Nightingale and R. H. Goddard (Salisbury, 1891).

A Collection of Ordinances and Regulations for the Government of the Royal Household (Society of Antiquaries, 1790).

The Coventry Leet Book, ed. M. D. Harris, 4 vols (Early English Text Society, 1907–13).

Devon Inventories of the Sixteenth and Seventeenth Centuries, ed. M. Cash (Devon and Cornwall Record Society, new ser., xi, 1966).

A Discourse of the Common Weal of this Realm of England, ed. E. Lamond (1893).

Dudley Probate Inventories, 1544–1603, ed. J. S. Roper (Dudley, 1965).

Dudley Probate Inventories, 1605–1685, ed. J. S. Roper (Dudley, 1966).

Early English Meals and Manners, ed. F. J. Furnivall (Early English Text Society, 1868).

The Edwardian Inventories for Bedfordshire, ed. F. E. Eeles and J. E. Brown (Alcuin Club Collections, vi, 1905).

The Edwardian Inventories for Huntingdonshire, ed. S. C. Lomas and T. Craib (Alcuin Club Collections, vii, 1906).

EVELYN, JOHN. *The Diary of John Evelyn*, ed. E. S. de Beer, 6 vols (Oxford, 1955).

Expeditions to Prussia and the Holy Land made by Henry Earl of Derby in the years 1390–1 and 1392–3, ed. L. Toulmin-Smith (Camden Society, new ser., lii, 1894).

Farm and Cottage Inventories of Mid-Essex, 1634–1749, ed. F. W. Steer (Chelmsford, 1950).

The Fifty Earliest English Wills in the Court of Probate, London, ed. F. J. Furnivall (Early English Text Society, 1882).

HALYBURTON, A. *The Ledger of Andrew Halyburton* (Edinburgh, 1867).

HARRISON, WILLIAM. *The Description of England*, ed. G. Edelen (New York, 1968).

Historical Manuscripts Commission: Calendar of the Salisbury MSS.

'Household expenses of Princess Elizabeth during her residence at Hatfield, 1.10.1551–30.9.1552', *The Camden Miscellany, Volume Two* (Camden Society, lv, 1853).

Household and Farm Inventories in Oxfordshire, 1550–1590, ed. M. A. Havinden (1965).

'The household goods, etc., of Sir John Gage, of West Firle, Co. Sussex, K. G., 1556', ed. R. G. Rice, *Collections of the Sussex Archaeological Society*, xlv (1902).

'Household inventories of the Lancashire gentry, 1350–1700', ed. O. Ashmore, *Trans. Historic Society of Lancashire and Cheshire*, cx (1958).

The Household Papers of Henry Percy, Ninth Earl of Northumberland (1564–1632), ed. G. R. Batho (Camden Society, 3rd ser., xciii, 1962).

The Household Roll of Richard de Swinfield, Bishop of Hereford for 1289–90, ed. J. Webb, 2 vols (Camden Society, old ser., lix and lxii, 1853–55).

Hustings Wills, see *Calendar of Wills*.

The Inventories of Church Goods for the Counties of York, Durham, and Northumberland, ed. W. Page (Surtees Society, xcvii, 1897).

Inventories of the Goods and Ornaments of the Churches of Surrey, in the reign of King Edward the Sixth, ed. J. R. D. Tyssen (1869).

'Inventories made for Sir William and Sir Thomas Fairfax, Knights of Walton and of Gilling Castle, Yorks., in the sixteenth and seventeenth centuries', ed. E. Peacock, *Archaeologia*, xlviii (1884).

'An inventory of the effects of Henry Howard K.G., Earl of Northampton, taken in 1614', ed. E. P. Shirley, *Archaeologia*, xlii, pt 2 (1869).

'On an inventory of the household goods of Sir Thomas Ramsey, Lord Mayor of London, 1577', ed. F. W. Fairholt, *Archaeologia*, xl (1866).

Italian Relation of England: A Relation or rather a True Account of the Island of England, ed. C. A. Sneyd (Camden Society, xxxvii, 1847).

'Jacobean household inventories', ed. F. G. Emmison, *Bedfordshire Historical Record Society*, xx (1938).

Journals of the House of Commons

Lincoln Wills, A.D. 1271 to A.D. 1526, ed. C. W. Foster (Lincoln Record Society, v, 1912).

Lists of Foreign Protestants and Aliens, Resident in England, 1618–88, ed. W. D. Cooper (Camden Society, old ser., lxxxii, 1862).

The Little Red Book of Bristol, ed. F. M. Bickley, 2 vols (1900).

The Local Port Book of Southampton for 1439–40, ed. H. S. Cobb (Southampton, 1961).

The Local Port Book of Southampton, 1435–6, ed. B. Foster (Southampton, 1963).

London Consistory Court Wills, 1492–1547, ed. I. Darlington (London Record Society, iii, 1967).

Manners and Household Expenses of England in the Thirteenth and Fourteenth Centuries, Illustrated by Original Records, ed. T. H. Turner (Roxburghe Club, 1841).

Memorials of London Life in the XIIIth, XIVth, and XVth Centuries, ed. H. T. Riley (1868).

Munimenta Gildhallae Londoniensis, i, Liber Albus, ii, Liber Custumarum, ed. H. T. Riley (1859–62).

Nottinghamshire Household Inventories, ed. P. A. Kennedy (Thoroton Society Record Series, xxii, 1963).

PEPYS, SAMUEL. *The Diary of Samuel Pepys M.A., F.R.S.*, ed. H. B. Wheatley, 10 vols (1912–18).

PLINY, SECUNDUS, C. *Historia Naturalis*.

The Port Books of Southampton for the Reign of Edward IV, ed. D. B. Quinn and A. A. Ruddock, 2 vols (Southampton, 1937–38).

The Port Books of Southampton, 1427–30, ed. P. Studer (Southampton, 1913).

Probate Inventories of Lichfield and District, 1568–1680, ed. D. G. Vaisey (Staffordshire Record Society, 4th ser., v, 1969).

'Probate inventories of Worcester Tradesmen, 1545–1614', *Miscellany II*, ed. A. D. Dyer (Worcestershire Historical Society, new ser., v, 1967).

'Probate inventory of Sir John Eliot, late prisoner in the Tower (1633)', *Camden Miscellany XVI*, ed. F. J. Fisher (Camden Society, 3rd ser., lii, 1936).

Register of the Freemen of the City of York, 1272–1558, ed. F. Collins (Surtees Society, xcvi, 1896).

Register of the Freemen of Leicester, 1196–1770, ed. H. Hartopp (Leicester, 1927).

The Registers of Edward the Black Prince 1346–65, 4 vols (1930–33).

The Regulations and Establishment of the Household of Henry Algernon Percy the Fifth Earl of Northumberland at his castles of Wresill and Lekinfield in Yorkshire, begun A.D. 1512, ed. T. Percy (1827).

Rotuli Parliamentorum, 6 vols (1767–77).

Sedgley Probate Inventories, 1614–1787, ed. J. S. Roper (Dudley, 1966).

'Some early inventories of pewter in country houses', ed. R. J. A. Shelley, *Apollo* (Oct. 1947).

Somerset Medieval Wills, 1501–1530, ed. F. W. Weaver (Somerset Record Society, xix, 1903).

Statutes of the Realm, 11 vols (1810–28).

Stourbridge Probate Inventories, 1541–1558, ed. J. S. Roper (Dudley, 1966).

SWEETING, J. *A Declaration of Sundry Grievances concerning Tinne and Pewter* (1645).

THEOPHILUS. *On Divers Arts: The Treatise of Theophilus*, ed. J. G. Hawthorne and C. S. Smith (Chicago, 1963).

'Transcript of two Rolls containing an inventory of effects formerly belonging to Sir John Fastolfe, 1459', ed. T. Amyot, *Archaeologia*, xxi (1827).

Tudor Economic Documents, ed. R. H. Tawney and E. Power, 3 vols. (1924).

Two Early London Subsidy Rolls, ed. E. Ekwall (Lund, 1951).

Two Italian Accounts of Tudor England, ed. C. V. Malfatti (Barcelona, 1953).

'Two seventeenth-century inventories', ed. E. W. Crossley, *Yorkshire Archaeological Journal*, xxxiv (1939).

The Universal British Directory (1791 and 1798 edns).

Universal British Directory, Supplement (1792).

'Visitations of certain churches in the patronage of St. Paul's Cathedral Church between the years 1138 and 1250', ed. W. S. Simpson, *Archaeologia*, lv, pt 2 (1897).

'Visitations of churches belonging to the Dean and Chapter of St. Paul's Cathedral in the years 1249-52', ed. W. S. Simpson, *Camden Miscellany, Volume Nine* (Camden Society, new ser., liii, 1895).

Visitations of Churches belonging to St. Paul's Cathedral in 1297 and 1458, ed. W. S. Simpson (Camden Society, new ser., lv, 1895).

WALLER, T. *A General Description of All Trades* (1747).

Wills and Inventories Illustrative of the History, Manners, Language, Statistics, etc., of the Northern Counties of England from the Eleventh Century Onwards, ed. J. Raine etc. (Surtees Society, 1835-1929).

Wills and Inventories from the Registers of the Commissary of Bury St. Edmunds and the Archdeacon of Sudbury, ed. S. Tymms (Camden Society, old ser., xlix, 1850).

'The will and inventory of Robert Morton, Gentleman, 1486-8', *Journal of the British Archaeological Association*, xxxiii (1877).

The York Memorandum Book, ed. M. Sellars, 2 vols (Surtees Society, cxx, cxxv, 1912-15).

PRINTED SECONDARY SOURCES

Agrarian History of England and Wales, IV, 1500-1640, ed. J. Thirsk (Cambridge, 1967).

ALEXANDER, D. *Retailing in England During the Industrial Revolution* (1970).

AYRTON, E. R., CURRELLY, C. T. and WEIGALL, A. E. P. *Abydos*, iii (1904).

BALSDON, J. P. V. D. *Life and Leisure in Ancient Rome* (1969).

BAPST, G. Études sur l'étain dans l'antiquité et au moyen âge (Paris, 1884).

BARATIER, E. and REYNAUD, F. Histoire du commerce de Marseille, II: de 1291 à 1480 (Paris, 1951).

BELL, M. Old Pewter (1905; 1913).

BEVERIDGE, W. H. Prices and Wages in England from the Twelfth to the Nineteenth Century (1939).

BRADBURY, F. History of Old Sheffield Plate (1912).

BREARS, P. C. D. The English Country Pottery: its history and techniques (Newton Abbot, 1971).

BRIDBURY, A. R. Economic Growth: England in the later Middle Ages (1962).

British Museum Guide to the Antiquities of Roman Britain (1st edn, 1951).

BROWN, P. D. C. 'A Roman pewter mould from St Just in Penwith, Cornwall', Cornish Archaeology, ix (1970).

BURT, ROGER. 'Lead production in England and Wales, 1700–1770', Economic History Review, 2nd ser., xxii (1969).

Cambridge Economic History of Europe, iii, ed. M. M. Postan, E. E. Rich, and E. Miller (Cambridge, 1963).

CARUS-WILSON, E. M. Medieval Merchant Venturers (1954; rev. edn 1967).

CHARLESWORTH, M. P. The Lost Province or the Worth of Britain (Cardiff, 1949).

CLARKSON, L. A. The Pre-Industrial Economy in England, 1500–1750 (1971).

COLLINGWOOD, R. G. and MYRES, J. M. L. Roman Britain and the English Settlements (2nd edn, Oxford, 1937).

COLLINGWOOD, R. G. and RICHMOND, I. A. The Archaeology of Roman Britain (rev. edn, 1969).

COTTERELL, H. H. and HEAL, A. 'Pewterers' trade-cards', The Connoisseur, December 1926; and 'About pewterers' trade-cards etc.', The Connoisseur, February 1928.

COTTERELL, H. H. *Old Pewter, its Makers and Marks* (1929).

COTTERELL, H. H. 'The pewterers of Newcastle-upon-Tyne', *The Antique Collector*, November 1935.

DAVIES, K. G. *The Royal African Company* (1957).

DAVIES, M. G. *The Enforcement of English Apprenticeship 1565–1642: a study in applied mercantilism* (Cambridge, Mass., 1956).

DAVIES, O. *Roman Mines in Europe* (Oxford, 1935).

DAVIS, D. *A History of Shopping* (1966).

DAVIS, R. 'English foreign trade, 1660–1700', *Economic History Review*, 2nd ser., iv (1952).

DE NAVARRO, A. *Causeries on English Pewter* (New York, 1911).

DOUCH, H. L. 'Cornish potters and pewterers', *Journal of the Royal Institution of Cornwall*, new ser., vi (1969).

DU BOULAY, F. R. H. *An Age of Ambition* (1970).

DUNNING, G. C., HURST, J. G., MYRES, J. N. L. and TISCHLER, F. 'Anglo-Saxon pottery: a symposium', *Medieval Archaeology*, iii (1959).

ELTON, G. R. *Reform and Renewal: Thomas Cromwell and the Common Weal* (Cambridge, 1973).

ENGLEFIELD, E. *Treatise on Pewter and its Manufacture* (1933).

EVANS, NANCY GOYNE. 'A Directory survey of pewter and Britannia craftsmen working in Birmingham, England, until 1860', *Bulletin of the Pewter Collectors' Club of America*, December 1969.

FAGNIEZ, G. *Études sur l'industrie et la classe industrielle à Paris, au treizième et au quatorzième siècle* (Paris, 1877).

FIELD, R. K. 'Worcestershire peasant buildings in the later Middle Ages', *Medieval Archaeology*, ix (1965).

FISHER, F. J. 'The development of London as a centre of conspicuous consumption in the sixteenth and seventeenth centuries', *Trans. Roy. Historical Society*, 4th ser., xxx (1948).

FORBES, R. J. *Studies in Ancient Technology*, vol. ix (Leiden, 1964).

FOX, A. *South West England* (1964).

FRANK, T., ed. *An Economic Survey of Ancient Rome*, 6 vols (1933–40).

FRANSSON, G. *Middle English Surnames of Occupation, 1100–1350* (Lund, 1935).

GARNER, F. H. *English Delftware* (1948).

GIBBS, F. W. 'The rise of the tinplate industry', *Annals of Science*, vi (1950) and vii (1951).

GLADSTONE, J. H. 'On metallic copper, tin and antimony from Ancient Egypt', *Proceedings of the Society of Biblical Archaeology* (1892).

GOWLAND, W. 'Analyses of metal vessels found at Appleshaw, Hants., and of some other specimens of Roman pewter', *Archaeologia*, lvi, pt 1 (1898).

GREEN, F. 'Pembrokeshire in by-gone days', *West Wales Historical Records*, ix (1920–23).

HAEDEKE, H-U. *Zinn: Ein Handbuch, für Sammler und Liebhaber* (Brunswick, 1963).

HAEDEKE, H-U. *Metalwork* (1970).

HAGGAR, R. G. *English Country Pottery* (1950).

HATCHER, J. *English Tin Production and Trade before 1550* (Oxford, 1973).

HAVERFIELD, F. 'Cornish Tin', *Mélanges Boissier* (Paris, 1903).

HAWKINS, J. 'On the intercourse which subsisted between Cornwall and the other commercial states of antiquity, and on the state of the Tin-trade during the Middle Ages', *Trans. Royal Geological Society of Cornwall*, iii (1824).

HAZLITT, W. C. *The Livery Companies of the City of London* (1892).

HEDGES, E. S., ed. *Tin and its Alloys* (1960).

HEDGES, E. S. *Tin in Social and Economic History* (1964).

HENCKEN, H. O'N. *The Archaeology of Cornwall and Scilly* (1932).

HERBERT, W. *The Twelve Great Livery Companies*, 2 vols (1834–36).

HOLE, G. *English Home-Life, 1500 to 1800* (1947).

HOSKINS, W. G. *The Midland Peasant: the economic and social history of a Leicestershire village* (1957).

HOSKINS, W. G. *Provincial England* (1965).

HUNT, R. *British Mining* (2nd edn, 1887).

KAUFFMANN, H. J. *The American Pewterer: his techniques and his products* (New Jersey, 1970).

KELLETT, J. R. 'The breakdown of gild and corporation control over the handicraft and retail trade in London', *Economic History Review*, 2nd ser., x (1958).

KERFOOT, J. B. *American Pewter* (Boston, 1924).

KINGSFORD, C. L. 'Essex House, formerly Leicester House and Exeter Inn', *Archaeologia*, 2nd ser., xxiii (1923).

KRAMER, S. *The English Craft Gilds* (New York, 1927).

LABARGE, M. W. *A Baronial Household of the Thirteenth Century* (1965).

LE PATOUREL, H. E. J. 'Documentary evidence and the medieval pottery industry', *Medieval Archaeology*, xii (1968).

LEWIS, G. R. *The Stannaries: a study of the medieval tin miners of Devon and Cornwall*, Harvard Economic Studies, iii (Cambridge, Mass., 1903).

LIPSON, E. *The Economic History of England*, 3 vols (1949–56 edns).

LIVERSIDGE, J. 'A new hoard of Romano-British pewter, from Icklingham', *Proceedings of the Cambridgeshire Antiquarian Society*, lii (1959).

LIVERSIDGE, J. *Britain in the Roman Empire* (1968).

LONGFIELD, A. K. *Anglo-Irish Trade in the Sixteenth Century* (1929).

LUCAS, A. 'Notes on the early history of tin and bronze', *Journal of Egyptian Archaeology*, xiv (1928).

LUCAS, A. *Ancient Egyptian Materials and Industries* (3rd edn, 1948).

LUMSDEN, H. and AITKEN, P. H. *History of the Hammermen of Glasgow* (Paisley, 1912).

MARÉCHAL, J. R. *Prehistoric Metallurgy* (Lammersdorf, 1963).

MARKHAM, C. A. *Pewter Marks and Old Pewter Ware, domestic and ecclesiastical* (1909).

MASSÉ, H. J. L. J. *Pewter Plate: a historical and descriptive handbook* (1910).

MASSÉ, H. J. L. J. *Chats on Old Pewter* (1911; rev. edn, 1949).

MASSÉ, H. J. L. J. *The Pewter Collector* (1921; rev. ed, 1971).

MATHIAS, PETER. *The Brewing Industry in England* (Cambridge, 1959).

MERRIFIELD, R. *Roman London* (1969).

MICHAELIS, R. F. *Antique Pewter of the British Isles* (1955).

MICHAELIS, R. F. *British Pewter* (1969).

MINCHINTON, W. *The British Tinplate Industry* (Oxford, 1957).

MITCHELL, B. R. and DEANE, P. *Abstract of British Historical Statistics* (Cambridge, 1962).

MOLLAT, M. *Le Commerce maritime normand à la fin du moyen âge* (Paris, 1952).

MORY, L. *Schönes Zinn* (Munich, 1961).

MOTTRAM, A. S. 'Roman pewter dishes from Shingham', *Norfolk Archaeology*, xxxv, pt 1 (1970).

MUMFORD, W. F. 'Terciars on the estates of Wenlock Priory', *Transactions of the Shropshire Archaeological Society*, lviii (1965).

MYERS, A. R. *The Household of Edward IV* (Manchester, 1959).

NEF, J. U. 'The progress of technology and the growth of large-scale industry in Great Britain, 1540–1640', *Economic History Review*, v (1934–36).

NEUMANN, B. *Die Metalle* (Halle a.s., 1904).

PATTEN, J. 'Village and town: an occupational study', *Agricultural History Review*, xx (1972).

PEAL, C. A. 'Romano-British pewter plates and dishes', *Proceedings of the Cambridgeshire Antiquarian Society*, lx (1967).

PEAL, C. A. *British Pewter and Britannia Metal for Pleasure and Investment* (1971).

PENNINGTON, R. R. *Stannary Law: a history of the mining law of Cornwall and Devon* (Newton Abbot, 1973).

PHELPS BROWN, E. H. and HOPKINS, S. V. 'Wage rates and prices: evidence for population pressure in the sixteenth century', *Economica*, xxiv (1957).

Pigot's New Commercial Directory, 1828–29.

POLLARD, S. and CROSSLEY, D. W. *The Wealth of Britain* (1968).

POUND, J. F. 'The social and trade structure of Norwich, 1525–75', *Past and Present*, xxxiv (1966).

POWER, E. and POSTAN, M. M., eds. *Studies in English Trade in the Fifteenth Century* (1933).

POWICKE, F. M. and CHENEY, C. R. *Councils and Synods and other documents relating to the English Church* (Oxford, 1964).

RAMSAY, G. D. *English Overseas Trade during the Centuries of Emergence* (1957).

READ, C. H. 'List of pewter dishes and vessels found at Appleshaw and now in the British Museum', *Archaeologia*, lvi, pt 1 (1898).

REANEY, P. H. *A Dictionary of British Surnames* (1958).

Report of the Commission on London Livery Companies (1884).

RICHMOND, I. A. *Roman Britain* (rev. edn, 1963).

RICHMOND, I. A. and SMYTHE, J. A. 'A Roman cup of tin', *Proc. Univ. Durham Philosophical Society*, x (1938).

ROE, F. G. *English Cottage Furniture* (1961).

ROGERS, J. E. T. *A History of Agriculture and Prices in England*, 7 vols (Oxford, 1866–1902).

ROWE, J. *Cornwall in the Age of the Industrial Revolution* (Liverpool, 1953).

RUDDOCK, A. A. 'London capitalists and the decline of Southampton in the early Tudor period', *Economic History Review*, 2nd ser., ii (1949).

SCHUMPETER, E. B. *English Overseas Trade Statistics, 1697–1808* (Oxford, 1960).

SHELLEY, R. J. A. *Brief Notes on Wigan Pewterers* (Wigan, 1936).

SHELLEY, R. J. A. 'Wigan and Liverpool Pewterers' *Transactions of the Historic Society of Lancashire and Cheshire*, 1946.

SHILLINGTON, V. M. and CHAPMAN, A. B. W. *The Commercial Relations of England and Portugal* (New York, 1907).

SMOUT, T. C. *Scottish Trade on the Eve of the Union, 1660–1707* (1963).

SMYTHE, J. A. 'Notes on ancient and Roman tin and its alloys with lead', *Transactions of the Newcomen Society*, xviii (1937–38).

SPILLER, B. *Victorian Public Houses* (Newton Abbot, 1972).

STEEL, A. *The Receipt of the Exchequer, 1377–1485* (Cambridge, 1954).

STONE, L. *The Crisis of the Aristocracy, 1558–1641* (Oxford, 1965).

TARDY. *Les Étains français* (Paris, 1959).

TAWNEY, A. J. and TAWNEY, R. H. 'An occupational census of the seventeenth century', *Economic History Review*, v (1934–35).

THIRSK, J. *English Peasant Farming: the agrarian history of Lincolnshire from Tudor to recent times* (1957).

THRUPP, S. L. *The Merchant Class of Medieval London* (Michigan, 1948).

THRUPP, S. L. 'Medieval gilds reconsidered', *Journal of Economic History*, ii (1942).

TIMMINS, S., ed. *Birmingham and the Midlands Hardware District* (1866, repr. 1967).

TOUCHARD, H. *Commerce maritime breton à la fin du moyen âge* (Paris, 1967).

TYLECOTE, R. F. *Metallurgy in Archaeology* (1962).

UNWIN, G., ed. *Studies of Finance and Trade under Edward III* (1918).

UNWIN, G. *The Gilds and Companies of London* (4th edn, 1963).

UNWIN, G. *Industrial Organization in the Sixteenth and Seventeenth Centuries* (2nd edn, 1957).

URE, A. *Dictionary of Arts, Manufactures and Mines* (1839).

VEAL, E. M. 'Craftsmen and the economy of London in the fourteenth century' in A. E. J. Hollaender and W. Kellaway, eds, *Studies in London History* (1969).

VERSTER, A. J. G. *Old European Pewter* (1958).

VICTORIA AND ALBERT MUSEUM. *Art Nouveau Pewter* (Catalogue of Exhibition, 1973).

Victoria History of the Counties of England: Cornwall, ed. W. Page, vols i and ii and parts 5 and 8.

Victoria History of the Counties of England: Devon, ed. W. Page (1906).

WARNER, O. *A History of the Tin Plate Alias Wire Workers Company of the City of London* (1964).

WEATHERILL, L. *The Pottery Trade and North Staffordshire, 1660–1760* (Manchester, 1971).

WEDLAKE, W. J. *Excavations at Camerton* (Camerton, 1958).

WELCH, C. *History of the Worshipful Company of Pewterers of the City of London*, 2 vols (1902).

WEST, J. *Village Records* (1962).

WHEELER, R. E. M., ed. *London in Roman Times* (1946).

WILKINS, D. *Concilia Magnae Britanniae et Hiberniae*, 4 vols (1737).

WILLAN, T. S. *The English Coasting Trade, 1600–1750* (Manchester, 1938).

WILLAN, T. S. *The Early History of the Russia Company, 1553–1603* (Manchester, 1956).

WILLAN, T. S. *Studies in Elizabethan Foreign Trade* (Manchester, 1959).

WOLFF, PH. *Commerces et marchands de Toulouse, vers 1350–vers 1450* (Paris, 1954).

WOOD, L. I. *Scottish Pewter-Ware and Pewterers* (Edinburgh, 1905).

WOODBURY, R. S. *History of the Lathe to 1850* (Ohio, 1961).

WRIGHT, T. *A History of Domestic Manners and Sentiments in England during the Middle Ages* (1862).

WRIGLEY, E. A., 'A simple model of London's importance in changing English society and economy, 1650–1750', *Past and Present*, xxxvii (1967).

UNPUBLISHED SECONDARY SOURCES

ARCHER, J. L. 'The Industrial History of London, 1603–40: with special reference to the suburbs and those areas claiming exemptions from the authority of the Lord Mayor (London, M.A. thesis, 1934).

BARTLETT, J. N. 'Some Aspects of the Economy of York in the Later Middle Ages, 1300–1550' (London, Ph.D. thesis, 1958).

DYER, A. D. 'The City of Worcester in the Sixteenth Century' (Birmingham Ph.D. thesis, 1966).

FISHER, F. J. 'The Influence and Development of the Industrial Gilds in the Larger Provincial Towns under James I and Charles I' (London M.A. thesis, 1931).

Index

Aberdeen, pewter industry, 126–7, 299
Abingdon, pewter industry, 74, 177–8, 256, 259, 260
Abington Piggots, Romano-British pewter from, 17
Abbotsbury Abbey, sepulchral chalice, paten from, 27
Abydos, Egypt, pewter flask from, 6
Adam de Stanton, 43
Advertising of pewterware
    rules governing, 183
    use of marks in, 184–5
Africa, export of pewter to, 268–9
Aikin, Mr., 321
Alexander, D., 285 n. 1
Alexander, Thomas, 231
Aliens, prohibition on employment of, 117, 152
Alloys
    control of constituents, 145, 152, 161, 162, 163–5 and n. 1
    for Britannia metal, 287–8 and nn. 5, 1
    in Romano-British pewter, 14–15, 16–18, 224
    in traditional pewter manufacturing process, 224–5
    innovations introduced by Taudins, 225–7, 228
    maintenance of standards, 306–7
    price of different, 228
    resistance to technical advances in, 208
    tin-rich, main uses of, 1
Americas, American colonies
    dependence on scrap for raw materials, 240
    export of pewter to, 139, 267–8, 269, 290–2, 320
Amiens, pewter industry, 78
Amphorae, pewter, 21
Andrees, Henry, 257
Angers, pewter industry, 78
Antimony, use in pewter and bronze alloys, 8, 227–8, 288 n. 1
Antoniniani, 9
Appleford, Romano-British pewter from, 11
Appleshaw, Romano-British pewter from, 11, 14, 16, 17, 18 n. 4
Apprenticeship, apprentices
    and division of labour in pewter industry, 223–4
    cost of being bound, 247, 295
    rules, ordinances governing, 146, 148, 149, 151, 153, 154, 159, 161, 187–92, 194–6 and n. 1, 207–8
    sale of, 190 and n. 2
    social background, 250
    trends in numbers, 194–6 and n. 1, 241–2, 272, 273, 293–8
Aquitaine, import of pots from, 61

342 *Index*

Archer, William, 157
Aristocracy *see* Nobility
Armourers' Company
　in joint action to curb hawking, 186
　incorporation, 149
Arsenic, use in manufacture of bronze, 5
Art nouveau pewter, 315
Artisan classes
　pewter in homes of, 34, 42–3, 105–6
Ashbourne, search of 1640 in, 258, 259, 260
Ashburton, pewter industry, 128
Ashebourne, William, 124
Asia Minor, export of pewter to, 266
Association of British Pewter Craftsmen Ltd., 322
Astlyn (Astelyn), Laurence (Lawrence), 231, 313
Ath, early pewterers' gild, 36
Atherstone, Atherstone Fair, search of 1640 in, 258, 259
Auckland, Durham, Collegiate Church of, pewter collection, 56–7
Augsburg, pewter industry, 36, 77, 265
Austin Friars, Pewterers' meetings in, 150
Australia, export of pewter to, 290–1
Aylesbury, searches in, 178, 256

Baltic area, export of pewter to, 265
Banbury, Banbury Fair, searches in, 178, 256, 259
Banffshire, pewter industry, 299
Banks, Robert, 248, 251, 262
Bapst, G., 44
Barcelona, pewter industry, 266 n. 2
Barnstaple, pewter industry, 128
Baron, Jonathan, 248

Barrett, Ann, 80
Basins, bronze, 60
Basins, pewter
　competition offered to other materials by, 59
　ecclesiastical, 28, 29
　export to China, 269
　household utensils, 1
　manufacturing technique, 209
Basins, pottery, 135
Bath
　decline of pewter industry, 297 and n. 2
　distribution of pewter made in, 257, 258
　searches in, 177, 257
Bayonne, demand for English tin in, 36
Beakers, pewter, 165
Bedfordshire, patterns of pewter ownership in, 92, 95, 96–7, 99–100, 102
Beer consumption, significance of increase in, 289–90
Beer pots *see* Pots, Tankards
Bell, Malcolm, 315
Bells
　alloys used for, 20, 21, 23
　medieval pewter, 28
Benefactions managed by Pewterers' Co., 312–14, 318–19
Berey, Robert, 255
Berkshire, medieval pewter craftsmen from, 73–4
Beverley, medieval pewter craftsmen from, 74
Bewdley, pewter industry, 298 and n. 6
Bicester Market, searches in, 256
Biddulph, Michael, 111–12
Biggs, — (Bromsgrove), 262
Billesdon, Robert, 232
Billing, — 262
Billingsgate, a centre of London pewter industry, 119
Biringuccio, Vanoccio, 67, 213–14, 228

Index 343

Birmingham
 pewter industry, 128, 297 n. 2, 298–9, 320
 searches, 178
Bishop, Peter, 266
Bishopsgate, a centre of London pewter industry, 119
Bismuth, addition to pewter alloys, 224–5, 227, 228–9, 241
Black Death, economic repercussions, 45–6 and nn. 1, 2, 62–3, 72
Black Prince, 44, 229
Blackjacks, leather, competition offered by pewter to, 60
Blacksmiths, in joint action to curb hawking, 186
Blake, John 43
Blandford Forum, searches in, 177, 257
Blansone (Blonsone), — 256, 258, 259
Blundell, Nicholas, 283 n. 1
Boddam, Nicholas, 182
Bohemia, tin resources, 22 n. 3, 36, 131 and n. 2, 138, 264
Bolsover, Mr., 287 n. 5
Bordeaux, pewter industry, 78
Boston, Thomas, 232
Boston, Lincs., pewter industry, 74, 128
Bourne, Samson, 257
Bourne, Samuel, 261, 262
Bowls, pewter
 alloys used for, 166
 displacement by silver, 107
 ecclesiastical lavers, 114
 Romano-British, 10–11
Bowling, John, 245–6
Boxes, pewter, Romano-British, 19
Bradshawe, Christopher, 257
Brass
 competition offered to pewter by, 137
 ecclesiastical furnishings made from, 30
 pewterers working in bronze and, 241 n. 3

Brentford, medieval pewter craftsmen from, 74
Breslau, pewter industry, 77
Brewers' Company, incorporation, 149
Brice, John, 58, 59
Bridgewater, pewter industry, 74, 177–8
Brigham and Wemmes, attempt to pre-empt tin production, 235
Brighton, size of pewter industry, 299
Brislington, Romano-British pewter from, 17, 18 n. 4
Bristol
 delftware industry, 133
 distribution of pewter from, 257, 262
 export of pewter from, 266 n. 2, 267
 growth, decline of pewter industry, 74, 125, 127–8, 297–8, 299, 300
 pewterers' gild in, structure, policies, 70–1, 73, 151, 161, 186, 305
 searches in, 177, 178
 supplies of tin for pewter industry, 239, 305
Britain, Roman, pewter industry, 8–19
Britannia metal (white metal)
 manufacturing techniques, centres, 2, 298, 299
 origins, competition offered to pewter by, 141, 227–8, 287–8 and nn. 5, 1, 294
 resistance to introduction of, 208
British Pewter Designs Ltd., 322
Britanny
 export of tin to, 78
 pewter industry, 61, 79
Bruton, search in, 257
Broadhead, Gurney, Spark and Co., 287 n. 5
Broklesbury, (Brocklesbury), Peter, 167 and n. 3, 237

Bronze
  candlesticks, 60
  distribution of manufacture in Roman Britain, 14 n. 3
  ecclesiastical uses, 30
  ewers, 60
  historical importance, 5
  import into Roman Britain, 10
  manufacture in Saxon England, 23
  pewterers working in brass and, 241 n. 3
  problem of verdigris, 20–1 and n. 1, 35, 135, 137
  tableware, decline of, 59
  vessels, utensils, in Middle Ages, 32–3 and n. 3, 34
Brooches, dating of, 19
Brown and Englefield, 301
Browne, John, 232
Bruges, early gild of pewterers in, 36
Buckinghamshire, medieval pewter craftsmen from, 73–4
Bullardyne, Robert, 201
Bulmer, Bevis, attempt to preempt tin production, 235
Burford, medieval pewter craftsmen from, 74
Burnishers, 221–3
Burt, R., 295 n. 3
Burte, Widow, 258
Burton, Robert, 246
Burton, searches in, 257, 258, 259
Burwell, Romano-British pewter from, 17
Bury St Edmunds, pewter industry, 74, 128
Butcher, Robert, 177
Butcher, Thomas, 177
Butsyd, Thomas, 231
Buttons, pewter, alloys used for, 164
Byshoptree, William, 124

Caerwent, Romano-British pewter from, 12
Cairo, pewter industry, 79
Cambridge
  pewter industry, 74, 124–5, 128
  searches in, 177
Cambridge University, pewter collections in colleges of, 56, 63, 112–13, 275–6, 292
Cambridgeshire, pewter industry, 73–4, 299
Camerton, Romano-British pewter from, 12, 15
Candle moulds, alloys used for, 164
Candlesticks, copper, 27, 29
Candlesticks, latten, 29
Candlesticks, pewter
  alloys used for, 164, 166
  competition offered to other materials by, 60
  ecclesiastical, household uses, 1, 28, 39 and n. 1, 114, 137
Candlesticks, pottery, 135
Candlesticks, silver, 29
Candlesticks, tinplate, wire, brass, 137
Cantelowe, Thomas, 232
Canterbury, pewter industry, 69 n. 4, 74
Capitulare Aquisgranense, 21
Cardiff, pewter industry, 240
Carew, Richard, 233–4
Carlisle, pewter industry, 74, 128
Carrawburgh, Romano-British pewter from, 12
Carter, Anthony, 256
Casting, in traditional pewter manufacturing, 208, 209–18, 221–3
Castor potteries, 10
Catcher, Edward, 313 n. 1
Catcher, John, 167 n. 3, 168–9, 236, 245
Cave, Philip, 256, 262
Censers
  latten, 29
  pewter, 28
Chalices
  pewter, 22, 24–30, 114
  silver, 24, 25–6, 29–30

Chalices—*contd.*
 tin, copper, 25 and n. 6
Chamberpots, pewter, 1, 108 n. 5
Chamberlain, Robert, 150
Chamberlayne, Richard, 266
Chargers, pewter
 alloys used for, 165–6
 competition offered to other materials by, 59
 displacement by silver, 107
 manufacturing technique, 209
 medieval domestic, 39
Charitable trusts managed by Pewterers' Company, 312–13
Charles II, King of England, support of Taudin, 226 and n. 3
Charles VI, King of France, 44
Chartres, pewter industry, 78
Chats on Old Pewter, H. J. L. J. Massé, 315
Cheshire, Thomas, 255, 257, 258, 259, 260
Cheshire, size of pewter industry, 299
Chester
 rise, decline of pewter industry, 71, 74 and n. 2, 124, 128, 296–7
 supplies of tin for pewterers, 239
 use of scrap from Ireland, 240
Chevisaunce, prohibition of, 185 n. 2
Chichester, medieval pewter craftsmen from, 74
Child, John, 237, 246
Childe, Robert, 257
China, challenge offered to pewter by, 281–5
Chipping Norton, distribution of pewter made in, 256, 259
Chrismatories, pewter, 28, 29, 39
Church, The, demand for, use of pewter vessels, 21–2, 23, 24–30, 35 and n. 1, 37, 113–14
City and Guilds of London Institute, support from Pewterers' Company for work of, 314, 316, 322
Clay vessels, in Middle Ages, 32, 33, 34; *see also* Pottery
Clifford's Inn, pewter purchases, 113
Clonmel, pewter industry, 127
Closestool pans, pewter, 108 n. 5, 166
Cloth trade, economic importance of exports, 67–8
Clothworkers' Company, pewter collection, 113 and n. 4
Clothere, — 257
Cockayne, William, 236
Coffee houses, increasing popularity, 133–4 and n. 1
Coffee pots, pewter, 1
Coinage
 bronze, introduction in Britain, 7
 dating of, 19
 debased tin-rich Roman, 9
Colchester
 rise, decline of pewter industry, 74, 128, 296–7
 value of lists of chattels as sources, 34
Coldham, John, 265 and n. 3
Coleraine, export of English pewter to, 267
Collier, Nicholas, 235
Cologne, pewter industry, 77, 265
Common informer, role in control of pewter industry, 174 and n. 3
Communion vessels, pewter, 114; *see also* Church, The, *and individual items*
Competition between pewterers, gilds' policies on, 154, 163, 179, 183–4, 207–8
Constantyn (Constantine), Richard, 42, 287 n. 5
Copper
 alloys with tin, historical importance, 5

Copper—*contd.*
  candlesticks, 27, 29
  chalices, 25 and n. 6, 29
  problem of verdigris, 20–1 and n. 1, 23, 35
  supplies for pewter industry, 228–9, 241
  tableware, decline of, 59
  use in Middle Ages, 32–3
  see also Alloys
Coppersmiths, inclusion in Pewterers' Company, 241 n. 3, 271–2 and n. 1
Cordwainers' Company, incorporation, 149
Cork, pewter industry, 127
Cornhill, a centre of London pewter industry, 119
Cornwall
  export of tin to France from, 78
  medieval export of pewter from, 65 n. 5
  exploitation of tin deposits, 6, 8–9, 13, 40–1 and n. 2, 229, 285–6
  pewter industry, 40, 128
  Romano-British pewter manufacture in, 13, 15
Corp, Thomas, 42
Cosyn, William, 42
Cotterell, Howard H., 315–17, 316 n. 2, 320
Cotton, Thomas, 260, 261, 311
Counterfeit ware *see* Sadware
Court of Assistants, constitutional role, 155–61
Coventry
  medieval pewter craftsmen from, 74
  pewter industry in, 124–5, 128
  rules, policies of pewterers' gild in, 71, 73, 151, 161, 186
  searches in, 177, 255, 258, 259
Cowes, Henry, 237
Cracow, pewter industry, 79 n. 3
Craft gilds
  basis of power, effectiveness, 142–4

  constitutions, structure of policy-making bodies, 154–5
  order of precedence, 79–80
  parliamentary action to restrict powers, 153
  pewter collections, 57, 113
  see also individual gilds
Craftsmen *see* Artisan classes
Crane, John Caruthers, 298 n. 6
Cranked wheel and cord driven lathes, 220–1
Cricklade, search in, 257
Crooked Lane wares *see* Tinplate
Crowe, John, 232
Cruets
  alloys used for, 164, 166
  pewter, 21, 27, 28, 29, 30, 39, 42
  Theophilus' account of manufacturing technique, 210–13, 218, 219
Cumberlidg, Stephen, 262
Cups, earthenware, 134
Cups, pewter
  alloys used for, 166
  competition offered to other materials by, 60
  ecclesiastical uses, 29
  household, 1
  Romano-British, 10–11, 12, 17, 19
Cutlers' Company, in joint action to combat hawking, 186
Cutlers' Hall, meetings of Pewterers' Company in, 318

Dadley, Edward, 307, 308–9
Danzig, export of English pewter to, 266
Dark Ages, pewter manufacture during, 19–23
Dating of Romano-British pewter, 18–19 and n. 4
Deacon's mark, 184
Debt, handling of cases of, 247
Defaulters, gilds' control over, 142–3, 149, 150, 151–2, 153–4, 161–79, 203–5, 245–6, 255–61, 302–4

Delftware, development of, 132, 133 and n. 3, 281-2, 284
Derby, Henry, Earl of, 51-2
Derby
  distribution of pewter made in, 258
  rise, decline of pewter industry, 74, 296-7
  searches in, 258, 259
Dere, William, 80, 266
Deuxell (Duxell), Henry, 167 n. 3, 245, 246
Devizes, pewter industry, 128, 177
Devon
  exploitation of tin deposits, 41 n. 2, 229
  export of tin to France from, 78
  patterns of ownership of pewter in, 92, 94, 96-7, 105
  pewter industry, 73-4, 123
Dictionarius, John Garlande, 47-8
Dijon, pewter industry, 45, 78
Dinant, pewter industry, 78, 265
Diodorus, account of tin mining in Cornwall, 8
Dishes, pewter
  alloys used for, 164, 165-6
  competition offered to other materials by, 59
  displacement by silver, pottery, 107, 135
  household utensils, 1, 34, 35, 39, 42
  price levels, 275
  Romano-British, 10-11 and nn. 1, 2, 14, 15-16 and n. 2, 17
Diss, pewter industry, 128
Dixon, Charles, 287 n. 5
Dixson, William, 169
Dogowe, John, 230-1
Doncaster, pewter industry, 124, 178
Dorchester, pewter industry, 124, 257
Dorset, medieval pewter craftsmen in, 73-4
Dounton, Thomas, 68-9 and n. 1, 80, 243 and n. 3, 266

Dover, size of pewter industry, 299
Drapers' Company, incorporation, 149
Dresden, pewter industry, 77
Dressers, for the display of plate, 47, 50 and n. 1, 54
Drinking vessels
  attractions of pottery, silver, glass, 133-5
  demand for pewter, from taverns, 114-15
  see also Tankards
Dublin
  export of English pewter to, 267
  pewter industry, 127
  source of scrap pewter, 240
Dudley, patterns of ownership of pewter in, 93, 96, 98-9, 205
Dundee, pewter industry, 126-7
Durham, pewter industry, 42, 128, 178
Dutch refugees, and the problem of immigrant labour, 198-9
Dutton, Christopher, 257
Duxell *see* Deuxell

Earthenware, challenge offered to pewter by, 282-3, 284, 285, 289 and n. 3; *see also* Pottery
East Anglia, Romano-British pewter finds, 12, 13-14
East India Company, dealings in tin, 287, 305, 311-12
East Indies, export of pewter to, 290
Eastcheap market, specialist pewter stalls, 253
Edinburgh, pewter industry, 75, 126-7, 299
Edward II, King of England, attempt to pre-empt tin production, 229
Elderton, John, 170
Eleanor, Queen, bronze effigy of, 37

Elizabeth I, Queen
  attempt to pre-empt tin production, 235
  household expenditure on pewter, 109
Emigration of English pewterers, restrictions on, 117, 152, 198, 200–1
Englefield, W. J., 315, 316
Englefields, of London, 320
Essex
  patterns of ownership of pewter, 93, 95, 96–7, 105
  pewter industry, 73–4, 123
Étain sonnant pewter alloy, 226–7
Etiquette, value of handbooks on, as sources, 31
Europe
  demand for English pewter, 65–7
  development, exploitation of tin deposits, 6, 7
  imports of pewter from, 76–7 and nn. 1, 3, 77–9, 116–18
  increase in pewter production, 34–6, 44–5, 75–6 and n. 1, 77–8
Evelyn, John, 133
Ewers, bronze, 60
Ewers, pewter
  alloys used for, 166
  displacement by silver, 107
  ecclesiastical uses, 28, 29, 114
  household, 1
  Romano-British, 10–11, 15, 18–19
Ewers, pottery, 135
Exeter
  burgess occupations, 73 n. 1
  pewter industry, 74, 128, 299
  searches in, 177–8
Exeter, Bishop of, (d. 1310), character of tableware, 33
Exeter Cathedral, sepulchral chalice, paten, 27
Exports of English pewter
  character, distribution of, 263–9
  control, curtailment of, 116–18, 169–70
  decline, 300
  medieval trade, 45 and n. 4, 50–1, 64–8, 76–7
  modern, 320
  prices, 305–6 and n. 1
  trends in, after 1700, 290–2
  upsurge in later seventeenth century, 138–9

Fairfax of Gilling, Sir William, 111
Fairs and markets, role in retail distribution of pewter, 252–4
Fashion in pewterware, control of changes in, by gilds, 166–7
Field, R. K., 57
Fishmongers' Company, incorporation, 149
Flagons, pewter
  domestic, 1, 35
  ecclesiastical, 21, 114
  Romano-British, 12, 16
Flatware *see* Sadware
Font bowls, basins, 28, 114
Forster, Stephen, 232
Founders' Company, in joint action to curb hawking, 186
Fowey, export of pewter from, 65 n. 5
Fox, John, 256, 260
France
  exports of pewter to, 265, 267
  importance in tin trade, 36, 78 and n. 3
  increased use of pewter in, 44–5, 50–1
  pewter imports from, to England, 76–7, 78–9
Frankfurt, pewter industry, 36, 77
Freemen pewterers, numbers in London Company, 271–3; *see also* Pewterers' Company of London
Freiburg, pewter industry, 77
French refugees, and the problem of immigrant labour, 198–9

Frewin, Henry, 256
Fryer, Sir John, 115 n. 4, 190–2, 247
Fulham, John, 237
Fussell, Juliana, 33

Gage, Sir John, 109–10
Galway
 export of English pewter to, 267
 pewter industry, 127
Garlande, John, 47–8
Gascony, export of tin to, 78
Gateshead, size of pewter industry, 299
Geoffrey le Peautrer, 38
George Johnson and Co. (Birmingham) Ltd., 320–1
Gerefa, 22 and n. 5
Germany
 exports of English pewter to, 265, 267
 imports of pewter from, 76–7 and n. 3, 77–9
 inferior quality of medieval tin, pewter, 67
 pewter industry, 36, 301 and n. 3
 tinplate industry, 135–6
Gesson (Gesonn), George, 255, 258, 259, 260
Gesson, Thomas, 258, 259
Gibbins, Robert, 256
Gibbons, Edward, 177
Gibbs, Harry Carr, 318
Gibson, Henry, 257, 258, 260
Gibson, James, 257, 258
Gilding of pewter, prohibition of, 208
Girdlers' Company
 opposition to tinplate manufacture, 136
 proportion of practising girdlers, 202
Glasgow, pewter industry, 126–7, 299
Glass
 challenge offered to pewter by, 134–5, 300–1
 competition offered by pewter to, 59, 62
 drinking vessels, 60, 134–5
 Rhenish, import into Roman Britain, 10
Gloucester
 distribution of pewter made in, 256, 257
 rise, decline of pewter industry, 74, 124–5, 128, 299
 searches in, 177, 257
 supplies of tin for, 239
Gloucestershire, pewter industry, 73–4, 123
Glover, Richard, 113 n. 6, 235
Glover, Roger, 235, 246
Glovers' Company, proportion of practising glovers, 202
Goblets, earthenware, 134
Goblets, pewter
 displacement by silver, 107
 modern, 320
Gold
 chalices, 24, 25–6
 competition offered by pewter to, 59, 60
 medieval tableware, 32, 33, 50
Goldsmiths' Company
 basis of power, effectiveness, 143
 incorporation, 149
 ownership of pewter tableware, 57
 price of being bound apprentice in, 295
Goldsmith, John, 257, ?258
Goodluck, Thomas, 231, 243 n. 5
Gorton, — 262
Gower, Nathan, 287–8 n. 5
Grant, C., 321
Graves, K., 321
Great Fire of London, repercussions in pewter industry, 140–1
Grene, Henry, 215–16, 220, 251
Greves, Francis, 113 n. 6
Grey, Thomas, 266
Grocers' Company, incorporation, 149

Grocers' Hall, Pewterers' Company meetings at, 318
Griges, George, 258
Gugge, John, 266
Guillaume de Bosc, 45
Guinea, export of pewter to, 267–8
Guinea basins, 166, 269

Haberdashers' Company
  competition offered to pewterers' retail trade by, 186
  incorporation, 149
Hamburg gild of pewterers, 45
Hammering
  and division of labour in pewter manufacturing, 223–4
  in manufacturing process, 169–70 and n. 6, 209
Hammermen of Scotland, 75, 126–7
Hammers, 209, 221–3
Hampshire, size of pewter industry, 299
Hampton, William, 232
Hancock, Joseph, 287 n. 5
Hanseatic towns, League
  commercial dominance, 77–8 and n. 1
  export of pewter to, 265, 266
Harby, Sir John, 236
Hard metal
  development of, 140, 227–8
  price, 140
Harries, Nelson G., 319–20
Harris, John, 260
Harrison, William, 66, 83–6, 87
Harry Carr Gibbs scholarships, 318, 322
Haseler, W. H., 301 n. 3
Hatfield, William, 177
Haukins, Edward, 257, 258
Hawking, hawkers, sale of pewterware by, 185–7, 199–200, 239–31, 252, 254, 285 n. 1
Hawksford, Roger, 173
Heal, — 262

Henry III, King of England, bronze effigy of, 37
Henry VI, King of England, policy on incorporation of gilds, 149–50
Henry VIII, King of England, household expenditure on pewter, 109
Hereford, pewter industry, 124, 257, 259, 260
Hertfordshire, pewter industry, 73–4
Hewtrell, Edward, 168
High Rochester, Romano-British pewter from, 12, 17
Hiltone, John de, 164 n. 1
Hiring out of pewterware, 52, 113
Hodge, Robert Piercy, 295–6
Hollowware
  alloys used for, 164, 166
  marking with maker's touch, 170–1
  price levels, 275–6
  traditional manufacturing technique, 209, 213–14, 218, 221–3
Holy water vats, sprinklers, pewter, 28
Household furnishings
  medieval, 46–50, 52–4
  rise in standards, 82–8
  see also Households
Households
  consumption of pottery, glass utensils, 135
  patterns of ownership of pewterware, 43–4, 51–2, 91–103
  value of accounts as sources, 31–3, 56–7
Housing, rise in standards, 82–8
Hudson, George, 168
Hull, pewter industry in, 74, 124, 127, 128
Humber, Bartholomew, 245
Hur, William, 166
Hurdman, William, 237

Husbandmen, improved standards of living, 82–8
Huy, pewter industry, 78

Icklingham, Romano-British pewter from, 11, 14, 17, 210 n. 1
Immigrant labour, restrictions on employment of, 198–9, 207–8
Imperfect wares *see* Defaulters, Pewter manufacture
Imports of pewter
 impact in England, 76–7 and n. 1, 77–9
 restrictions on, 152, 198
 see also individual European countries
Incense boats, pewter, 28, 29
Incorporation of craft gilds, trend towards, 149–51; *see also individual gilds*
Industry in England, expansion of, 81–2
Inflation, causes, effects, in sixteenth, seventeenth centuries, 82
Ingles, Jonathan, 169
Ingole, Daniel, 313 n. 1
Ingots, pewter, Romano-British, 14 and n. 4
Inkpots, pewter, 1
Innholders' Company of St Albans, inclusion of pewterers, 124
Inns of Court, pewter purchases, 57, 113
Institutions, pewter purchases, collections, 54–7, 112–14
Inventories, value as sources, 31, 33, 44–5, 54–7, 60, 85, 86, 87 and n. 2, 88–103, 123
Ipswich, pewter industry, 74, 124, 128
Ireland
 export of English pewter to, 267
 pewter industry, 127
 source of scrap pewter, 240

Iron
 tinning of, in Saxon England, 23
 use for domestic utensils in Middle Ages, 32–3, 34
Iron ore working, in Saxon England, 22
Italy
 exports of pewter to, 265–6, 267
 pewter industry, 79

James I, King of England, attempt to pre-empt tin production, 235
James, — 262
Jeanne de Presles, 44
Jewellery, pewter, 6–7, 23 and n. 1
John, King of England, attempt to pre-empt tin production, 229
John le Peautrer, 38
Johnson, C. J., 321
Johnson, G. B., 321
Johnson George & Co., Birmingham 320–1
Jones, John, 313
Journeymen pewterers
 constitutional role, 157–9 and n. 3
 examination of skills, 167 and n. 2
 numbers, 241–4, 274
 regulations governing admission as masters, 197 and n. 6
 restrictions on mobility, 200–1
 working conditions, status, 192–4
Jugs, pewter, 10–11, 12, 15, 18–19
Jurdeine, Nicholas, 204–5 and n. 1

Kendale, John, 266
Kent, decline of pewter industry, 299
Kidwelly, Geoffrey, 232
King, Gregory, 101, 129
King's College, Cambridge, pewter purchases, 112

King's Lynn, pewter industry, 74, 128
Kinsale, pewter industry, 127
Kitchenware
  range of utensils in Middle Ages, 47-8
  tinplate, 136, 137
  see also individual items
Knighton, Henry, 53

La Rochelle, medieval demand for English tin from, 36
Labourers, unfree, in pewter industry
  constitution role, 158
  gild policies on employment of, 199-200
  role in manufacturing process, 223-4
Labouring classes, ownership of pewter, 96-103, 131; *see also* Peasantry
Ladles, in pewter manufacturing, 209-18
Lambert le Peuterer, 38
Lancaster, pewter industry, 128
Langtofte, Thomas, 52
Lansdown, Bath, Romano-British pewter industry at, 13
Large, William, 150
Lathes, in pewter manufacturing
  in traditional techniques, 15-16, 209, 210-18
  technological advances, 219-21
Latten utensils, vessels, 29, 30, 60
Launder, John, 251
Lavers, pewter, 114
Lead
  health hazards from, 18, 42-3 and n. 3
  increased production in Europe, 76 n. 1
  medieval domestic uses, 42-3
  mining in Saxon England, 22
  price of, 43 n. 3
  supplies for pewter industry, 228-9
  see also Alloys

Leathersellers' Company, incorporation, 149
Leatherworkers' gilds, 143
Lee, Richard, 232
Leeds, pewter industry, 128, 299
Leicester, pewter industry, 73, 74, 128, 177, 255, 259
Leicester, Robert Dudley, Earl of, 108
Leicestershire, pewter industry, 73-4
Leipzig, pewter industry, 77
Leodgotan, functions in Saxon England, 21-2
Lewes, medieval pewter craftsmen from, 69 n. 4, 74
Lewis, G. R., 63
Lewis, John, 232
Liber de Utensilibus, Alexander Neckham, 47-8
Liberty's, marketing of new pewter, 301 n. 3
Lichfield
  patterns of ownership of pewter in, 93, 95, 99-100, 101, 105, 111-12
  searches in, 177, 258, 259
Liège, pewter industry, 78, 265
Lime Street, Pewterers' Company premises in
  aquisition, 150-1 and n. 1
  income from, 314
  modern development of site, 317-18
  removal from, 311-12
Limoges, gild of pewterers in, 45
Lincoln, pewter industry, 74, 124-5, 128
Ling, Richard, 321
Liquids, storage of, pewter vessels for, 59-60
Lithuania, pewter industry, 79
Liverpool
  rise, decline of pewter industry in, 127, 297, 298, 299, 300
  supplies of tin for, 239
Liverymen pewterers
  constitutional role, 157-9, 160-1

Liverymen pewterers–*contd.*
  number of apprentices permitted to, 196
  social standing, 307–8
Lobb, William, 168
Lock, Robert, 185
London
  delftware industry, 133
  distribution of pewter made in, 257, 259, 262–3
  export of pewter made in, 45 and n. 4, 76–7, 263–9
  role in history of English pewter, 38–40, 63–4, 68–9 and n. 4, 115–19, 130–2, 241–51
  tin trade through port of, 230–2
London, Bishop of (d. 1303), character of tableware, 33
'London' mark, 184, 206; *see also* 'Made in London'
Longford
  distribution of pewter made in, 255–61
  search of 1640 in, 255
Low Countries, export of pewter to, 265, 266, 267
Lowton, William, 113
Lübeck, pewter industry, 36, 77, 265
Ludlow, pewter industry, 74, 128
Ludlow Castle, pewter cruet from, 28
Luke, Richard, 124
Lumney, Richard, 266

Macon, pewter industry, 78
'Made in London' mark, 206, 225 n. 2
Maidstone, decline of pewter industry, 296–7
Maker's touch marks
  introduction of compulsory, 152, 153–4, 161, 170–1
  loss of right to strike, 171–2
  regulations governing, 183–5, 303–5, 307
  W. J. Englefield, 1913, 315

Malaga, import of pots from, 61
Malaya, supplies of tin from, 138
Mallets, in traditional pewter manufacturing technique, 209
Malpas, Philip, 232
Manchester
  size of pewter industry, 297, 299
  Romano-British pewter from, 12
Manton, Wiltshire, Romano-British pewter from, 18 n. 4
Margery le Peautrer, 38
Market Harborough, search of 1640 in, 255, 259
Markets, role in retail distribution of pewter, 252–4
Marlborough
  distribution of pewter made in, 257–8
  pewter industry, 128
Marseilles, pewter industry, 78–9
Marsh, R. G. B., 319–20
Mason, Daniell, 169–70
Massé, H. J. L. J., 315
Master of Pewterers' Company, functions, 155–7, 158, 160–1
Master pewterers
  numbers in London Company, 270–3
  numbers of apprentices permitted to, 196
  see also Pewterers' Company
Meare, Somerset, Romano-British pewter from, 18 n. 4
Mearse, John, 247
Measures, pewter
  competition offered to other materials by, 60
  domestic, 35
  for taverns, 114–15, 172–3
Mediterranean area, export of pewter to, 265–6
Mendip Hills, exploitation of lead deposits, 13
Mercers' Company, incorporation, 149

Merchant classes
  attempts to control craft gilds, 154 and n. 2, 155
  ownership of pewter, 34, 42–3, 54–7, 105–6
  power to enforce gild ordinances, 146–7
Merchant Taylors' Company, pewter collection, 113
Meuse Valley, pewter industry, 78
Middle Ages
  domestic usage of pewter, 30, 34–44
  effect of distribution of wealth on demand for, use of pewter, 46–59
Middle classes
  improved standards of living, 86–8
  ownership of pewter, 34, 42, 45, 54–7, 96
  rise, 52–4
Mildenhall, Romano-British pewter from, 17
Milford, import of scrap from Ireland, 240
Miller, Nicholas, 43
Monasteries, use of pewterware, 21–2, 23, 42, 54, 56 n. 1
Monkton Farley, search of 1640, 257
Monopolies
  basis of power of craft gilds, 142, 146
  supply of tin to London pewterers, 131
Mons, pewter industry, 78
Montacute, pewter industry, 74
Montpellier, pewter industry, 78
More, John, 58, 59
More, Robert, 258
Morlaix, pewter industry, 79
Moulds
  in traditional manufacturing techniques, 210–18, 221–3
  Romano-British, 12–14, 210 and n. 1

sharing of, 249
technical developments, 218–19
Mumford, W. F., 58
Munich, pewter industry, 77

Namur, pewter industry, 78
Neckham, Alexander, 47–8
Netherlands
  expansion of pewter industry, 77–9
  export of pewter to, 265
New England, export of pewter to, 267–8
Newbury, pewter industry, 128
Newcastle on Tyne, rise, decline of pewter industry in, 74, 124–5, 128, 174 n. 2, 178, 298
Newgate, a centre of London pewter industry, 119
Nicholas de Ludgate (Nicholas le Peudrer), 38, 39, 230
Nicholas le Graunt, 34
Nicholas, Christopher, 258, 259
Nicholas, Richard, 256, 259
Nicholas, William, 255, 256, 257, 258, 260
Nicholas, — 257
Nicholls, — (Walsall), 262
Nicholls, — (Worcester), 262
Night working, prohibition of, 146, 161, 197
Nobility, ownership of pewter, 42, 43–4, 45, 51–2, 57, 106–12
Norfolk, John Howard, Duke of, 75 and n. 3
Norfolk, medieval pewter craftsmen from, 73–4
Norfolke, Thomas, 168
Normandy
  export of tin to, 78
  import of pots from, 61
Norris, Sir William, 110–11
North, John, 204
Northampton, Henry Howard, Earl of, 108
Northampton, pewter industry, 74, 124, 128, 177, 255, 259

Northamptonshire, medieval pewter craftsmen from, 73–4
Northumberland, Henry Percy, 5th Earl of, 52
Northumberland, Henry Percy, 9th Earl of, 108
Norwich, pewter industry, 71, 73, 124–5, 128
Nottingham, pewter industry, 74, 127
Nottinghamshire, patterns of ownership of pewter in, 92, 94, 96–7, 98, 103
Nüremberg, pewter industry, 36, 77, 265

Oat Lane, opening of Pewterers' Hall in, 319
Offertory plates, pewter, 114
Old Pewter, Malcolm Bell, 315
Old Pewter: Its Makers and Marks, H. J. Cotterell, 317
Ordinances of pewterers gilds, 145–7, 161–79
Ornamentation of pewterware, 16 and n. 2, 45, 139–40
Oxford, pewter industry, 74, 128, 256, 259
Oxford University, pewter collections in colleges of, 56, 63, 112–13, 275–6, 292
Oxfordshire
 ownership of pewter in, 92, 94 96–7, 97–8, 103, 105
 pewter industry, 73–4, 123

Pace, J. W., 318–19
Painting of pewterware, prohibition of, 208
Papacy, purchase of English pewter, 50–1
Paris, John, 80, 231, 243, 266
Paris, pewter industry, 35–6, 78
Partnerships, regulation of, 197
Pascoll, — 257
Patens, pewter, 26–7
Paumer, Edith, 33
Peal, C., 14

Peasantry, ownership of pewter, 34, 43, 45, 57–9, 96
Peautrer, John, 40
Peautrer, Le, emergence of surname, 38
Pellytory, Matthew, 245
Pembrokeshire, use of pewter in, 130 n. 1
Pensioners of London Company, 311, 312–13
Pepys, Samuel, 226 n. 2
Perth, pewter industry, 126–7
Pepper pots, 1
Peutrer, John, 73
Pewter
 basis of valuations for inventories, 90 and n. 1, 91, 103–5
 challenge of other materials to, 107–9, 132–8, 141, 281–5, 300–1
 competition offered by, to other products, 59–63
 connoisseurs of old, 315–17
 defined, 1
 design, workmanship in seventeenth century, 139–40
 distinction between fine, lay, 164
 earliest reference to medieval domestic, 34
 effect of distribution of wealth on medieval demand for, 46–59
 examples from ancient world, 6–8 and n. 2
 hire of, for large feasts, 52, 113
 medieval domestic, 30, 34–45
 patterns of ownership, 34, 42–5, 51–2, 54–9, 83–8, 91–115, 129–30
 prohibitions on sale of second-hand, 197 and n. 3
 recycling of scrap, 131–2, 141, 164, 181, 229, 239–41, 292
 Romano-British, 8–19, 210 and n. 1, 224
 social, economic significance, 2, 54

Pewter–*contd.*
see also Alloys, Prices *and under individual aspects, utensils*
Pewter Collectors' Society, 315–17, 319–20
Pewter Guild, The, 321–2
Pewter manufacturing, pewter industry
  factors affecting rise, decline, 46–59, 138–9, 280–1, 292–300
  importance of London, 115–19, 130–2, 296–7
  in English provinces, 119–26, 127–9
  in Ireland, 127
  in Scotland, 126–7
  regulation, maintenance of standards, 115 and n. 1, 140, 142–3, 145–7, 150, 151–2, 153–4, 161–79, 207–8, 245–6, 302–4, 321–2
  revival in modern times, 320–1
  Romano-British sites, 12–14
  structure of industry, 223–4, 241–51, 304–5
  supply of raw materials, 228–41
  technology, 14–19, 37, 140, 199, 208, 218–21, 221–3
Pewter Plate, H. J. L. J. Massé, 315
Pewterers
  costs of setting up in business, 247–51
  early ordinances, 38–9, 43 and n. 3
  emergence of specialist, 37–41, 124
Pewterers' Company of London
  aquisition of drinking glasses, 134
  associate membership, 174
  C. Welch's *History*, 315
  collection of old pewter, 319–20
  constitution, structure of policy making body, 155–61
  control of exports, 169–70
  dealings in tin, 131, 159–60, 230–6 and n. 3, 237, 238, 305–6, 308–11

  disciplining of errant members, 167–8, 203–5
  distribution of grants, 202 and n. 1
  existence of secret rules, 144, 149
  extent of powers, 201–9
  finances, 308–14, 317–19
  founder members, 241
  hiring out of pewter, 113
  in joint action to curb hawking, 186
  incorporation in 1474, 69, 149–51
  maintenance of standards, 75 and n. 4, 140, 149, 150, 151–2, 173–9, 302–4, 322
  meetings in coffee houses, 134 n. 1
  numbers, composition, 202, 270–3, 274, 292–8, 307–8, 314
  opposition to tinplate manufacture, 136
  origins, 68–70, 79–80, 144–8
  premises, 150 and n. 1, 311–12, 317–19
  reaction to restrictions in 1504 Act, 153–4
  regulation of partnerships, 197
  report of 1791, 306–7
  searches, 119–26, 140–1 and n. 2, 151–2, 161, 163, 174–9, 206, 254, 255–61, 302–4
  strength in sixteenth and seventeenth centuries, 115–19, 140–1
  value of search records as sources, 119
  support for connoisseurs of old pewter, 315–17
  support for modern Pewter Guild, 321–2
Pewterers' gilds
  basis of power, effectiveness, 142–4
  combination with other craft gilds, 124

Pewterers' gilds–*contd.*
  decline in powers of provincial, 205 and n. 2
  early continental, 35–6, 45
  expansion outside London, 70–5
  limitation of competition, 77, 154, 163, 179, 183–4
  see also Apprenticeship, Pewter manufacturing, Pewterers' Company of London
Pewterers' Hall, Lime Street
  aquisition, surrender of premises, 150 and n. 1, 311–12
  development of site, 317–19
  preservation of panelling, 318 n. 1
Pichon, Baron, 44
Pitchers, pewter, 34, 42, 60; *see also* Ewers
Plague, economic repercussions, 45–6 and nn. 1, 2, 62–3
Plates, pewter
  alloys used for, 164
  dressers for display of, 47, 50 and n. 1, 54
  medieval domestic, 1, 42
  price levels, 275
  Romano-British, 10–11, and n. 1, 12, 14, 15–16, 17, 19
Platters, pewter
  alloys used for, 165–6
  competition offered to other materials by, 60
  displacement by silver, 107
  medieval domestic, 35, 39
Plomer, (Plumer) Robert, 257
Plumbism, from lead poisoning, 18
Plumbers' Company, in joint action to curb hawking, 186
Plymouth, export of pewter from, 65 n. 5
Poitiers, pewter industry, 36, 78
Poland, pewter industry, 79 and n. 3
Poorer classes, ownership of pewter, 96–103; *see also* Labouring classes, Peasantry

Population growth, effects of, 82 and nn. 1, 2, 129 and n. 1
Porcelain, competition offered to pewter by, 132–3, 281–5
Porringers, pewter, 1, 59, 164, 166
Portugal, export of pewter to, 266 n. 2
Pots, pewter
  alloys used for, 164, 165–6
  medieval domestic, 35, 39
  regulations governing outwork, 245
  see also Tankards, Taverns
Pottery industry,
  challenge of pewter, 59, 61–2
  competition offered to pewter by, 61–2, 132–4, 135, 141, 281–5, 294
  regression in Dark Ages, 19–20
Powell, Ralph, 167 n. 3
Price of pewterware
  fixing by gilds, 144 and n. 2, 149, 152, 153, 161, 162, 179–82
  impact of fluctuations in tin prices, 285–7
  in seventeenth century, 131, 138
  medieval, 41, 63
  new, secondhand distinguished, 292
  of different alloys, 228
  of exports, 269
  of hard metal, 140
  retail, of new, 275–6
  significance of scrap trade, 239–41, 249 n. 5, 292
Principalia, in medieval peasant holdings, 57–9
Punishments for default, nature of, 167–9
Purling, Major, 137
Putting out of work, regulation of, 244–5, 250, 252
Pyxes
  latten, 29
  pewter, 28, 29

Quarterage, payment by pewterers, 69–70

Raleigh, Sir Walter, 159, 232
Ramsay, Sir Thomas, 111
Reading
    distribution of pewter made in, 256
    pewter industry, 74, 124, 128
    search in, 177
Regensburg, pewter industry, 77
Repair of pewter, demand for, 37, 132, 185–7
Research scholarships, Pewterers' Company support for, 322
Retail trade in pewterware
    internal organisation, 251–61
    itinerant dealers, hawkers, 185–7, 199–200, 239–41, 252, 254, 285 n. 1
    numbers of shopkeepers in London, 270–3, 274
    overseas, 263–9
    regulations governing, 185–7
    significance of dealings in scrap, 239–41
    trends in relation of vendors to manufacturers, 304–5
Rheims, Archbishop of (1389), 45
Rheims, Council of, 21–2, 25
Richard I, King of England
    attempt to pre-empt tin production, 229
    ransom, 26 n. 1
Richard de Swinfield, Bishop, expenditure on tableware, 32
Riche, Richard, 232
Robbins, John, 313
Roberts, Robert, 256, 257
Robins, John, 237
Rodes, Nicholas, 203, 204, 238 n. 6
Roger le Peautrer, 38
Rogers, Thorold, 62, 112
Roman Britain, pewter manufacture in, 8–19
Rome, Ancient, use of tin for utensils, 7–8 and n. 2
Rose and Crown mark, 184
Ross, search in, 257
Rotherham, false pewter seized from, 74

Rouen, pewter industry, 45, 78, 79
Rouen, Synod of, 25
Royal African Company, pewter shipments, 268–9
Royal households, ownership of pewter, 44, 50–1, 109
Russia
    export of pewter to, 267, 269
    pewter industry, 79
Rutland, medieval pewter craftsmen from, 74

Sadlers' Company
    hiring of pewter to, 113
    incorporation, 149
Sadware
    alloys used for, 164, 165–6
    costs of production, 249 and n. 5
    defined, 59
    price levels, 180–1, 275–6
    traditional manufacturing techniques, 169–70 and n. 6, 209, 210, 213–14, 218, 221–3
St Albans
    pewter industry, 74, 124
    Romano-British pewter from, 18 n. 4
St Andrews, pewter industry, 126–7
'Salers', pewter, 39
Salford, size of pewter industry, 299
Salisbury
    distribution of pewter made in, 257–8
    pewter industry, 74, 124, 128
    search in, 258
Salt cellars, pewter
    alloys used for, 165–6
    competition offered to other materials, 59
    displacement by silver, 107
    medieval, 34
Samian ware, import into Roman Britain, 9–10
Sandys, William, 227, 251

Saracen pots, 61
Saucers, pewter
  alloys used for, 164, 165–6
  displacement by silver, 107
  medieval, 39
  Romano-British, 11
Sawnderson, John, 201
Saxony, exploitation of tin resources, 22 n. 3, 36, 131 and n. 2, 138, 264
Scarborough, medieval pewter craftsmen in, 74
Scattergood, Thomas, 313
Schipwaysshe, Ernald, 38, 241
Scotland
  compulsory touch marking in, 171 n. 4
  export of English pewter to, 267
  interest in old pewter, 315
  pewter industry, 126–7 and n. 3
Scottish Pewterware and Pewterers, L. Ingleby Wood, 315
Scrap pewter, significance of recycling of, 131–2, 141, 164, 181, 229, 139–41, 249 n. 5, 292
Searches, *see* Pewterers' Company
Sedgley, ownership of pewter in, 93, 105
Seeley, — 262
Senere, (Sinay) William, 256, 259
Seneres, Thomas, 258, 259
Seney, Robert, senior, and junior, 258
Senores, Robert, 258, 259
Sepulchral chalices, pewter, 26–7
Seynerdy, Richard, 256, 259
Shabroles, Mark Henry, 199
Shapworth, Somerset, Romano-British pewter from, 18 n. 4
Sheffield
  Britannia metal industry, 298, 299–300
  modern pewter industry, 320, 321
Sherbrone, search in, 257
Shingham, Norfolk, ornamentation on pewter found at, 16 n. 2

Shorey, John, pewterer, 113 n. 4
Shrewsbury, rise, decline of pewter industry, 124, 299
Silver
  challenge offered by pewter to, 59, 60–1
  challenge offered by porcelain to, 133
  cost, value, in sixteenth, seventeenth centuries, 107–8 and n. 3
  displacement of pewter by, 107
  drinking vessels, 134
  ecclesiastical vessels made from, 24, 25–6, 29–30
  import into Roman Britain, 10
  use for medieval tableware, 32, 33, 34, 50
Silvorum, 137, 208
Skinners' Company, incorporation, 149
Slipware, development of, 132, 133, n. 3
Smallwood, William, 151
Smith, Lovell, 255, 256, 258, 260
Smith, Thomas, 113 n. 6, 235, 237
Smith, — (of Coventry), 262
Smith, — (of Rugby), 262
Snandon, Thomas, 72
Solder, soldering
  control of standards, 164
  in traditional manufacturing techniques, 209, 223
Somers, Robert, 203–4
Somerset
  medieval pewter craftsmen from, 73–4
  Romano-British exploitation of coal fields, 13
  Romano-British pewter from, 13, 18 n. 4
Soranzo, Giacomo, 67
South Africa, export of pewter to, 290
Southampton
  pewter industry, 64 and n. 2, 74, 124, 128, 296–7

Southampton—*contd.*
  role in tin trade, 230, 231, 265 n. 3, 266 n. 2
Southwark, composition of Romano-British pewter from, 17
Spain
  export of pewter to, 267
  pewter industry, 79, 266 n. 3
  Roman exploitation of tin mining, 8, 9
Spice boxes, 107
Spinning of pewter, resistance to, 208
Spirit pots, pewter, 166
Spoonmakers, numbers in Pewterers' Company of London, 274
Spoons, pewter, 1, 10–11, 19, 28, 29, 60, 107
Spring-pole-and-treadle-drive lathes, 219–20
Spurriers' Company, in joint action to curb hawking, 186
Staffordshire
  size of pewter industry, 299
  ownership of pewter in, 93, 95, 96–7, 102, 111–12
Stamford, medieval pewter craftsmen from, 74
Stamping of pewter, resistance to, 208
Stanford Bridge fair, sale of pewter at, 254
Stanley, John, 124
Stannaries *see* Tin production
Staple, Richard, 245, 246
Stephen le Straunge, 38, 241
Stevenes, — (of Northampton), 255
Stewards, numbers of apprentices permitted to, 196
Stills, pewter, 164
Stokesley, Romano-British pewter from, 12
Stoneware, 282, 284
Stourbridge, ownership of pewter in, 92, 96, 98, 105

Stourbridge fair, sale of pewter at, 253
Stratton, Bartholomew, 232
Stray, Ralph, 313 n. 1
Subcontracting, regulations governing, 244–5
Suffolk, pewter industry, 69 n. 4, 73–4, 123
Sumptuary statutes, 53
Surrey, medieval pewter craftsmen from, 73–4
Sutton, Cambridgeshire, Romano-British pewter from, 17
Sutton Hoo burial treasure, tinning in, 21
Sweden, export of pewter to, 268
Symkin, James, 267
Synaky, William, 257, 259
Syward, John, 38, 241

Tableware, medieval domestic usage, 34–44, 47–8, 58–9
Tableware, pewter
  challenge offered to, by pottery, 281–5
  displacement by silver, 107
  in medieval England, 31–4, 34–44
  Romano-British, 9–10, 17, 18–19
Tailors' Company, incorporation, 149
Tailors' Company of Ipswich, inclusion of pewterers, 124
Tan Hill Fair, search in, 177–8
Tanfeld, John, 253
Tankards, pewter
  alloys used for, 164, 166
  control of standards, 60, 172–3
  decline in demand for, 300–1
  displacement by silver, 107
  for taverns, 60, 114–15, 172–3, 275, 289–90, 300–1
  Hanseatic pot-bellied, 78 n. 1
  manufacturing techniques, 223 and n. 1
  medieval domestic use, 1
  modern, 320

Tankards, pewter—*contd.*
  regulations governing outwork, 245
Taudin, Daniel, 199
Taudin, James, 140, 199, 225–7, 228
Taunton, pewter industry, 74, 128
Taylor, John, 201
Tazza, pewter, Romano-British, 10–11
Tea drinking, impact on demand for pewter, pottery, 280–1
Teapots, pewter, 1
Tedman, Humphrey, 255
Templars, household inventory of 1307, 35
Thame, distribution of pewter made in, 256
Theophilus Presbyter, 37, 210–13, 218, 219, 224
Thistle mark, 184
Thomas atte Vigne, 43
Thomas de Weston, 40
Thomas le Peautrer, 38
Thomas Townends and Co. Ltd., 317–18
Thirty Years' War, effects on tin production, 131
Tin
  attempt to prohibit export of, 236
  chalices, 25 and n. 6
  cost, in Middle Ages, 43 n. 3
  dealings in, by pewterers' companies, 131, 159–60, 201–2, 230–6 and n. 3, 237, 238, 305–6, 308–11
  development of alloys based on, 1, 5
  English, French demand for, in Middle Ages, 36
  export to France, 75–6, 78 and n. 3
  impact of fluctuating prices on pewter industry, 62–3, 183, 285–7
  use in ancient world, 6–8
  see also Alloys, Tin production

Tin production
  control of quality, 238 and nn. 5, 6
  fluctuations in levels of, 20, 21–2 and n. 3, 40–1, 62–3, 65, 131, 132, 138, 291–2
  in ancient world, 5–6
  in Bohemia and Saxony, 22 n. 3, 36, 131 and n. 2, 138, 264
  in Cornwall, 6, 8–9, 13, 40–1 and n. 2, 229, 285–7
  rights of purchase, 118, 159–60, 201–2, 228–41
Tin Plate Alias Wire Workers' Company, 288–9
Tinning, practice of, 20–1, 23, 135–6, 137
Tinplate manufacture
  competition offered to pewter by, 135–8, 141, 288–9, 294
  development of industry, 136–7
  export of, 136–7
  resistance to, 208
Tonges, Richard, 179, 256
Tonkin, Digory, 251
Torel, William, 37
Touch marks
  introduction of compulsory, 152, 153–4, 161, 170–1
  loss of right to strike, 171–2
  regulations governing, 183–5, 303–5, 307
  W. J. Englefield, 1913, 315
Toulouse, pewter industry, 78
Townend, Thomas & Co., 317
Towsen, Peter, 217
Toys, pewter, alloys used for, 164
Trade secrets, gilds' policies on preservation of, 198
Tradesmen, ownership of pewter, 105–6
Trenchers, exports of Russian, 269
Trifling ware, alloys used for, 164, 166
Trowbridge, search in, 177–8
Troyes, Bishop of (1370–1), 45
'Tudric ware', 301 n. 3

362 *Index*

Turkey, export of pewter to, 268
Turning, in traditional manufacturing technique, 209
Turnour, Robert, 52

United States of America, export of pewter to, 320

Vases, pewter, Romano-British, 11
Venetian glass, popularity for drinking vessels, 134
Venice, pewter industry, 79
Verdigris, problem of, in metal vessels, 20–1 and n. 1, 35, 135, 137
Vickers, James, 287–8 n. 5
Vickers and Son, 287 n. 5
Villedieu, pewter industry, 78
Vintners' Company, incorporation, 149
Virginia, emigration of pewterers to, 200

Wages in the pewter industry, 62–3 and nn. 1, 7, 193
Wakefield, pewter industry, 128, 299
Walbrook, Romano-British pewter from, 10, 19 and n. 2
Wallingford fair, search in, 256, 259
Walsall
  competition offered to York pewterers by, 205 n. 2
  distribution of pewter made in, 255–61
  pewter industry, 125, 127, 128, 178
Wardens of London Pewterers' Company
  functions, 155–7, 158, 160–1
  numbers of apprentices permitted to, 196
Ware, medieval pewter craftsmen from, 69 n. 4, 74
Warwick
  pewter industry, 128
  searches in, 178, 179, 256, 259

Warwickshire, searches in, 175–6
Water pitchers, pewter, 27; *see also* Ewers
Watson, Edward, 186 n. 3
Wealth
  causes, effects of increase in, 82–8
  relation to ownership of pewter, 94–5, 103–5
Wedgwood, Josiah, 282, 286
Weetwood, Humfry, 171–2
Welch, Charles, 315
Wellingborough, pewter industry, 128
Weoley Castle, pewter cruet from, 28
West, Robert, 172, 173, 252
West Africa, export of pewter to, 268–9
West Indies, export of pewter to, 268, 269, 290
Westminster Abbey, sepulchral chalice, paten from, 27
Westminster, Council of, 1175, 25
White metal *see* Britannia metal
Wigan
  competition offered to York pewterers by, 205 n. 2
  distribution of pewter from, 261
  ordinances of pewterers' gild in, 161
  rise, decline of pewter industry, 74 and n. 2, 125–6, 127–8, 141, 207, 297, 298, 299
  supplies of tin for, 239
Wilkes, Thomas, 255, 256, 258, 259, 260
Wilkie, I., 320–1
William de Ordesale, 40
William de Suttone, 38, 39
Williams, Martin, 217–18, 249
Wills, value as sources, 30–1, 33, 42, 43, 54–7, 60
Winchester, pewter industry, 64 n. 2, 74, 128, 177
Winchester College, purchases of pewter, 56, 63, 112–13, 275–6

Winchester, Council of, 1076, 25
Wine barrels, ecclesiastical, pewter, 28
Wolsey, Cardinal, 108–9
Wood, L. Ingleby, 315
Wooden vessels
  competition offered by pewter to, 59, 62
  medieval use of, 32, 33, 34
Woodstock, distribution of pewter made in, 256
Woodworkers' gilds, 143
Wookey, medieval pewter craftsmen from, 74
Worcester
  distribution of pewter made in, 257
  ownership of pewter in, 106
  pewter industry, 74, 123, 124–5, 128
  searches in, 256, 257, 259
Worcestershire, ownership of pewter in, 92–3, 96–7, 98–9
Workmen, unfree, gilds' policies on employment of, 199–200
Worm makers, 295–6 and n. 6
Wylkinson, Robert, 253

Yarmouth, medieval pewter craftsmen from, 74

Yates, Thomas, 290–1
Yeomen pewterers
  constitutional role, 157–9 and n. 3, 160–1
  numbers in London Company, 271, 274
Yonge, William, 232
York
  competition offered to pewter industry by Wigan, Walsall, 205 n. 2
  emergence of specialist pewterers in, 40
  regulation of partnerships, 197 and n. 6
  rise, decline of pewter industry in, 40, 125, 127–8, 241, 297
  rules, structure of pewterers' gild in, 70–3, 75, 148–9, 161, 167, 173 n. 4, 188, 196
  stock of moulds, 249
  working conditions of journeymen, 193
Yorkshire
  medieval pewter craftsmen from, 73–4
  Romano-British pewter manufacture in, 14
Youghal, pewter industry, 127